BALLOTS &
BANDWAGONS

2

Books by RALPH G. MARTIN
  BOY FROM NEBRASKA
  THE BEST IS NONE TOO GOOD

Co-author with Morton D. Stone:
  MONEY, MONEY, MONEY
    Wall Street in Text and Pictures

Co-author with Ed Plaut:
  FRONT RUNNER, DARK HORSE

Co-author with Richard Harrity:
  THE HUMAN SIDE OF F.D.R.
  ELEANOR ROOSEVELT: HER LIFE IN PICTURES
  MAN OF THE CENTURY: CHURCHILL
  MAN OF DESTINY: DE GAULLE OF FRANCE
  THE THREE LIVES OF HELEN KELLER
  WORLD WAR II: FROM D-DAY TO V-E DAY

BY RALPH G. MARTIN

 BALLOTS &
BANDWAGONS

★ ★ ★ ★ ★ ★ ★ ★ ★ ★ ★ ★

RAND McNALLY & COMPANY

CHICAGO • NEW YORK • SAN FRANCISCO

The author and the publishers wish to thank the following for permission to quote material from the publications listed:

BRANDT & BRANDT: *Released for Publication* by Oscar King Davis, Houghton Mifflin Company, copyright 1925 by Oscar King Davis; *The Incredible Era* by Samuel Hopkins Adams, Houghton Mifflin Company, copyright 1939 by Samuel Hopkins Adams.

DORRANCE & COMPANY: *Back Stage in 1912* by Victor Rosewater.

DOUBLEDAY & COMPANY, INC.: *The Happy Warrior* by Emily Smith Warner, copyright © 1956 by Emily Smith Warner; *Front Runner, Dark Horse,* by Ralph G. Martin and Edward Plaut.

DUELL, SLOAN & PEARCE: *FDR, His Personal Letters* 1928–1945, edited by Elliott Roosevelt and Joseph P. Lash.

JAMES A. FARLEY: *Jim Farley's Story: The Roosevelt Years,* Whittlesey House.

WILFRED FUNK, INC.: *Western Democrat* by Arthur Mullen; *Tale of Two Conventions* by William Jennings Bryan.

HARCOURT, BRACE & WORLD, INC.: *Behind the Ballots* by James A. Farley, copyright 1938; *Theodore Roosevelt: A Biography* by Henry F. Pringle, 1931; *Affectionately Yours* by James Roosevelt and Sidney Shalett, 1959.

HARPER & ROW, PUBLISHERS INCORPORATED: *As I Knew Them* by Henry L. Stoddard; *It Costs To Be President* by Henry L. Stoddard; *Working With Roosevelt* by Samuel I. Rosenman; *Garner of Texas* by Bascom Timmons.

HARVARD UNIVERSITY PRESS: *The Letters of Theodore Roosevelt,* Elting E. Morison, Editor, Cambridge, Mass., copyright 1951, 1952, 1954 by the President and Fellows of Harvard College.

HOLT, RINEHART AND WINSTON, INC.: *The Life and Times of William Howard Taft* by Henry F. Pringle; also to Charles P. Taft and the Taft family for permission to reprint quotes from letters written by William Howard Taft which appear in the book.

HOUGHTON MIFFLIN COMPANY: *Beveridge and the Progressive Era* by Claude G. Bowers; *Crisis of the Old Order* by Arthur Schlesinger, Jr.

THE JOHNS HOPKINS PRESS: *A Carnival of Buncombe* by H. L. Mencken.

THE MACMILLAN COMPANY: *Autobiography of William Allen White,* copyright 1946 by The Macmillan Company; *Memoirs of Herbert Hoover,* Volume 1; *Interpretations* by Walter Lippmann, 1932.

McNALLY & LOFTIN: *I Write For Freedom* by T. M. Storke.

PUTNAM'S & COWARD-McCANN: *Power and Glory: Life of Boise Penrose* by Walter Davenport, copyright 1931 by Putnam's & Coward-McCann; *The Mirrors of Washington* by Anonymous, copyright 1921.

RANDOM HOUSE, INC.: *Mr. Sam* by C. Dwight Dorough, copyright 1962.

CHARLES SCRIBNER'S SONS: *Theodore Roosevelt: An Autobiography; Across the Busy Years* by Nicholas Murray Butler; *From McKinley to Harding* by H. H. Kohlsaat; *Our Times* by Mark Sullivan, Vol. 6; *Selections from the Correspondence of Theodore Roosevelt and Henry Cabot Lodge.*

SIMON AND SCHUSTER, INC.: *My Life: The Memoirs of Claude Bowers* by Claude Bowers, copyright 1962 by Simon and Schuster, Inc.

THE VIKING PRESS: *Teapot Dome* by M. R. Werner and John Starr; *You're The Boss* by Edward J. Flynn.

WORLD PUBLISHING CO.: *The Man Behind Roosevelt* by Lela Stiles.

Jacket photograph: United Press International.

For My Dear Friend,
DEBS MYERS,
who first pulled me into
the excitement of politics

ACKNOWLEDGMENTS

MY PERSONAL APPRECIATION TO MY EDITOR, AS well as my friend, Cynthia Smith Vartan; to my dear friend Paul S. Green, always so willing to help in every way; to James and Virginia Eisenstein who helped with both research and excellent criticism; to Mari Walker who did the typing, often under trying circumstances; and to Shirley L. Warren.

Again, my thanks to the staff of the Franklin D. Roosevelt Library at Hyde Park, for their courteous and complete co-operation, particularly its director, Elizabeth R. Drewry and Joseph Marshall, Jerome Deyo, William Stickle, Mrs. Anne Morris.

To the New York State Library in Albany, especially the head of the Reference Section, Mason Tolman and his staff Ida M. Cohen and Joseph Menditto, and senior librarian Marion Hemstead.

To a large number of anonymous people at the Library of Congress.

To the small, but hard-working staff of the Oyster Bay Public Library who have been of such enormous help in getting me some of the books and material I needed, especially, Library Director Ruth P. Greene, Mrs. Annette S. Macedonio, and Mrs. Christine Lane.

To my collaborator on our book *Front Runner, Dark Horse*, (Doubleday), Ed Plaut, for permitting me to reprint a section of our book, a section which we both had researched and which I wrote.

My gratitude to Jean Gildea for permitting me access to the files of James Finnegan.

My special thanks to all those people who so kindly gave me of their time and memory:

John F. Kennedy, Ted Sorenson, Eleanor Roosevelt, Adlai Stevenson, James Roosevelt, Franklin D. Roosevelt Jr., James A. Farley, Samuel Rosenman, George Ball, Senator Stuart Symington, Senator Hubert Humphrey, Senator Paul Douglas, Senator Gale McGee, Senator George Smathers, Senator Joseph Clark, former Senators Richard Neuberger and Estes Kefauver, Jim Rowe, John Sharon, Hugh Sidey, Phil Potter, Bill Haddad, Earl Mazo, Michael DiSalle, Abe Fortas, Sam Brightman, Neil Stabler, Tom Quimby, Marquis Child, Eric Severeid, Jack Arvey, Porter McKeever, Bill Blair, Dixon Donnelly, William Wirtz, Newt Minow, Ed Morgan, Hy Raskin, George Backer, Ivan Nestingen, Oscar Chapman, Fishbait Miller, Representative Hale Boggs, Representative Richard Bolling, Arthur Schlesinger Jr., Sidney Shore, Representative Frank E. Smith, Herb Waters, Max Kampelman, Torbert Macdonald, Clark Clifford, Tom Winship, Sargent Shriver, Al Weisman, Dave Talbot, John Powers, Robert Albright, Abba Schwartz, Stan Fike, Robert Kennedy, Stephen Smith, Ken O'Donnell, Ted Reardon, Evelyn Lincoln, Fran Halberg, Sue Sideman, Helen Fuller, Louis Lyons, Joseph Lyford, Larry O'Brien, Ed Welsh, Joseph Kennedy Sr. and former President Harry S Truman.

A final note of personal appreciation to Jerry Moonelis, for his technical assistance.

RALPH G. MARTIN
East Norwich, N.Y., 1964

TABLE OF
CONTENTS

INTRODUCTION

"A NATIONAL CONVENTION IS AS FASCINATING as a revival or a hanging," wrote H. L. Mencken. "It is vulgar, ugly, stupid, and tedious, to be sure, and yet there suddenly comes a show so gaudy and hilarious, so melodramatic and obscene, so unimaginably exhilarating and preposterous that one lives a gorgeous year in an hour."

If Americans are basically spectator citizens, then surely the National Political Convention is one of the most exciting spectacles of them all—and it is an excitement uniquely American.

Attending a national convention with a British reporter of the *Manchester Guardian*, Anne O'Hare McCormick of the *New York Times* reported that the Englishman was fascinated by "the doves wheeling in the tropic glare, the girls in kilts, the bands in fur shakos parading impartially for every candidate, the radio singers whooping it up on top of the Chairman's desk . . . the cinematic effects of mass and color, of grotesque shadows thrown against the human horizon, beyond the imagination of Hollywood."

Somebody asked the British reporter how American politics thus illustrated, compared with English, and he looked surprised.

"Politics?" he repeated. "Politics? How should I know? So far, I have seen everything here except politics."

This book is about the politics of national conventions that the Englishman didn't see, that few Americans ever see or hear or know about: it's the story of what happens behind the ballots and behind the bandwagons; it's the story of the wheeling and the dealing; it's the story of the men and maneuvers that create Presidents of the United States—and this behind-the-scenes show is even more fascinating than the showcase.

As much as anything, this fascination comes from the constant air of political unpredictability that hangs over a national convention. No matter how seemingly controlled a convention, no matter how certain a candidate's selection, there is always the feeling that an unexpected deal, a hot speech, a personal revelation, a newspaper headline, a thousand other things can convert a divided crowd of delegates into a single mood and a single mind, can create a bandwagon psychology that can overturn the tightest political clique. It partly happened in 1900 when a majority of Republican delegates wanted Theodore Roosevelt for Vice-President and both President William McKinley and national political boss Mark Hanna definitely didn't want him. It happened in the Republican convention of 1920, one of the tightest controlled of them all, which nominated Warren Gamaliel Harding for President, when a seemingly complacent convention suddenly came alive and refused the "official" candidate for Vice-President, and nominated their own, Calvin Coolidge. It happened in 1940 when Republicans surprisingly picked Wendell Willkie instead of one of the party "regulars," and in 1952 when Democrats really drafted Adlai Stevenson.

While each national convention has its own political profile and personality—and all of them belong in a definitive two- or three-volume history which I someday hope to write—the selection of sample conventions came from a twin standard: drama and importance.

Drama alone would have qualified many: the Republican convention that produced Willkie in 1940, the Democratic convention that drafted Stevenson in 1952, the 103 ballots of the 1924 Democratic convention, among many others. But all these produced losing candidates, and the simple problem of space eliminated them.

Of others that qualified in both categories of drama and importance—the 1912 Democratic convention that nominated Woodrow Wilson and the 1952 Republican convention that picked Dwight D. Eisenhower—the decision was more difficult. The choice then boiled down to a further definition of the word "important." Different conventions highlight different political problems and principles. In both the 1912 and 1932 Democratic conventions, the featured factor of control was the two-thirds majority rule, with the candidates maneuvering on the extra ballots to create a bandwagon. Each had its own high drama, its own importance in history, and each might have belonged in this book. The choice became almost the toss of a coin.

In the 1952 Republican convention, the key Eisenhower-Taft fight had an original hinge of controversy on the Credentials Committee's recognition of delegations. Taft's control of that committee and that committee's recognition of contested delegations in Taft's favor ballooned into a hot bubble that broke the convention toward Eisenhower. The 1912 Republican convention hinged similarly, but much more importantly, on the Credentials Committee. The 1912 convention also featured the fight between two former friends—former President Theodore Roosevelt and his hand-picked successor William Howard Taft, then running for renomination. It was unquestionably the most exciting national political convention of the twentieth century. As a result of it, Roosevelt broke away from the Republican party, held his own Progressive party convention, became its nominee and thus insured the election of Woodrow Wilson.

Space stopped other conventions from fighting into the book, including some conventions in which I was personally and actively involved. One other convention, of which I was a part and which is included—the 1956 Democratic convention—concentrates here on the open race for the vice-presidential nomination between Senators Estes Kefauver and John F. Kennedy. Millions of Americans were caught by the dramatic close vote, warmed to the gracious speech of concession by the young Senator Kennedy. That

convention converted Kennedy from a relatively unknown freshman Senator to such a national political celebrity that he felt immediately able to start his race for the presidential nomination in
1960. Had Kennedy won that vice-presidential nomination, had
the Stevenson-Kennedy ticket lost to Eisenhower, as was likely,
many critics could have blamed the defeat on Kennedy's Catholi-
cism and it would have killed his political future.

On the other hand, Kennedy's defeat in that 1956 vice-presidential race was the defeat that made a President.

The story of a convention is never simply the story of a week
in a convention city. No convention better illustrates this than the
1920 Republican convention that selected Warren G. Harding
in a supposed "smoke-filled" room. The prologue to that convention goes back a generation when an unsuccessful Ohio politician
named Harry Daugherty saw the political potential of a handsome,
casy-moving country editor "who looked like he should have been
President." The story of a convention must begin at different
beginnings.

The selected conventions: the Republican conventions of 1900,
1912, and 1920 and the Democratic conventions of 1932 and 1956.

Commenting on national conventions, one critic said with
finality, many years ago, "It is a relic. It cannot survive the radio.
As an institution, it is already as dead as a chicken, flopping around
after its head is cut off."

But an earlier critic, himself three times a presidential nominee,
William Jennings Bryan said, perhaps more truly, "The convention
is, in a way, a photograph of the nation. All the great forces that
exert a potential influence in our country are here in person or by
proxy."

The excitement of a national convention is the excitement of
these forces in conflict. It is the excitement of a political World
Series. It is the excitement of watching the ripples of a thousand
political pebbles. It is the excitement of seeing a sword of uncertainty hanging over a glorified national town meeting, mixed with
a sense of circus and a huge tremor of hope and history.

THE UNITED STATES moved into the twentieth century with prosperity at a peak after four years of President William McKinley's "full dinner pail" (even though an ad for a cashier's job offering a ten-hour working day and a six-day week for eight dollars got 725 replies within 48 hours).

But the bulk of our seventy-six million citizens seemed highly satisfied, and in a feisty mood. We had just completed a short, dramatic "splendid little war" with Spain over Cuba, pushing our country into a new, higher gear of world importance. This crisis over Cuba still simmered in 1900 as a political issue with Republicans calling this expansionism our "manifest destiny," and Democrats calling it imperialism.

Women won the right to vote in four thinly-populated western states, but most women seemed more concerned about the rising cost of food (eggs, fourteen cents a dozen; sugar, four cents a pound; and twenty cents for a turkey dinner); the quality of their corsets—tight enough so that the waist "could be easily clasped with two hands"; and the length of their dresses—long enough to hide their ankles. No ad yet dared mention that women might someday buy and smoke cigarettes.

Some 8,000 automobiles bumped along on the country's ten miles of concrete road (one-third of the cars were electric and the rest operated on steam). The Literary Digest flatly predicted that the car could never replace the bicycle in popularity. The Digest would prove itself more fatally wrong within forty years when it prophesied the overwhelming election victory of Alfred Landon over President Franklin D. Roosevelt.

At the turn of the century, Roosevelt (Theodore) was the Republican governor of New York and Dewey (George) was an outstanding Democratic presidential hopeful. Two other prominent Democrats competing for vice-presidential mention were Stevenson (Adlai, Sr.) and Nixon (Lewis). Still another name that would have future meaning, was the dictator of Venezuela, Castro (Cipriano). A conflict between General Castro and European powers soon raised disturbing questions in regard to the Monroe Doctrine.

But the keynote of America's mood came from thirty-seven-year-old United States Senator Albert J. Beveridge of Indiana, fresh from a visit to the Philippines, who said in his maiden Senate speech, ". . . And of all our race, He has marked the American people as His chosen Nation to finally lead in the regeneration of the world. This is the divine mission of America, and it holds for us all the profit, all the glory, all the happiness possible to man."

REPUBLICAN NATIONAL CONVENTION OF 1900

THE 1900 REPUBLICAN NATIONAL CONVENTION WAS seemingly a stage set without drama. After all, the presidential candidate was obvious. No Republican politician in his right mind would stir against the renomination of President William McKinley. McKinley men already had settled on his campaign slogan, *"Four More Years of The Full Dinner Pail."*

The convention then seemed cut and dried.

There was one small political problem. Vice-President Garrett Hobart died in office on November 21, 1899. But, even so, all McKinley had to do was to crook his finger toward his choice and the deed was done.

Still, it wasn't that simple.

That was mainly because of the cast of characters: three political bosses divided into two camps, a string of vice-presidential possibilities who didn't want the job, and a colorful convention personality named Theodore Roosevelt who wasn't really sure what he wanted.

Of these key characters, the most pivotal and primary was United

States Senator Marcus Alonzo Hanna, America's first and greatest national political boss. A heavy-set man with piercing eyes, Hanna was caricatured by opposition newspapers as an obese money bag, marked with dollar signs, lugging a hurdy-gurdy with McKinley as a dejected monkey hitched to his master's wrist. The truth was much more complex. No one questioned Hanna's political power. Almost single-handedly, he had converted McKinley from a defeated Congressman to the President of the United States within fourteen years. Somebody wrote, "the two men were so closely bound together that they merged into a single personality." So enormously successful was his handling of the previous presidential campaign in 1896, that Hanna had become the single most important person in the United States, with the sole exception of McKinley himself. Some rumors even circulated that Hanna might replace McKinley as the Republican presidential nominee in 1900. But Thomas Reed, Speaker of the House of Representatives and a long-time political power, said, "Hanna run for the Presidency in 1900? Why should he snatch at the shadow when he has the substance?"

Long before, Hanna had confided to a friend that he would never exchange his personal power with that of the President. And yet, even though McKinley let Hanna organize the national political power, even though McKinley let Hanna do what he wanted with the conduct of the campaign, the basic truth was that McKinley operated the hurdy-gurdy and Hanna was the monkey tied to his master's wrist. Nothing proved this more conclusively than the 1900 Republican National Convention.

Hanna had a neat political mind. When he wrapped a political package, he wanted all the corners carefully folded and closed—no loopholes. But with the upcoming convention, Hanna saw the vacant Vice-Presidency as a gaping loophole, fraught with political danger. And this was a package he wanted knotted tightly.

Soon after Hobart's death, Hanna asked McKinley to fingerpoint the new vice-presidential nominee.

McKinley indicated a preference for Senator William Allison of

Iowa, one of the prime conservative powers in the Senate, who had been a presidential rival of McKinley's at the previous convention. But Allison, then serving his fifth term in the Senate as its outstanding authority on all matters of finance, had refused Cabinet offers from previous Presidents and wanted no part of the Vice-Presidency.

Hanna then suggested Cornelius N. Bliss, McKinley's Secretary of the Interior, and an intimate Hanna friend, and McKinley agreed. But Bliss didn't. Like Hanna, Bliss had been a highly successful merchant and organizer and Republican party fund-raiser, and so Hanna put on all his personal pressure of friendship, and Bliss wavered, finally agreed to accept the Vice-Presidency if his wife similarly agreed. That's when Hanna gave up. Mrs. Bliss still hadn't forgiven Hanna for persuading her husband to become Secretary of the Interior.

Who else? Elihu Root, McKinley's new Secretary of War? Henry Cabot Lodge reported to a friend that Root was offered the nomination, and refused it.

That left a string of other possibilities: Representative Jonathan Dolliver of Iowa, a genial giant who mannered his speech after Lincoln and was destined to succeed Allison in the Senate; former Secretary of the Navy John D. Long, a safe, conservative Republican; Charles Fairbanks, the senior Senator from Indiana, also a "stand-pat" man in the Hanna tradition; and Timothy Woodruff, the wealthy lieutenant governor of New York, who was low on the list.

McKinley refused to name any of them, or any other. No matter how hard Hanna persisted that McKinley must make the choice in advance of the convention, McKinley flatly refused.

But there was one man whom neither Hanna nor McKinley wanted as Vice-President: Theodore Roosevelt.

Roosevelt had served as McKinley's Assistant Secretary of the Navy under John Long, from 1897 to April 1898, and Long had called him "a bull in a china shop." President McKinley and Hanna had both hoped to preserve peace with Spain over Cuba, but Roosevelt seemed hot for war and told Hanna, "We will have this war for the freedom of Cuba, Senator Hanna, in spite of the timidity of commercial interests." Pennsylvania Congressman Butler said of Roosevelt then, "He came down here looking for war. He did not care whom we fought as long as there was a scrap."

Hanna called Roosevelt "a wild man," "impulsive, frivolous, unsound." As for McKinley, his feeling for Roosevelt was not softened by a Roosevelt remark made to newspaper publisher H. H. Kohlsaat, "McKinley has a chocolate eclair backbone."

But Roosevelt's political status now came from the fact that he was governor of New York State, and any New York governor was automatically a presidential possibility.

This clear fact became clearer in June, 1899. Roosevelt then attended a reunion of his Rough Riders, the colorful unit he led so dramatically in the Spanish-American War. Arriving in Las Vegas, Roosevelt found a wild, tumultuous reception waiting for him, his Rough Riders wearing printed cards in their hatbands, "ROOSEVELT IN 1904." Roosevelt wrote home that he had been greeted "exactly as if I had been a presidential candidate," and the New York Times reported that so exciting was the reception that it had started Roosevelt thinking about his presidential chances in 1900.

Similar thoughts uncomfortably crossed Hanna's mind. Kohlsaat, a friend of both Hanna and Roosevelt, traveling with Roosevelt at that time, persuaded him to send a telegram to President McKinley telling him he had found much western sentiment for McKinley's renomination and offering his own personal support. When Roosevelt agreed, Kohlsaat wired the Associated Press correspondent to meet the Governor's train at Albany, and Roosevelt gave an interview repeating with emphasis what he had said in the telegram.

If this made Hanna happier, and resulted in a McKinley invitation for Mr. and Mrs. Roosevelt to spend Sunday at the White House, it also worried close Roosevelt associates.

To one of them, shortly afterward, Roosevelt wrote: "For

Heaven's sake, don't think I have any Presidential or Vice Presidential ambitions just at present. I am trying to be a middling good Governor of New York, that is all."

But that wasn't all. Roosevelt's closest political adviser, Senator Henry Cabot Lodge of Massachusetts, outlined for his friend two possible roads to the Presidency: another Roosevelt term as Governor—which unfortunately would end in 1902, still two years away from the 1904 presidential convention; and, more ideally, said Lodge, the Cabinet job of Secretary of War where "your services would make you President without serious opposition."

Any chance of getting that Secretary of War job, which Roosevelt did want, went out of the window when Roosevelt sent McKinley his telegram of support. His friends felt that if Roosevelt had maintained his mystery without declaration, he could have hand-picked his place on the Cabinet as his political price. His premature telegram of support carned him a White House social invitation, but cost him the War Cabinet job—which went to Elihu Root.

Blocking Roosevelt's other road to the Presidency—his re-election as Governor—was the still-formidable figure of Thomas Collier Platt, the so-called "Easy Boss" of New York.

Platt and Roosevelt had had a previous history of conflict. The two had clashed some five years before when Roosevelt was head of the New York City Police Board. Platt then felt that the unbending Roosevelt righteousness might split Republicans and result in returning Tammany Hall to power. President Harrison had once introduced Roosevelt to an audience, saying, "He is a young man, impatient for righteousness. He wants everything done before nightfall; some of us can wait until tomorrow." Roosevelt had shown this same righteousness when he was Civil Service Commissioner and a losing reform candidate for mayor of New York. The two men had bumped heads in all these areas.

But they had made a tentative peace when Roosevelt wanted to be Assistant Secretary of the Navy to John D. Long and had to go hat in hand to Platt, asking his approval of the application.

At that time Platt had said of Roosevelt, "I do not particularly like Theodore. He has been a disturbing element to every situation to which he has been a party. I have no reason to believe the leopard changes his spots. But he is not essentially harmful and can probably do less harm to the organization as Assistant Secretary of the Navy than in any other office that can be named."

Before approving the application, however, Platt got Roosevelt to attend a "harmony" dinner for Platt's personal bid for the United States Senate, and Roosevelt later wrote "a very strong letter" to the exclusive Metropolitan Club in Washington "much annoyed over the alleged opposition to Senator Platt's election to the club."

Now, in the upcoming state election of 1899, Platt needed Roosevelt even more.

It was Boss Platt who had picked Roosevelt to go for governor. As soon as Colonel Roosevelt and his Rough Riders returned from the war to their bivouac area in Montauk, Long Island, there was a Boss Platt emissary waiting to see the Colonel, to query his interest in the governorship of New York and to extract a single promise that he would "not make war on him [Platt]." Roosevelt answered well enough and Boss Platt maneuvered the nomination.

With a lingering corruption issue facing the voters, Boss Platt needed a war hero to win, and even so, Roosevelt barely squeaked into the governorship by some 17,000 votes.

Every Sunday morning, Governor Roosevelt visited Boss Platt's suite at the Fifth Avenue Hotel for breakfast and political discussion, and one columnist called it, "Platt's 'Sunday School Classes.' " The two men seemed to have an arrangement about patronage distribution, and while it is true that Roosevelt generally went along with Platt's requests, it is also true that Platt "eased along" with Roosevelt's pet welfare legislation.

But the two men split on several strong issues: Roosevelt's franchise tax on business and Platt's candidate for Superintendent of Insurance. On the franchise tax, Platt wrote Roosevelt:

"When the subject of your nomination was under consideration,

there was one matter that gave me real anxiety. . . . I had heard
from a good many sources that you were a little loose on the relations of capital and labor, on trusts and combinations. . . .

"At the last moment [of the recent legislature], and to my very
great surprise, you did a thing which has caused the business community of New York to wonder how far the notions of Populism,
as laid down in Kansas and Nebraska, have taken hold upon the
Republican party of the state of New York. . . ."

As for reappointing Platt's Superintendent of Insurance, who
had jurisdiction over the powerful insurance companies, friendly
and generous to Platt in their financial support, Roosevelt pointed
out that this Platt man, with a salary of $7,000 a year, had man-
aged to borrow a half-million dollars for himself from these insurance companies. Roosevelt vetoed his appointment calling it "a
stench in the nostrils of the people."

While Roosevelt did finally compromise with Platt on another
candidate for Superintendent, Platt made a basic political decision
on Roosevelt: he wanted him out and away. As he once answered
McKinley on his approval of two New York appointees to foreign
embassies, two men Platt didn't particularly like: "the foreigner
the better."

For Platt, the political problem of Roosevelt had special perti-
nence because the state convention and the question of Roosevelt's renomination for Governor, would happen only several
months after the national convention. Platt's concern crystallized
with Hobart's death: he would get Roosevelt kicked upstairs to
the hidden quiet of the Vice-Presidency. A joke current at that
time was about the two brothers: "One ran away to sea, the other
was elected Vice-President, and nothing was heard of either of
them again." John Adams, the first Vice-President of the United
States, called it "the most insignificant office that ever the inven-
tion of man contrived or his imagination conceived."

Platt's plan demanded careful political detailing. The hurdles
seemed enormous. Platt knew of Hanna's estimate of Roosevelt as
"erratic, unsafe . . . too ambitious." Platt also knew the mood of

President McKinley. James Rhodes, Hanna's brother-in-law, later wrote, "President McKinley, in an inobtrusive way, let it be known that he did not want Roosevelt as his running mate." And Platt knew of Hanna's simmering resentment against Platt—because Platt had nominated Congressman Reed for President in 1896 against McKinley and because Platt had helped force Hanna to accept the gold standard plank as part of the party platform.

Platt joined forces with Matthew Quay, still the supreme political boss of Pennsylvania. Quay had minimal interest in Roosevelt but a maximum interest in Hanna. What kept rankling Quay was that Hanna—who had replaced him as chairman of the Republican National Committee—had also cast the deciding vote in the United States Senate denying Quay his Senate seat because of a questionable certificate of appointment. (At the turn of the century, state legislatures—except for Minnesota—still hand-picked their candidates for the United States Senate, then called "a rich man's club." The Pennsylvania state legislature had a tie vote on Quay, but the Governor had signed Quay's certificate of appointment. A protest of Quay's status put the issue before the Senate for decision.)

As Boies Penrose, Quay's upcoming successor, warned Hanna: "Quay had a hell of a memory."

Penrose attended the initial meeting at the Walton Hotel in Philadelphia between Quay and Platt, in which Platt described Roosevelt as "a bloody anarchist" and "an enemy of the people." Penrose listened to Platt's lengthy bitter attack and then tried to summarize it: "What you mean to say, Senator, is that you want to force Hanna to take Theodore for vice president, but that you know Hanna won't if he can help it and that Theodore will balk because you want to get rid of him and is afraid he'll be just another vice president, a political corpse."

It was an apt summary.

Then Penrose offered his personal advice:

"I went to college with Theodore," he told Platt and Quay. "I know Theodore very well. If you can get enough people hollering for him to take the job—common people, mind you, not nice people—he'll insist on being vice president. Just tell Theodore the people need him in Washington and then start the people out west writing to him, begging him to take it. I've known Theodore a long time."

It worked out much that way.

Platt promptly stirred up political friends in the West to start the letter-writing campaign to Roosevelt. Platt also made a personal pitch to Roosevelt. He intimated that Roosevelt would have a rough fight for re-election as Governor because he had antagonized business by his franchise tax, and antagonized labor by calling out the state militia to quell a strike at Croton. Platt even vigorously tried to persuade Hanna that he was wrong about Roosevelt, and that Roosevelt on the ticket could guarantee New York's electoral vote for McKinley. A political reporter commented that, after every meeting with Platt, Hanna carefully searched his pockets to make sure Platt had not dropped Roosevelt into one of them.

Unexpected support for the Platt plan came from none other than Roosevelt's close friend, Lodge, who now saw this as a new road to the Presidency for his friend and wrote:

"Your interests and your future have been constantly in my mind. The general impression of course is that you would be very foolish to take the Vice Presidency. . . . I would put it most tersely by saying that if I were a candidate for the Presidency, I would take the Vice Presidency in a minute at this juncture. . . . My belief in your taking it arises from my conviction that it is the true stepping-stone for you, either toward the Presidency or the Governor Generalship of the Philippines. . . . I think the Vice Presidency is the better path to better and more important things. . . ."

On December 11, 1899, Roosevelt wrote Lodge:

". . . It seems to me that the chance of my being a presidential candidate is too small to warrant very serious consideration at present. To have been a good Colonel, a good Governor, and a good Assistant Secretary of the Navy is not enough to last four years. If McKinley were to die tomorrow I would be one of the men seriously considered as his successor—I mean that and just no more. But four years hence, the Spanish War will be in the very remote past and what I have done as Governor will not be very recent. Nobody can tell who will be up by that time. . . .

"The Vice Presidency is a most honorable office, but for a young man there is not much to do. . . . If I am Vice President, I am 'planted' for four years. Here I can turn around. Platt told me definitely that of course he was for me for a renomination.

". . . Some of the Western men are wild to have me go on to strengthen the ticket, but it scarcely seems to me that the ticket needs strengthening. . . ."

But, that same week, in a note to his sister, Roosevelt said, ". . . Of course, were my renomination out of the question, I should accept the Vice Presidency were I offered it. . . ."

Platt busied himself on both sides of the political street. With Roosevelt, Platt kept his pressure on a "soft sell" basis, but planting all the seeds of question in his favor. Elsewhere, especially in Washington, Platt played it hard.

Word of all this finally reached Roosevelt, and he quickly wrote Lodge:

"I hasten to write you because of a most unexpected bit of information. I find that after Platt's return from Washington he *did* tell a couple of New York politicians that I would undoubtedly have to accept the Vice Presidency; that events were shaping themselves so that this was inevitable. He gave me no hint of this, taking exactly the opposite view, and I do not understand what was up, or for that matter what is up now. . . ."

Roosevelt's confusion quickened. Platt started sending people to Roosevelt with an entirely different idea: if he did become Vice-President, they told him, he could then resign to accept the Governor Generalship of the Philippines, which he *did* want.

Countering that, Roosevelt received a visit from his lieutenant governor, Timothy Woodruff who said that he didn't ever want to be governor, because of the hard knocks and the responsibility, but that he very much wanted the titular dignity of the Vice-Presidency, "chiefly because he had plenty of money and could entertain."

"Woodruff is a most good-humored, friendly fellow," Roosevelt wrote Lodge, "wild to have me nominate him for Vice President, which I suppose for my sins I might have to do (not if *I* can help it!), and he is amusingly and absolutely certain that nothing can prevent his nomination."

Roosevelt then pointed out to Lodge that the money question was a serious one with him, especially since his children were grown and their education a matter of pressing importance. Furthermore, he said, the social side of the Vice-Presidency would involve a serious financial drain, which he could not afford.

But Platt increased his pressure. Several members of the Republican National Committee, led by Henry C. Payne, visited Roosevelt in Albany, added their urgings that Roosevelt accept the Vice-Presidency. Roosevelt refused them gently, saying he feared a political reaction in New York if he left the state, but he still left a large door open. And, in Washington, Platt and Quay had helped stir a consensus of Republican congressmen to announce that Roosevelt was the logical vice-presidential candidate since New York was a crucial state, and Roosevelt was also so popular in the Midwest and West. They also urged that Roosevelt might make the Vice-Presidency an important office, that he would be in the public eye at all times as presiding officer of the Senate, without running the risks always present in the problems of governorship.

But in a letter that day to Platt, Roosevelt took a different tack:

". . . As you know, I am of an active nature . . . but as Vice President, I don't see there is anything I can do. I would be simply a presiding officer and that I should find a bore. . . ."

The next day he wrote to Henry C. Payne in the same vein:

". . . There would be nothing in the world for me to do once I became Vice President. I could work at my historical studies, but after all I could do that better if I were professor of history at some college. . . ."

And the day after, in a letter to Lodge, which began, "Now this letter is to be strictly secret . . ." he wrote:

"I have found out one reason why Senator Platt wants me nominated for the Vice Presidency. He is, I am convinced, genuinely friendly, and indeed I think I may say really fond of me, and is personally satisfied with the way I have conducted politics; but the big-monied men with whom he is in close touch and whose campaign contributions have certainly been no inconsiderable factor in his strength, have been pressing him very strongly to get me put in the Vice Presidency, so as to get me out of the state. . . ."

Three days later, on February 6, Roosevelt told reporters, "It is proper for me to say definitely that under no circumstances could I or would I accept the nomination for the Vice Presidency. My duty is here to the state whose people chose me as Governor. I am happy to state that Senator Platt cordially acquiesces in my views in the matter."

Of course he was wrong. Platt may have seemed cordial, but he did not acquiesce. Roosevelt wrote Platt that he would not accept the nomination for the Vice-Presidency even if it were unanimous, and pointed out that Platt could prevent such a unanimity if he wanted to. He also added that he favored Woodruff for the job. Then, in an official statement, Roosevelt said on February 12, that he was a candidate for the governorship and not the Vice-Presidency.

That almost seemed to settle it. Hanna sent a quick note to Roosevelt, "Your reasoning in the political situation in New York seems to be good and I think should be conclusive."

But if Hanna closed the books on the Roosevelt candidacy, Platt did not.

Roosevelt soon started hedging. At a dinner in March, Roosevelt surprised John McCook by asking whether he thought it might not be better to accept the Vice-Presidency rather than disrupt the state Republican party. And, on April 23, Roosevelt wrote to Lodge: "I did not say that I would not under any circumstances accept the Vice-Presidency. I have been careful to put it exactly as you advised." He was on a seesaw of political indecision.

He talked to friends about the New York State voters being "entirely ephemeral" and that "nobody can tell . . . whether the machine intends to renominate me next fall or not . . . there is no question whatever that if the leaders can, they will upset me." He also wondered aloud whether the party would ever offer him anything again if he flatly refused the Vice-Presidency.

Yet, three days after writing that letter to Lodge, he told reporters that he would return to private life before accepting the Vice-Presidency. And, two weeks after that, he was in Washington repeating to McKinley that he intended to run again for governor. In Washington, he told his friend Elihu Root of all his objections to the Vice-Presidency and Root smiled and said, "Of course not, Theodore, you're not fit for it."

To buttress himself, he even dredged up a piece of political history about a New York governor named Silas Wright, who refused to accept the nomination of Vice-President with President Polk and returned to New York to win re-election as governor by an even greater majority.

At the same time, he told his friend James Bishop, "If I were actually nominated; and I were unable to stem the convention's desire to nominate me, it might be impossible to refuse." He also told Benjamin Odell, New York State Republican Party Chairman, that he would support Odell for the Vice-Presidency, if he wanted it. Odell didn't.

Odell was Platt's ambitious lieutenant, ambitious to succeed Platt as party boss, ambitious to succeed Roosevelt as governor, and he would do both. But, at that point, Odell gave some practical political advice to Roosevelt: First, Roosevelt must stay away from the convention, then he must state "positively and explicitly" that he would not accept the nomination if tendered. If he did that, said Odell, he might be certain with my help and influence that he would not be nominated.

Roosevelt refused pointblank to stay away from the convention because he would be "looked upon as a coward."

"I told him that he would then be nominated in spite of himself," said Odell.

Lodge said much the same thing:

"If you go to that Convention . . . you will be nominated . . . and if you are nominated . . . you will be unable to refuse. If you stay away with your absolute declination, which you already have put out, I do not think you will be nominated."

Roosevelt worried aloud about all this and Secretary of State John Hay had a soothing statement, "I think you are unduly alarmed," Hay told him, "there is no instance of an election of a Vice President by violence."

As convention time came closer, Platt used everything short of violence. His greatest pressure was indirect, spreading the mood among western delegates that Boss Hanna was trying to cheat Roosevelt out of his political future. As one western delegate put it in print—he wanted Hanna to stop kicking their friend in the face. Hanna, of course, long ago had stopped kicking because he firmly thought the dark horse was dead.

But the whir of Roosevelt's indecision had never stopped. The *New York World* featured a cartoon of Roosevelt on a horse saying, "Nay! Nay!" to Platt who was holding out a bucket of feed to lure Roosevelt into the vice-presidential stockyard.

Platt's pushing of Roosevelt for the Vice-Presidency was more complex than the pure wish to get the man out of the state. Platt felt that Roosevelt would add enough strength to the McKinley ticket so that he (Platt) could nominate and elect almost any Republican candidate for governor. In a single move, as Mark Sullivan put it, "Platt could get rid of Roosevelt, put Roosevelt where he did not want to be, and at the same time make use of Roosevelt's popularity for ends that Roosevelt abhorred."

As Platt's manipulations became more obvious, Hanna stirred himself to greater activity on pinpointing a candidate. Platt's man, Frederick Gibbs, New York representative on the Republican National Committee, and also a member of its executive committee, reported to Platt from Philadelphia, about a week before the convention opening, that Hanna was still trying to get Bliss to change his mind, and seemed convinced he could.

Platt told Gibbs not to worry, that he still felt certain it would be Roosevelt. To another cohort, he added, "Roosevelt might as well stand under Niagara Falls and try to spit water back as to stop his nomination by this convention." As if to confirm this, Platt's political partner, Matthew Quay reported, "Our babe is in the manger. The kings have seen his star in the east and are come to worship him."

Shortly before the New York State delegation left for Philadelphia, Mrs. Roosevelt found herself discussing the upcoming convention after dinner at the State Executive Mansion with Chief Judge Alton B. Parker of the New York Court of Appeals. Mrs. Roosevelt turned to Parker for his political judgment: did he think that Theodore could avoid the Vice-Presidency?

Judge Parker, a tall, distinguished looking man with a flowing mustache, told Mrs. Roosevelt that he didn't think her husband was so very anxious to avoid that nomination. And then he presented his vision of what would happen:

". . . And then—just a bit late—you will see your handsome husband come in and bedlam will break loose, and he will receive such a demonstration as no one else will receive. And, being a devoted wife, you will be very proud and happy. Then some two or three days later, you will see your husband unanimously nominated for Vice President of the United States."

But Roosevelt's political seesaw had turned to the firmly negative side, and so outspoken was it that a *New York Times* analysis of vice-presidential possibilities, three days before the convention opening, didn't even list the Roosevelt name. Dolliver was much mentioned; Long was listed as a dark horse administration favorite, although the analyst failed to see what strength Long could add to the ticket; and Fairbanks was added as a possibility. The *Times* added, "Well informed politicians believe New York will not present a candidate for Vice President."

Aggressive Timothy Woodruff was not to be sidelined that

swiftly. Hanna was already in Philadelphia holding conferences with party leaders, including New York County chairman L. E. Quigg, and Woodruff sought out Hanna to make a personal pitch for Hanna's support.

Hanna asked Woodruff, "Do you think that the Convention would nominate you for the Presidency?"

Woodruff said no.

"Then, don't you know," said Hanna, "that there is only one life between the Presidency and the Vice Presidency and that it would be foolhardy to nominate a man for Vice President who would not be big enough to be President?"

Woodruff felt that his hopes for the nomination were finished.

As delegates poured into Philadelphia, they found few posters or banners appealing for their support for any vice-presidential nominee. Somebody described the general attitude of these delegates as "listening."

Resting at his friend's home in Philadelphia, one of the best listeners was Mark Hanna. Platt's carefully planted talk of Roosevelt continually increased. The newly-arrived California delegation declared loudly for Roosevelt. National Committeeman Saunders was busy circulating among the receptive intermountain delegates, pressing the Roosevelt idea, ably aided by Senator Wolcott of Colorado.

Then, on Saturday, June 16, Theodore Roosevelt himself arrived in Philadelphia.

"Immediately on reaching Philadelphia," Roosevelt later wrote, "I was made aware that there was a very strong movement outside the state of New York in favor of my nomination, the motive of these men outside of New York being the exact reverse of the motives of the politicians in New York; for the men outside of New York wished me nominated because they believed in me and wished me to continue in public life. . . ."

The intensity of Roosevelt's dilemma soon multiplied.

Kansas came first, their delegates led by J. R. Burton, a candidate for the United States Senate, who felt a Roosevelt on the ticket would also heighten his own election chances. Roosevelt told Burton, "My dear fellow, I want to do what is right by the party, but I honestly believe that my path of duty lies in New York State."

Burton tried to shrug it off, "Well, if we don't vote for you, we'll vote for Woodruff."

But, outside the room, Burton told reporters that Kansas didn't care what Roosevelt's private preference might be because they still planned to work for his nomination. More imprudently, Burton added that he cared nothing about Roosevelt personally, but that Roosevelt's name on the ticket would ensure his own election to the Senate. (Burton later won that election.)

The Kansas delegation wore huge artificial sunflowers on their lapels, and when they turned back their coat lapels, these read:

"I'M FROM KANSAS!
NOW, DAMN YOU, LAUGH!"

Roosevelt hedged a little more carefully with the next group, the Iowa delegation, headed by Colonel Lafayette "Lafe" Young and pledged to Dolliver. Young asked for Roosevelt's intentions and desires:

"It is easy to say what I desire to do," said Roosevelt laughing. "I desire to be Governor of New York again, and I do not care to be nominated for Vice President of the United States."

"Can you give us an idea of what you *intend* to do?" asked one of the delegates.

"Well, these fellows have placed me in an awful position," Roosevelt said. "I want to be Governor of New York for another term at least, and I do not care to be nominated for Vice President. But they are forcing the matter on me on all sides, and it is going to be very difficult to decline it. If I refuse, the people will say that 'Roosevelt has the big head and thinks he is too much of a man to be Vice President.' I do not care to be placed in such a position, for it is not true that I hold any such opinion of myself."

"Then why don't you take the stand taken by Senator Allison

when they tried to get him to take the place," a delegate suggested. "He simply said, 'I don't want it, gentlemen. I will not take it. Good day.'"

"Possibly the pressure brought to bear upon me is somewhat stronger than that placed upon the Senator," said Roosevelt.

Young then interrupted, trying to point up the problem:

"The situation is right here, Governor. These people who are trying to get you to take this place don't care anything for you. They simply think that you, of all men, can lend strength to the ticket. They think that you can carry the state of New York. They do not care to have you carry it for the Republican party. They know you can carry it either as Governor or as Vice President. They want you to carry it as Vice President for their own purposes and they are unwilling that you should carry it for your own purposes or for the good of the party. Now, if you accept the nomination, you are simply playing into their hands and making yourself a party to their schemes."

Roosevelt laughed. "Oh, come now Young," he said. "You are too hard."

"I am not hard at all," said Young. "I am simply stating the situation as I know it exists, as you and everybody else know it exists. These men cannot hurt you if you decline to take the nomination. No man can hurt Roosevelt save Roosevelt himself."

"Well, gentlemen," said Roosevelt, "I have said all that I can say at the present time. Mr. Hanna and a number of other gentlemen are waiting to see me and I will be glad to see you all at any time."

"Then you cannot give us any positive assurance at this time as to what you will do," persisted a delegate.

"I have said all that I can say at the present time."

To the waiting press outside the room, Young tried to sum up the interview: "He [Roosevelt] did not say he would and he wouldn't, and, as we came out of his room, Mark Hanna was waiting to see him to urge him to refuse the nomination and Henry Cabot Lodge was waiting to urge him to take it."

Squeezing in before Hanna was the South Dakota delegation. To them Roosevelt said, "Gentlemen, I am placed in a great and serious quandary. I am not unmindful of the honor which you all want to confer upon me. I do not scorn it or scoff at it, but I believe that I can better serve my party in New York State than in the nation, and I am of the mind that I should not be nominated for Vice President but for Governor of New York."

"Will you refuse?" a delegate asked. Roosevelt hesitated, then said slowly, "I don't see how I could," and then added quickly, "but I have not yet entirely made up my mind."

"Who will be nominated?" another delegate asked.

"I don't know," said Roosevelt, "what do you hear?"

The Hanna-Roosevelt meeting had an important prelude.

Roosevelt's personal emissary in Philadelphia was Nicholas Murray Butler and a small group whom he had sent ahead to discourage delegates from voting for him for Vice-President. Butler was a prominent New York educator who had helped found Teacher's College at Columbia University, and would soon be the university president. Roosevelt had months before sent Butler to tell both McKinley and Hanna that he could not and would not accept the Vice-Presidency. Hanna had exploded at this, banged the table, saying that he would control the convention and Roosevelt couldn't and wouldn't be nominated under any circumstances.

But now, at Philadelphia, the Roosevelt talk kept increasing. The pivotal Pennsylvania delegation had announced its entire group would vote for Roosevelt. Seriously concerned that Roosevelt might be drafted against his will, Butler and Frederick Holls went to see Hanna and said, "You cannot beat somebody with nobody. . . ." The only alternative, they said, was for Hanna to produce a candidate whose personality and fitness were so compelling that the convention would rally to him quickly.

"Hanna greeted these statements with another outburst of profanity," wrote Butler later, "and again affirmed with all vehemence that Roosevelt would not be nominated because he, Hanna, would not permit it."

Butler and Holls persisted in the search for an alternative, and Hanna finally mentioned former Secretary of the Navy Long. Butler and Holls both doubted that the convention would prefer Long to Roosevelt, and the meeting ended.

Now here was Butler, Lodge, and a few other close Roosevelt associates meeting with Hanna for a showdown, all of them agreeing with Hanna that Roosevelt should refuse the possible nomination. Roosevelt's friends felt firmly that if he didn't really want the nomination, it should not be forced on him.

"I think we can nominate someone else besides Roosevelt," Hanna told the group.

"For God's sake, go ahead and do it," said Roosevelt.

"That's right, do it," said Lodge. "Let's go ahead and nominate some other man."

"What's the matter with Long?" said Hanna.

"Nothing," said Lodge, "go ahead and nominate him."

"Well what's the matter with Fairbanks?"

"Nothing in the world," said Lodge. "Go ahead and nominate him. Nominate anybody you can. We are all standing ready to help you."

The conference lasted forty minutes. Roosevelt promised to issue a statement to the press at 4:00 P.M. Interviewed outside the room, Hanna was asked, "Do you think Roosevelt wants the nomination?"

"Well, I don't know," said Hanna. "He knows how he can stop it."

Hanna then hurried off to another room at the Walton Hotel, where he met with Bliss, Allison, Lodge, and several others. One of them opened with, "If you propose to nominate an administration candidate, it is high time that he be decided upon."

As the group talked, their feeling was that neither Dolliver nor Long could get delegate support away from Roosevelt.

Meanwhile, in Roosevelt's room, Butler was busy persuading Roosevelt that his single hope to stay out of the race was to issue an absolutely flat and final statement of declination to the press.

"What is it you want me to say?" said Roosevelt. "I am willing to say it."

Butler then wrote a brief statement ending with the thought that he could not accept even if nominated. Mrs. Roosevelt read it and approved it, then handed it to her husband, and Butler told him, "If you will sign that paper and give it out this afternoon, you will not be nominated."

"T. R. screwed up his face as he had a way of doing when in perplexity," Butler wrote afterwards, "and said he was in favor of the statement but thought he could improve its phrasing. So he sat down at the desk and wrote a statement of his own. Having finished, he handed it to us and said, 'There, that is what you want.' I read it carefully and then, after reading it a second time, said; 'Theodore, if that is all you will say, you will certainly be nominated. You have taken out of the statement all of the finality and definiteness that was in mine.' "

Roosevelt argued with them vigorously but refused to budge from his position. "I then began to suspect for the first time," said Butler, "that he was really willing to be nominated. . . ."

Exactly at four, Roosevelt called, "Come in, gentlemen," and reporters so overflowed the room that some of them even stood on the bed. Standing in a corner, behind the bed, Roosevelt took up his statement and said, "I shall read very slowly." Not only did he read slowly, but he even announced the different punctuation marks:

"In view of the revival of the talk of myself as vice presidential candidate, I have this to say: It is impossible too deeply to express how touched I am by the attitude of those delegates who have wished me to take this nomination.

"Moreover it is not necessary to say how thoroughly I understand the high honor and dignity of the office, an office so high and so honorable that it is well worth the ambition of any man in the United States.

"But while I appreciate all this in the full, nevertheless I feel most deeply that the field of my best usefulness to the public and to the party is in New York State and if the party should see fit to renominate me for governor, I can in that position help the national ticket as in no other way.

"I very earnestly ask that every friend of mine in the convention respect my wish and my judgment in this matter."

And then Roosevelt added, "That's all. I have nothing to add. Don't ask me any more questions."

Instead of squelching the question, Roosevelt had raised it to a new crescendo. At the press conference, Butler watched the faces of Platt's son, Frank H. Platt, and his henchman, Lemuel Ely Quigg "both of whom had their eyes fixed upon Roosevelt with closest attention. When they heard the words of the statement, their faces were wreathed in smiles and they darted for the door to report to Senator Platt that all was well. . . ."

Just as Platt saw the statement, so did Hanna. He and his group were still in hot discussion about an alternative candidate when somebody broke into the meeting with a copy of Roosevelt's words. They all read it quietly and one of them said, "A flat bid for the nomination."

But nobody seemed to be absolutely sure. To the press, Hanna highly praised the Roosevelt statement as a definite declination, then said, "I have no candidate. The choice of the convention will be my candidate. The Administration is not dictating what will be the action of the convention." Hanna then sent men to various delegations, spreading this declination interpretation, telling everybody that the Roosevelt boom had busted, and that Long was the man. Hanna then personally appealed to Lodge to hold New England delegates for Long.

Lodge still seemed to feel that Roosevelt really didn't want the nomination and so he said he was for Long first, last, and always, that Massachusetts was for Long and that Long would be nominated if New York could not agree upon a candidate from their own state. Lodge wore a huge blue silk badge which said in bold gilt letters: FOR VICE PRESIDENT, JOHN D. LONG.

As usual, rumors ran wild. One really wild one, and highly popu-

lar, said that every Long button was a potential vote for Roosevelt
and that Lodge and Hanna would arrange for a Roosevelt nomination supported by New York.

The next day's *New York Times* headline read: LONG GAIN-
ING GROUND.

The *Times'* reasoning was that Long would not run unless he
knew he was satisfactory to the Administration. "This idea," said
the *Times* analyst, "received encouragement in quarters which
made the man a prime favorite."

Later that day, a reporter asked Roosevelt, "Governor, is there
any change in the situation?"

"I don't know what the situation is," said Roosevelt.

"Have you escaped?" Roosevelt looked at his well-wishing
friends who wanted him to run, "Judging from the sour expressions, I should say that I had."

The escape, however, was not that simple. Platt and Quay that
night planned their next strategy—to stampede his nomination and
force his acceptance. Quay and Penrose already had pledged their
word to the Pennsylvania delegation at its caucus that Roosevelt
would accept the nomination, and the delegation then voted for
Roosevelt 53–4.

At the New York caucus, at 8:00 A.M. the next morning, June
18, the corridors were so crowded with the curious, the local police
were needed to screen New York delegates. On Roosevelt's arrival
into the caucus room, the crowd burst into applause. But the meeting lasted only ten minutes; some committees were selected, Platt
picked as permanent chairman of the delegation, and no mention
made of a vice-presidential nominee.

Platt, in a plaster cast, suffering from a broken right rib, retired
to his rooms. Asked if Roosevelt could be defeated, Platt said, "I
think so." National Committeeman Gibbs told a reporter that
Roosevelt had personally asked him to help knock out any potential Roosevelt boom. A reporter also quoted Odell as saying he
did not think Roosevelt would accept the nomination.

And Platt's man Quigg was quoted: "If a New York man is

chosen, it will be Roosevelt. If he is not named, the west will select a man."

There was still much Dolliver talk but Fairbanks had pulled himself out of the picture. Woodruff announced to the press that he would be the New York favorite son, but that New York would support Roosevelt if he were nominated by another state. States everywhere were holding caucuses, and a reporter described their general mood as resembling "dumb, driven cattle" and reported overhearing this conversation:

"Whom are you for Vice President?"

"I don't know; I haven't been told yet."

The early caucus showed a remakable amount of "no preference," or "any good man" or as the Arkansas delegation put it, "anybody the leaders wanted." The California caucus agreed on no candidate but added, "Roosevelt is the strongest man who could be named . . . and if it was not for McKinley, he would be the man in the party for President." Generally, the New England states stayed with Long, the Midwest leaned toward Dolliver or Roosevelt, and Florida made the most honest political announcement of them all, saying, "We cannot deliver our electoral vote and we believe in supporting the party leaders when it comes to the selection of candidates."

Hanna men were still busy circulating for Long, trying to persuade Illinois to switch from Dolliver to Long, trying hard to unite the splintered anti-Roosevelt factions. What hurt Hanna most was McKinley's silence and his own inability to openly and loudly proclaim anybody as an administration candidate. And what confused the caucuses most was the bevy of Roosevelt friends assigned to plead with them not to vote for Roosevelt. Once such close Roosevelt friend was General Francis V. Greene, and if he put more fervor into his pleading, the cynics said it was because he himself was a hopeful vice-presidential nominee.

But despite Greene's pleading, Kansas caucused again that night, kept firm for Roosevelt. So did Wisconsin, the Indian Territory, and a strong core of others. However, there was a growing uncertainty and confusion. If the confusion seemed general, the Platt-Quay political mind kept clear. They had a great ace to play, but the time was not yet right.

On the afternoon before the convention opening, Greene came to see Platt, a final futile attempt to dissuade Platt from pushing Roosevelt. Greene told Platt about a Roosevelt press interview that day in which he supposedly said he would positively not accept the nomination if offered, that he was acting on the advice of his close and valued friends.

During the discussion, Senator Penrose burst excitedly into the room to tell Platt that the Pennsylvania caucus again had given Roosevelt almost unanimous support.

Platt pointed to Greene, and told Penrose:

"This gentleman, who is a close friend of Governor Roosevelt, has just informed me that the Governor has given to the newspapers a statement to the effect that he will not accept a Vice Presidential nomination."

Penrose simply said, "He better go back to the Governor and tell him it is high time he learned who his real friends are."

New York held a caucus that night. Bedded by his broken rib, Platt sent for Hanna, and Hanna came. The two men talked alone. Platt played his political ace.

In his autobiography, he detailed it:

"Since we were greatly outnumbered by the administration forces, some strategical operations were deemed advisable in order to demoralize and, if possible, disorganize the administration opposition to our plan.

"Accordingly Mr. Quay let it be known that he intended, upon the assembling of the convention, to offer a resolution reducing the representation in the convention of certain Southern States upon the basis of the voting population. A large measure of the strength of the opposition lay in the South, and the proposition of Senator Quay created great consternation in the administration forces."

While Quay was spreading the plan to key delegates, Platt presented the details to Hanna. For Hanna, the plan spelled havoc.

The South was his sewed-up bailiwick, and any tampering with his control of it would mean an ugly floor fight with such confusion that it might even result in an uncontrolled convention where anything could happen—conceivably even a *presidential* nomination for Roosevelt. And it would certainly cut his future political effectiveness as a national boss.

"At first, Senator Hanna obdurately opposed my efforts to convince him of the party necessity of nominating Mr. Roosevelt," wrote Platt later, "but finally I won him over to my idea, and he left the room promising to issue that night a public statement that, in his judgment, Mr. Roosevelt should be the candidate of the convention. This promise he faithfully kept, and from that moment, the nomination was assured."

(Platt's memory served him badly on this point: Hanna issued no such statement that night. If anything, his anti-Roosevelt activity heightened and he was on the phone to President McKinley trying to get him to issue a flat statement of support for Long. McKinley refused.)

Platt felt he had Hanna, that Hanna must succumb to his threat on the southern vote. In the meanwhile, up in Roosevelt's room, the Governor again seemed convinced that he must *not* accept the nomination, and his statements to everybody took on a more unequivocal tone.

"I heard of this," said Platt, "and asked my son Frank to go in to him and say that he would be nominated; that he could not stop that, and I wanted his promise that if he were made McKinley's associate, he would run.

"Roosevelt and my son came to my rooms. The Governor was in a state of rare excitement, even for him.

" 'I shall go into the New York caucus and tell the delegates that I shall, if nominated for Vice President, arise in the convention and decline. I can serve you, Senator Platt, far better as Governor than as Vice President,' said Roosevelt pugnaciously [according to Platt].

" 'But you cannot be renominated for Governor; and you are

going to be nominated for Vice President,' was my retort.

" 'I cannot be renominated?' queried Roosevelt.

" 'No, your successor is in this room,' said I, pointing to Chairman Odell.

" 'Now, I want your promise, that if you are endorsed by the New York caucus, you will not refuse, and that, if you are nominated by the convention, you will run,' I added.

"Roosevelt showed his teeth, paced up and down the room, and chafed as a horse does under a tight rein and curbed bit.

" 'Well, Senator Platt,' finally returned Roosevelt reluctantly, 'I will pledge myself not to formally decline the New York caucus endorsement, but I shall certainly urge the caucus to name another,' he added.

" 'And remember, I shall pinch you if I see any signs of your getting up and declining,' put in my son.

" 'All right, you may pinch me as hard as you like,' answered Roosevelt as he and Frank hurried to the caucus of the New York delegation."

Roosevelt, in *his* autobiography, differs in his description of what happened in Platt's room. After receiving Platt's invitation, Roosevelt writes he went upstairs to see Platt, was told he would be nominated as Vice-President and would have to yield.

"I answered that I was sorry to be disagreeable," wrote Roosevelt, "but that I regarded the movement as one to get me out of the governorship for reasons which were not of a personal but of a public character; that is, for reasons connected with the principles in which I so heartily believed, and that I would not and could not consent to go back on those principles, and so I would refuse to accept the nomination for Vice-President. Senator Platt then said I would have to accept, I would be beaten for the nomination for Governor, and some one else nominated for Governor in my place. I answered, in effect, that this was a threat which simply rendered it impossible for me to accept, that if there was to be war there would be war and that was all there was to it; and I bowed and left the room."

Roosevelt then said he went directly to the New York caucus meeting, promptly informed a half-dozen delegates of everything that had happened in Platt's room. He also said he told them: "I intended to announce immediately that I was a candidate for Governor and would fight for the nomination, and that every man who voted for my nomination as Vice President must do so with the understanding that I would see that the people in their turn understood that he was thus voting at the direction of Mr. Platt, in order to remove me from the Governorship; that I should make this statement instantly in the full meeting; that I would make it to the newspapers afterwards, and that I would fight for the nomination on this issue."

". . . There was a great confusion," continued Roosevelt, "and one of Senator Platt's lieutenants came to me and begged me not to say anything for a minute or two until he could communicate with the Senator, whom he was certain must have been misunderstood by me. I laughed and said I had very clearly understood him, but that of course I would wait for a few minutes until he could be communicated with. In three or four minutes, this gentleman came downstairs saying that the Senator wished to see me again, that he was very sorry he had spoken in a way that caused me to misunderstand him, that he was under the influence of opiate to reduce the pain caused by the injuries he had received, and that he supposed he had expressed himself badly in consequence.

"Accordingly I went upstairs and Mr. Platt substantially repeated this explanation to me, saying that he was sorry he had shown temper or expressed himself badly, but that, of course, in view of my feeling, the effort to nominate me for Vice President would be abandoned, and that he wished me to be assured that he and all his friends would favor my renomination as Governor."

"I thanked him, bowed, and went downstairs," said Roosevelt.

Platt says nothing of all this, nothing about a second Roosevelt visit that night, nothing about reneging on the nomination.

Whoever's version comes closer to truth, here's what happened at the caucus:

Roosevelt reiterated his intention not to be a vice-presidential candidate. Some of the delegates then spoke in dignified and forceful language that Roosevelt's wishes in this matter should be respected. But delegate Edward Lauterbach advanced to the front row, where Roosevelt was seated, pointed his finger almost in Roosevelt's face and said:

"Your very presence at this convention as a delegate-at-large is an allurement to the convention to nominate you. You come here, and moving among the delegates, associating with your old friends from the West, and for that matter in all parts of the country, with the glamor of the Spanish War resting on you, you tempt the delegates to support you and make you the candidate, regardless of what you may say as to your wishes in the matter."

Later in that meeting, according to Platt, Nicholas Murray Butler and some others clustered around Roosevelt, asking him, "Say you'll decline if nominated, Governor."

At that moment, according to Platt, Platt's son Frank pinched Roosevelt in the leg, and whispered, "Remember your contract with the Senator, Governor."

(Platt later referred to that as the pinch that made a President.)

Pinch or no pinch, the clear point is that Roosevelt did not put his refusal in the most final terms.

However, most New York delegates felt the Roosevelt statement was final enough so that they voted to support Timothy Woodruff.

("It might taper down to Tim," Platt had once said.)

And where was Platt's firm hand? Did this mean that Roosevelt's version of a second meeting was accurate? It seems so. On the other hand, a Times reporter, analyzing the caucus result, felt it was an old Platt political trick to permit the delegation to hold an open meeting, arriving at an open decision, so that he could put on record all those delegates who were more pro-Roosevelt than pro-Platt. It is true that Platt later blackballed twenty-one of them.

The New York caucus vote had a brush-fire effect, and the convention confusion increased. The Arkansas delegation chairman expressed this confusion when he said, "We don't propose to be carried off our feet, but I think we will support any gentleman whose nomination is desired by the Administration. We did want Roosevelt; I don't know who we want now."

But Kansas had no qualms. A delegation with their silken sunflowers told Roosevelt, "Governor, we have heard your wishes. Now listen to our demands. You must be the candidate for Vice President. . . .

"Whatever might be your wishes, ambition or final decision, this delegation proposes to vote for you at all hazards. Nothing that you could say would stop us from using all our efforts in your behalf, both in preliminaries, in the corridors and on the floor of the convention."

Louisiana also stayed steadfast for Roosevelt; Indiana put Roosevelt first choice, Dolliver second; Kentucky, who had wanted Roosevelt, was now unsure; California, strong for Roosevelt, now trended to Long.

Roosevelt's close friend Lodge kept acting as if Roosevelt was definitely out of it. Not only did he busy himself corralling specific first ballot commitments for Long from all the New England delegations (except Connecticut, which still wavered), but he also wired Long that he would nominate him. Delegates from Nevada, Missouri, Michigan, and Illinois also assured Lodge that Long would get at least some of their votes. New Jersey also seemed to be for Long, but refused to be bound. Pennsylvania had not caucused again. There seemed to be little question that if Roosevelt had stayed away from the convention, Long would have been the nominee.

Somebody quoted the New York Stock Exchange odds then against Roosevelt as ten to one, and the unhappiest man at the convention seemed to be the familiar figure of "Buttons Bim" Bimberg who had ordered thousands of emblems announcing a McKinley-Roosevelt ticket. "If it isn't Roosevelt," a reporter noted, "there will be a dent in the Delaware River caused by Bim committing suicide."

But the convention opening on June 19 was not suicide weather —a breezy, cool day with a bright sky, the fresh air blowing into the Exposition Auditorium, the hot air blowing out.

Excitement on opening day seemed minimal, and there was no physical confusion because well-trained ushers were everywhere to help find seats for delegates.

It was a convention conspicuously dominated by United States Senators. Senator Hanna, as Chairman of the National Committee, was scheduled to call the convention to order; Senator Wolcott, Temporary Chairman, whose keynote address would be the campaign document; Senator Lodge, picked as the convention Permanent Chairman; Senator Fairbanks, as Chairman of the Committee on Resolutions preparing the platform; Senator Foraker, given the honor of nominating McKinley; Senators Thurston and Depew to help second it; and then, of course, Senators Platt and Quay.

Senator Mark Hanna walked into the Exposition Auditorium about 11:30 and the band struck up, "Hail to the Chief" and many observant delegates noted that there was more political truth than poetry in that musical reception. One reporter remembered the joke of the child who had asked her parent: "If McKinley should die, will Hanna still be President?" and the parent answered, "I'm afraid so, my child."

But it was a power Hanna didn't feel at that moment. He saw it as a convention of loose ends with strings he couldn't pull. The Platt-Quay threat on the southern vote still loomed large. McKinley was still silent. And nobody knew what Roosevelt might do.

It took time for the hall to fill up and Hanna finally gavelled the convention to order about thirty-five minutes late.

While Hanna's heavy gavel thumped for order, in walked Theodore Roosevelt, his figure made more obvious by his famous broad-brimmed black hat, the same hat he had worn in his race for the governorship.

Wayne MacVeagh, who had been Attorney General under President Garfield, turned to his friends and said, "Gentlemen, that's an Acceptance Hat."

To the crowd, it looked like Roosevelt's Rough Rider hat, and their applause went wild.

Roosevelt kept his face frozen, he didn't acknowledge the applause, didn't even remove his hat during the two minutes it took to find his seat. The New York delegates seated all around him wore Woodruff buttons.

The band then started playing, "The Star-Spangled Banner," and Roosevelt was first on his feet. Somebody said he jumped up almost as if he had been sitting on a tack. He kept his hat over his heart during the anthem. As soon as it was over, a swarm of some two-hundred delegates came to shake his hand.

On the platform, Hanna was obviously not smiling.

Talking to the convention that day, Hanna said something about a different political situation existing this year and, almost with a tone of prophecy, added:

"At this convention, if ever, the vice presidential nomination should be made a serious question and a man chosen who would . . . give the country an administration equally as good as that of McKinley if he should, by any mishap, ascend to the first place."

Talking about the tone of the administration, Hanna said, "Do we want a change? Let well enough alone. . . ."

Applause was on the listless side, the dullness of the convention mood shown by the absence of delegates marching in bodies to their seats cheering their favorite sons, the absence of state leaders moving around to get support from other delegations. The only noise came from an intermittent buzzing of ordinary conversation and the playing of a single band. It was almost as if the average delegate felt that somebody else would arrange everything, that only their approval would be necessary.

The hall had only one very narrow gallery along an end wall and a green fence surrounded the delegates and alternates. Spectators were seated in a square doughnut shape on an incline around it. And the strongest stir came during the touching ceremony of introducing individually the thirteen survivors of the first National Republican Convention held in Philadelphia in 1856.

Temporary Chairman Senator Edward O. Wolcott of Colorado gave the keynote address in a strong, clear voice, striding freely and easily on the platform while he praised the "stand pat" concept of Hanna, praised the full dinner pail of McKinley prosperity, denounced the previous Democratic Cleveland administration. The greatest applause came from his comments on the expansionism of America. But he spoke so long that it caused an obvious restlessness in the audience.

Quickly afterward, the usual committees appointed, the first day's session adjourned.

Backstage maneuvering had more meaning. Western delegate pressure intensified on Roosevelt to run, but he still resisted.

"Frederick Holls and I had been out for a walk with T. R.," said Nicholas Murray Butler, "during which he had insisted with all the emphasis at his command that never, no, never, would he be browbeaten by Platt and Quay into accepting the nomination for Vice President! When we got back to the Hotel Walton, we stood at the bottom of the elevator shaft and, after waiting several minutes, were told that the elevator was out of commission for a bit, and that we must either wait or walk upstairs to our room on the seventh floor. While we were waiting, Lemuel Ely Quigg and Frank H. Platt joined us and after taking Roosevelt aside for a few minutes walked up with him to a room on the mezzanine floor. There he talked with Senator Platt personally. An hour later T. R. joined us in our headquarters; his tail feathers were all down. The fight had gone out of him and he changed his former tune to that of, 'I cannot disappoint my western friends if they insist etc. I cannot seem bigger than the party etc.' "

To Republican Party Chairman Odell of New York, Roosevelt soon afterward said more flatly, "If the West nominates me, I will take it."

What happened in that room with Platt? What did Platt say to Roosevelt alone in that room? Roosevelt never revealed it. Neither did Platt. But there is no question that Roosevelt had serious concern about his renomination as Governor. Back on April 16, in a letter to New York district leader Norton Goddard, Roosevelt said, ". . . Nobody can tell, and least of all the machine itself, whether the machine intends to renominate me next fall or not. If for some reason I should be weak, whether on account of faults or virtues, doubtless the machine will throw me over. . . ."

Platt had previously indicated to Roosevelt that he intended to name Odell either to the governorship or the Vice-Presidency, saying "Odell would fill the place to a dot." But Odell had declined the Vice-Presidency, preferred the governorship, and Platt might have detailed this handwriting on the wall. Platt and Odell completely controlled the New York State party machinery which even a fighting Roosevelt might find hard to buck. So, perhaps instead of bucking, he buckled. Or perhaps the Platt pitch was made on the loftiest terms of public duty and duty to the party, perhaps Platt told him that the western states would go for Bryan, unless there was a Roosevelt name on the ticket with McKinley.

Whatever was said then, nobody knows.

But everybody knows what happened. After resolving the Roosevelt situation, Platt decided his aching rib needed home treatment and he left the New York delegation under Odell's charge.

The final move of the Platt-Quay plan happened on the convention floor the next day soon after Platt took his train home. It was Senator Quay's single chance to make Hanna squirm and he milked his moments.

Recognized soon after the convention started its second day, Senator Quay listened to the crowd cheer him for seven minutes before he finally took the platform. The cheers surprised nobody. They came from a Quay claque, packed and planted by Quay's Mayor Ashbridge of Philadelphia. As the absolute boss of Pennsylvania, this was Quay's home ground.

Permanent Convention Chairman Senator Henry Cabot Lodge greeted Quay on the platform. One reporter described the look on Lodge's face as "a sneering smile."

Quay's suggested amendment proposed that national conventions should base state representation on the size of the Republican vote in the previous presidential election. Southern delegates saw this as disaster. It not only stripped Republican leaders of their power but it also eliminated the bulk of Negro delegates, then notoriously purchasable and largely controlled by Hanna. While southern Republicans yelled for recognition, Quay proposed that this resolution be held up another day. Quay knew that southern delegates would quickly crowd in on Hanna to pay the Quay price for killing the amendment. The Quay price: Hanna and the southern delegates must support Roosevelt.

During the reading of the platform, spectators left by the hundreds. The platform had been completed by a minority within a minority, and not one in ten delegates knew anything about it until it was adopted, and it was adopted unanimously without discussion and without a single dissenting vote. Hanna himself had written the plank on "trusts" openly placing the party on the side of organized capital and corporate expansion, but adding the word "honest" before the phrase "aggregations of capital." Proudly the Republicans claimed to have restored prosperity "by means of two legislative measures—a protective tariff and a law making gold the standard of value." "Every American dollar is a gold dollar or its assured equivalent, and American credit stands higher than that of any nation."

On foreign issues, Republicans favored "the construction, ownership, control and protection of an isthmian canal," "approved the annexation of the Hawaiian Islands" and pledged "independence and self government for Cuba."

It was a short session and newspapers indicated an early recess was necessary to give the convention something to do the following day since they had a three-day contract with Philadelphia.

Now the delegate pressure was heavy on Hanna, southern leaders converged on him to kill the Quay amendment. Throughout the crowded halls of Hotel Walton, delegates were marching and yelling, "We want Teddy . . . we want Teddy. . . ." Charles G. Dawes of Illinois, a chief Hanna lieutenant in that state who had helped organize it for McKinley in the 1896 election, now sought out Hanna, told him of the dangers within the convention of those who felt Roosevelt was being trampled by the bosses. Hanna insisted to Dawes that he was only carrying out the President's wishes. Dawes, a reflective pipe-smoker who later became Vice-President under Coolidge and was awarded the Nobel Peace Prize for his Dawes Plan on war reparations, now decided to take the peace initiative in this political war and personally called President McKinley on the new long distance telephone gadget. Dawes detailed the risk of the administration in committing itself to any uncompromising opposition to the general mood of the convention.

George W. Perkins of New York, who was later to initiate the name of Woodrow Wilson into national politics, also called McKinley, strongly advocating Roosevelt's nomination.

McKinley's official biographer Olcott, reported on this phone call to McKinley:

"The Roosevelt boom is let loose and it has swept everything. It starts with the support of Pennsylvania and New York practically solid and with California and Colorado back of it also. The feeling is that the thing is going pell-mell like a tidal wave."

William Allen White once wrote of McKinley, "He walked among men a bronze statue, for thirty years determinedly looking for his pedestal." But White also noted that McKinley knew that the first maxim in politics is to take care of yourself; the second maxim is to take care of your crowd. And "Uncle Joe" Cannon, the powerful future Speaker of the House and a McKinley contemporary, saw another side of the President: "McKinley keeps his ear to the ground so close that he gets it full of grasshoppers much of the time."

But this time, there were no grasshoppers in McKinley's ear. George Perkins even hired a special train from Philadelphia to Washington to make a personal appeal to McKinley on Roosevelt. Fairbanks and Allison both had sent word to McKinley that they agreed with Dawes and Perkins.

McKinley listened long, made his decision. Through his secretary, George B. Cortelyou (who would later be Roosevelt's secretary, then his Secretary of Commerce, then National Chairman of the Republican party), McKinley sent this message to Dawes: "The President's close friends must not undertake to commit the Administration to any candidate. It has no candidate. The convention must make the nomination; the Administration would not if it could. The President's close friends should be satisfied with his unanimous nomination and not interfere with the vice-presidential nomination. The Administration wants the choice of the convention and the President's friends must not dictate to the convention."

Dawes privately showed the message to Hanna. Faced with these orders from the President, and the Quay resolution on southern votes, Hanna surrendered. Shortly before, Hanna had told Roosevelt, "By God, Teddy, you know there's nothing in this country which can compel a man to run for an office who doesn't want it." Now he called Roosevelt, said simply, "Teddy, you're it."

Hanna called a meeting of party leaders. Odell later told newsmen, "'The whole matter got into a snarl and was left to Senator Hanna to arbitrate and his decision is that the Vice-Presidency should go to New York and Roosevelt will be nominated."

This left the show of power still with Hanna, but the victory was Platt's and Quay's. It was a bitter political pill for Hanna to swallow, but he swallowed it like a professional. In his statement to the press, he said, "The Administration has had no candidate for Vice-President. It has not been for or against any candidate. It has desired that the Convention should make the candidate and that has been my position throughout. It has been a free field for all. Under these circumstances, several eminent Republicans have been proposed, all of them distinguished men with many friends. I may now say on behalf of all of these candidates, and I except no one, I have within the last twelve hours been asked to give my advice. After consulting with as many delegates as possible in the time at my disposal, I have concluded to accept the responsibility involved in this request.

"In the present situation with the strong and earnest sentiment of the delegates from all parts of the country for Governor Roosevelt, and since President McKinley is to be nominated without a dissenting voice, it is my judgment that Governor Roosevelt should be nominated for Vice-President with the same unanimity."

The Hanna surrender came at midnight. Some said that McKinley had used this means to cut Hanna's political size because he had been irritated by the growing international publicity comparing Hanna to a German Chancellor and a British Warwick, and those cartoons of Hanna at the hurdy-gurdy and McKinley as the monkey. Now there was no question of who operated the hurdy-gurdy and who was the monkey hitched to his master's wrist.

The quick switch caught most of the New York delegation still wearing their Woodruff buttons, but "Buttons Bim" Bimberg didn't have to dent the Delaware River. Prices for convention tickets quadrupled on Thursday morning. Built to seat less than 16,000, the hall was jammed with close to 20,000.

Hanna's old opponent in Ohio, Senator Foraker, made the nominating speech for McKinley. For the first two days of the convention, Hanna had sat on the platform, usually hidden from the audience, behind some of his national committeemen. But when McKinley was nominated, such was the emotional relationship between the two men, despite the Roosevelt situation, that Hanna jumped on a table, "grabbed a pampas plume and began to yell like an Apache for five minutes."

Introduced to make a seconding speech for McKinley, Roosevelt got such an ovation that he "stood flushed and almost dazed by the tremendous character of his greeting." Roosevelt had a typewritten copy of his speech, but he seldom looked at it. Not many months before, Roosevelt had told Willis J. Abbott, editor of the New York Journal, that McKinley was a weakling who could not be relied upon in "a serious crisis whether it took the form of a soft money craze, a gigantic labor riot, or danger of a foreign conflict." But now, in this speech, he saw McKinley as one of the great Presidents of our history, "who will rank next to Lincoln during the whole nineteenth Century in point of great work worthily done."

With McKinley nominated by acclamation, next came the vice-presidential nominations. Alabama yielded to Iowa. Iowa withdrew the name of its favorite son, Jonathan Dolliver, and its chairman, Colonel Lafayette "Lafe" Young made the nomination speech for Roosevelt, and Roosevelt got 925 out of the 926 votes (the total lacking, presumably, Roosevelt's own vote). No other candidate was nominated.

As the Roosevelt vote was announced, he got the greatest cheers of the convention and the band played, "There'll Be a Hot Time in the Old Town Tonight." Roosevelt's wife gasped momentarily at the final vote and cheering, then smiled.

Platt was exultant. The *New York Tribune* ran a cartoon showing Platt as a railroad workman throwing the switch which turned the Roosevelt train off the governorship track onto a siding for the Vice-Presidency. And the *New York Journal* also had a cartoon, and the caption read, "Rounded Up," and showed Platt triumphant on a cow pony, with a lariat labeled, "Vice Presidency" to catch Roosevelt's foot and throw him.

Later, Platt would say gleefully, "Yes, I am going to Washington to see Theodore Roosevelt take the veil."

Roosevelt himself had few illusions about his future. Henry Cabot Lodge tried to buck him up by saying, "Theodore, the way to break a precedent is to make one." Historian Henry Adams, who knew both men well, later wrote that Lodge had jealously resolved to "cut the throat" of Roosevelt by recommending the Vice-Presidency because no man since Martin Van Buren, who had been Vice-President, had ever been elected President afterward. Another friend, Winthrop Chanler, wrote Roosevelt, "Well, well, well! Long ago, when you first got the nomination for governor, the astute Cabot told me he wanted you to be Vice-President . . . the Wily One has won the day, in spite of your titanic struggles to disappoint him. It is the first time you have been beat, old man. . . ."

It was strange. Why would Henry Cabot Lodge want Roosevelt to be Vice-President? Since their young manhood together, Lodge had constantly advised, nurtured, promoted every major political move of Roosevelt. It was Lodge who stopped Roosevelt from bolting the party with a group of Independents in the presidential election of 1884. It was Lodge who kept Roosevelt from openly fighting Platt during his governorship. It was Lodge who had written Roosevelt in 1895, "I am glad that I have known you long and loved you well . . . for you are rushing so rapidly to the front that the day is not distant when you will come into a large kingdom and by that time I shall be a back number. . . ."

If there was envy here, this was the nub of it. True, he had helped steer and push the Roosevelt hope, but was there a resentment that the hope had soared so high so fast? Was this why Roosevelt's friend Owen Wister regarded the Lodge influence over T.R. as that of "an evil genius?" Was this why historian Henry Adams wrote, "the most dangerous rock on Theodore's coast is Cabot. We all look for inevitable shipwreck there."

Was Roosevelt's nomination to the Vice-Presidency, the seeming political dead end, "the inevitable shipwreck?" Why was Lodge so curiously contented with Roosevelt's nomination? He was eight years older than Roosevelt. Somebody had said of him that he was "thin soil highly cultivated," but he saw himself as Roosevelt's superior. After all, wasn't he Roosevelt's teacher? And now he would be a United States Senator and Roosevelt was an insignificant Vice-President, and who was now the "back number?"

If all this was supposition, there was no question about Roosevelt's feeling for his new job.

The "adventurous amateur" felt shelved. He wrote to his friend, Edward S. Martin, "I do not expect to go any further in politics."

Harper's Weekly sounded a more optimistic note for Roosevelt: "We cannot escape the conviction that the old order of things is about to change, and that the vice-presidency, instead of being a graveyard of political ambition, will turn out to be something radically different—something like a dynamo, for instance, with a large number of live wires attached to it."

But from his friend, Judge Alton B. Parker, Roosevelt got some personal advice: since he would have so little to do in Washington, why not enroll in law school? (Four years later, the Judge and the would-be law student faced each other as presidential rivals.)

The Democrats had their convention scheduled two weeks later, and William Jennings Bryan, their candidate in 1896, seemed an obvious choice for renomination. McKinley faced the upcoming campaign confidently and complacently—after all, he had beaten Bryan before. He even seemed more relaxed about the Republican convention. "It was a very nice convention," he said.

But Hanna was not mollified. When Roosevelt was nominated, he had told friends, "Don't you realize that there is only one life between this madman and the White House?" And now, he told McKinley, "We have done the best we could. Now it is up to you to live."

THE DISCO SELF-STARTER

The Sensation of 1912

The most marked advance shown for motor cars for 1912 is the Disco Self-Starter. Safe-Sure-Simple. We can make your car self-starting and up-to-date in three hours.

THERE WERE ALL kinds of other sensations: the first air-mail letter flown from Nassau Boulevard on Long Island to nearby Mineola, on Long Island.

Then somebody stole the Mona Lisa from the Louvre, leaving behind the glass and the frame.

And everybody talked about the maiden voyage of the Titanic, the most modern ship in the world. It had everything from Turkish Baths to the new-fangled electric elevators—it had everything except enough lifeboats, and so 1,198 people were drowned on a smooth sea when the ship hit an iceberg.

Europe was dividing, as usual, with the British on one side and the Germans on the other, and the British were saying that Germany was building up her war machine, increasing her naval budget and that war seemed increasingly imminent—but nobody seemed to be listening.

American prosperity was still in high gear and most people were dancing the Bunny Hug or the Turkey Trot or the Grizzly Bear. Most popular song was "Alexander's Ragtime Band" and the best selling book, Zane Gray's Riders of the Purple Sage. Movies had moved out of nickelodeons into theaters.

We had long since pulled our troops out of Cuba, our second military occupation of that country. China dumped its Manchu Dynasty and became a republic. And the United States decided to charge tolls at the Panama Canal. ("We own the canal," President Taft told Congress. "It was our money that built it. We have the right to charge tolls for its use." But the British called it "barefaced robbery.")

Women were smoking openly now and moving out of the hobble skirt into the sheath dress, still at ankle length. But the biggest butt of national humor was the New York parade of 10,000 suffragettes—many of them on horseback.

"Sell" was suddenly a fresh word in the American language, and everybody was doing it.

REPUBLICAN NATIONAL CONVENTION OF 1912

"Or ever the knightly fight was on,
The skirmish of smear and smudge,
I was a king in Washington
And you were a county judge.
I saw, I took, I made you great,
Friendly, I called you 'Will.'
And back in Nineteen Hundred and Eight,
Out in Chicago, Ill.,
I made the convention nominate,
And now—the terrible chill."
                    (by FRANKLIN P. ADAMS, New York World)

THE TERRIBLE CHILL FROZE THE CLOSE FRIEND-
ship of two Presidents, Theodore Roosevelt and his hand-picked
successor in 1908, William Howard Taft—whom Roosevelt had
predicted would be "the greatest President, bar only Washington
and Lincoln."

The terrible chill tore apart and transformed the Republican
party, resulted in the birth of the short-lived Progressive party and
the consequent election of a Democratic President.

The terrible chill, rooted in the magnetism of political power, created such national heat that it turned the 1912 Republican National Convention into a historically dramatic event.

And how did it all begin? And why?

"I don't know what I have done to offend Theodore," Taft told a relative. "I can think of only two things, and both of these are trivial. I have heard that he is offended because we did not do enough for Mrs. Roosevelt while he was in Africa. My other offense, I am told, was that I mentioned Charley in that letter in which I thanked Theodore for what he had done for me. What else could it have been?"

(Roosevelt described the "Charley" incident to a friend: "He [Taft] said he owed his nomination and election to the Presidency to me and his brother Charley. I sent back word that 'his brother Charley gave him money, but I gave him the Presidency.'")

It was Roosevelt who had pushed his dear friend, William Howard Taft, into national prominence. True, Taft had his own high record of respectability. His father had been President Grant's Attorney General, and he, himself, had ranked second in his class at Yale, served successfully as a lawyer and Superior Court Judge in Ohio, and for a brief time was a United States Collector of Internal Revenue. But the Roosevelt-Taft friendship grew fast and firm when both men worked in Washington as President Harrison appointees, Roosevelt as Civil Service Commissioner and Taft in the superior job of Solicitor General. Both men were then still in their early thirties. They stayed in federal government under President McKinley, Roosevelt as Assistant Secretary of the Navy and Taft as head of the Philippine Commission.

Then Roosevelt stepped on the political skyrocket: Spanish-American war hero, Governor of New York, Vice-President and then—after the assassination of McKinley—President of the United States. As Roosevelt rose, so quickly rose the fat, friendly shadow of Taft. Roosevelt appointed him Governor General of the Philippines, then Secretary of War, replacing Elihu Root.

Roosevelt originally wanted Root to succeed him as President, but Root refused. It was then Roosevelt turned to Taft. "Root would make the best President," Roosevelt told a friend, "but Taft the best candidate."

Another friend put it more bluntly to Roosevelt: "Colonel, all your enemies and a few of your friends think that you broke with Taft because you could not control him, and that you, therefore, are more to blame than Taft."

". . . I never asked him to do a single thing," Roosevelt bristled, then added, "There was no one incident on which I broke with Taft. It was a series of incidents, an accumulation of disappointments. . . ."

Taft never overwhelmingly wanted to be President. Some of the background for this beginning happened after dinner in the second floor library of the White House in January, 1908. Reclining in an easy chair, surrounded by some guests including the Tafts, Roosevelt dramatically closed his eyes and said, "I am the seventh son of a seventh daughter. I have clairvoyant powers. . . .

"I see a man standing before me weighing about 350 pounds. There is something hanging over his head. I cannot make out what it is; it is hanging by a slender thread. At one time it looks like the Presidency—then again it looks like the Chief Justiceship."

"Make it the Presidency," said Mrs. Taft.

"Make it the Chief Justiceship," cried Mr. Taft.

Roosevelt made it the Presidency. It meant jamming his personal candidate through a reluctant convention, and the mistake was major.

"Mistake, hell, it was a disaster," said his friend William Allen White, publisher of the *Emporia Gazette*.

Another friend and publisher, Henry L. Stoddard, of the *New York Evening Mail*, pleaded with Roosevelt, "Let the party pick its own man. It may make a mistake. If it does, it will be the party's mistake—not yours. . . . I am urging you not to take the responsibility when you are not to have the power."

The transition from power to powerless came hard for Roosevelt. Here he was, a former President at fifty, totally blind in one eye, overweight and slightly soft, a trace of Cuban fever in his blood, a driving energy, and unemployed. Who wants to hire an ex-President? Where can you climb after you have reached the top of the tallest mountain?

Taft was properly appreciative. During his campaign, he said, "If defeated because I am close to Roosevelt then . . . I ought to be defeated. . . . My strength is largely as his friend." Then, after his election, Taft wrote Roosevelt, "I can never forget that the power I now exercise was voluntarily transferred from you to me, and that I am under obligation to you to see that your judgment in selecting me as your successor and bringing about the succession shall be vindicated."

Roosevelt sent a short note: "Ha ha! you are making up your Cabinet. I in a light-hearted way have spent the morning testing the rifles for my African trip. Life has compensations!"

The "ha-ha" soon disappeared. Taft sent him a bon voyage present of a gold expandable ruler, and the "Charley" letter.

It took Taft time to get used to the Presidency. "When I hear somebody say, 'Mr. President,' I look around expecting to see Roosevelt," he said. Talking to his wife another time, he referred to Roosevelt as "the President," and his wife quickly corrected him, "You mean, the ex-President."

'I suppose I do dear, but he will always be the President to me."

But he soon moved on his own, even replaced several Roosevelt favorites, including the Ambassador to France, Henry White, whom Roosevelt regarded as "the ablest man in the foreign service." To his friend Senator Henry Cabot Lodge, Roosevelt wrote, "Taft not only told you, but he told me that he [White] was to stay in Paris. . . . It was, of course, not a promise any more than my statement I would not run again for President was a promise. . . ."

It was a strange coupling of comments.

Lodge wrote him that there was a "constantly growing thought of your return to the Presidency." Roosevelt's reaction: "I've had all the work and all the fun, all the honor and all the glory through seven full years. I'm through." And he joked about the lion hunting, saying he knew that Wall Street "hoped every lion would do its duty."

"Of course I shan't make a prediction of any kind about my future," he wrote Lodge in another letter. "I shall not discuss with any human being anything so absurd as the question as to whether I shall ever return to political life in any shape or form. . . . The chances are infinitesimal."

Elihu Root, who had refused Roosevelt's offer of support for the presidential nomination in 1908 (before Roosevelt turned to Taft), and who had served as Secretary of State for both men, described the transition from Roosevelt to Taft "like changing from a new automobile to a horse cab." Yet, as far as Roosevelt was concerned, it was Root who helped push Taft into the horse cab. Freshly appointed as the senator from New York, Root pressured Taft to fire Chief Forester Gifford Pinchot, a key man in Roosevelt's conservation program. Pinchot publicly opposed Taft's Secretary of the Interior Ballinger on his return of public power sites to private use. Pinchot hotfooted to Europe to meet Roosevelt and present his case and Lodge appealed to Roosevelt not to show he was upholding Pinchot against the Administration. Roosevelt persuaded Pinchot not to take any open position against Taft because of the probable need to support him for re-election in 1912.

Roosevelt, however, privately made his petulance plain to a friend, Gilson Gardner: "It is true he [Taft] has never originated anything that would savor of progressiveness, but he has been close enough to this Administration to know what it stands for."

Later, he would say, "Taft means well, but he means well feebly." And to journalist Mark Sullivan, Roosevelt said of Taft: "He's weak."

Following the Pinchot crisis, William Allen White quoted, "There stands Taft like the statue of Louis XV in the Tuileries Gardens, smiling and formidable, but without heart or guts."

Roosevelt spelled out his own position on Taft months later, in a letter to Pinchot, "I very keenly share your disappointment in Taft, and in a way perhaps feel it more deeply than you do, because it was I who made him President. . . . He has not proved a good leader, in spite of his having been a good first lieutenant . . . a rather pitiful failure because he had no strong man on whom to lean. . . .

"Incidentally I may add from my own standpoint . . . I could see very ugly times ahead for me, as I should certainly not be nominated unless everybody believed that the ship was sinking and thought it a good thing to have me aboard her when she went down."

During all this, Roosevelt was still touring Europe, but all kinds of former friends managed to catch up with him for conversation, much of it political. Taft privately protested to his military aide, Archie Butt, who also had been Roosevelt's military aide. Butt put everything down in a daily detailed diary. "Archie," said Taft, "I am greatly distressed [about Roosevelt]; he sees no one but my enemies, and if by chance he sees any supporters of the Administration, he does not talk intimately with them. . . . I hardly think he [Roosevelt] is playing it exactly square with me."

Butt added his own comment on Taft: "I have never known a man to dislike discord as much as the President. He wants every man's approval, and a row of any kind is repugnant to him."

Before the Pinchot problem, Taft refused to consider any rumored possibility that Roosevelt might run again in 1912. "Theodore wouldn't do that," he said. And then he added, later, "If I am defeated for the next nomination, I think it will be by Hughes [Charles Evans Hughes whom Taft soon appointed to the United States Supreme Court]. . . . I do not think Theodore Roosevelt will allow his name to come before the convention. I may be mistaken, and many around me tell me I am, but nevertheless that is my firm conviction. He will have his own way of doing it, but I think you will find I am right in my judgment of the man."

Taft amplified this to Frank Kellogg, a trust-busting special counsel in both administrations, then head of the Minnesota State Central Committee: "One thing I feel certain of, Frank, and that is that he [Roosevelt] will never be President again. I base this belief entirely on the anti-third term sentiment in this country. It is much deeper than is supposed. People are afraid of it, more afraid of it in a man like Roosevelt than in a weaker man like Grant."

But after he fired Pinchot, Taft was asked by a friend if he thought Roosevelt might be a candidate in the upcoming election, and Taft answered, "I don't think he will want to, but the country may demand it of him; and if he does, he will most certainly be elected."

Taft finally persuaded himself to write a long, poignant letter to Roosevelt. He added up his fifteen months in office and said, "I do not know that I have had harder luck than other Presidents, but I do know thus far I have succeeded far less than have others.

"I have been conscientiously trying to carry out your policies but my method of doing so has not worked smoothly."

Roosevelt received Taft's letter just before he sailed home from Southampton, England. Taft told close associates that he felt sorry for Roosevelt coming home because Theodore would have a hard time in a difficult role, "even more difficult than the one I have to play. Every man with an ambition, every new movement will try to drag to him and to it the ex-President, and whether he will be able to keep out of it all I don't know."

Nobody knew, least of all Roosevelt. He wrote Lodge, "Ugh! I do dread getting back to America and having to plunge into this cauldron of politics." And, again, "I most emphatically desire that I shall not be put in the position of having to run for the presidency, staggering under a load which I cannot carry; my present feeling is that Taft should be the next nominee."

He seemed to be trying to convince himself to withhold judgment. "I don't want you to think that I have the slightest feeling of personal chagrin about Taft," he wrote Lodge. "I am sincere when I say I am not sure whether Taft could with wisdom have followed any course save the one he did."

Henry Pringle, biographer of both Taft and Roosevelt, wisely said of them: "Roosevelt, out of office, typified an ideal. Taft, in office, was imperfect reality." On the homecoming of the "ideal" Roosevelt, the country's eyes turned to him as the first citizen of the world. He had been away for sixteen months, and the American people had read the rich details of his African safaris, his sightseeing views on everything from royalty to religion.

Archie Butt reported that Taft was "white-looking and his pallor does not seem healthy," and he added, it was "hard on any man to see the eyes of everyone turn to another person as the eyes of the entire country are turning to Roosevelt." Taft finally decided it was not within the dignity of his office for him to meet Roosevelt's incoming boat, but he did send Archie Butt, a naval yacht, and some top government officials to represent him. In addition there were vast crowds, bands, a delegation of Rough Riders, and Roosevelt spoke of their country's future and said, "I am ready and eager to be able to do my part so far as I am able in helping solve problems which must be solved if we . . . are to see its destinies rise."

Taft Republicans quivered at the phrase "ready and eager."

Taft felt then that if Roosevelt wanted to be renominated again "nothing could prevent it." At the same time he said, "There's no use trying to be William Howard Taft with Roosevelt's ways . . . our ways are different." And to somebody else, he said, "I am determined to paddle my own canoe."

To clear up any question about his own candidacy, Roosevelt told a Taft friend, "Of course I am for Will's nomination and his re-election; there can be no question about it." To the press, he said, "One thing I want now is privacy." He wanted to go home to Sagamore Hill in Oyster Bay and "I want to close up like a native oyster." To Taft, he wrote, "I am of course much concerned about some of the things I see and am told; but what I have felt it best to do was to say absolutely nothing—and indeed to keep my mind as open as I kept my mouth shut!"

Talking to Archie Butt about Roosevelt, Taft said, "Whether he has any ambition to be President again, I don't know either. He will have to fight that out by himself, for there is no way that a discussion of it can ever come between us."

The two men did meet at the end of the month at Taft's summer White House at Beverly, Massachusetts. It was outwardly cordial: "How are you Mr. President? This is simply bully," said Roosevelt.

"See here now," said Taft hitting Roosevelt on the shoulder gently, "drop the 'Mr. President.'"

"Not at all. You must be Mr. President and I am Theodore. It must be that way."

". . . The force of habit is very strong in me," said Taft. "I can never think of you save as Mr. President."

But if their talk was friendly, and it was, their aides followed careful instructions not to let them be alone together. The wish was mutual.

A residue of bitterness was beginning to show through in the inner circles. Commenting on Roosevelt's arrival, one Taft aide said, "He will come to see the President today and bite off his leg tomorrow." Roosevelt bit, but not immediately.

Taft, he said, was an admirable fellow, good natured, feebly well meaning, "but totally unable to grasp or put into execution any really great policy." As a leader, Roosevelt described Taft as "utterly commonplace," and yet, he said, "I do not believe he has been a bad President, and I am sure he has been a thoroughly well-meaning and upright President. I think he is a better President than McKinley and probably than Harrison, but the times are totally different and he has not the qualities that are needed at the moment."

The play-acting of an oyster in Oyster Bay soon seemed silly. The parade of politicians and friends and self-seekers to Sagamore Hill never stopped. Taft was right about that—Roosevelt had a hard role to play. One thing was certain: Roosevelt's visitors included more Taft enemies than Taft friends. One of the Oyster Bay luncheon guests was Miles Poindexter, from the state of Washington, an insurgent candidate for the United States Senate against Taft's Secretary of the Interior Ballinger. Poindexter not only was a bitter critic of Taft but he had openly endorsed Roosevelt's renomination for President in 1912. And he came out of the lunch telling reporters, "We . . . found ourselves in entire agreement." The press immediately applied this statement to the Poindexter campaign, and Roosevelt repudiated it, but Taft saw it as glove slapping in his face and he said, "I do not see how I am going to get out of having a fight with President Roosevelt."

Taft's wife had a prediction for her husband: "Well, I suppose you will have to fight Mr. Roosevelt for the renomination, and if you get it, he will defeat you," she said, referring to T.R.'s growing enmity. "But it can't be helped. If possible, you must not allow him to defeat you for the renomination. It does not make much difference about the re-election."

But there was much pressure from some Roosevelt friends urging him not to run. One of these was William Allen White in Kansas who advised Roosevelt to keep clear of the 1912 nomination and wait until 1916 when "you would take us a long way ahead." Another was Victor Rosewater, National Committeeman from Nebraska, who would soon be the Chairman of the Republican National Committee and cross the Roosevelt path at a point of crisis.

"I am not and shall not be a candidate for President," Roosevelt wrote Rosewater. "It remains for Taft to show us whether we can support him for re-election. He has made mistakes but I am going to do nothing and say nothing that will prevent me being for Taft and I wish that you and all my friends would do the same."

Out of his supposed shell, Roosevelt now saw reporters and one of them asked, "Well, Colonel, how about the White House again for yourself?"

Roosevelt replied instantly with a characteristic gesture, snapping his thumb and forefinger with a motion as if he was tossing something very light over his shoulder. "I don't care that for it," he said. "To go to the White House again simply for the sake of being President doesn't interest me in the least. There are so many things that I haven't yet done and that I want so much to do."

But this did not preclude politics. Charles Evans Hughes, then Governor of New York, persuaded Roosevelt to make a public appeal for a new primary law in New York. Roosevelt did, but it was badly beaten anyway. This political blunder brought Roosevelt head-on against the New York Republican boss, William Barnes, an Albany newspaper publisher and the Republican party chairman. Barnes was a Taft field marshal, a political boss with brains and daring, and the two men were set to keep clashing. To fight back, Roosevelt tried to get the New York State Committee to name him Chairman of the State Republican Party Convention later that fall, but the committee, under Barnes, voted twenty to fifteen to recommend that the state convention name Vice-President Sherman as its temporary chairman. At the meeting, Barnes insinuated that this had Taft's approval.

Taft officially denied this, but Archie Butt's diary provides some evidence. Butt told of Taft saying casually to his private secretary, Charles Dyer Norton, "Have you seen the newspapers this afternoon. They have defeated Theodore."

Norton, a Chicago banker who had been an Assistant Secretary of the Treasury and a constant critic of Roosevelt, began to chuckle and then President Taft joined in and the two started laughing together, and then Norton said, "We have got him—we've got him—we've got him as sure as peas we've got him." Then they both laughed again.

They were both wrong, not only about Roosevelt, but about New York. Roosevelt fought Barnes all the way into the convention, and New York's delegates voted 568 to 443 to reject the state committee advice and selected Roosevelt instead of Sherman as their convention chairman. Roosevelt then helped push the nomination of his friend (and Root's law associate) Henry Stimson as the Republican candidate for governor. "We are going to beat them to a frazzle," he told the crowds, "remember the word frazzle."

Frazzle, however, was not the word. Barnes still controlled the state committee and they still endorsed Taft and the tariff.

Through all this, the Taft-Roosevelt bitterness deepened. The strangeness of it was the almost utter lack of communication between them, two men who had been the warmest, dearest of friends.

"If I only knew what the President [Roosevelt] wanted, Archie, I would do it," said Taft, "but you know he has held himself so aloof that I am completely in the dark. I am deeply wounded and he gives me no chance to explain my attitude or learn his."

"Since he has come back," said Taft of Roosevelt, "he has seared me to the very soul."

Roosevelt, on the other hand, felt piqued, as he wrote Root, because he felt himself "neither consulted nor considered." He found that he had "no share in directing party policy." And, while party officials called for his help in stump speeches around the country for that midterm congressional election year, ". . . In spite of their anxiety to use me at the moment, [they] were exceedingly anxious to limit that use before elections with the understanding that I should have no say afterward."

Roosevelt and Taft met again in New Haven, Connecticut toward the end of September, a strained meeting, ostensibly concerning New York politics. As Butt then put the question: "Comes he in peace or comes he in war?"

The preliminary was peace, the aftermath was war.

"Taft and Norton were more than cordial, and made a point of being as pleasant as possible," Roosevelt wrote later. "Of course I did not ask Taft's aid or support in any shape or way, and it would never have entered my head to do so; although of his own accord, he volunteered the statement that Barnes and Company were crooks, and that he hoped we would beat them. But Norton, who is evidently a little too slick for genuine wisdom, with or without Taft's connivance, got all the newspapermen to publish the statement that I had asked to come because I was in difficulties and needed Taft's support. . . . It is all the more outrageous because it was Norton who asked Griscom to get me to call.

". . . hundreds of good people have kept asking me why I did not call and see the President, why I did not talk with him; and if they ask me anything more about it, I shall simply tell them that this experiment has shown that when I do call, those close to the President industriously seek to try to humiliate me and put me in a wrong position because I have called."

What actually happened was that the Roosevelt man did make the first overture to have the meeting, although the Taft man might have urged him to make it. As for the meeting itself, although Roosevelt denied he had asked Taft's help, Taft wrote his wife that Roosevelt did ask for that help. However, Taft told Butt that he, unsolicited, offered to help Roosevelt because he knew Theodore was going to ask for it anyway.

Whatever did happen, the friendship was finished. Except for an onstage meeting at a dinner for Cardinal Gibbons in Baltimore the following June, where both men put on their act for the public, chatting cheerfully like old friends—this was their last full meeting. They still kept writing to each other for awhile, they still sometimes talked about each other wistfully, but their paths were turned and their split was set.

Taft said of Roosevelt shortly afterward, "If you were to remove Roosevelt's skull now, you would find written on his brain, '1912.'"

But at least part of Roosevelt's brain concentrated on 1916. It was the kind of thinking William Allen White had urged, the idea that 1912 was going to be a Democratic year anyway. ". . . and therefore for every reason I most earnestly hope to retain sufficient control, to make Taft's nomination inevitable," Roosevelt wrote an English friend. "Only after the defeat would it be possible to reorganize the party under "capable and sane progressive leadership."

Roosevelt worked hard that midterm election year to retain that personal political control. He took a stump-speaking trip of some sixteen states, covering 5,000 miles in his special train, and he wouldn't let the Republican National Committee sponsor it. "My speeches on the trip will represent myself entirely, nobody else."

And so they did. At Osawatomie, Kansas, he talked the doctrine of a New Nationalism that chilled conservatives. "I stand for a square deal," he said. "The New Nationalism . . . demands of the judiciary that it shall be interested primarily in human welfare rather than in property . . . there must remain no neutral ground to serve as a refuge for law-breakers of great wealth. . . . We must drive special interests out of politics. . . ."

He also hit the new tariff law because "the big special interests and the little special interests" helped set the rate schedules in it.

The *New York Evening Post* promptly denounced him as "the most radical man in public life in our time."

Wherever he spoke, the crowds were huge, the reception exhilarating. But the November results swept in Democrats, even defeated Roosevelt's candidate for governor in New York, Henry Stimson. In his own home district, his congressman was defeated. "In New York State, the hatred of me amounted to a mania," he said. But if Republican regulars were routed in the East, Republican progressives survived in nine western states. One of the eastern Democrats moving in as governor of New Jersey was the former president of Princeton University, Woodrow Wilson, whom Roosevelt had met and liked and congratulated on previous occasions. Another successful Democrat was a young State Senator in New York, a Roosevelt cousin whose wedding he had attended, and who had fought a strong fight against Tammany Hall bosses. The former President wrote the future President, Franklin D. Roosevelt: "Just a line to say that we are all really proud of the way you have handled yourself. Good luck to you! Give my love to dear Eleanor."

The plain fact of the total election however spelled a definite personal defeat for Theodore Roosevelt and he tried to brush it lightly: "Every dog has his day," he said, "but the nights belong to the cats. It is just thirty years this Fall since I began my work in politics. I have had a great run for my money. . . . One result I think will follow which will be to me an unmixed blessing, and that is doing away with the talk of nominating me in 1912."

But even then, he hedged: "To have me come out and make the announcement that I would not take the nomination of 1912 would merely have been to play into my enemies' hands. But at present it looks as if the situation then will be as impossible as it is now. Taft is President, and the tradition is very strong to give a President a second nomination, even where, as in the case of Harrison, it is unlikely that he can win."

He widened this hedge, saying he knew he had not one chance in a hundred for the presidential nomination, but that he declined to make a flat refusal of it "because I do not wish to put myself in the position where if it becomes my plain duty to accept I shall be obliged to shirk such duty because of having committed myself."

He now wanted to go back to being an oyster in Oyster Bay. To Henry Wallace in Iowa, father of a future Vice-President, Roosevelt wrote, "what is needed for me is to follow the advice given by the New Bedford whaling captain to his mate when he told that all he wanted from him was silence and damn little of that."

With the Roosevelt defeat, Taft even relaxed enough to invite him again to the White House and Roosevelt politely refused, "I think you are a trump to ask me to come to the White House. . . ."

Roosevelt himself relaxed by writing books, working as an editor at The Outlook magazine, and settling into a quiet obscurity. But the political darkness proved only an eclipse.

One of those who relished the Roosevelt situation was Senator Robert La Follette of Wisconsin, the energetic man with the bushy hair and dynamic voice that created a binding electrical current among the nation's progressives. La Follette knew the pivotal value of Roosevelt support. If the Roosevelt-Taft breach widened enough, if Roosevelt really wanted to wait until 1916 for the presidential race, and if Roosevelt would throw the full force of his power and personality behind La Follette, he could most probably control the Republican National Convention and make La Follette the Republican presidential nominee.

However, La Follette mistrusted Roosevelt as a man who would too often "take half a loaf." La Follette had said of him, "Theodore Roosevelt is the ablest living interpreter of what I would call the superficial public sentiment of a given time, and he is spontaneous in his reactions to it."

Translated into political terms, this meant expediency.

Their first intermediary was the Washington correspondent for the Scripps syndicate, Gilson Gardner, and he gave La Follette the Roosevelt message that he wouldn't enter the 1912 presidential race under any circumstances, nor would he accept the nomination if tendered to him.

Early in 1911, it really did seem that Roosevelt had pulled himself out of the race. "Taft is stronger than he was," he wrote, "because his opponents in his own party have largely gone to pieces, and his worst advisors have been eliminated from their positions of power. . . . Most of my particular supporters are still against him, but not as violently as before. . . . I think all danger of my own nomination has vanished."

Roosevelt also felt then that the public would resent his nomination, "would feel in some way I had intrigued to bring it about, and would experience a revulsion of feeling about Taft and think I had treated him badly."

Taft's own feeling at the time was that Roosevelt expected to be a candidate in 1912, "but before that time comes, I think he will change his mind . . . he will see that his candidacy will split the party, and he may feel that he owes enough to it to withdraw. . . . But what I expect to see more than anything else is his withdrawal for fear he may not be able to win."

Roosevelt's mental energy now focused in another area. He had declined all speaking invitations for more than five months, wrote friends that he was sure Taft would be nominated on the first ballot, and what really excited him was the increasing talk of possible war in the Far East or Mexico. He even wrote Taft asking if he could be permitted to raise a division of cavalry if war came, and Taft agreed.

"My present intention is to make a couple speeches for Taft, but not to go actively into the campaign," he wrote a friend. "I hope we can carry Taft through, and there would be a fair chance against Harmon, although much less of a chance against Wilson."

In the coming months, though, Roosevelt seemed increasingly

critical in his *Outlook* articles of Taft policies, and Taft again talked to close friends about the possibility of an "open rupture," and La Follette then felt the time was ripe to make a full pitch for Roosevelt support. The two men met in May.

"Now, Colonel," asked La Follette, "can't you consistently give this movement the benefit of your great name and influence?"

Roosevelt wasn't prepared to go that far, but La Follette afterwards claimed he went far enough.

"Roosevelt had entirely changed his mind regarding a progressive candidate against Taft," he said. "He now believed that the progressives should put forward a candidate, that I should be that candidate, and that I should get into the fight at once. . . . He, Roosevelt, could not oppose Taft, whom he had made President . . . could not for the same reason openly advocate my candidacy against Taft . . . but he would commend my work from time to time in *The Outlook*, and help along."

Roosevelt followers now flocked to the La Follette cause, including money man Medill McCormick. La Follette hopes now ran high. Taft seemed to be alienating everybody. In the *American Federationist*, labor branded the Taft government as "defiant uncompromising hostility."

Taft's program of trade reciprocity with Canada alienated farmers and high protectionists and his increased enforcement of antitrust laws caused big business resentment.

La Follette buoyantly scheduled a National Progressive Convention in Chicago in October, 1911, with representatives from thirty states to advocate his candidacy. La Follette supporters even claimed up to 350 delegates at the upcoming 1912 Republican convention.

In an article on social reform in *The Outlook*, Roosevelt wrote, "We can now . . . look for leadership in Wisconsin."

The La Follette political balloon was blowing hard.

But a *New York Times* political analyst dropped a cynical note, suggested that the La Follette candidacy was merely a decoy for Roosevelt, and would switch to him at the proper time.

Roosevelt's criticism of Taft policies increased and although he issued a public statement that he would not be a candidate in 1912, he added he would not support anybody else for the nomination. The Taft-Roosevelt cooling quickened. The last note between them was a short one from Taft, dated June 18, thanking Roosevelt for his gift for their silver wedding anniversary.

Then came the trigger to the time of tension. On October 26, the Taft government filed an antitrust suit against United States Steel Corporation and specified the acquisition of the Tennessee Coal and Iron Company during the 1907 panic. Since the antitrust suit revealed that Roosevelt had okayed the deal, the government petition practically described Roosevelt as a dupe. Roosevelt was furious, quickly commented that Taft had been in his Cabinet at the time, had heard the deal outlined in detail and had been enthusiastic in his support of the Roosevelt action.

Archie Butt saw Roosevelt's sister, and she said:

"Oh Major Butt, it is too late now. If it had not been for the Steel suit! I was talking to Theodore only last week, and he said he could never forgive."

"Of course you know," said Butt, "that the President never saw that suit until it was filed."

"Yes," she said, "Theodore knows that, and that in his eyes is the worst feature of the case—that such a thing could have been done without his knowledge."

Butt reported this conversation to Taft, and he said, "He would understand if he wanted to understand, but this is just what he wanted to happen. . . . I fear things are going to become very bitter before long." Another time, Taft told Butt, "It is hard, very hard, to see a devoted friendship going to pieces like a rope of sand." And to H. H. Kohlsaat, Taft said, his eyes filled with tears, "I am so distressed it keeps me awake nights."

If Taft quivered, he did not crack. He told Butt, "Archie, I am going to defeat him in the Convention. He may defeat me for re-election, and he probably will, but I think I will defeat him in the Convention."

To test public opinion, Taft went on a nationwide speaking tour that fall and Roosevelt men circulated the quip that public reaction to Taft was so cool that it forced the President to change his itinerary in the middle of the tour to include a few southern states so he could thaw out.

All this so depressed Taft that he publicly admitted to a *New York Times* reporter in Denver that there was a strong possibility of his defeat the next year.

Taft asked his wife, "Well, you are not hopeless about the nomination."

Mrs. Taft spoke slowly as if she was carefully trying to find the right words. "No, I think you will be renominated, but I don't see any chance for the election."

"Well, I am chiefly interested in the renomination," said Taft, "so don't get disconsolate over that. If we shall lose the election, I shall feel that the party is rejected, whereas if I fail to secure the renomination, it will be a personal defeat."

All kinds of rumors reached Taft. One of them said that Roosevelt wanted Taft to get so discouraged that he would withdraw his name as a candidate, and then Roosevelt would run. But if Taft didn't back out, the mutual friend said, Roosevelt wouldn't accept the nomination no matter how hard he was pressed—because Roosevelt expected Taft to be defeated and that he (Roosevelt) would be renominated and elected four years later.

"That is my opinion too," said Taft.

Meanwhile, at Oyster Bay, the politicians converged on Roosevelt and their pressure multiplied. Three Republican State Chairmen—Walter Brown of Ohio, Edward Lee of Indiana, and Frank Knox of Michigan—all made the same plea: unless Roosevelt consented to run in 1912, the party outlook was "hopeless."

The three men had just come from a Republican National Committee meeting in Washington where they had discussed the time, place, and tone of the upcoming convention. The failure of the Taft tour had made it a meeting of gloom. Not only did the National Committee veto Senator Borah's idea for a national primary to pick convention delegates, but they also intimated that perhaps the time had come to drive insurgents out of the party.

The three men told all this to Roosevelt.

"I am not in this situation," he answered, "and I am not going to be dragged into it. Taft created it and let Taft take his spanking for it. There is no reason why I should. If I wanted four years more in the White House I would say so and go after it; but I don't want it. I've had enough. I couldn't go back without risking all I gained in the seven years I was there."

Frank Knox interrupted. "Colonel, I never knew you to show the white feather, and you should not do so now."

"What do you mean by that?" said an angry Roosevelt.

"Why you are basing your refusal on the possibly bad effect another term might have on your reputation," said Knox. "I contend that you ought to look at this thing from the party's interests and not your own. The party has honored you, and it now turns to you to do a service for it. It is in distress and it needs you."

"By George," Roosevelt said, "that would be a good argument if I were the only man available, but I am not. I agree that Taft cannot be elected. I do not know that any Republican can be elected, but if the party can win I am not the only Republican with whom it can win. I am not ungrateful for the honor I have had, but I think I have repaid in service. When I left the White House, every state we had any right to expect was in the Republican column. It's not my job to put them back again."

The three men left Sagamore Hill convinced Roosevelt would not run. But the question wouldn't quiet, and a headline in the *New York American* put it compactly:

T. R.: R U or R U NOT?

Dan Hanna, Mark Hanna's son, published a strongly pro-Roosevelt editorial in his paper, and Roosevelt wrote him, "I am not and will not be a candidate. . . . I have not and would not declare that I would under no circumstances accept the nomination."

Oscar King Davis, familiarly known to Roosevelt and everybody else as "O.K. Davis," a *New York Times* Washington correspondent, in an article in *Hampton's Magazine* earlier had suggested Roosevelt's possible nomination, intimating that if the call was made, Roosevelt was not the sort of man who would refuse that call. Roosevelt answered, "The article was all right . . . except that I am by no means certain that I would not refuse the nomination, even if it came to me unanimously."

Roosevelt forces meanwhile busied themselves elsewhere. At the Progressive Convention, Roosevelt's former Secretary of the Interior, James Garfield, struck the only discordant note in the La Follette nomination, saying, "This endorsement is to be regarded as a recommendation rather than a committal of the movement to any one man." And Gilson Gardner, the Roosevelt intermediary reported the Oyster Bay word to La Follette: "Roosevelt is not only surprised at the development of your candidacy, he is disappointed." Some Roosevelt men, on their own, urged La Follette to step aside in favor of Roosevelt, and he flatly refused.

La Follette then tried to get Roosevelt to declare himself. At a private party at Carnegie Hall in New York, in La Follette's honor, Roosevelt was scheduled to come, but instead held his own dinner that night inviting top Progressives, who originally intended to go to the La Follette meeting. The press headlined the obvious snub.

In his last intermediary dispatch to La Follette, Gardner said, "T. R. does not say 'I will not be a candidate,' but he does say, 'I am not a candidate.'"

His "devout wish," Roosevelt said, was that "other candidates should develop such overwhelming strength that there will not possibly be any tendency to come to me."

Throughout his letters at that time there was a repeated reference to a nagging piece of conscience. H. H. Kohlsaat summed it up for Roosevelt:

"I'll tell you what is the trouble," said Kohlsaat. "You foolishly issued a statement the night of your election in 1904, saying you would not be a candidate in 1908 for what you called a 'third

term,' which was not a third term, as you were serving out Mc-
Kinley's second term. You could have been renominated easily if
it had not been for that declaration."

Kohlsaat said that Roosevelt screwed up his mouth and said:
"I would cut that hand right off there," putting his finger on his
wrist, "if I could have recalled that statement given to the Associated Press."

Roosevelt men now hit harder at Taft. Gentlest was Senator
Dolliver of Iowa who described Taft as "an amiable island entirely
surrounded by men who knew perfectly what they wanted." But
Roosevelt now called him "a flubdub with a streak of the second
rate and common in him. . . ."

"Taft is utterly hopeless," Roosevelt said.

Taft's own view of Roosevelt's future stayed flexible. Now he
told Archie Butt: "I don't believe he can be nominated. He will
not dare to take it as long as I am in the field, for he will not
underestimate my friends in this country. He will be forced to
support me also. If he does not, he will be charged with my defeat
in case I fail to be elected, and should I be elected, he will get
none of the credit for it. That's how I read the signs."

In a final burst of confidence, he added, "Archie, I am going to
be renominated and re-elected."

A Taft friend suggested he attack Roosevelt openly and boldly,
and Taft patted him on the arm and said, "Not yet, old man. That
is not my method."

Some Roosevelt friends increasingly questioned the Roosevelt
idea of waiting until 1916. Advised journalist Mark Sullivan: the
time to set a setting hen was when the hen wanted to set. "There
was no use in sitting back and waiting for another year when somebody entirely different might do best as a leader."

Author Henry Adams described Roosevelt followers as "squirming like a skinned eel, not knowing what to do."

Roosevelt agreed, "My silence is deliberately misrepresented by
my enemies." And, after a dinner at the Aldine Club in New
York on January 9, 1912, when the press quoted that he was not

a candidate but would not refuse the nomination if offered, Roosevelt complained, "I am the most misrepresented man in America."

But how misrepresented was he anyway? There was a turmoil in the man. It was as if he was walking a tightrope and everybody wanted to push him, and he didn't know where to fall. He had rationalized all the reasons for not running. His political sense pointed out all the obvious dangers. And yet, there was this pull of an invisible destiny. Here were all these people anxious to wrap around him the cloak of indispensability, and it became a kind of call that superseded sense.

"Almost overnight has this Roosevelt obsession risen and spread until it has become the dominant feature in the political discussions of the country," editorialized the magazine *Current Literature*. "The Roosevelt campaign ark is afloat," editorialized friend William Allen White in his *Emporia Gazette*.

"If the call does come," said Frank Munsey on the front page in his *Washington Times*, "Roosevelt will buckle on his armor."

Answering Munsey in a sixteen-page letter on January 16, Roosevelt said, "If at this particular crisis, with the particular problems ahead of us at this particular time, the people feel that I am the one man in sight to do the job, then I should regard myself as shirking a plain duty if I refused to do it."

And then he added, "The right motto for any man is, 'Spend and be spent.'"

It sounded firm enough for Roosevelt men to start their switch from La Follette to Roosevelt: the Pinchot brothers, Bill Flinn of Pennsylvania, and Medill McCormick. Governor Hiram Johnson of California visited Roosevelt to get a firmer word before switching because he then faced a wide-open fight in his state against die-hard La Follette people. Governor Glasscock switched to Roosevelt from Taft. And a friend wrote Victor Rosewater in Nebraska that "Roosevelt is rarin' to go."

Archie Butt, military aide to both Roosevelt and Taft, and devoted to both, paid a social visit to the Roosevelts at Oyster Bay at the end of January. He left with the thought, "He is not a candidate, but if he can defeat the President for renomination, he will do it."

Back at the White House, Taft was waiting with the question: "And the Colonel, Archie?"

"He said nothing sir. I don't believe he is a candidate, but I simply caught this from the atmosphere; but he will never forgive the Steel Trust suit, in my opinion."

"If he is not a candidate," said Taft, "why is he sending for governors and delegations all the time?"

"It's all a mystery to me," said Butt, "but the fact that he would not send a message to you by me was significant."

It was significant to Taft, too:

"Archie, I am going to say something which may surprise you," Taft said, "and therefore you must not say anything about it. Do you know those presentiments which sometimes come over one, even against his reasoning? Well I have a strong presentiment that the Colonel is going to beat me in the Convention. It is almost a conviction with me. I shall continue to fight until the last moment, but when you see me claiming victory, or my friends claiming victory for me, remember that I feel I am losing a battle, and that I am not blind myself, no matter what my friends may put out."

He added a footnote: "But don't think me capable of quitting. I can fight just as well when losing as when certain of victory. . . . I hope we can keep the fight from becoming personal."

Butt erred. Maybe the Oyster Bay atmosphere didn't have a campaign feel, but the campaign was already in gear. Various governors had been urging Roosevelt to issue a public statement, and Senator Albert Beveridge from Indiana made a particular plea. Young, impressive, Beveridge himself was a potential dark horse candidate waiting in the wings.

The public statement must still not seem an acceptance, but it would open the door publicly, officially—and wider. As T. R. somehow rationalized it to himself, he would seek the nomination without "the slightest manipulation" by anybody. By anybody, that is, but Roosevelt himself. Roosevelt decided to capitalize on the queries from governors, have a letter framed which they would then send him and which he would then answer. It would all be very neatly packaged.

To prepare the package, Roosevelt wired Frank Knox, Republican State Chairman of Michigan, and a former member of the Roosevelt Rough Riders. Knox came, drafted a letter for the governors to sign. "T. R. suggested a couple of added sentences emphasizing that the nomination must come as a real popular demand and declaring that the Governors were taking their action, not for his sake but for the sake of the country."

Knox soon had the letter signed by seven governors: Walter R. Stubbs of Kansas, Chase S. Osborn of Michigan, Chester H. Aldrich of Nebraska, Herbert S. Hadley of Missouri, Robert P. Bass of New Hampshire, William E. Glasscock of West Virginia, and Joseph M. Carey of Wyoming.

With Medill McCormick money, a Roosevelt National Committee was set up in Chicago and a national meeting set for February 10, to include the governors plus some fifty-six delegates from thirty states to form a national permanent organization.

"I cannot decline the call," Roosevelt said at an editorial conference of The Outlook magazine on January 22.

During all this, La Follette simmered and stewed. It was as if he were chained to a rock when the tide was coming in. And there was nothing he could do except to wait for the waves of history. His Roosevelt followers had departed in wholesale lots, especially the money men. Some of his most faithful friends were trying to persuade him to withdraw in favor of T. R. when the time came. One of his strongest Midwest backers, William Allen White, had taken a private poll of La Follette's political strength and found it wanting, so much so that White predicted La Follette couldn't even beat Taft in Kansas. On top of everything there was an invitation to speak at the annual banquet in Philadelphia of the important 800 members of the Periodical Publishers Association, most of whom hated his guts—this on the day before his daughter was having a serious operation.

The date was too important to cancel, especially since it might seem to confirm the rumor that he was withdrawing in favor of Roosevelt; so he went, tired, discouraged, still weak from a previous attack of ptomaine poisoning. Woodrow Wilson was on the program with him, spoke first and effectively and the toastmaster introduced La Follette after ten in the evening. He had the original copy of a long speech which he had cut to a half hour, but had no time to retype.

He started to read his speech, which was unusual for him, and things went smoothly for the first ten minutes, and then he put down his manuscript to emphasize a point. It was an attack against the money trust and publishers. It was late and some people started leaving and La Follette shook his fist at them, "There go some of the fellows I'm hitting. They don't want to hear about themselves."

"He continued his speech," said author Owen Wister, who was there, "and a new astonishment came over us; whole passages were being repeated. At first one was not sure, then it was obvious. And the repetitions made havoc with his coherence. In fact, all consecutive meaning disappeared."

At first Woodrow Wilson took notes on the La Follette speech, but then Wilson realized what was happening and Wilson's face seemed to share the La Follette suffering.

Those nearest to La Follette noticed that he wasn't even laying down his finished pages, but reshuffling them inside the other pages, and consequently repeating them again.

All this for more than two hours, raging in a fury at the top of his voice. Once he yelled, as part of his speech, "Is there a way out?" and somebody in the audience yelled, "I hope so." Soon there were shouts of "Sit down," but he ignored them, raging on in his incoherence. Long past midnight, he finished, slumped into his seat, his head sinking to the table.

The next morning's headline:

LA FOLLETTE ILL
VIRTUALLY OUT OF PRESIDENTIAL RACE

Wiring a reply afterward on his rumored resignation, La Follette said, "Always remember, I never quit. . . . There won't be any funeral unless it's a real one with music and flowers."

And the *New York Tribune* editorialized: "He is being hustled ruthlessly inside the hearse, although he still insists that he is strong enough to occupy a seat alongside the driver."

It was part of the price of politics. A man spends a lifetime to create a name of political strength, pushes himself within visible reach of the highest prize and then it all disappears through an invisible door, sometimes in a steady slicing operation, sometimes in the force of a pulverized moment. The requested price for the Presidency is simple perfection. No show of weakness, no double meanings, no buried past, no wrong words, no bad pictures. Perfection is the price and the measure is always.

But if Robert La Follette became a broken man with a broken dream, he still came away from that dinner with enough political strength to break the dreams of others.

Sensing political disaster from a potential split of the Progressive vote, mutual friends of La Follette and Roosevelt suggested a combined ticket with Roosevelt for President, La Follette for Vice-President. La Follette coldly and quickly refused. Even though Taft once had called La Follette "a yellow dog," William Allen White openly worried about the two forces combining to crush Roosevelt at the convention.

Meanwhile Roosevelt changed his "maybe" to "yes."

At the home of a Roosevelt relative, in New York City, a small group of his top advisors settled on the hair-covered chairs and sofas of the "back parlor," with the Colonel in a high-backed armchair directly in the center of the room under the chandelier.

"Every man gave his frank opinion," said New York editor Henry Stoddard, who was there, "as to his own state as well as the nation. Finally, we had our say. There was an interval. Many of us began exchanging views in a low tone, while waiting for the Colonel to speak. He was evidently doing some hard thinking. Suddenly he raised his hands high, outstretching them as though in benediction. Quickly closing them he brought his fists down in a flash, each fist striking an arm of his chair with a bang and in a tone almost a shout, exclaimed: 'Gentlemen, they're off.' "

The race was on.

To his son-in-law, Nicholas Longworth, who would run for Congress in a Taft district in Ohio as a Taft man, Roosevelt wrote: "If I were longer doubtful, I would telegraph you to come and talk with me, but it would not be any use now, Nick, I have got to come out."

At another meeting of party leaders, Roosevelt said he felt the probabilities were all against his nomination because a President in office had all the party machinery on his side, that his only hope was to reach the popular vote in the primaries, but that this breach was necessary for the health of the Republican party.

"But the situation is complex, I suppose? You would like to be President?" asked William Roscoe Thayer.

"You are right, it is complex," Roosevelt said. "I like power; but I care nothing to be President as President. I am interested in these ideas of mine and I want to carry them through."

Publicly, Roosevelt said he had received a letter from the governors and would not make his decision public until he spoke at the Ohio Constitutional Convention on February 21.

The letter from the governors, as finally written, said:

"We believe your candidacy will insure success in the next campaign. We believe that you represent, as no other man represents, those principles and policies upon which we must appeal for a majority of the votes of the American people. . . .

"In submitting this request, we are not considering your personal interests. We do not regard it as proper to consider either the interests or the preferences of any man as regards the nomination for the presidency. We are expressing our sincere belief and best judgment as to what is demanded of you in the interests of the people as a whole. . . ."

The other part of the prepared package, the Roosevelt answer, was also written and ready, but Roosevelt couldn't keep a secret.

To a reporter's question the next day, he blurted, "My hat's in the ring! The fight is on and I'm stripped to the buff!" To another reporter who asked, "Do you intend to support the Republican nominee, no matter who he will be?"

"Of course I shall," answered Roosevelt.

Just before all this, Taft made a speech at the New York Republican Club in which he said, "Such extremists are not progressives, they are politically emotionalists or neurotics." Everybody saw this shaft aimed directly at Roosevelt, although Taft insisted he didn't intend that. But there had been enormous publicity in the press about a Dr. Allen McLane Hamilton who used *New York Times* columns to seriously question the Roosevelt sanity. Then there was a long Freudian analysis by Dr. Morton Prince suggesting that the subconscious Roosevelt desire to be re-elected in 1912 had poisoned his emotional system even before T. R. left the White House. And a Rudolph Patterson, who listed himself as a real estate expert, offered $5,000 to charity if a Sanity Commission expert determined that Roosevelt was not insane. All three men admitted to reporters that they were Taft supporters.

In spite of the Taft speech, William Allen White insisted to Roosevelt that Taft had told him "nothing would induce him to say—or allow anyone whom he could control to say—anything against you personally."

More prophetically, *Harper's Weekly*, published by Woodrow Wilson's strong friend, George Harvey, wrote, "Hate, not hat, is in the ring."

Roosevelt now released his more formal reply to the governors:

"I absolutely agree with you that this matter is not one to be decided with any reference to the personal preferences or interests of any man, but purely from the standpoint of the interests of the people as a whole. I will accept the nomination for President if it is tendered to me, and I will adhere to this decision until the convention has expressed its preference."

The preliminary flash on the Roosevelt announcement came over the Associated Press wire into the White House while the

Tafts were at dinner, and they both read it and Mrs. Taft said, "I told you so four years ago and you would not believe me."

The President laughed good-naturedly and answered:

"I know you did, my dear, and I think you are perfectly happy now. You would have preferred the Colonel to come out against me than to have been wrong yourself."

The full Roosevelt letter soon arrived, and President Taft read it aloud and the room was soon full of critical comments.

Taft, however, said: "No, he could not have made it any stronger. It is characteristic of him, and it will be a rallying cry to the Progressives of the country and to the discontented, but I think that you will find that in a week or ten days it will have lost much of its clarion note, and there will be a great sag in the sentiment which will at first be aroused by it."

But it was not the lasting sound of the clarion call that worried the most savvy political professionals in the Roosevelt camp—it was the timing. Most of the state conventions in southern states—the so-called Republican "rotten boroughs" because they had so few Republican votes—already had selected their convention delegates. As always, they were administration men tied tightly by office holders and patronage. They now constituted a strong, solid Taft bloc. Roosevelt pros insisted that if the Roosevelt decision had been made six weeks earlier, they could have moved into the South with money and organization, sewed up those votes and clinched the nomination.

Roosevelt men still moved swiftly to salvage what they could. In charge of this southern operation was a tall, big-eyed, sharp-featured North Dakota lawyer with iron gray hair and a high-pitched musical voice named Ormsby McHarg. During the 1908 campaign, McHarg had a similar job of sewing up southern delegates for Taft. Since then he had been an Assistant Secretary of Commerce, and when fired, became counsel for two Indian tribes. When fired from this job, he switched from Taft to Roosevelt.

McHarg's tactic was to contest every southern delegation, regardless of the merits of the case. With a free use of money,

McHarg helped set up rump conventions, search out questions of legality, switch the supposedly set votes. To persuade switchers, McHarg's argument to patronage-hungry delegates was that Taft couldn't possibly win the election and therefore his patronage promises for the future meant nothing, but that Roosevelt would win, and so his patronage promise had meaning.

But Taft's campaign manager, again touring the South, had a more powerful persuader—*immediate* patronage. Taft's manager was Representative William B. McKinley, a bald-headed, blue-eyed little man, quiet, careful, boyish-looking but a first-class political pro, the head of the congressional campaign committee. McKinley simply pinpointed any possible Roosevelt sympathizers among southern office holders, and fired them quickly and without qualm. This included every political level up to Cecil Lyon who had been the supreme Republican boss of Texas controlling some 5,000 jobs. McKinley fired Lyon. The rooting out reached into the postmaster level and one such letter got into Roosevelt hands and was widely publicized. It was from a Republican State Chairman to a small town postmaster and it was blunt: "If you will bring a delegation to the state and district convention instructed for Taft, I will see that you are reappointed."

Sometimes it backfired. So heavy-handed was the Taft intervention in North Carolina in the selections of six postmasters and two customs collectors that the local group defiantly organized a pro-Roosevelt delegation.

McHarg's main point of publicly contesting the southern delegates was to offset the psychological advantage of listing the delegates for Taft before Roosevelt could even get started. Putting these delegates in the "contested" column instead of the "Taft" column minimized some of the opposition's preliminary bandwagon strategy.

In that way, it did help. More practically, the Roosevelt people knew their main hope was in the direct primary. It was the final note in the Roosevelt answer to the governors:

"I hope that so far as possible the people may be given the

chance, through direct primaries to express their preference as to who shall be the nominee. . . ."

Writing in *Colliers* in mid-February, Mark Sullivan stated: "The presidential primary means that you can go to the polls (if you are a Republican) and say whether you want Taft or Roosevelt. If you don't do the choosing, the bosses will."

First order of business was public pressure in the various states for laws permitting direct primaries. These already existed in seven states and Roosevelt forces helped push them in six others: Illinois, Maryland, Massachusetts, Ohio, Pennsylvania, and South Dakota. As a grand propaganda gesture, with little hope of success, Roosevelt leaders threw down the gauntlet to Taft's manager McKinley: nation-wide presidential preferential primaries to finally determine the Republican presidential nominee.

McKinley simply answered: "I do not favor changes in the rules of the game while the game is in progress."

Roosevelt promptly sent a telegram of challenge to Taft, with little positive effect except publicity, and then Roosevelt wrote:

"Their feeling is that politics is a game, that the people should simply sit on the bleachers as spectators, and that no appeal lies to the people from the men who, for their own profit, are playing the game . . . practically the entire body of professional politicians are pitted against us in this contest. . . ."

That was hardly fair and hardly true, but it was politically par for the course. All this quickening controversy made Taft writhe.

"The truth is that I am not very happy in this renomination and re-election business," Taft wrote his half-brother Charles. "I have set my teeth and go through with it as best I can. I am not going to squeal or run away. . . . But after it is all over, I shall be glad to retire and let another take the burden. . . . The day of the demogogue, the liar and the silly is on. . . ."

Later, Taft added, "I am not conscious of having done anything which disentitles me to stand as a candidate for a second term or requires a departure from the time-honored and very safe tradition against a third term. . . . I feel certain that if Theodore Roosevelt were nominated, he would be stronger the day of the convention than ever before and there would rise up against him in four months discussion of the real reasons why he should not be made more deserving than Washington, Jefferson, Jackson, Lincoln, or Grant."

The third term thing bothered Roosevelt, too, and some of the "silly" that Taft talked about, came out in a Roosevelt simile that backfired to haunt him.

"Frequently, when asked to take another cup of coffee at breakfast," Roosevelt said, "I say, 'No, thank you, I won't take another cup.' This does not mean that I intend never to take another cup of coffee during my life; it means that I am not accepting the offer as applying to that breakfast. . . ."

The New York Tribune promptly printed a cartoon showing a waiter serving a cup of coffee to Taft, and Roosevelt, next to him, saying, "Hey, waiter! Bring that over here. When I said I wouldn't take a third cup a little while ago, I only meant I wouldn't take it on top of the other two." And the Taft people soon circulated the gag, ". . . Have another cup of coffee. . . ."

Soon after the silly came the stronger demagogic tone of the opposition press on this third term issue.

"Does any sane person believe," asked the Philadelphia Evening Telegraph, "that if Theodore Roosevelt is nominated and elected in November, he will ever quit the Presidency alive. . . . An election in 1912 will be equivalent to an election for life and hereditary succession. . . ."

"Unless he breaks down under the strain and is taken to a lunatic asylum," editorialized the Louisville Courier Journal, "there can be in his name and person but one issue—life tenure in the executive office."

And the New York Sun ran a Rollin Kirby cartoon showing Roosevelt holding a document reading, "THEODORE ROOSEVELT FOR PRESIDENT FOR EVER AND EVER AND EVER. . . ."

While Taft had the bulk of press support, Roosevelt did have the string of Munsey papers, plus Nelson's *Kansas City Star and Times*, Valkenberg's *Philadelphia North American*, Stoddard's *New York Evening Mail*, and the *Chicago Tribune*. Small county papers stayed solid for Taft because of the usual strong ties between local organization politicians and local editors.

But the Taft men had no monopoly on money. Roosevelt had his own quota of "fat cats" and the two biggest and best were Perkins and Munsey. George W. Perkins was a partner of J. P. Morgan and Company, and a director of United States Steel; Frank Munsey, worth an estimated forty million dollars, published magazines, newspapers from Baltimore to Boston and had a chain of grocery stores. William Allen White said Munsey had "the morals of a green goods grocer" and Louis Brandeis, later a Justice of the United States Supreme Court, called Perkins the Prime Minister of the Rooseveltian party and asked, "Was it not like serving both God and Mammon at the same time?"

La Follette disciples also spread the talk that Munsey and Perkins both backed Roosevelt to prevent any possibility of a La Follette nomination, and to soft-pedal any platform plank on trusts.

Whatever their reasons, the sharper fact is that these two men ardently admired Roosevelt and backboned his campaign for almost a million dollars. Without them, there probably would have been no Roosevelt candidacy in 1912.

Roosevelt's campaign manager was Senator Joseph M. Dixon of Montana who still maintained his North Carolina accent even though he had moved to Montana. A smooth-shaven, soberminded man, Dixon was talkative, excitable, and impressive. He had headed the Speaker's Bureau of the Republican party for four years and had key contacts everywhere. For his publicity man, Dixon had O.K. Davis.

When Munsey met the two of them, he said, they talked of initial expenses and Munsey simply said, "Figure out how much you want."

Dixon jotted some figures on paper, finally said, "We ought to be sure of $50,000."

BALLOTS & BANDWAGONS

"I'll underwrite that much if you two will take the midnight train back to Washington and start work tomorrow morning," said Munsey. "Done!" they both said.

Munsey papers also pushed hard on the primary, his papers and magazines headlining, "GET THE DIRECT PRIMARY FOR YOUR STATE."

Munsey's Magazine also ran a series of articles straight through the primaries called "Catching up with Roosevelt," aimed at showing that Taft couldn't hope to do it. Munsey men distributed more than a million copies of that series.

But just before the primaries started, Roosevelt almost pushed his candidacy past the door of invisibility.

It was a speech scheduled at the Ohio State Constitutional Convention. He hadn't even wanted to go, but Republican State Chairman Walter Brown persuaded him by saying, "Colonel, Wilson came out to Columbus and didn't cause a ripple. Taft came out and there was not enough of a crowd to halt a trolley car; if you will come there will be such a crowd that the whole traction system of Columbus will be tied up."

What should he talk about? He had written an article for *The Outlook* six weeks before called "Judges and Progress" dealing with the recall of judges, which he once firmly opposed, but which he now favored, mostly due to the pressure of his western friends who stressed that this was the burning issue of the political west, where judges in many states were not even subject to removal by governors. The article created no stir at the time. But, of course, he had not been a declared candidate then, and the weight of his words had a different scale.

Roosevelt himself saw the speech as middle of the road, somewhat more conciliatory to business, and his board of business backers all read the speech, approved it. As Brown predicted, huge crowds stalled the Columbus traction system, arriving despite a hard snow on the city. (Afterward, Stoddard wired Perkins, "It looks to me as though we had tied up the whole campaign as well as the Columbus trolleys.")

Roosevelt called the speech, "A Charter of Democracy," and in it he said that the rich man "holds his wealth subject to the general right of the community to regulate its business use as the public welfare requires." He then went on to advocate initiative, referendum of legislation by the people and, most important of all, recall of judicial decisions. "It is both absurd and degrading," he said, "to make a fetish of a judge or of anyone else."

With the swift stroke of a few phrases, Roosevelt sliced off some of his strongest and most conservative supporters. His firm supporter, Senator Borah of Idaho, said, "The recall of judicial decisions is bosh." The *New York Sun* wrote, "Roosevelt proposed to establish on the street corners a higher court of law, the Court of the Crowd, with supreme jurisdiction—the craziest proposal that ever emanated either from himself or from any other statesman." Close friend William Allen White wrote of it afterward, ". . . it crippled him more than any other one thing he did in his life. For his speech shocked millions of his countrymen whom he had gathered about him as followers."

William Roscoe Thayer wrote flatly that the speech cost Roosevelt the nomination. Oscar Straus, a Cabinet member under both Roosevelt and Taft, afterward wrote, "I believe that but for this unfortunate statement regarding judicial decisions, Roosevelt would have been elected President in 1912."

But Roosevelt's greatest loss through that speech was the support of two of his oldest friends and advisers, Senator Henry Cabot Lodge and Elihu Root. Lodge wrote Roosevelt, "I have had my share of mishaps in politics, but I never thought that any situation could arise which would have made me so miserably unhappy." Lodge added, that, of course, he "would not think of supporting anyone else." Still, Lodge publicly disagreed with Roosevelt, and this open disagreement with its favorite son had a critical meaning in the upcoming Massachusetts primary.

As for Root, he coupled his shock with cynicism: "I have no doubt he thinks he believes what he says, but he doesn't," said Root. "He has merely picked up certain popular ideas which were at hand as one might pick up a poker or a chair with which to strike."

Root's importance was to prove even more politically pivotal—he was scheduled to act as Temporary Chairman at the upcoming Republican National Convention.

It did Roosevelt little good to explain that this concept of public recall of judicial decisions applied to state law and not national law, to constitutional law and not to criminal law.

If the West liked it, the East shuddered. Before the speech, a close canvass of Republican leaders in the country forecast a convention majority for Roosevelt; after the speech his political stock seemed to sag. Some careful analysts suggested that the speech had cost him more than twenty-nine delegates at the convention. These were controlling votes in that convention. It also intensified other opposition against him. It forever lost any possibility of weaning back business support which had been antagonized by Taft's increased trust busting.

The split which had started because of personalities now took on a new tone of principles.

"Death alone can take me out now," said Taft.

Lines were now more sharply drawn. Hearing the continued rumor that his 1908 campaign manager, later his Postmaster General, Frank Hitchcock, secretly supported Roosevelt, Taft openly confronted him at a Cabinet meeting, pointed his finger at him and said, "Frank! Are you for me or against me?"

Flushing, Hitchcock stood up stiffly and said, "I am for you, Mr. President."

The parade of primaries started badly for Roosevelt. The one in New York on March 26 had special meaning. It was his home state, the scene of his political start and of his recent fight for party control in which he had helped nominate a gubernatorial candidate—who had lost. Bill Barnes was now ready; Roosevelt was not. It was almost that simple.

Both sides had money. Taft's brother Charles quickly provided $50,000; Roosevelt's friends Munsey and Perkins each contributed

$15,000, as a starter. Analysts estimated that Roosevelt forces spent four dollars for each of the 15,000 votes they got in Manhattan. But it wasn't money; it was organization. True, the ballot was long and complex and only the well informed understood it. Also true, at least 400 of the 1,699 election districts in New York County lacked either ballots, election officials, or tally sheets.

This prompted Roosevelt men to call it "a criminal farce" and "a scandalous spectacle." But, again, it was not so much a case of corruption but of organization. Barnes men made sure that their votes came to the polls, that their voters had ballots, tally sheets, and election officials.

Barnes was no fool; he knew how much the public focus was on the New York primary. Barnes knew all the election tricks, and he had used them with cold efficiency to keep Albany heavily in the Republican column. His election returns sometimes showed as many Republican votes as there were voters in a particular precinct. Barnes carried on in the tradition of his grandfather, the long-time New York boss Thurlow Weed.

But this time Barnes played it so clean and careful that, despite their denunciations, Roosevelt people did not contest the New York primary at the convention.

Barnes was enough of a pro not to let his personal bitterness toward Roosevelt obstruct his political flexibility. More than anything else, he was a bandwagon boss—he wanted a winner. Reports came to Victor Rosewater from a New York committeeman that Barnes thought seriously of switching his support to Roosevelt, even made overtures through his lieutenant, County Committee Chairman Sam Koenig, but that it didn't work out. If it had, the final vote of delegates, eighty-three for Taft, seven for Roosevelt, would have been reversed and would have made Roosevelt a sure nominee.

"Under the New York law," Rosewater was told, "it is not a question of public sentiment but of the use of the party machinery."

A string of state conventions in some of the border states made the New York primary look mild-mannered. So many delegates carried ball bats at the Missouri convention that it became known as "the ball bat convention." And in Oklahoma, two-hundred unseated Roosevelt delegates stormed the convention hall and took possession. Three men were carried out after fist fights, one dropped dead from the excitement, and the presiding chairman was warned that if he caused any trouble he wouldn't walk out of the hall alive—and there was a man standing behind him with a loaded gun to show they weren't fooling. Roosevelt won well in both those conventions: in Oklahoma, he swept the state's ten delegates-at-large and six of the district delegates. Two of the four Taft delegates were later successfully contested at the convention.

North Dakota's primary, a week before the one in New York, represented the La Follette challenge. This was his area, and he fought with a fury on a five-day tour calling Roosevelt a tool of the money powers, loudly noted that the conservative Republican organization in that state backed Roosevelt in "an unholy alliance of enthusiasts and standpatters," and he added, "I want the names of all those who are ready to fight for La Follette to the end."

Old Guard Republicans adopted the "blanketing" technique, supporting Roosevelt verbally, but not physically. Roosevelt people were inexperienced, hesitated too long on withdrawing from the race, and Democrats saw a strong chance of humiliating Roosevelt by crossing lines and voting for La Follette.

Strong support came from Representative Charles Augustus Lindbergh (father of the famous flier), originally a La Follette man (who switched to Taft after the convention). To Lindbergh, Roosevelt wrote: "It seems to me that in North Dakota, a vote for Senator La Follette is a vote for Mr. Taft and will be so accepted by the country. Can't you say this to them?"

Expecting certain defeat in the primary, and trying to minimize its psychological effect nationally, Roosevelt told Dixon to issue a statement on election morning "claiming an immense progressive victory," emphasizing that the expected La Follette victory could still be counted as a Roosevelt delegation once it had cast "a complimentary vote for La Follette." This did little to lessen the La Follette bitterness as he won a sweeping victory.

Roosevelt philosophized about the situation to his friend, Missouri Governor Hadley: "The amusing thing is that in the Dakotas I am being opposed on the ground that I am a conservative and in the East on the ground that I am a radical."

But the most telling aftereffect of the primary was the Taft finger-pointing to the crossover of Democrats as an example of the ineffectiveness of the direct primary system as a true popularity gauge of the party.

Facing similar defeat in the well-organized Taft state of Indiana, Dixon's preliminary broadside to the press announced, "We do not propose to be robbed of our victory by any of the numerous forms of political burglary of which the Taft managers are masters." A specific instance of this tactic was the use of hand ballots pushed through a hole in a wicker basket; nobody seemed to know what happened to them afterward. That was in Indianapolis. Indiana gave Taft twenty-two out of thirty delegates.

A state convention in Michigan which featured a Taft man throwing a football block on a Roosevelt speaker, and the convention splitting in half, each electing its own chairman, also officially went for Taft. So did Kentucky, selecting twenty-three for Taft, only three for Roosevelt.

"From the outset," said Dixon, "the scheme to renominate Taft was a scheme to steal the nomination." Dixon even wrote an open letter to Taft, "You will become a deliberate receiver of stolen goods." All this sounded like the usual squeals of political losers, but the sound soon changed.

The big turn came in Illinois on April 9. Thanks to the steady pressure of publicity by the *Chicago Tribune*, which included a special canvass to show the popularity of the primary idea with the people, the Governor called a special session of the state legislature, passing a law for a direct primary only ten days before.

Roosevelt polled twice as many votes as Taft, won fifty-six Illinois delegates to Taft's two, his first national primary victory.

Dixon men used the term "Before April 9th Men," for all those Roosevelt supporters who favored him before the Illinois primary brightened his prospects.

The next day Maine and Vermont slightly muddied the picture. Aggressive, experienced Roosevelt leadership in Maine at the state convention won four delegates-at-large, after winning eight district delegates. That same day in Vermont, less experienced Roosevelt leaders lost to Taft men who got the four delegates-at-large while Roosevelt won two district delegates. Dixon promised to protest the Vermont decision: "We have won Vermont by fair means. We do not propose to have the state stolen from us."

New Hampshire also gave two-thirds of its delegates to Taft, despite a vigorous campaign by Governor Bass for Roosevelt. Wrote Roosevelt to Bass: "I am very sorry to hear what is happening in New Hampshire. As you say, every Federal officeholder, the whole Congressional delegation, all the old-school politicians, all the newspapers, and an unlimited supply of money make a hard combination to fight. It is the kind of combination that is against us practically everywhere."

The picture changed again in Pennsylvania in mid-April. Roosevelt people gave Boss Penrose ten days "to think it over" before he made his political decision of support. When Penrose went for Taft, the main campaign attack hit at Penrose rather than Taft. The publisher of the *Philadelphia North American*, E. A. Van Valkenburg drafted a University of Pennsylvania Professor of Surgery, James Allen White, to organize a campaign of amateurs. These amateurs combined with the professionals of Bill Flinn, a Penrose rival, and the combination gave Roosevelt fifty-five of the state's sixty-four district delegates in the primary, and a dozen more delegates-at-large at the state convention on May 1.

Talking of the Pennsylvania defeat, Taft said, "Of course such a defeat is very significant in the hold which Roosevelt still has over the plain people. . . . We had hoped by May 1 to have enough votes to nominate but now we may have to depend on the May states. I shall not withdraw under any condition."

The political wind now with him, Roosevelt no longer charged "bare-faced frauds." In Nebraska, local Roosevelt and La Follette groups combined on a single slate of delegates pledged to the one who came out best in the balloting. The combined slate beat Taft by 50,000 votes, and Roosevelt swamped La Follette by 46,795 to 16,785. This gave all sixteen Nebraska delegates to Roosevelt. The sweep defeated Victor Rosewater, who tried to stay in the middle of the road. But Rosewater still had an important part to play in the T. R. future. Rosewater's elected successor tried to replace him before the convention opening because Rosewater was slated to head the National Committee investigation of contested cases, but this was so much against party tradition that Dixon refused to support the insurgent claim.

Neighbor state Kansas also went big for Roosevelt, but Roosevelt complained about his speaking schedule which now added up to ten speeches a day. "I got through Nebraska and Kansas all right," he wrote O.K. Davis, "and it was necessary to make the speeches, but my voice has gone and there must be no repetition of such a program as that in Nebraska and Kansas, for the simple reason that halfway through, my voice would go completely. I do not even know whether I will be able to speak in North Carolina. You must arrange in Massachusetts next week that there is no effort to have me make speeches from the end of the car, or many speeches of any kind. . . ."

Roosevelt attacks on Taft switched to a new emphasis: Taft was bowing to the bosses. He cited Penrose of Pennsylvania, Cox of Ohio, Aldrich of Rhode Island.

"Association with them, when it is by and for Roosevelt, has nothing evil in it," Taft wrote his brother. "It is only when they support me that bosses are wicked."

Roosevelt also openly accused Taft of being "disloyal to our past friendship, disloyal to every canon of ordinary decency." Finally, on April 26 in Boston, four days before the start of the Massachusetts primary, President Taft made one of the most poignant, most personal speeches ever made by an American President. It was a two-hour speech that filled ten newspaper columns and it concerned "one whom in the past I have greatly admired and loved."

"I am here to reply to an old and true friend who has made many charges. I deny all of them. I do not want to fight Theodore Roosevelt, but I am going to fight. . . . Mr. Roosevelt prides himself in being a true sportsman. . . . The maxim which he has exalted above all others is that every man is entitled to a square deal. . . . Is he giving me a square deal?"

At the finish of his speech, Taft returned to his private railroad car, put his head in his hands and wept. Outside a crowd sang, "We'll hang Teddy's hat to a sour apple tree. . . ."

Taft's successive speeches were in the same personal tone: "This wrenches my soul. . . . I have been a man of straw, but I have been a man of straw long enough."

And then, a phrase that came back at him in a constant campaign ricochet: "I am a man of peace. I don't want to fight. But when I do fight, I want to hit hard. Even a rat in a corner will fight."

". . . Even a rat in a corner will fight. . . ."

"I look back now with amazement," said O.K. Davis, "on the readiness with which we rang the changes on that unhappy sentence, and almost daily quoted the President's description of himself as a cornered rat."

If Taft could tell a *New York World* reporter, "Roosevelt was my closest friend. . . ." and then weep openly, Roosevelt had neither time nor taste for tears. He said simply to the press, "Mr Taft is President only because I kept my promise in spite of infinite pressure to break it. It is a bad trait to bite the hand that feeds you." Roosevelt then wrote O.K. Davis, "I am glad you liked the way I answered Taft . . . I think stamping on a man I have knocked down is both useless and discourteous."

No matter how hard Roosevelt's friends tried to paint him as a martyr, the paint looked thin. William Allen White explained it: "He did not have a drop of martyr's blood in his veins. He told me so. . . . He wanted to be a victor. . . ."

That wasn't easy in Massachusetts. The strange primary law permitted each delegate to label himself for a specific presidential candidate. Voting for eight delegates-at-large, voters confusingly found nine proposed delegates for Taft and eight for Roosevelt.

To confuse the confusion, the Roosevelt force was made up mostly of well-meaning amateurs, mostly young—the oldest was forty-two—wealthy Harvard graduates, all from the eastern part of the state with a basic political ignorance. "I have just come back from Massachusetts," Roosevelt wrote. "I think that Taft will carry the state because ours is only a fight of minutemen under sergeants and corporals, all the generals and mercenaries are against us." Roosevelt sent in Bill Flinn to help, but the help was too little and late. Lodge's public opposition to Roosevelt on the judicial recall issue hurt Roosevelt, but they still stayed friends. In fact, Roosevelt wrote Lodge about the campaign result.

"Well, isn't the outcome in Massachusetts comic?" he asked Lodge.

The comic quality came from the fact that Taft won the overall preferential vote by 86,772 to 83,099. However, eight delegates-at-large, pledged to Roosevelt, defeated the Taft slate by some 8,000 votes. Roosevelt publicly requested these eight "to disregard the pledge to support me" and accept the preferential vote to support Taft. (The eight refused to do this and voted consistently with Roosevelt at the convention). In the district contests, Taft received eighteen of the twenty-three delegates.

Roosevelt won all ten delegates in the Oregon primary. Washington found itself with two full rival slates of delegates each claiming authority, the Roosevelt group accusing the Taft organization of hand-picking delegates. And, in Maryland, with another complicated primary law, Taft forces now accused the Roosevelt group of buying votes in critical counties. O.K. Davis admitted later that Dixon "gave a little money to pay for some printing and some other expenses" to three voters providing a winning margin in a key county. The two candidates evenly split the state in delegates even though Roosevelt had won the overall primary by 3,000 votes.

California voted its entire delegation of twenty-six for Roosevelt, with Taft claiming two district delegates in the San Francisco area. The bitterness in that fight had been between the partisans of Roosevelt and La Follette. In New Jersey, where both candidates campaigned hard, Roosevelt took all the twenty-four district delegates and also won the four delegates-at-large. South Dakota was another Roosevelt state and Arizona had two rival conventions going on in the same convention hall with the results contested.

But probably the most significant primary of all was Ohio, Taft's home state. Its psychological importance was obviously enormous. Both men traveled in private railroad cars, an estimated 1,800 miles a week, Roosevelt making ninety scheduled speeches, Taft fifty-five. One evening in Steubenville, their private trains were both alongside each other on the same railroad platform, separated only by the warm air and the cold silence. The commentary was political; the tragedy, social.

This fight was bitter back-alley, no holds barred.

"Dangerous demagogue . . . egotist," said Taft of T. R.

"Fat head . . . puzzlewit," said T. R. of Taft.

Both men brought in their biggest batteries of names including senators and governors. It was the bandwagon testing time. Henry Stimson, whom Roosevelt had unsuccessfully supported for Governor of New York and whom Taft had promoted to a Cabinet job, now openly supported Taft. But Taft wrote his brother, "Root has failed me. He is bitterly against Roosevelt, he tells me, but he will not come out to Ohio to help me."

Elihu Root wrote Taft, "I hope you will pull through. I believe you will. I think it should be a great misfortune if you should not." And then he added, "My fighting days are over."

Complicating the clear issue, La Follette also moved into Ohio to campaign, saying, "I'm nobody's cloak. I'll fight to the finish."

Another factor of more personal complication for Roosevelt was his son-in-law, Nicholas Longworth, running for Congress from the Cincinnati area, the stronghold of Boss Cox, a Taft supporter. In deference to Longworth, Roosevelt stayed out of there, and lost the district. But Roosevelt carried sixty-nine out of Ohio's eighty-eight counties, while Taft took only nineteen, with a Roosevelt majority of 31,977 over Taft and La Follette combined. Of the forty-two district delegates, Roosevelt won thirty-four.

There was also the upcoming state convention selecting six delegates-at-large, and Roosevelt announced, "Any attempt to give Mr. Taft a single delegate-at-large would mean to sanction an effort to defraud the people." And Taft wired his Ohio campaign manager, National Committeeman Vorys, demanding a "last ditch" fight for those delegates-at-large. Taft also closely consulted Warren Gamaliel Harding, whom Roosevelt had unsuccessfully supported for Governor of Ohio two years before, and who was now a Taft man. Harding was badly hissed when he spoke for Taft at the state convention. But Taft forces had maneuvered well at the county conventions, and Roosevelt campaign manager in Ohio, Walter Brown, Chairman of the Republican State Committee, accused Taft of applying job pressure on all federal officeholders, especially in Cuyahoga County (Cleveland). Taft men at the state convention controlled all committees and the six delegates at large all went to Taft by a vote of 390 to 362½.

Roosevelt called it "burglary." "They succeeded in getting from the city of Cleveland, which had repudiated Mr. Taft three-to-one at the polls, a delegation of politicians which was ten-to-one in his favor. This delegation turned the scale at the state convention," said Roosevelt.

Of the thirteen primaries, Roosevelt claimed 278 delegates, more than twice the total for Taft. The total popular vote in those states: 1,157,397 for Roosevelt, 761,716 for Taft, and 351,043 for La Follette. Taft could only claim weakly that they included a lot of Democrats who voted for Roosevelt to embarrass the Republicans.

Dixon predicted that Roosevelt would have six-hundred votes on the first ballot and would be nominated "without the aid of a single deserter from the Taft forces who wishes to get on the bandwagon, and without asking the help of a single uninstructed delegate."

The more impartial Associated Press had these statistics on
June 10:

Total in convention (majority 540)	1,078
Instructed for Roosevelt, uncontested	411
Instructed for Taft, uncontested	201
Instructed for La Follette uncontested	36
Instructed for Cummins, uncontested	10
Uninstructed, including New York	166
Contested	254

The fascinating figure was the final one: 254. And, on that, the
major fight would be fought.

The Taft gloom was on and Taft wrote his brother that he expected the seats on the Roosevelt bandwagon to become increasingly popular "when it becomes apparent . . . that I cannot win."

Talk now increased about compromise candidates, and Taft
wrote his brother: "I said I had no great desire to run again provided I could get somebody who does not represent what Theodore
Roosevelt represents; but that I would not withdraw in favor of
La Follette, Cummins, or Roosevelt; and that if he [Root] or
Hughes or a man of like conservative standing were to be seriously
suggested, he would find no difficulty with me."

Root ruled himself out of the race "if for no other reason, because I shall be sixty-eight years old at the time of the next in-
auguration, and no man of that age is fit to be President."

Roosevelt ruled himself in, dismissed all thought of a compromise candidate. "I'll name the compromise candidate," said
Roosevelt. "He'll be me. I'll name the compromise platform. It
will be our platform."

Asked whether he would attend the national convention, Roosevelt said, carefully spacing his words, "if——circumstances——demand——of——course——I——shall go!"

In Chicago, the first contingent of uniformed Roosevelt Rough
Riders was already practicing parade formation in the city parks.
Elsewhere in Chicago, the Republican National Committee started

to assemble to decide the contested cases of the 254 delegates.

The upcoming meeting had the smell of danger and the stronger smell of defeat. Whatever happened, it could only hurt the Republican party. It might split the crack into a canyon. It might stir up a hate and an ugliness that wouldn't heal. And, worst of all, it might lose the election. A dozen top Republican leaders met to talk about it. They were all Taft men: "Uncle Joe" Cannon, Elihu Root, W. Murray Crane of Massachusetts, Jim Watson of Indiana, Bill Barnes, and Boies Penrose. The men talked of alternative candidates, and somebody mentioned Governor Hadley of Missouri, because Roosevelt liked him.

"Uncle Joe" Cannon, speaking caustically from his authority of power, broke in and said that if the Republican party was going to surrender to Roosevelt, "ain't we wasting our time by not calling him in and getting our orders early?"

Then Boies Penrose stood up, paced the floor, talking as he walked:

"Here we sit," he said, "a group of supposedly practical men, trying to deceive ourselves that the people want us. They are tired of us. They're tired of the Republican Party. They're tired of Boies Penrose. They're tired of Murray Crane. They're tired of Joe Cannon and Jim Watson. They're tired of the whole damned lot of us. We're going to lose this election; for God's sake, don't let us lose control of ourselves.

"There's only one way to go and that's straight ahead. We've got to stick to the road we're on. I know damn well it leads straight over a precipice. You know it, too. But that's what we've got to do. All right, let's drive the old machine into the chasm.

"After the crash, we can pick ourselves out of the wreck—those of us who survive. With what's left of the machine, we can begin building another. It's an outworn model anyway. In the reconstructed machine, we'll ride back home."

To Bill Barnes, Penrose had added, "Bill, a wiser man than you —Governor Ben Odell of your own state—told me something a few years ago. He told me that when it came to deciding between losing an election and losing control of the party—lose the election. And Bill, he was right by God!"

Right or not, this was the Taft Republican road: no compromise with Roosevelt.

Pressed for a statement, Roosevelt said he expected fair treatment from the National Committeemen on the contested cases because "they have to go home and spend the rest of their lives with their constituents."

This was mostly political wind-whistling. But the greatest wind-whistler of them all was William L. Ward, National Committeeman from New York who had traveled the country talking to other committeemen in favor of Roosevelt. Of the fifty-three members of the Republican National Committee, Ward claimed that twenty-nine were for Roosevelt, "at least not FOR Taft."

"With this anti-Taft majority on the National Committee," Ward continued, he expected a high-powered steamroller to start going about the time the convention started in Chicago, and "this is the way it will work:

"The national committee names the Temporary Chairman of the Committee, and he'll be a Roosevelt supporter, probably ex-Senator Beveridge of Indiana. The Temporary Chairman appoints the Credentials Committee, and he'll name a committee favorable to Roosevelt. The Credentials Committee decides contests among the delegates. So there you are. Taft loses and Roosevelt wins by virtue of the anti-Taft majority in the National Committee."

That was not exactly the way it worked out.

The fifty-three members of the Republican National Committee were largely the hand-picked friends of the "in" President. They always were. This meant, simply, that this time they were mostly Taft's friends. The current primaries and state convention selections didn't affect them. They all served four years from the end of the previous convention to the beginning of this one. Their replacements, therefore, wouldn't take over until the convention officially started. All this had more meaning now than ever before in Republican history because these "yesterday" committeemen, these Taft friends, would decide the contested cases of the "today" delegates. More than that, since each state's vote counted the same on the National Committee, the strength of the South was highly disproportionate, especially since the combined popular Republican vote of Florida, Louisiana, Mississippi, and South Carolina added up to less than 34,000 votes. And the South was the firmest Taft stronghold, the firmest for any "in" President, because so many of those few Republicans represented federal officeholders.

William Jennings Bryan spelled it out for the public: "It has been customary in all parties for the Committee which conducts a campaign to retain its authority until the next convention is permanently organized. In ordinary times, the power thus conferred upon an old Committee is not misused, but in times of upheaval and change, the power is subject to abuse."

Then he added the obvious political truth: "If the Roosevelt men had control of the National Committee, there is no doubt that they would have seated their men, and it is quite probable that they would not have been looking for precedents to sustain the position they are taking."

With the strangeness of history, it was Roosevelt himself who had framed the scale of his own predicament, who had resolved his own future. At the end of President Roosevelt's term in 1908, a specific proposal was presented to the National Committee to change the disproportionate representation of the South by more closely apportioning the number of delegates in each state to the number of their Republican votes in the previous election. Roosevelt's personal influence vetoed that proposal. He similarly helped kill another idea to seat newly-elected committeemen immediately after their election. Either one of these proposals would have drastically changed the picture and the prospects in 1912.

It took a majority to demand a roll call on the National Committee. Roosevelt now wanted this changed so that eight or ten delegates could demand a roll call (which represented most of Roosevelt's extended strength on the committee). The committee, of course, refused to do this. But four years before, under Roosevelt's insistence as President, they would have changed that rule, or almost any other.

The result of this on the upcoming cases: no roll calls.

Since the National Committee made up the roll of the convention, deciding on contested delegations, and since these contested delegates then had the right to vote permanent organization of the convention, and since this organization would then decide the ultimate right of these same contested delegates to sit in that convention—their importance was obvious.

It was a stacked deck, and the dealer was Taft, but it could have been Roosevelt.

When the committee refused to cut the majority needed for a roll call, it prompted a Roosevelt blast: "It is expected that outrages will be perpetrated in the National Committee in the next ten days that will make insignificant crimes of similar nature in the past and yet there will be no record to show who the perpetrators were."

Committee Chairman Victor Rosewater, the small, quiet man who published the *Omaha Bee* in Nebraska made a struggling show of impartiality. This struggle had cost him his place on the National Committee in the earlier primary—but he still kept this position until the convention was permanently organized.

Rosewater counted himself a confidant of both candidates although he had written Taft a letter of "staunch adherence" before the primary. Still, on a trip East before the committee meeting, when President Taft invited him to be his guest in his railroad car for the ride from Princeton to Washington, Rosewater made it a public point immediately afterward to confer with Roosevelt's manager, and then with the La Follette representatives.

The key committee question was whether to make hearings secret or public.

Taft sent a suggestion to Rosewater: ". . . I am really in favor, I think you will believe, of acting impartially. . . . I have had a talk with General Clayton of Arkansas and he brought to my attention the wisdom of having the Committee sit not with open doors, but with representatives of the principal contestants present when each contest is heard, together with some four or five representatives of the press associations, as well as a stenographer, that they may get a fair account of what has happened."

Rosewater accepted the Taft suggestion.

Taft discussed the contested cases in a letter to a friend, ". . . some . . . of course, which Roosevelt ought to win," but added, "We do not propose to be defrauded or bulldozed out of it."

That likelihood was little.

The *New York Times* gave Roosevelt only four "sure" votes out of the fifty-three on the committee and intimated Roosevelt's only hope was the pressure put on committeemen by hometown "bread and butter" politicians on a lower level who wanted to win the election and saw Roosevelt as the most likely winner.

But what were these contested cases anyway?

About one-third of the 254 contested seats were southern. "Of the strictly southern state contests," said Rosewater, "not over a dozen rested on plausible grounds."

However, the most remarkable admission on the southern contests, was printed in the *Washington Times*, a pro-Roosevelt Munsey paper, which revealed the Ormsby McHarg strategy in the South—and it was printed the week of the committee opening:

"On the day when Roosevelt formally announced that he was a candidate," the analyst said, "something over a hundred delegates had actually been selected. When Senator Dixon took charge of the campaign, a tabulated showing of delegates selected to date would have been hopelessly one-sided. Moreover a number of southern states had called their conventions for early dates and there was no chance to develop the real Roosevelt strength in the great northern States till later.

"For psychological effect, as a move in practical politics, it was necessary for the Roosevelt people to start contests on those early Taft selections in order that a tabulation of delegate strength could be put out that would show Roosevelt holding a good hand. In the game, a table showing Taft 150, Roosevelt 19, contested none, would not be very much calculated to inspire confidence, whereas one showing Taft 23, Roosevelt 19, contested 127—looked very much different. That is the whole story of the larger number of southern contests that were started early in the game. It was never expected that they would be taken very seriously . . . they served a useful purpose."

How useful the purpose really was even La Follette acknowledged. "Beyond question," he said, "it is true that during the last few weeks preceding the convention, many delegates were elected for Roosevelt because of the false claims put forth by his managers that he had a large lead in the contest. . . ."

As for the disposition of the contested cases, the pro-Roosevelt *Review of Reviews* expressed a widely held public opinion: "The country would have applauded . . . if both sets of delegates from these manipulated rotten boroughs had been thrown out. . . ."

But the steamroller already seemed set. In fact, a local Hearst reporter even hired a steamroller, parked it in front of the Chicago Coliseum where the committee meeting was scheduled, and asked Rosewater to pose in the driver's seat for a picture. Rosewater unsmilingly refused. Then it began, alphabetically by states, numerically by Congressional district.

One of the early cases that caused an uproar, dividing the Committee—so much so that even Rosewater voted against seating Taft delegates—was the Ninth Alabama Congressional District.

The case turned on the legality of a district convention call, and it hinged on the vote of a single pivotal vote on the district party committee. The yes or no of that vote would supply the majority vote to a split committee and determine whether or not that convention would be called. According to the evidence, Roosevelt representatives presumably persuaded the delegate to resign from the committee, and not to attend the decisive meeting so that a Roosevelt man could be appointed to his place. But then, afterward, Taft representatives also contacted this same man and persuaded him to attend the meeting. But the district committee chairman, a Roosevelt man, already had appointed a new committee member. So, on the day of the meeting, both men showed up—the man who was supposed to stay away and the new appointee.

The confusion resulted in two convention calls and two sets of delegates from the same district.

"The impression I gained," Rosewater said, "was that both sets seemed to be tarred with the same stick. I would have been disposed to exclude both."

However, the Taft set was selected, even getting the vote of pro-Roosevelt committeeman Cecil Lyon of Texas. That was because the Texas case was coming up and Lyon told Rosewater, "I think it's always good policy to line up with the regular organization," adding hopefully, "We're all in the same boat."

The Texas boat seemed equally sinkable.

Cecil Lyon had controlled political patronage in Texas for twelve years, for both Roosevelt and Taft, and was known there as "the whole works" because he maintained a closed corporation of retainers and relatives. His will was law on five-thousand jobs—more than any four United States Senators. Every man he recommended was appointed. His tactic of control was to stack committees in district conventions, alloting disproportionate representation to the most sparsely settled 126 counties where there were so few Republicans that Lyon, a strong Roosevelt man, could hand-pick his candidates for delegates. In those counties that voted for Taft delegates, Roosevelt men simply withdrew and chose their own delegates. Both sides challenged different district results, and the committee finally gave Taft thirty, Roosevelt two.

As one delegate put it, "In our opinion, the Texas case stands out conspicuously as the one in which expediency is the controlling factor in the decision of the majority." Rosewater felt the decision could have gone either way on many of the Texas contests but Roosevelt called the final decision "indefensible."

Arizona's double set of delegates were both elected in the same hall. Roosevelt men protested the chairman's (a Taft man) method of preparing the temporary roll call at the state convention so they simply escorted their own man to the platform, elected him as

temporary chairman and each chairman selected a separate credentials committee. It was Arizona's first appearance at a national
convention with statehood status and the National Committee
gave all its six delegates to Taft.

California's case was much more complicated. Governor Hiram
Johnson put through a new state primary law giving its solid slate
to a single winning candidate. He asked for, and received, signed
certificates from all presidential candidates, including Taft, agreeing to accept this law. Roosevelt then won by seventy thousand
votes, and received all the states twenty-six delegates.

So far, so simple.

However, a Republican National Committee rule provided that
no state election could prevent election of district delegates by
voters of that district. And, in the California Fourth Congressional
District, in San Francisco, two Taft delegates polled more votes
than their Roosevelt opponents. Taft people then claimed those
two delegates on party rules.

Governor Johnson refused to appear before the committee. "I
will not submit to a trial of the title of property by the thief who
steals it."

Californians flooded the committee with letters and telegrams
of protest, but the committee still accepted the two Taft delegates.

"The contest for the Republican nomination," said Roosevelt,
"has now narrowed down to the naked issue of right and wrong.

"Hitherto, it was supposed that the National Committee was
content with the political emoluments of pocket-picking and
porch-climbing," Roosevelt continued. "Today, however, they as-
sayed the role of the apache and the garoteer."

The pro-Taft newspaper, the *New York Sun* commented, "So
much for the naked issue . . . now for the naked truth," and
proceeded to tear down the Roosevelt case, especially on the
southern credentials. Then it parodied the rest of the Roosevelt
statement:

"The bestial nature of the indecent hordes of pirates, second
story men, porch climbers, gun men and short card dealers who

oppose me is now perfectly manifest. . . . I denounce it as a machination of the special interests in their loathesome campaign for the submergence of innocence, childhood, motherhood, womanhood and Abraham Lincoln. . . ."

Back at the committee hearings, the parade of cases continued:

Washington's conflict concerned a primary, which Roosevelt won, declared illegal by the Taft-controlled state committee which promptly certified fourteen Taft delegates. The charge against the Taft delegation from Kentucky involved committee-stacking and federal job pressure, although an outside observer noted that Taft had replaced only 20 per cent of federal officeholders in that state compared to an 80 per cent replacement by Roosevelt during his presidential term. In the Indiana case, affidavits were shown claiming that Taft forces had sent truckloads of voters to one ward after another, wherever extra votes were needed. Louisiana had one district where an eight-man "convention" selected two delegates, sent them affidavits to return saying they would be for Taft. One man signed, the other didn't. The National Committee ratified only the man who signed the affidavit for Taft.

Taft's case in Missouri however was so weak that the Taft Committeemen feared a swing of the more independent committeemen to Roosevelt and thought that it might have a bad psychological effect. They then called a recess, arranged a compromise giving Roosevelt some delegates and permitting Governor Hadley to remain as Chairman.

The meetings had streaks of humor as well as starts of fist fights.

One claimant from Florida described how the Roosevelt delegates had been kept out of a local convention: "We walked in, and then, in a couple minutes, we were walked out again." When he persisted on trying again, he said, "one of the men wheeled on me and I wheeled on him and they wheeled me out."

There was also the case of a contested Mississippi district, another double-header convention, one for Taft inside the hall, the other for Roosevelt in the courtyard. But there was little physical problem on this one: both conventions picked the same delegate to represent them, and he had credentials from each in his pocket. The National Committee decided that he, Perry Howard, was a Taft delegate, (but inside the Convention Hall, Howard later voted for Roosevelt).

It created some stir when Mississippi delegate Charles Banks sent a letter to Taft manager William McKinley, referring to a thousand dollars given him for expenses for ten Negro delegates. "I am returning the money," he said, "and you can do as you see fit." McKinley denounced the Banks letter as a betrayal of confidence, noted that it was sent from Roosevelt headquarters, generally intimated that perhaps Banks got more money elsewhere. But Banks was also the business agent for noted Negro educator Booker T. Washington—who was strong for Roosevelt.

Recognized Taft leader within the committee was Senator W. Murray Crane of Massachusetts, a long man with a long face topped by a tuft of brown hair. Crane had a soft voice and he kept it as faint as his barely visible mustache. He worked through others as a steerer and prompter. The main voice of Crane was Senator Charles "Colonel" Dick of Ohio, formerly an advance man for Mark Hanna in the McKinley days. Dick was a man with piercing eyes, a receding forehead backed by long, fluffy gray hair, an angelic smile, but a hard man on witnesses.

Featured on the Roosevelt side was Senator William E. Borah of Idaho, a heavy set man with broad shoulders and thick brown hair, a jutting jaw and a habit of asking questions that ended with, "That's so, is it not?" Borah called Rosewater, "Schoolmaster." In contrast there was Francis J. Heney, a great California lawyer who kept reminding everybody how he had just sent Boss Abe Ruef of San Francisco to jail. A shrewd looking man with a long nose and a large mouth, he looked as if he had a steady smirk on his face. It was Heney who maintained a steady loud tone of protest, saying nobody would be recognized on the committee "but a hand-picked machine-made crook."

When it was all over, the National Committee had seated 164 delegates for Taft, unanimously or because of contest withdrawal, and 19 delegates for Roosevelt. Of the 254 contested cases, only 65 were seated by a split vote of the National Committee—and these were given to Taft.

"A fraud as vulgar, as brazen, and as cynically open as any ever committed by the Tweed regime in New York forty years ago," said Roosevelt.

But others noted that there must have been some criteria for judgment based on some fact since there were cases where red-hot Roosevelt supporters refused to support claims for some Roosevelt delegates. Similarly, in the split votes, even a few Taft men voted for certain Roosevelt delegates.

After going over the disputed documents with some aides, La Follette felt that only sixty-five delegates given to Taft might have gone to Roosevelt. "These figures," said La Follette, "can fairly be reduced. They cannot with the least show of fairness be increased." The *Chicago Tribune*, a pro-Roosevelt paper, listed only fifty-seven cases in real question.

However, Governor Hadley of Missouri, prepared a list of seventy-two which the committee minority for Roosevelt agreed on, and signed. Long afterward, Nicholas Murray Butler, then President of Columbia University, asked Hadley how he arrived at the precise figure.

"Governor Hadley smiled and said: 'I will tell you. After the National Committee had heard the various contests and reached their conclusions, Borah, Frank Kellogg and I decided that in 24 cases we had been literally defrauded of our representation. We recognized that we had a very strong case in respect to other contests, but that there were debatable questions, every one of which, however, had been decided against us. . . . So we three went to Colonel Roosevelt and told him this fact. We said we were going to contest these twenty-four seats on the floor of the convention. On hearing this statement, Colonel Roosevelt cried with great vehemence: 'Twenty-four seats! Twenty-four! What is the use of contesting twenty-four? You must contest seventy-four if you expect to get anywhere.' So we raised the number to 74." (The final list presented on the convention floor was seventy-two.)

So much public fury for both sides followed the National Committee result that humorist Finley Peter Dunne converted it into a column:

"I had no idee it was so bad. I wint to bed last night thinkin' th' country was safe, so I put out th' cat, locked th' dure, counted th' cash, said me prayers, wound th' clock, an' pulled into th' siding for th' night. Whin I got up I had a feelin' that somethin' was burnin', th' same as I had th' mornin' iv th' big fire. But I cudden't find anythin' wrong until I opened up th' pa-apers an', much to me relief, found that it was not me pants but th' republic that was on fire. Yes sir; th' republic is doomed to desthruction again."

Slightly more seriously, Roosevelt man George Ade said, "The National Committee fixed things so that they couldn't be fixed by anything short of an earthquake."

Of course, political earthquakes *had* happened in national conventions before. And this one, particularly, had a looming unpredictability about it. The National Committee action on contested cases still needed approval from convention delegates themselves. The personal excitement of the Roosevelt personality always had explosive possibilities. A big bloc of votes supposedly tied to Taft might unexpectedly break for Roosevelt or push for a compromise candidate. Many Negro delegates were reported as "straining at the leash to vote for Roosevelt."

Before the convention opened, these large questions seemed even larger.

One of the immediate questions was the selection of a Temporary Chairman. The National Committee named Elihu Root. The choice was shrewd. Root had presided over the 1904 Republican National Convention that had nominated Roosevelt, had served as Secretary of State and Secretary of War, United States Senator, was probably the most distinguished corporation lawyer and one of the foremost conservative Republicans in the country. Roosevelt had said "I would rather see Elihu Root in the White House than any other man . . . I would walk on my hands and knees from the White House to the Capitol to see Root made President. . . ."

Opposing Root seemed at first an untenable position for Roosevelt. He hedged. For reporters, he quoted the Illinois delegation who considered the Temporary Chairmanship as too unimportant for a showdown fight. It took pressure from western delegates to force Roosevelt's move on Root. Westerners saw Root in the bold color of a Taft conservative who must be fought on principle or else invite defeat in November. Similar reaction came from those close to the La Follette Progressives. An added factor might have been a growing ridicule in the press poking at Roosevelt's fear to fight Root.

As preventive politics, Bill Barnes of New York had wired all delegates, except those pledged to Roosevelt: "The National Committee has selected Senator Root for Temporary Chairman of the convention at Chicago. It is reported that the Roosevelt forces will oppose the action of the Committee. I am wiring . . . to ask for your support. . . . We believe this contest is the most serious one which has afflicted the Republican Party, and that the attempt to nominate Mr. Roosevelt can only lead to disaster. . . . Will you please wire me, New York City collect, whether we can rely on your support for Senator Root for Temporary Chairman?"

After a six-hour conference at Sagamore Hill with close advisers, Roosevelt announced: "In the past, Mr. Root has rendered distinguished service as Secretary of State and Secretary of War. But in this contest, Mr. Root has ranged himself against the men who stand for progressive principles within the Republican Party . . . he is put forward by the bosses and representatives of special privileges. . . ."

Roosevelt took time to decide on his own candidate. There had been talk of Borah, then Roosevelt tentatively approached Hadley of Missouri, whom he described in a letter as "a Progressive with the bridle on."

Then came a political brainstorm, a seemingly obvious way that might sew up the convention. Roosevelt wrote about it to Dixon:

"Wish you would think over whether it would not be wise to have McGovern [Governor] of Wisconsin Permanent Chairman. . . . McGovern is a fine fellow. Our choice of him would emphasize, as nothing else would, the fact that we wish all Progressives to stand together. . . ."

Dixon agreed and Roosevelt wrote a confidential letter to Mc-Govern, making the pitch on the chairmanship, and adding, "What I should like particularly to see at Chicago is an immediate and close alliance between the Roosevelt and La Follette men. . . ." McGovern answered promptly, assured his agreement, then said, "now all who think alike should act alike until we are assured that the fruits of victory shall not be stolen from us."

The liaison seemed perfect. (The offer of Permanent Chairman changed into the Temporary Chairmanship.) It did not attempt to swerve McGovern and his group from their commitment to La Follette, but it did seem to coalesce a united strength against Taft that could block his organization of the convention and probably prevent his nomination.

"Taft cannot possibly win now," Roosevelt wrote McGovern, "except by deliberate highway robbery. He himself lacks the strength and courage to perform such highway robbery, but he has all the viciousness and ethical dishonesty necessary for the end, and the ability and nerve will be supplied by the unscrupulous people around him if the chance arises."

Taft had similar doubts, similar confidence. "It is possible that by bulldozing, bribery and other dishonorable means," Taft wrote Archbishop Ireland, "he may reduce my vote to slightly less than enough to nominate, but I very much doubt he can nominate himself as long as I stay in the field—and I shall stay as long as my remaining will interfere with his success."

Both candidates picked men to nominate them. Taft wanted former governor of Ohio Warren Gamaliel Harding, (who would one day turn tables and appoint Taft to his lifetime dream job, Chief Justice of the United States Supreme Court). Taft told Harding about the nominating speech: "I know you can do it well, and I shall be delighted to have it done by a man who represents his state so worthily as you do."

"Prendergast [of New York] is to nominate me," Roosevelt told Dixon, "Hiram Johnson to second me. I should like to have two other men second me, one of them Dean Lewis [the University of Pennsylvania's Dean of Law], the other some first-class business-man or lawyer from the Middle West. . . . I think that with Hiram Johnson to second me, the Far West will be content." Later, Roosevelt had a further idea, "I want some colored man to second my nomination."

Rumors now got thicker, uglier. Back in Oyster Bay, Roosevelt felt impelled to deny that he was a drunkard. "I never drink whiskey at all," he wrote, "and on none of these trips have I even drunk any wine."

But Roosevelt had more immediate concern than rumors. His Chicago field marshals had retired to a quiet corner to count names and noses of delegates. Boies Penrose already made the statement that the indications showed Taft with a slight majority on the first ballot unless there was a big break in the New York delegation. He also added that if the convention agreed with the National Committee and decided contested cases on their merits, that Roosevelt would be about one hundred short of a majority.

After a meeting with other leaders, Dixon had a letter written to Senator Beveridge: ". . . considering the closeness of the vote . . . I believe that the Colonel's presence would add material strength and enthusiasm to his followers. We have broken all precedents in our campaign to nominate Mr. Roosevelt and we might as well go even further and have him personally at the head of his forces. . . . I firmly believe that you are the one to put this up to Colonel Roosevelt and convince him that the best interests of the cause demands his presence."

Roosevelt needed little convincing. "This convention is no place for anybody who doesn't love a fight," he said, and Roosevelt loved a fight. Little of this discussion went over Roosevelt's direct telegraph line to Chicago because O. K. Davis strongly suspected their wire was tapped. Roosevelt left for Chicago with a small family group that included wife, children, and cousins, and their train narrowly escaped a serious accident en route. Waiting for them at the Chicago station was a huge crowd mixed with Roosevelt's uniformed Rough Riders, buttons and badges everywhere, people yelling, ". . . We want Teddy . . . we want Teddy . . ." and bands playing tunes reminiscent of Roosevelt's Cuban campaign as well as the popular hits such as "Everybody's Doin' It, Doin' It, Doin' It . . ." Somebody had printed ten thousand handbills the day before which read:

At Three O'Clock
Thursday afternoon
Theodore ROOSEVELT
WILL WALK
on the
WATERS OF LAKE MICHIGAN

And then there he was, wearing his new felt hat and a wildly-colored necktie, a ready Roosevelt smile, and his hand out for shaking. "They greeted him as they might have greeted a successful Roman general returning from the wars," wrote the *New York Times.*

It took a large wedge of men to clear him to his car, which moved slowly through the streets to the Congress Hotel. There he had a suite of four rooms, overlooking Lake Michigan. On a lower floor, near the Florentine Room, a large ballroom, the Roosevelt group had a string of offices.

But long after he checked in, the crowd was still packed outside, wouldn't go away until he spoke to them, and so he did. He went out on the balcony of the second-floor room and told them: "It's a naked fight against theft and the thieves will not win. . . ."

And the crowds yelled, "Soak 'em Teddy. . . ."

"If ever an American was a hero of a hot and crowded hour," wrote William Allen White, "it was Theodore Roosevelt that day in Chicago."

But Presidents are not made in such fevered hours and nobody holds a hand over the heads of presidential candidates to register the applause for them on a meter.

"Taft men speak more deliberately, show less animation . . . are more inclined to view with alarm than to enthuse," wrote William Jennings Bryan in his convention column. "As for Roosevelt men," he said, "largely of the aggressive type . . . have already decided matters and have no doubts to settle . . . they don't talk in whispers . . . Mr. Roosevelt's friends take it for granted that he can win. . . ."

Further describing this Roosevelt public support, William Allen White insisted Roosevelt had little labor backing, that his supporters were mainly middle class, "the little businessman, the country lawyer, the doctor, the teacher, the preacher, the real estate dealer, the skilled worker."

New York boss, Bill Barnes, speaking at Taft pep rallies all over the city, painted the Roosevelt picture in more vivid colors. "We have got to save our country, save the Constitution, save our liberty. We are in danger of monarchy. The country must be saved!" A prejudiced Roosevelt observer noted of the Barnes performance: "It was made all the more preposterous by the fact that a very ancient colored gentleman stood back of Barnes, and whenever Barnes paused, would point to the crowd and feebly begin clapping his hands. They would then slowly and very politely take up the applause, in every case waiting for his signal. It was almost pathetic."

But there was nothing pathetic about the Taft mood. That weekend before the convention opening, Taft forces retained a tone of calm and confidence, claiming 590 carefully counted votes.

"The X, or unknown quantity in the Republican situation," said Democratic reporter William Jennings Bryan, "is the colored vote from the South. It is the weakness of the Taft cause not only because it does not represent a voting strength proportionate to its influence in the convention, but a weakness also because it cannot be depended upon to stand tied."

It was no secret that Negro delegates were carefully housed, fed, and guarded by Taft men, who seriously worried about Roosevelt raids—and with good cause. It was also no secret that money flowed liberally from both sides into many pockets. "In fact," added the prejudiced Bryan, "it looks now as if this convention might turn on the size of the 'honorarium.'"

The more important political persuasion, however, to white as well as black, was that of power and patronage. When Taft people announced pep rallies in ballrooms, Roosevelt men usually followed them, yelling derisively, "All postmasters attend." The point Roosevelt advocates made persistently to delegates, was: What's the point of nominating a man who can't win? Taft can't; Roosevelt can. And if you don't get a winner, you won't get patronage, and your political power in your state will be a paper power.

With the highly organized and enthusiastic Illinois delegation as their hub, the Roosevelt force worked hard all weekend, often greeted incoming delegates with a band (even marched a Roosevelt band with banners after a Taft delegation).

For the candidate, there was still occasional time for the quiet moment. Beveridge recorded this: "We sat together alone in his room for, I suppose, upward of an hour. I recall nothing more curious than that conference. Here we were with his fate, the fate of the party, almost the fate of the country at stake; yet both of us felt it so keenly that our talk was about almost everything else. It was casual, even trivial. T.R. was in one of his sweetest and most human moods, and I felt pretty human myself. I was interested in his health, how he was standing the strain, etc.; and he wanted to know all about the campaign I had made for him, how much it had cost me, whether my voice stood up well, how Mrs. Beveridge was, and what she thought about it. And I on my part wanted to know how Mrs. Roosevelt took it and what her judgment was etc. In this talk, T.R. grieved about Taft; what a disappointment he had been, how shamefully he had betrayed T.R., and the trust all of us had in him. Strangely enough, T.R.'s talk was not bitter—its tone was that of a deep regret. . . ."

That quiet was the calm in the eye of a hurricane. Out front in the Florentine Room, a platform had been set up for the constant stream of stump speeches which somebody described as a "steam gauge." People crowded that ballroom to near suffocation. The packed quality gave the room its own electricity, and the current was always charged, always on.

This electricity reached the floodlight stage the night before the convention at a huge Roosevelt rally of 5,000 people in the Auditorium, Chicago's second largest hall. It was a boomer's meeting: flags for everybody, cheering squads, a glee club singing patriotic hymns, bands everywhere. So many of the delegates there had never before been to a convention (a quick reporter's count showed only one convention veteran each in the California and New Jersey delegations).

"The National Committee! What are they?" Roosevelt told his audience. "About fifty people with the ratio of honesty ranging from about fourteen to twenty and the remaining thirty sure-thing men. . . . It is bad enough to have the victory stolen by the bosses that are living, but it is an added outrage to have it stolen by bosses that are among the unburied dead. . . ."

"Say that again! . . ." the crowd shouted. "Tell us that again. . . ."

"He condemned the members of the National Committee, jointly and severally, individually and in groups," wrote William Jennings Bryan. "He described them by naming characteristics, discussed them biographically, and singled them out by name. He analyzed them in their representative character and in their lack of character. The words 'theft,' 'crime,' 'stolen,' 'shame,' 'treason' were interwoven with the names of Senators, ex-Senators, bosses, ex-bosses, leaders, ex-leaders and 'sure-thing' men. . . . The Arabs are said to have seven hundred words which mean 'camel'; Mr. Roosevelt has nearly as many synonyms for 'theft', and he used them all tonight."

Mixed with the Roosevelt metaphors were some stinging statistics: "Of Mr. Taft's delegates," Roosevelt said, "over half come from territories and from states that have never cast a Republican electoral vote since the days of the reconstruction. . . ."

"Over half the remainder," Roosevelt continued, "are boss-picked delegates from northern states where there have been no open primaries. About one-eighth represent theft pure and simple . . . about one-eighth of his delegates represent a real sentiment for him."

Roosevelt then described the fight as being between the plain people and the special privileges, and Bryan noted that it "sounded so much like Senator La Follette's speeches during the last eight years and like Democratic speeches during the last sixteen years that one could hardly believe it was being applauded by a Republican audience."

But the most moving words that night were these:

"What happens to me is not of the slightest consequence; I am to be used, as in a doubtful battle any man is used, to his hurt or not, so long as he is useful and is then cast aside and left to die. I wish you to feel this. I mean it; and I shall need no sympathy when you are through with me. . . .

"We fight in honorable fashion for the good of mankind, unheeding of our individual fates; with unflinching hearts and undimmed eyes; we stand at Armageddon, and we battle for the Lord. . . ."

It had a ring to it, almost a rhythm of religious fervor. The boomer's meeting seemed suddenly converted into a religious revival. The fervor in that hall sounded like the start of the Crusades.

Walking along Michigan Avenue immediately afterwards, William Allen White and Senator Borah both tried to analyze the speech. As an orator himself, Borah was aware of how Roosevelt had done it. "He was tremendously impressed with it," said White, "but he was a little frightened, as I was. We had no idea of the hidden forces beneath our feet. . . ."

The Armageddon phrase prompted songs, poems, and some ridicule. British historian John Morley described Roosevelt as "Half St. Paul, half St. Vitus." And the New York Sun jeered:

"In spite of some hesitances of pronunciation, the brethren get a holy joy out of 'Armageddon.' There is a mystical wonderful charm to it like 'Abracadabra' or 'parallelopipedon,' a word of might and magic in the vowels and bowels of it. Seth Bullock believes it to be a township in Oklahoma. The Hon. Angelo Perkins is positive that it is Welsh. Medill McCormick holds that it was an early skirmish in the Revolution. . . ."

The poked fun detracted little from the emotional impact of that phrase and that speech.

Again, however, you cannot counter arithmetic with emotion. The statistic was simple. The Roosevelt strength was not sufficient to organize the convention or even deadlock it—unless the convention gave them more of their contested seats, or unless they could combine with La Follette.

At first, it seemed set. After all, how could the La Follette Wisconsin delegation refuse to vote for their own Governor McGovern for Temporary Chairman. And, with McGovern in to name the committees, help set the rules and recognition, they had a real hope of overturning the National Committee on the contested cases.

Hope heightened when Roosevelt men reported a possible beginning break in the New York delegation—the single political fear of Bill Barnes. "Timothy Woodruff is wavering," they said, "with four other delegates, and will soon fall to us," and they told of other delegates "flopping over, here and there."

The key, however, was still La Follette, and the key wouldn't turn. He wouldn't co-ordinate, he wouldn't compromise; he could neither be coaxed, bluffed, nor bribed. He saw himself in the light of a Roosevelt political pigeon, and he would fly no more for him. His hatred of Roosevelt was deep. The fatal crimp on La Follette's own candidacy had come from Roosevelt, and now La Follette promised to return the favor.

When Roosevelt picked McGovern as his candidate for Temporary Chairman, La Follette tried to get McGovern to refuse, but McGovern wouldn't. La Follette then worked on his own delegations of Wisconsin and North Dakota, worked on them with a fury that could not be resisted. On the night before the convention opening, the Wisconsin delegation caucused in Room 200 of the Grand Pacific Hotel and the critical motion came up on supporting their own Governor for Temporary Chairman. Fighting for McGovern was Henry Cochems, who had nominated La Follette for President in 1908 and now planned to nominate McGovern for Temporary Chairman. So fiery was the split caucus that it adjourned without decision.

During the adjournment, a call came in Cochems' room. It was La Follette. A mutual friend answered the phone because Cochems said his voice was too hoarse to talk. La Follette asked if Cochems had anything to say. "Yes," said Cochems, "say to Bob if he presses his motion to a vote, it will result in a split in the delegation."

"Let the split come then," said La Follette.

It came with a 15-11 caucus vote against supporting McGovern.

The kick hurt. Something else that revealed the seriousness of the situation was an intercepted telegram "from Murray Crane to his nephew saying that Crane and Barnes would 'fight or ruin' and that it was now 'use any means and sacrifice the Republican Party.'" It was a slightly distorted version leaking out of the secret meeting of top Republican leaders when they had decided not to compromise on a Roosevelt-favored candidate.

With the political wind now shifting fresher for Taft, the Roosevelt bandwagon lost some of its attractiveness. Governor Walter Roscoe Stubbs of Kansas, one of the original signers of the letter to Roosevelt urging his candidacy, suddenly decided there were all kinds of vital matters needing his personal attention in Kansas. Stubbs, who had made his fortune as a railroad contractor, and spent thousands of dollars on the long distance telephone to help organize the Progressive party in his state, had a political reputation as a slugger and a salesman. But, that night, the salesman had sold out on the slugger, and Stubbs reported to the unofficial state party boss, Colonel William Rockhill Nelson, owner of the *Kansas City Star*.

"Colonel, I find I have to go to Topeka. They need me there."

The old Colonel's face flushed, first with anger, then with contempt and his voice boomed, "So you are going to run away from us, are you!"

Stubbs stayed.

A Roosevelt staff announcement said:

"The fight at the outset is expected to be possibly without precedent in a national convention. But it will be conducted, on the Roosevelt side, entirely in accord with parliamentary rules and, if there are any violations to these rules, they will come from the Taft side."

This statement seemed necessary to counteract the spreading rumor that Roosevelt men planned to rush the convention hall and refuse to admit contested delegates. One newspaper even headlined it:

> GAVEL TO BE SEIZED
> BY FORCE IS PLAN OF
> ROOSEVELT CHIEFS
> 600 Police to Club Back Rioters are Put on Guard
> By Taft Forces; Borah to Lead Colonel's Fight

The story had this much truth: In the words of James Amos, Roosevelt's valet, here is what happened on the night before the convention opened:

"Quite late I heard a racket outside the door," said Amos, "and a voice raised in anger threatening to shoot the detectives [on guard]. I went outside and found a western delegate who had been a Rough Rider and was an old friend of Mr. Roosevelt's demanding admittance and threatening to shoot his way in. The detectives saw he was half-filled with liquor and tried to pacify him."

Amos admitted the delegate who then went up to Roosevelt and said, "Now look here Teddy, what are we goin' to do about this tomorrow?"

Roosevelt said they would have to wait and see what happened, and the westerner said, "There's no use monkeyin' around with these guys any longer," and he pulled out two enormous pistols from his tailcoat. "As soon as Rosewater makes the ruling, I'm goin' to fill him full of lead," he said. "Then I'm goin' to plug that old guy Root."

Roosevelt then had the detectives take his western friend in tow, and the man finally passed out.

Without knowing any of this, humorist Finley Peter Dunne, in his column, quoted Penrose telling Rosewater, "Victor, as soon as you make that ruling, you had better take a running jump off that platform before some one can take a shot at you."

And Dunne's syndicated Mr. Dooley promised the public that the convention would be "a combination iv th' Chicago fire, Saint Bartholomew's massacree, the battle iv th' Boyne, th' life iv Jessie James, and th' night iv th' big wind. . . ."

Big wind or no, the convention was still the big show in the country, and scalpers' minimum price for tickets started at $100. In charge of convention arrangements was the former chairman of the National Committee, Harry S. New, a hard-working man of few words and quick decisions whose trademark was a sugar-loaf, straight-brimmed, black felt hat.

Who got how many tickets became a fact of prime political importance.

"Yesterday I wired Harry New asking for courtesy of an allotment of tickets for the Roosevelt family and immediate friends," Dixon wired Rosewater. "I have a telegram from New saying not a single ticket will be allotted for that purpose notwithstanding the fact that he has allotted to Mr. Taft for his relatives and friends."

By this time New had called Dixon "a pettifogging falsifier" and Sergeant-at-arms William F. Stone, answering another Roosevelt request for tickets, said, "Not a damned ticket to any Roosevelt man." William Jennings Bryan got his ticket to the convention from Rosewater by writing, "If you will send me a ticket, I will agree not to say anything worse about Taft or Roosevelt than they say about each other—a promise I feel sure I can live up to." Then came Bryan's postscript, "By the way, suppose you have two

Republican conventions, to whom shall I apply for admission to the second?" And Bryan's brother, Charles, later Governor of Nebraska, asking Rosewater for his ticket, added, "If your steamroller is overworked or out of repair, wire me ànd I will express you another one. The Democrats will have no need for one at Baltimore."

Those unkind cuts barely scratched Rosewater; he had the more urgent worry—the inevitable political explosion on opening day.

Here was this small, thin, young man with a small voice and a fierce pride and he would be the first man on the podium with the gavel, and so the explosion would head for him.

How can you control an explosion?

Through a mutual friend, a Kansas City real estate operator, E. Mont Reilly (who later became Governor of Puerto Rico), Victor Rosewater arranged a midnight meeting with Roosevelt in his private suite at the Congress Hotel. This was still the night before the convention opening.

The night had been crowded for both men, and this was a kind of climax. They shook hands, sat together on a sofa in an empty reception room, talked for twenty minutes.

"He seemed to have the idea," said Rosewater, "that none of the contested delegates seated by the National Committee should be allowed to participate in the organization of the convention, but I told him that as Chairman of the Committee, though I had voted 'No' on placing some of the names on the roll, I could not change or discredit the roll as made up by that Committee, nor was there any other roll which I could go by."

Roosevelt then started to discuss some of the contested cases and Rosewater firmly indicated that he had no intention of rehashing the evidence at that time, that all he wanted was an orderly, fair convention. Roosevelt said they also wanted no violence, but would insist on their full privileges. Roosevelt then designated Hadley as his representative and Rosewater agreed to recognize Hadley on any debatable question.

Rosewater then talked to Hadley who told Rosewater his intention to challenge the temporary roll immediately—even before Rosewater gave up his gavel to any selected Temporary Chairman. Rosewater doubted his parliamentary right on this, but agreed to discuss it further with Hadley at 9:30 that morning.

If Rosewater had not prevented an upcoming explosion, at least he now knew some of its force and direction.

The Hadley meeting at the Blackstone Hotel lasted a half-hour that morning. Hadley admitted he had no real precedents for his proposal "but all precedents must have a beginning." Rosewater answered that this meant "all precedents are against you." Hadley then cited the 1892 convention when McKinley, as convention chairman, permitted discussion before ruling on a point of order, and asked Rosewater to permit similar discussion on his proposal.

Rosewater saw the proposal as a Pandora's box, hesitated, said he would give his decision at 11:30, a half-hour before the convention opened. Meanwhile, Rosewater wrote a summary of their conversation and both men initialed it. Next stop for Rosewater: a meeting with Barnes, Penrose, Root, Crane, Butler, and some others, plus a quick consultation en route with one of the convention's two parliamentarians (there were two because the first one had turned out to be a Roosevelt man from Ohio).

The small group of Republican leaders discussed without deciding, and so the small man with the small voice made his own decision: recognize Hadley immediately after the reading of the convention call; permit him to submit his proposal, grant him twenty minutes for argument, and then make the formal ruling. Rosewater then went to Hadley, told him. "He seemed thoroughly content with my decision," said Rosewater, "and we returned together to the convention hall."

As the two entered the hall, it was twenty minutes to noon, Tuesday, June 18.

Much already had happened in that hall.

The Coliseum was a huge place, its walls supporting arching girders and an arching roof, all of which had been painted a bright canary yellow to make things more cheerful. But there was no cheer in the faces of the six hundred policemen scattered through the hall, many of them strategically placed in front of the platform, facing the delegates to prevent any jammed rush towards the speaker.

The railing approaches to the podium were wound with barbed wire, carefully concealed under the bunting. As for the ticket takers, they were so expectant of trouble that their hands trembled. To get in, ticket holders had to pass muster three different times, had to surrender the day's coupon so they could not return if they left.

For the early arrivals, the band broke out with "My Country! 'tis of Thee," followed it with "The Star-Spangled Banner," and people stood and bared their heads. Earliest of the delegations to arrive were some from New York, Mississippi, and Texas.

One of the New York delegates was former Senator Chauncey Depew, a jaunty man with thick white eyebrows and muttonchop whiskers. Some newsmen cornered him and said that Roosevelt leaders claimed a majority of forty and Taft leaders also claimed a majority of forty, and what did Depew think that really meant? Depew laughed. "That means," he said, "there are at least eighty liars in the convention."

An assistant sergeant-at-arms unwrapped the three-piece silver water service from the tissue paper, polished it until it shone. Two stenographers wandered through the hall familiarizing themselves with delegation positions. The parliamentarians not only brought stacks of books but also stacks of typewritten parliamentary opinions on what could and could not be done.

The reading clerk had his megaphone and the messengers had a plentiful supply of cards and pencils to thrust at delegates to record any unheard comments they had made except "violent and profane language."

The Coliseum had started to fill up. The California delegation marched in with their gold silk banners featuring their Teddy bear and the motto, "The people will rule." Somebody started a cheer for West Virginia and then a New Jersey group broke in:

"Rah rah rah, who are we
We are the delegates from New Jer-see
Are we in it?
Just you wait.
Till we give Teddy, twenty eight straight!"

The band then played "Dixie" and Florida delegates for Taft
stood on their chairs and sang, then shouted yells of defiance at the
New Jersey Roosevelt delegates across the aisle. Helping clear the
aisles, along with others, was a famous former Yale football guard,
W. W. "Pudge" Heffelflinger, now an assistant sergeant-at-arms.

Floor leaders for both candidates were already working in the
hall, Bill Barnes of New York for Taft, Bill Flinn of Pennsylvania
for Roosevelt, both of the same political boss breed.

Directly facing the platform, on floor level, were the 1,078
delegates sitting on kitchen chairs, almost knee to knee in a space
little larger than the orchestra section of an average theater. Behind the delegates sat their alternates, and surrounding them on
three sides sat the spectators on a rising slope of seats that merged
with the balcony that seemed to hang from all four walls.

The platform seemed half the width of the Coliseum, but so
poorly constructed and arranged so low, that any speaker was
forced to stand in front of the presiding officer. In order to bridge
the newsmen who sat near the platform, a gangplank jutted like a
wharf from the mainland, cutting the press section in two.

When Victor Rosewater walked the gangplank to the podium,
nobody seemed to know who he was. And the 15,000 people in
that huge hall, while they were not yelling now, still maintained
a drowning din of murmuring that he couldn't quiet with his
gavel.

Author Owen Wister described Rosewater as "a sort of fluttering
moth of a man, about as up to ruling those roaring waves as a cork
would have been. His hammering for order brought it no more
than the ticking of a watch." George Ade wrote in *Colliers Weekly*,
"Poor little Victor Rosewater with a timid ingrowing voice, says
something heard by no one except the reporter leaning confi-

dentially over his shoulder." The *Kansas City Times* reporter added, "When Mr. Rosewater dealt his first feeble whack with the gavel, he was asked if he didn't want a boy to help him."

During Rosewater's insistent gavelling, Wisconsin delegates marched in with a huge picture of La Follette and a California delegation started a cheer:

> "Eat 'em alive
> Eat 'em alive
> Roosevelt, Roosevelt
> Wow . . . wow . . . wow. . . ."

A reading clerk with a foghorn voice and his huge megaphone finally quieted the crowd telling them that a flashlight picture was to be taken of the convention, and would everybody please look pleasant, and a delegate yelled that this would probably be for the first and last time. This caused a wave of nervous laughter. Then the band again played "The Star-Spangled Banner" and they all stood, and many sang, and the foghorn-voiced clerk quieted them again and Rosewater said in a voice few heard, "The hour of twelve o'clock having arrived, and a quorum manifestly being present, the Convention will be in order while Father Callaghan invokes Divine blessing. . . ."

The Fifteenth Republican National Convention had begun.

Following the prayer came the reading of the official Call for the Convention, a dry detailed mass of words explaining the rules of delegate selection. Hardly was it finished when up jumped a handsome man with a boyish disarming smile, wearing a double-breasted, knee-length coat, one hand in his pocket, the other used for gesture. He was in his late thirties, had an air of chivalry and courtesy, a firm manner, a resonant voice. He was Herbert Hadley, Governor of Missouri, with a question and a proposal that eventually would twist and tear the pages of American history.

"Mr. Chairman," he said, "I rise to a question of information."

And the war was on.

Strip the Hadley statement of the technical and it added up

to this: he wanted the convention to substitute a list of seventy-two Roosevelt delegates for the National Committee list of seventy-two Taft delegates.

"I say to you, Mr. Chairman," said Hadley, "that this to my mind is more a question of principle than of precedent. We cannot here in this Convention close our ears to what the American people are saying today. The integrity of this roll has been challenged by fifteen members of the National Committee whose signatures I have here in my pocket, who say that seventy-two names have been placed upon that roll of delegates, not honestly elected, in place of the names of seventy-two delegates who have been elected by the honest votes of the Republican voters in the different states and Congressional districts. . . .

"I do not say to you that all these charges are true. I sat in some of the sessions of the National Committee, and in my judgment some of the charges are true, but whether true or false, let us meet them here now. Let us hear these fifteen members of the National Committee who say that delegates are sitting upon the floor of this Convention without any honest title to their seats . . . and then let the thirty-seven members of the National Committee, who are responsible for that roll, be heard in reply. You cannot settle a question of fundamental honesty, fair play by disregarding it."

Hadley had hit a sensitive note, and hit it hard.

The question boiled down to the amount of power a National Committee had in preparing the list of delegates, whether their decision was absolute or merely a recommendation to the convention. But a Taft delegate had a query:

"This is a question of order and orderly proceedings on one hand, and of possible chaos on the other. . . . How are you going to select from the list of delegates those who are entitled to seats in the Convention? Suppose this motion is put? Who will vote on the question—those on the list made up according to the usual manner by the National Committee or those on the list made up by the gentleman from Missouri?"

(". . . Thieves . . . thieves. . . ." yelled a California delegate.)

But it was a good question, and while the parliamentarians searched through their stacks of typewritten opinions for the proper precedents, other speakers made themselves heard.

"One amusing thing about it all," wrote William Jennings Bryan from the press box, "is the lack of frankness in the speeches. Each side gives reasons that do not influence the men who give them. . . .

"Convention audiences are not like juries, made up of those who are unprejudiced, nor like popular audiences, made up of people who act only for themselves and therefore are free to follow their inclinations," Bryan continued. "The delegates are sent there largely under instructions, expressed or implied, and they are there . . . to accomplish their purpose. Every delegate knew what the speakers seemed to overlook that the seating of the seventy-odd delegates would in all probability decide the convention's actions. The Taft men had charge of the National Committee. By seating the Taft delegates, they were able to give Mr. Taft's friends a majority on the temporary roll call. This majority could organize the convention and give Mr. Taft's friends the temporary chairman. As the Credentials Committee is made up from the delegates appearing on the temporary roll call, this would give the Taft men a majority of the Credentials Committee and secure them a majority report. The delegates on the temporary roll call would then approve the report and seat the Taft contestants."

Then Bryan posed the natural question:

"Did not the National Committee act in the same way four years ago when the friends of Mr. Fairbanks, Mr. Cannon and Mr. Hughes were complaining of the Roosevelt steamroller? And does anyone doubt that the Committee would have put on the Roosevelt delegates and kept them there if Mr. Roosevelt's friends had had control?"

After consulting with parliamentarians, Rosewater announced his ruling. "We are here now simply as a mass meeting," he said. "We have appointed a temporary chairman for the purpose of organizing that mass meeting and converting it into a convention of delegates. . . . It is not within the province of this unorganized assemblage to pass upon credentials . . . any such proposition therefore . . . is out of order. . . ."

Commenting in the *American Magazine*, Finley Peter Dunne wrote:

"He [Rosewater] made the decision, there is no doubt about that. It is in the official record, written down by the official reporter —the night before. But no one heard him make it. The actual physical disposition of the decision is unknown. The impression of those who sat in front of the chairman and watched the play of his throat muscles, was that he swallowed it."

Whether they heard him or not, Rosewater moved on, opened the nominations for Temporary Chairman and presented the name of Elihu Root.

Henry Cochems, waving for recognition and getting it, pushed his way onto the platform with the force of a former football player, which he was, and said: "As an individual delegate from the state of Wisconsin . . . I present the name of the brilliant, the able, the impartial and the fearless governor of my commonwealth, Hon. Francis W. McGovern. . . ."

Seconding Root was Job E. Hedges of New York who started out by saying, "I quote Mr. Roosevelt . . ." and the unexpectedness of this caused considerable laughter and confusion as Hedges continued, quoting Roosevelt as saying, "Elihu Root is the ablest man I have known in our government service. He is the ablest man that has appeared in the public life of any country in any position at any time."

A delegate yelled, "Nobody has said anything against Root. . . ."

Hedges continued: "I second the nomination of the man whom Theodore Roosevelt tells me is the ablest man in public life."

Much applause and cheers for Roosevelt, quickly suppressed, and Hedges continued, "You need not hesitate to cheer Roosevelt in my presence. I cheered him seven years, and I am just trying to take a day off, that is all. . . . (CONSIDERABLE LAUGHTER)

"I leave Elihu Root with you," finished Hedges. "He was good enough for Roosevelt and he is good enough for me."

Wise, witty, and he had left them laughing.

The mood soon changed.

"It was a crowd as smart as terriers," wrote Richard Harding Davis at the time, "as wise to the game of politics as are the bleaching boards to the other national game, a crowd ready to jump upon an error, to take advantage of a slip, to give a double meaning to any unstudied sentence. . . ."

Hadley's seconding speech made the point that McGovern had Roosevelt's unquestioned support, and he was followed by a Negro delegate from Kentucky, who began, "The Negro of this country looks to the Republican Party for ——

". . . Post offices," yelled one of the delegates.

The speaker continued, "The imputation has been made that the Negro will repudiate his instructions. The imputation has been made that the Negro is a traitor; but I stand here as the representative of my Race to say to you that the Negro is loyal and true, and he will obey the instructions of his constituency, and will cast his vote for Elihu Root."

(Observer W. O. Hart wrote: "The large number of colored delegates at the Convention reminded me somewhat of the Louisiana legislature during reconstruction times, and it was curious to note how carefully the colored delegates were watched. It was very seldom that one moved from his seat without being accompanied by another person.")

Bill Flinn of Pennsylvania, in a seconding speech for McGovern, added a warning note, ". . . unless you get 540 votes that are untainted, without fraud, for your candidate for Chairman, I doubt whether my constituents in Pennsylvania will ratify it. . . ."

"Will you bolt?" yelled a delegate.

Flinn hedged his answer.

Amid the bubbling fierceness of the delegates, there were still the flowers. Describing his state of Virginia, during a seconding speech for Root, the delegate said, ". . . ancient glories made her matchless among the states, whose devotion to principle made her the Mecca of the people of the South, and whose conservatism

and love of constitutional government made her the hope of the
Republican Party of the future. . . ."

A delegate caused a laugh by yelling, "Amen. . . ."

He was followed by a delegate who began, "The men—of Kenn-
tuck-ee, love—Kenn-tuck-ee!"

Then a delegate shouted, "Then go back to Ken-tuck-ee!"

And when a West Virginia delegate started out with the same
flowery oratory, "Gentlemen and fellow delegates, give me your
ears," he was so much hooted, that he changed tone fast and
pleaded, "Boys, give me a chance. . . ."

No speaker was safe.

Former Governor Fort of New Jersey, a Roosevelt man, had a
speech which said, "We must be firm at first, because later it will
be too late. But what he said, was, "We must be firm at first . . ."
and he hesitated, and it sounded as though the Roosevelt group
would later be prepared to surrender, and the crowd picked it up
fast and started laughing, then roaring, with New York delegate
James Wadsworth so carried away by it that he sat there kicking
his legs in the air, shrieking in mocking derision. And Fort tried
to make himself heard, saying, "I don't mean what you mean.
. . ." But his usefulness was finished.

A delegate who ran into real trouble with the crowd was California lawyer, and a seconding speaker for Roosevelt, Francis J.
Heney.

"Heney . . . could do nothing but call names," wrote Richard
Harding Davis. "No one likes to be called names. The more angry
Heney grew, the more angry grew the delegates. He went at them
like a two-gun man and they would not have it. They did not like
his method; they did not like what he said; they did not like him."

"Are the friends of Mr. Taft afraid to listen to the facts?" cried
Heney, as the disorder continued.

"Oh cut it out," yelled a delegate.

Heney went on to say, "The proposition is simply that a corrupt
judge shall sit in his own case to place himself upon this floor."
The audience noise kept growing louder and a red-faced Heney

turned to Rosewater, asking him to restore order. "I'm doing the best I can," said Rosewater, yelling and rapping for order.

"Fellow citizens, you may as well hear me out," said the perspiring Heney, "because you are going to hear me if it takes all summer."

"We will not wait that long," a delegate shouted.

The party kept getting rougher.

White-haired W. O. Bradley of Kentucky walked the gangplank to the platform, started to speak and somebody jeered, "You voted for Lorimer!" (a senator accused of corruption) "Yes, I voted for Lorimer," said Bradley, "and when I did, I voted for a man ten thousand times better than you."

Cries increased: "Lorimer! Lorimer! Lorimer!"

Losing his temper, his breath, and his dignity, Bradley said to Rosewater, "Mr. Chairman, with your consent, I will suspend for a few minutes to allow each fool in this Convention to get through with his interruptions before I resume. . . ."

"He voted for Lorimer and now he votes for Root," chimed in another delegate.

"We don't want any of this rough riding business," said Bradley. "If you gentlemen think you can override and bully this Convention you are mistaken."

"Steamroller!" shouted another delegate.

The audience imitated train whistles, others yelled, "Toot . . . toot. . . ."

"Steamroller, did I hear you say," said Bradley, shouting now. "Roosevelt ran the steamroller over me eight times in 1908. . . ."

"Bet your life, he ought to," derided another delegate.

"All we want in this Convention is regularity and justice," said Bradley. "I am not in any hurry at all," he said, and took a drink of water.

"Take another drink," yelled a delegate.

"I am afraid you have had too many drinks," said Bradley, coming back fast.

(Bryan told the story of a convention sixteen years before when a Louisiana delegate paused in his speech to take a drink of water. An interruption prevented him from speaking immediately, so he took another drink, and a third one. A delegate then suggested he take another drink and soon messengers were coming to the stage with buckets of water and convulsed the convention for a quarter of an hour).

Again, the man was old and the crowd was young, and the crowd won. But the bitterness was just beginning.

La Follette's campaign manager, Walter L. Houser added to it when he stood up to say that La Follette had refused "to enter into any combination or alliance with any candidate or set of men . . . the Wisconsin delegation voted decisively not to present a candidate for Presiding Officer of this Convention. . . ."

Cochems then jumped up on a point of personal privilege, with a warning, "I challenge any man in the Progressive delegation from the state of Wisconsin to rise in his seat and vote for Elihu Root in this Convention for Temporary Chairman, and return to that state. . . ."

The typical roll call is by states alphabetically, and, if there is a challenge of a state vote, the delegates of that state are polled individually. The struggling Chairman Rosewater, however, had set a pattern the night before, now proposed it—to everybody's surprise. "Following the precedent of the Convention of 1884," he said, "which is the only Republican National Convention which has been challenged, the Secretary will call the roll of delegates by name and each delegate will rise in his place as his name is called and answer with the name of his preference for Temporary Chairman."

Delegation chairmen announced they would not be bound to accept their contested delegates, but balloting began anyway. To keep it rolling, with minimal squabbles within states, Rosewater refused to recognize anybody during the roll call.

Alabama began, twenty-two for Root, two for McGovern.

A soft note in the fury, a kind of magic moment, came when the clerk, loudly and distinctly, said, "Mrs. Florence C. Porter."

She was a California delegate, a gray-haired, gentle-faced woman, the first woman ever to cast her vote in a National Convention— and the whole hall cheered.

The real fury of the fireworks came from Flinn of Pennsylvania. The clerk called the name of a Pennsylvania delegate, and he was absent, and so the clerk then called the name of his alternate. Flinn yelled that they had called the wrong alternate. As Rosewater tried to gavel him into silence, "You are raping your own roll . . . I protest . . . Steal! . . . Thief! . . . You are a pack of thieves, that is what you are . . . if you steal this vote, you will call no more rolls in this Convention today." (Cries of "Oh, Oh")

When the clerk announced the final Pennsylvania vote, Richard Quay shouted a final comment, shaking his fist at Rosewater, "You have stolen everything else, but you cannot steal Pennsylvania. . . ."

Barnes had predicted the night before that Root would win by ninety-two votes, but it was closer than that. Root had 558 to McGovern's 551, with a small scatter of fourteen votes for favorite sons, and five not voting. The Root majority was slim, only eighteen more than half the convention. The wise ones knew that a number of Root's votes came from delegates instructed for Roosevelt. That left the presidential situation still in doubt.

As Bryan put it, "Mr. Roosevelt may be nominated if he can get some of his contestants seated, or can make inroads upon the southern delegates."

Rosewater introduced Root in the manner of a man in a nervous hurry to get out of focus fast, and Flinn made a final shouting thrust, "Receiver of stolen goods! . . . Root advised the prosecution of the very people for whom he is now willing to act as a tool."

Root's first words were, "Gentlemen of the Convention: Believe that I appreciate this expression of confidence. . . ."

Root scarcely began when hundreds of delegates started leaving noisily and hurriedly, and Root scowled and stopped until they left. The band had been playing a lively tune while the sergeants-at-arms tried desperately to restore some order in a crowd that had yelled itself hoarse. When Root resumed, the entire rear part of the floor and gallery was empty; the rest of the hall was quiet while he talked, so quiet the boom in the chemical of an exploding flashlight for a photograph made everyone jump.

More complimentary critics had called Root "a piece of refined steel," "a thinking machine as inflexible and sure in its operation as a steel trap." One of his prominent corporation clients was quoted as saying that other attorneys had told him what he could not do, but that Root told him how he *could* do things.

It had taken seven tense hours—a record for any convention— to decide on its Temporary Chairman, but the thin-lipped man who now clicked his gavel on the marble block was a man of complete outer calm, impeccable dignity, and the measure of a man who had mastered crowds before. His voice was not very powerful, but there were no catcalls while he talked. His was a lawyer's speech, dry and detailed, a long speech of Republican party achievements, but with small space for cheers.

When Root finished, the convention got its temporary organization of work in gear, names were announced of all temporary officers, from doorkeepers to tally clerks, and delegates selected by their delegations to serve on the basic convention committees: Permanent Organization, Rules and Order of Business, Credentials, Resolutions.

Then, again, the slim young man who had won a convention's respect and quick affection, Governor Hadley of Missouri called for the substitution of the seventy-two names on the temporary roll call. The Reading Clerk with the megaphone then read Hadley's list of proposed names, and a motion was made to adjourn, with the understanding that the Hadley motion would be the first order of unfinished business the following morning.

It was 7:43 P.M. It had been a long, long day.

Back in Washington, Taft, highly satisfied with the day's results, wrote his brother: "Root's election as Temporary Chairman was satisfactory in several respects. First it showed that I have enough votes to nominate me, if they will stick. . . . Second, it established and organized a Convention with a fixed membership, which makes a standard of regularity and puts Roosevelt and his faction in the attitude of bolters if they leave the Convention. . . .

"One of the very funny phases of the situation," Taft continued, "is the anxiety of La Follette not to help Roosevelt. Some of his followers would desert for Roosevelt but for the fear of La Follette anger in Wisconsin. So the delegation is broken up and the delegates are calling each other names. . . ."

At the Congress Hotel, halls were so packed with people, that the servants' elevators, fire escapes, and rear stairways were all thrown open, but people still couldn't move much. Bands played everywhere, and everywhere were the strong voices of impromptu orators and, in the lobby, a quartet entertained, singing "Steam Roller Bill."

Inside the comparative quiet of private rooms, Roosevelt leaders discussed strategy, talked increasingly of a convention bolt. Those against it pointed out that the only way Root had won was to get seven of Roosevelt's instructed delegates in Maryland, three in Oregon, and four in Pennsylvania. All these men were under specific instructions from primaries and would have to vote for Roosevelt on a roll call.

Hadley talked more persuasively than anyone else against a bolt that first day, later regretted it, and said, "I am inclined to believe now that it was a mistake from my standpoint in staying in the convention and that, if the walkout had been permitted on the first day, it would have assumed much lesser proportions than it did later."

One of the most serious lacks in the Roosevelt camp was the scarcity of leaders as convention delegates. The ablest Roosevelt advisers were not delegates. Remembering the back-room talk, Hadley said, "We would agree on some proposition and some one would say, 'Borah, you take care of that.' And he would reply, 'I am not a delegate.'

" 'Well, then, let Kellogg handle it.'

"And Kellogg would answer, 'I am not a delegate either.' "

"And one after another," continued Hadley, "Stubbs, Garfield, Pinchot and the rest—would sidestep it and it would be put back to me or to Governor Johnson."

"We afterwards got some help from Henry Allen [of Kansas]" said Hadley, "but we were very short of spokesmen who could argue as lawyers or who were familiar with the contests or with convention procedures."

This very shortage of speakers had put the convention limelight on Hadley. "That night, up and down Michigan Avenue, in the hotel corridors, in committee rooms, bar-rooms, Gold rooms, Florentine rooms, the gossip, the surmise, the speculation was all of Hadley," wrote Richard Harding Davis, "and in the half-million words sent out over the country by the correspondents, the name of Hadley led all the rest."

William Jennings Bryan wrote, "There is still a way of escape for the present and past occupants of the White House. They can withdraw and allow a third man to be nominated. This would be the thing most likely at present."

Bryan also openly rubbed his hands in political glee. He had interviewed Republican leaders, he said, and "many of them are willing to admit confidentially that the Republican Party is in such a muddle that the Democrats now have the chance of a lifetime."

Nobody knew this better than Taft leaders especially since the closeness of the Root vote. Outwardly confident Bill Barnes, his hair always parted neatly in the middle, approached Borah, talked to him about possibly accepting second place on a compromise ticket with Charles Evans Hughes. Borah refused, although Barnes later tried him twice again, and others talked to him about taking the top job. Some were also busy sounding out Hughes. Senator Cummins of Iowa, controlling only ten electoral votes, was barely mentioned.

But the major compromise talk concerned Hadley. Few seemed to remember what he had said that had so deeply impressed them or what particular act of his showed any special strategy or statesmanship. It was a quality of the unexplainable, the quality of charisma, but that quality was there and the convention had caught it in a mass transference of emotion.

In the Taft camp, the man who talked most of Hadley was James Watson of Indiana, the man who would argue most with him on the convention floor. Watson and some close friends then approached Hadley, talked tentatively of a promise to seat Roosevelt delegates from Washington and Texas, if Hadley would replace Roosevelt as a compromise candidate.

Reporters, meanwhile, reached Roosevelt, who freely admitted to them about past prophecies of immediate victory, "I'm a better warrior than a prophet." He had been directing the convention hall battle over a telephone wire, specially installed without any switchboard connection so that he could not be overheard. Asked by *New York Times* reporter Arthur Krock why he still stayed in Chicago when Root's election seemed to prove the impossibility of defeating Taft, Roosevelt had a characteristic reply, "I intend to see that Mr. Taft is nominated." Krock's interpretation was that this affirmed Roosevelt's intention to make sure the convention did not settle on a compromise candidate.

Word got out now about the Taft camp compromise offer to Hadley. "Senator Dixon sent for me," said Hadley, "and told me he had heard of a movement on the part of the Taft people to get together on a new man, and [Dixon] wanted me to promise not to consider a nomination or accept it."

"Are you speaking for yourself or Colonel Roosevelt?" Hadley asked.

"I am speaking for myself," said Dixon, "but the Colonel knows about it."

"Well, then," said Hadley, "that's a matter, it seems to me, to be taken up with the Colonel himself, and not with a third party. If you will go with me to Colonel Roosevelt, I will go over it with him and let him know how I stand."

Roosevelt, meanwhile, sent for William Allen White, and asked him, "What do you know about Hadley, really?"

White knew a great deal. The two men were close friends.

White traced the Hadley story from his student capacity for poker at Kansas University, to his later capacity for prosecuting crooks and cleaning up corruption in Kansas City and his fine reform record as Governor of Missouri. White also mentioned something that caused Roosevelt to cry out audibly: the fact that Hadley currently had a touch of tuberculosis, and was working on the convention floor with a temperature ranging up to 103.

After the biography, Roosevelt snapped his teeth as he often did when something disturbed him, and said, "Well, they want to compromise on Hadley. He is going to see me in a few moments." Roosevelt hesitated, stayed silent, then said, "I can take Hadley, but they must purge the roll of the convention if they want to compromise with me, take off the fraudulent delegates. Let an honest convention assemble, and it can do what it pleases, and I'll help Hadley."

Roosevelt then asked White to wait with Mrs. Roosevelt in an outer room. Afterward, White wrote of her, "I never saw so calm a woman. She reminded me of Madame Defarge, but she was not grim. . . . There she sat high above the crowd, beside the hotel window, knitting."

Inside the Roosevelt room, Hadley had entered, and Roosevelt's cousin George also joined them.

"They have offered to nominate me," Hadley said.

"Are you certain that it is a genuine offer," asked Roosevelt.

Hadley said he wasn't positive, but that it seemed genuine. He also added that his health wasn't good, and that the Presidency might kill him. Roosevelt's answer was that the public service of the Presidency was worth any sacrifice.

Then Roosevelt came up with the kicker, saying that no honest man could accept the convention nomination unless the roll was first purged. If it was, said Roosevelt, he would be glad to support Hadley, or any man of progressive views. After more talk, Hadley left. Long afterward, Hadley told Rosewater:

"I soon found out that he [Roosevelt] was determined to nominate himself and no one else, and I was convinced that no other man could be nominated without his assent. He put it on the ground that his followers wouldn't stand for it, that they were so bent on nominating him and following only his leadership, that no one else could take his place. Seeing the situation, I assured him, of course, that I was not a candidate and would not think of becoming one under those conditions.

Both Frank Knox and Henry J. Allen insisted, however, that Roosevelt told them that he was willing to support Hadley "if at any time you feel Governor Hadley can lead you better than I or that he can be nominated when I cannot be nominated."

But Roosevelt always added the purged roll as the postscript.

The obvious political fact was that if the roll were purged, Roosevelt himself would sweep in, and there would be no need for a compromise candidate.

The early morning of the convention's second day saw a sea of empty chairs. Sergeant-at-arms Stone found three-hundred forgotten badges in a safe and distributed them to a waiting crowd of authorized employees.

Root, Hadley, and Watson all arrived early, discussed the upcoming debate, agreed to have three hours of it, equally divided, the time to be individually apportioned to Hadley and Watson.

Opening the session that morning was a Rabbi's prayer, ". . . truth prevaileth over the waves of passion. . . ."

Hadley started his statement by quoting Roosevelt as saying, "I have carefully examined the facts in these cases, and I say to you that there is no element of doubt that the men in question were honorably and legally chosen by the people, and that the effort of the majority of the National Committee to unseat them represents nothing but naked theft, carried on with the sole and evil purpose of substituting the will of the bosses for the deliberately expressed judgment of the people of the United States."

Hadley then added his own thought:

"I do not know whether a majority of this Convention agrees with me on the proposition that Theodore Roosevelt ought to be our candidate for President of the United States (APPLAUSE) but there can be no difference on the proposition in the mind of any intelligent man that his voice today is the greatest voice in the western world. He can command the support of more people, and he can lead a larger number of American voters in a cause for which he fights than any other man who lies beneath the folds of the American flag."

Finally urging that the seventy-two contested delegates should not vote on their own cases, Hadley said, "It is written in the law of England that no man shall be a judge in his own case."

California delegates busily brandished their new banner which read, "WE REFUSE TO TRY TITLE TO THE PROPERTY BEFORE THE THIEF WHO STOLE IT."

Talk of others turned to the so-called "pretended primaries," primaries they claim were illegally called. One delegate testified, "I have come from my far-off state to place my hand upon my heart and tell you that is the truth." Another delegate, who brought much more than his heart and hand, Henry J. Allen claimed to have 200 pounds of voting records ready to place in evidence. "I have the polling list containing the names of every man who voted and his place of residence," he said, talking about the contested Kings County primary in the state of Washington.

Several delegates later queried Allen: How many delegates did Roosevelt claim at the convention? Another shouted the question of whether Allen would abide by the convention's decision, whether he would support its nominee?

To the first delegates, Allen said, "Gentlemen, you have not got anything until this Convention is over, and then the Lord only knows what you've got." To the second insistent delegate, Allen shouted, "Sit down until I can answer you." When the delegate finally did, Allen said, "I want to support the nominee of the Convention more than I want to do anything else in all my life. I will support the nominee of this Convention, but only on one condition. . . ."

The convention murmuring grew louder.

"Hear me," continued Allen, "I will support the nominee upon the one condition that his nomination is not accomplished by fraud and thievery. (APPLAUSE) Let me ask you a question. Will you support the nominee of this Convention if he steals the nomination?"

And an Indiana delegate loudly spoke over the noise, "Who shall be the judge?" That was the convention's critical question: Who shall be the judge?

William Jennings Bryan, sitting in the press box, eating a sandwich, wrote of this: "All of which goes to show that a National Convention is not the best place in the world to decide questions of abstract justice. The temptation to gain an unfair advantage is so great that it is not always resisted."

Indiana's Watson tried to answer: "Gentlemen it is a very easy answer to talk about mob law, it is a very easy matter to say, 'Throw these men out of the Convention,' but gentlemen, that is not right, that is not fair, that is not Republican, that is not American."

Somebody suggested a break for lunch, but the crowd hooted it down and Root finally ordered a fifteen-minute recess for those who wanted to leave. Watson then continued, intimating that Hadley himself favored sending contested cases to a Committee of Credentials rather than deciding them on the convention floor and a cry came from the crowd, "Hadley! . . . Hadley! . . . and Watson yielded to Hadley.

As Hadley walked the gangplank to the platform, Pennsylvania delegate William Coleman rushed to the front of the platform with a megaphone and blared, "Three cheers for Governor Hadley, the next President. . . ." And Coleman jumped up and down, getting the three cheers, with other delegates yelling, "Hadley! . . . Hadley! . . ."

And it started.

"A convention is a splendid place to study human nature," Bryan had said. "Man in a crowd is quite a different creature than man acting alone. Enthusiasm is contagious. . . ."

Reporter Richard Harding Davis added, "For four hours now,

every delegate had been sitting on a kitchen chair that each minute grew harder, smaller, and nearer to those on either side of it. For four hours he had been without food, drink or a cigar. And he was bored irritated, insurgent. Veterans of many conventions say it is impossible to explain the psychology of a demonstration. What floated this one, possibly, was that the Roosevelt delegates were pleased when Root permitted Hadley, who already had addressed them, to speak again. They looked upon his having the last word as an advantage. And when he came down the gangplank, they cheered and applauded mightily. At this point, the enthusiasm was heartfelt and genuine, but no more violent than it had been on other occasions.

"People had time to say it was clever of Root to let Hadley speak again as nothing he could say could now alter the final vote, and the concession gave an impression of fairness, even of magnanimity. Then when the cheering reached a higher note, it took on a new and strange significance. As one man, each reporter reached for his watch. Hadley, who had raised his hand for silence, felt the change, and, lowering his arm, stepped back quickly. Just as quickly, but too late, Root saw the danger and shot forward. The cheers now were yells and halted him. A moment earlier, with a few raps of his gavel, he could have stopped it. Now thunderclaps could not have stopped it."

William Jennings Bryan had said that a demonstration was a hard thing to manufacture but an easy thing to enlarge.

Delegates were stomping, cheering, pounding chairs, doing a "grizzly bear" dance in front of the speaker's stand, and one delegate even threw an open umbrella over his head. State standards had been especially weighted in fixed positions so they could not be carried in demonstrations, but this stopped nobody. Standards were torn loose from their bases, and it took three men to carry a single standard, but off they went with the Missouri delegation starting it off, and the parade was on.

"The demonstration fed on itself," wrote Richard Harding Davis. "The delirium of one man affected the one next to him.

They became like dancing dervishes, like those at a Negro camp meeting who have found religion. Twenty Texans rose in a solid mass and flung their arms into the air like men at calisthenic exercises."

Then, suddenly, almost as if a wave had broken in the middle and changed course, the tide turned. Suddenly it was a Roosevelt demonstration, and the chant went up, "WE WANT TEDDY . . . WE WANT TEDDY . . . WE WANT TEDDY. . . ."

And, from other persistent delegates, "WE WANT HADLEY . . . WE WANT HADLEY . . . WE WANT HADLEY. . . ."

But the Roosevelt cheers soon swallowed the Hadley cheers, and now the frenzy reached a new pitch. The whole hall was on its feet now, jeering, cheering, hissing, howling, waving handkerchiefs, flags, newspapers, anything. When noise sank in one section, it exploded elsewhere. Now no delegate had age or status or respectability—all of them simply melted into a mass of sound and color. There was Governor Stubbs of Kansas, like anybody else, standing on a chair waving his hankerchief with an enthusiasm that a younger man could hardly have equaled.

At the height of it, Bill Barnes of New York, told a reporter, "I'm not disturbed. Reason eventually will be restored."

The convention mood did seem to settle slightly, and even the yelling in rhythm seemed to diminish, but suddenly something happened that captured the convention intact, a moment of magic.

It was a woman in a white dress, really a cream-colored linen, a blue straw turban hat, a bouquet of sweet peas, a radiant infectious smile, waving an oversize Roosevelt poster in time with the music as she leaned over the gallery rail. Then she gave a cheer for Teddy Roosevelt in a high thin voice that somehow carried through the hall like a faint wisp of a breeze. Now she was waving at the Roosevelt poster with her handkerchief in her other hand, then she started a speech in pantomime aimed in a kind of mute appeal to the Taft men on the platform as if asking them to be fair to her hero, and soon her mood changed again and she was throwing kisses at the Roosevelt delegates.

The whole convention was now with her, staring at her, cheering her. Another woman in white, at the 1896 Democratic National Convention, had similarly stampeded them.

While the whole convention was watching her, almost in a kind of hypnotism, her Roosevelt poster dropped from her hand, fluttering to the convention floor, and it was the flick that switched on the electricity again. They surged forward for the poster, brought it to her, then carried her down from the balcony, pushed past the police, paraded her up the hall, put her on the platform.

"She was a very excited, very good-looking young woman," wrote Davis. "The audience liked her so well that the tempest rose again, the rooftops seemed to sway and men and women went entirely crazy. Delegates who had sunk into the kitchen chairs, breathless and panting, unable even to whisper, returned to life at the sight of the girl in the blue hat. Unable to express themselves like ordinary human beings, they gave imitations of Indians, coyotes, cowpunchers, noon-day whistles, motor car sirens. Nothing could silence them."

The California delegation served as the woman's personal flying wedge, swept her down the aisles past the jam of howling men, lifted and dragged her to the reporter's tables.

"Three of her bodyguards were jostled off the tables," said Davis, "and disappeared beneath them. But no one sympathized with them. The lady and her guard of honor were kicking and tramping upon the instruments of the telegraph operators, and the telegraph experts were fighting mad and trying to hurl them into space, but no one sympathized with them either. Lifted high above the crowd in the aisle, with policemen plucking at her skirts, the lady in dumb show made a speech. At least we could see her lips moving, her eyes flashing, her clenched fists trembling on high. . . ." The woman's name was Mrs. W. A. Davis, wife of a Chicago lumber dealer, and what she had done, nobody could deliberately do.

At the height of the frenzy when a Missouri delegate knocked down a policeman and an Illinois delegate got a punch on the jaw, the dignified Nicholas Murray Butler, then President of Columbia University, a former Roosevelt enthusiast who had switched to Taft, turned to the calm Boies Penrose, who was slowly fanning himself. Butler asked Penrose how in the name of common sense men of that sort ever got themselves elected delegates to a national political convention. In his inimitable twang, Penrose said, "Oh, those are the corks, bottles and banana peels washed up by the Roosevelt tide."

The way a tide does, the sounds started to subside and Root moved in to gavel for order and the convention secretary listed and dismissed the forty-seven-minute fury with this single sentence in the Official Proceedings: ("At this point there was a demonstration.")

When it was all over, nobody seemed to know what it all really meant. Was it a boom for Hadley or a stampede for Roosevelt? Or was it just a lot of "corks, bottles and banana peels?"

Jefferson's "Manual of Parliamentary Procedure" now again took over, and Root pointed his gavel handle at a noisemaking Pennsylvania delegate who wouldn't give up, and said to him in an icy voice of authority, "If the delegate from Pennsylvania who is so disturbing this Convention does not take his seat, the Chair will order the Sergeant-at-Arms to eject him from the hall."

That did it. That so stripped the sound from the hall that a nearby reporter even heard Penrose snicker, "Hear how rough he talks to the Mayor of McKeesport."

When the quiet came, Hadley finally spoke, made the point that he had suggested contested cases could be decided by a Committee on Credentials, but only if no contested member voted on the selection of these committee members, or on their report. Opposition delegates quickly pointed out if Hadley's proposal were upheld, enough seats could be contested that there wouldn't be enough remaining delegates with votes to do convention business.

Root ruled then that no contested delegate could vote on the question of his own right to a convention seat, but that he could vote on the rights of the other seventy-one contested delegates.

Working committees were then formally appointed, and the Convention adjourned at 5:30 P.M. Feeling stayed heated in the hall, however, with many refusing to leave, a crowd chanting, "WE WANT TEDDY . . ." and the police threatening to turn the lights off unless everybody left. Police also advised Root not to leave the platform until the crowd had gone. Root stayed there for an extra hour, a semicircle of twenty policemen framed in front of him.

"A convention feels about demonstrations somewhat like the big man who had a small wife who was in the habit of beating him," wrote Bryan. "When asked why he permitted it, he replied that it seemed to please her and did not hurt him."

The factional fight continued on a smaller, sharper scale within the Committee on Credentials meeting to rehash the contested cases. There seemed small question of the outcome since the Taft forces had the same proportional strength as they had on the National Committee. But the official machinery had been geared, and the official motions must move in their ordered ways.

Tension was on a trigger and the committee meeting almost broke up before it started. Heney of California was in the middle of a speech, when New Jersey delegate, George L. Record, sidled up to him, whispered something in his ear. Heney said, "Wait a minute," and Record shook his head vigorously and said, "Now, now, this minute, he says." Then Record announced to the room, "All Roosevelt men walk out. . . . Everyone go to the Florentine Room at the Congress. . . ."

National Committee Secretary William Hayward, a big handsome man who wore his glasses attached to a long, black heavy cord, chased after the departing Roosevelt men, caught up with Heney and Record outside on the sidewalk and asked, "Why did you act this way. Why didn't you wait until some rules had been passed."

"We are acting under the orders of Colonel Roosevelt," said Record. "He told us to leave the room, and we did it."

After considerable pleading, Hayward persuaded five of the

departing twelve to return with him, promising fair discussion and fair rules.

What had happened was that Roosevelt heard that the committee already had set up some gag rules limiting discussion on each case to ten minutes, permitting no new evidence. Without double-checking the truth of this, Roosevelt telephoned Record and told him to tell Heney and the rest to walk out. At the same time, he scheduled a mass meeting at the huge Orchestra Hall for 1:00 A.M.

Meanwhile the Credentials Committee had softened its rules, increased the discussion time limit to thirty minutes for each case, and provided for general discussion. When Roosevelt heard about these rules, he canceled the Orchestra Hall meeting, told Heney, Record, and the others to return to the committee meeting.

Roosevelt and some of his group then convened for a conference and Roosevelt said, "Shut the door!" The door slammed in somebody's face just as he said, "But I'm a delegate . . . Everybody laughed one of the few laughs of the day, and Roosevelt said, "Let him in . . . I'll do anything for a delegate. . . ."

A crowd of many hundreds still packed in the Florentine Room, still waiting for word from Roosevelt that night. It was after midnight when he talked to them: "So far as I am concerned," he told them, "I am through."

A gray-haired man in the audience, tears streaming down his face, jumped up and said, "Oh don't say that. . . ."

"I went before the people and I won," Roosevelt said. "Let us find out whether the Republican Party is the party of the plain people or the party of the bosses. . . . If you are voted down, I hope you—the real and lawful majority of the Convention—will organize as such and you will do it if you have the courage and loyalty of your convictions."

Governor Hiram Johnson then jumped on a table and told the group, "If turned down in the convention tomorrow morning, we can march out and nominate Roosevelt. We can conquer the country and put man above dollars. . . ."

Commenting on the meeting, a *Chicago Tribune* reporter wrote that it sounded like the birth of a new party.

The decision was delayed. At the Coliseum the next noon, the crowd waited, the band and a woman singer ready for "The Star-Spangled Banner." The Credentials Committee, however, reported that it had been in continuous session but still wasn't finished. The convention adjourned until 4:06 P.M., but the committee was still not ready to report and so it adjourned a moment later until the next morning. Somebody spread the rumor that Roosevelt was coming to the convention hall that afternoon and a large crowd lingered, waiting, but finally ebbed away.

President Taft had a more relaxing day in Washington. He sat in the grandstand watching the Washington Senators beat the Philadelphia Athletics and move into second place. The next day he played eighteen holes of golf at the Chevy Chase Club with his son Robert (who would face his own presidential contest against another military hero at another Republican National Convention exactly forty years later.)

That day Taft wrote his friend, M. T. Herrick: "Chaos is still a proper word for conditions at Chicago as far as the Roosevelt forces are concerned. The question Roosevelt has to settle is whether to break now or wait and vote some more. He wishes to do so now. Many of his lieutenants are against his doing so. My lines are reported firm, but no one can tell when the break may come. There are men on both sides seeking a third candidate, but who shall it be. . . ?"

With Hadley out as a compromise candidate, Hughes became most mentioned in the inner circles. Hughes was a strong-willed forceful man and Republican leaders long ago had tagged him as a man who wouldn't "play the game." It took Roosevelt's full support to help elect Hughes governor of New York in 1906. Many Roosevelt leaders at this convention strongly believed that the Hughes support for Roosevelt in 1912 might have made the difference in insuring a Roosevelt nomination, but Hughes had kept judiciously quiet. Now he was forced into a decision on whether or not he wanted to replace Roosevelt as the candidate. He decided it must not happen, that he preferred being Chief Justice of the United States Supreme Court. He therefore sent Root two telegrams insisting that he must not be considered for the presidential nomination under any circumstances, that if he were nominated he would face the embarrassing necessity of declining the honor. Root kept the telegrams secret, showing them only to a few top leaders.

Hughes finally decided a public statement was necessary to forestall last-minute pressures. The newspaper headline read:

HUGHES WOULD
REFUSE, IF NAMED

Prefers U. S. Bench

Sees As High Duty in the Courts
As In The White House

Four years later, Hughes would change his mind, but then he said, ". . . No man is as essential to his country's well being as the unstained integrity of the courts. . . ."

On the convention's fourth day, the Credentials Committee still had unfinished work and hesitated on submitting a partial report. While they were discussing it among themselves, Root delayed the official opening and the band played while some of the state delegations demonstrated with new yells.

Ray ray ray
Pennsylvan i a
Sixty five votes for Roosevelt
Ray! Ray! Ray!

The band even had a sentimental song for William Jennings Bryan when he took his press seat that morning, "Should Auld Acquaintance Be Forgot . . ."

The Credentials Committee finally decided to go ahead, Root gaveled the hall to order, and somebody shouted from the gallery, "Play ball. . . ."

It was historically unheard of that a convention should still be temporary on the fourth day. Before beginning with its report on Alabama, the Credentials Committee Chairman reported, "Your Committee on Credentials has been in session continuously without intermission to secure either food or sleep, since nine o'clock yesterday morning. It is only fair to say that there are present in the meeting of the Committee men who, to say the least, are not assisting the Committee in concluding its deliberations. . . ."

His reference, of course, was to the Roosevelt minority, the "solid fourteen." For the next eight and a half hours, the committee reported the majority and minority statements on the different contested cases.

"The machine has been working beautifully all day," Bryan wrote. "It has not slipped a cog. When it was running at full speed, 'Toot . . . toot . . .' would occasionally come from the audience. Sometimes sounds arose that resembled escaping steam, but I am satisfied that no steam escaped; it was all being used, and at high pressure, too."

At one time, Root raised both hands for silence, and he looked so much like a railroad conductor giving the signal to start a train, that a young man yelled, "All aboard," and the whole convention roared with laughter, and even Root smiled.

In the roll call of states on whether to accept the majority or minority report on contested cases, one voting delegate was reported absent because of a broken leg. "Yes, he's got a broken leg," yelled delegate Calvin Palmer of Michigan, "but when the Republican Party comes out of this convention, it will have a broken back."

That started another round of "WE WANT TEDDY" cheers.

The hot vote of the day came on California, with Governor Johnson waving the Taft telegram agreeing to abide by the state law. And Johnson said, "The question is: shall the people rule?"

"Yes, yes, yes, let the people rule." came the roar from the crowd.

But the majority ruled. After convention adjournment that day, a newspaper headline read:

TAFTIES HAVE
CLOSE SHAVE
ON CALIFORNIA

Close on Fourth Day's
Session Finds Margin
Cut to Two Votes

Machine in Fright at Unexpected
Vote in Convention: 542 to 529;
Crowds Cry 'Choo Choo'

Conferences behind closed doors seemed continual.

The close California vote seemed the final crusher of any slim Roosevelt hope. Now the question was: what next?

Taft discussed it in a letter that week:

"Roosevelt is struggling to secure as many of his followers as possible to join him in the bolt, and it is their reluctance or refusal that makes the situation doubtful. He has given specific notice of his intention to bolt. If he does not do it at once, it will look like so many of his bluffs. They have bought delegates right and left. They have poured out money like water. If I win the nomination and Roosevelt bolts, it means a long hard fight with probable defeat. But I can stand defeat if we retain the regular Republican Party as a nucleus for future conservative action."

Queried by a friendly reporter, Roosevelt admitted that the California delegation was in favor of an immediate bolt, but that there were some strong differences of opinion among some of his Ohio supporters and others. "If the people want a Progressive Party," he said, "I'll be in it . . . I shall have to see if there is a popular demand for me to run."

Some of the strongest opposition to a bolt came from Borah. "History shows conclusively," he said, "that no successful party was ever born under such auspices. It would be created half-formed and would go into the fight with the likelihood of its parent wearing it down."

BALLOTS & BANDWAGONS

Roosevelt called a special meeting with two representatives from each state having Roosevelt delegates, and the caucus came up with a fresh concept—they unanimously decided to sit in their convention seats silently without voting.

"This is the shrewdest move we've made," said a Roosevelt man. "It will enable us to hold a genuine Republican Convention without having it said that we have bolted."

They felt that if they did bolt, the convention would simply fill their seats with other delegates, and pin on them the blame for a bolt. But by fighting this political sin with silence, they hoped to win some sympathetic votes away from Taft that could still deadlock the convention and change its course. The test would be the first ballot; if Taft didn't make it then, they felt he never would. At best, their chances seemed slim. Bitterness now was at its ripest, deep and purple. Tension was an open wire.

At this critical point, the night before the final day, a delegate approached O.K. Davis:

"I represent a group of about thirty delegates," he said, "partly from my own state, Michigan, and partly from others that have a good chance of going Republican at the election. We were all sent down here to beat Roosevelt but the thing that is going on is beating the Republican Party, and we are not for that. We have been talking the situation over among ourselves, and have made up our minds to submit this proposition to Roosevelt. We have noticed that, on every roll call thus far, Taft has won by a majority so small that, if we had voted the other way on any one of them, Taft would have lost. We are all instructed for Taft, but this is going beyond our instructions. So this is what we'll do. We will watch the roll call on nomination, and if it is going the same way that the others went, we will vote for any man you say, provided you will give a few votes to the same man, so that it will look like an effort at compromise. That will prevent Taft from going over on the first ballot, and I guess I don't need to tell you any more. Now can you take that to Roosevelt?"

This was it. The Presidency on a platter. If they deadlocked Taft on a first ballot, O.K. Davis saw the blocs break in an inevitable rush to Roosevelt.

The two men raced to the Roosevelt suite, the Michigan delegate waiting outside with "an alert expectancy." Inside, Davis only half-finished the explanation of the deal when Roosevelt exploded:

"No! No! No!" Roosevelt interrupted. "I won't hear of it. I won't have it. You needn't talk to me at all. You go back and tell your man that I won't have anything to do with it. You tell him that it is a crooked convention, and I won't touch it with a forty-rod pole. You tell him that the first thing they've got to do is purge the roll. I will support any man they want to nominate except Taft. I won't support Taft. But, until they purge the roll, neither I nor any other honest man, can touch this convention. Now you go tell him what I say."

Davis stared in amazement. Roosevelt wasn't just gently pushing it away—he was kicking it, breaking it, stomping on it.

Davis then reported all this to the waiting Michigan man outside. The Michigan delegate, a huge bulk of a man, listened to Davis, dazed, dumbfounded, and finally said, slowly, "Say, say that again." Davis repeated it, the man sighed deeply and said, "Say! Don't that beat hell." This wasn't the only Roosevelt chance.

Close Roosevelt friend, Lawrence Abbott, reported a southern delegate coming to Roosevelt, claiming he represented thirty-two southern delegates who would pledge to vote for Roosevelt provided they would be permitted to vote with regular Republicans on all motions referring to party organization and platform.

"Without a moment's hesitation," reported Abbott, "and in the death-like silence of the room, the Colonel's voice rang out, clearly and distinctly: 'Thank the delegates you represent, but tell them that I cannot permit them to vote for me unless they vote for all the progressive principles for which I have fought, for which the progressive element in the Republican Party stands and by which I stand or fall.'"

Abbott described the reaction in that room:

"Strong men broke down under the stress of that night. Life-long friends of Mr. Roosevelt endeavored to persuade him to reconsider his decision. After listening patiently, he turned to two who had been urging him to accept the offer of the southern delegates, placed a hand on the shoulder of each, and said: 'I have grown to regard you as brothers; let no act or word of yours make that relationship impossible.' "

The huge question was: Why?

Here was the Presidency all wrapped up, packaged politically and perfectly—why would he refuse it?

Of course it was a "deal."

But Roosevelt was a practical politician. He had made deals before.

He had made deals with Boss Platt when he was Governor of New York.

He had made deals with Boss Mark Hanna, when he was President of the United States.

He had made all kinds of deals organizing the "rotten boroughs" of the South and setting up the Republican National Convention of 1908 to insure the nomination of Taft to succeed himself as President.

Throughout the whole of his political career, from the very beginning, he had compromised on all kinds of questions, issues, platforms, candidates.

He had "played the game." Then, why not now?

Why not now, with the greatest prize of all at stake—not just the Presidency and not just his pride, but the final chance to shape the Republican party in his image. Why not now?

"Yes, I am a practical politician," Roosevelt later explained to Davis, "and I have played the game. But that was something different. There was a question of simple honesty involved in that fight in Chicago, the principle of right and wrong. It had gone far beyond the mere question of expediency or political shrewdness. It was a fundamental question of morality."

But it was more than that. Roosevelt had boxed himself in politically. So vigorously had he denounced the "crooked" convention, the theft of delegates, so righteously insistent had he been in demanding a purged convention before he would participate in it, so dramatically had he sided his battle with Armageddon and the Lord—that he had left himself no area of political flexibility.

To accept any deal then would seem like too large a moral stain. The Roosevelt personality, the Roosevelt explosive energy, the Roosevelt righteousness had killed his own chances. He had slammed his own door in his own face.

It was no longer a personal dilemma; it was a personal and political disaster. But it was still disaster with a shine of glory in it, like the man before the firing squad refusing the blindfold. If you have to make a gesture, somebody said—make a grand gesture.

The convention's fifth and final day continued with the Credentials Committee reports. The "solid fourteen" minority had a statement to make, which had already been distributed and printed in that morning's *Chicago Tribune*. It read in part: "This convention was called to contain 1,078 delegates. Of this, one-quarter were to come from States and Territories which have no part in Republican affairs, cast no Republican vote, and are practically destitute of Republican voters. Such delegates are always controlled by Federal office holders or others interested in the management of Federal office. As they live by politics, they form an efficient political machine.

"The combination between these and one-quarter of the delegates from the Republican states will form a majority of the convention. In other words, one third of the representative Republican states can, by manipulation, dictate to two-thirds of the Republican representatives.

"This year such a coalition was attempted, but a majority of the convention was not obtainable until members of the National Committee, who have been repudiated by their own states, seated a sufficient number of contested delegates to give a majority on the temporary roll call."

This minority report also accused the National Committee majority of sitting upon their own cases, acting as attorneys for the seated delegates, interfering with an orderly procedure, and bullying the witnesses of the contestants. "The hearing," it said, "if held in public, would have aroused the scorn of all spectators, and for this reason the public were excluded."

The minority also accused the majority of preparing set reports on cases beforehand, then adopting them as a formality. "It is therefore plain," the report concluded, "that if these contested delegates are seated, they will not only create a majority of which less than one-half represent Republican states, but that this majority will also be composed of delegates improperly seated in violation of good parliamentary law and common morals."

Taft committee members then made the point that Roosevelt delegates had left their committee hearing even before a single case had been heard, that three hours had been spent on the Alabama cases, five hours on Indiana, that the discussion had been full. A convention vote then upheld the majority; the remaining contested cases rushed to a finish.

Root recognized a Mississippi delegate on a point of order:

"The point of order is that the steam roller is exceeding the speed limit," said the delegate, and the crowd roared.

But Root had a ready answer: "The Chair is ready to rule upon the point of order. The point of order is sustained. The justification is that we have some hope of getting home for Sunday."

With the completion of the cases, a final vote transferred the names of the sitting delegates onto the permanent roll and Root was made Permanent Chairman. His first act then was to get unanimous consent for Henry J. Allen of Kansas to make his statement. If there is anything that a convention loves, it is a voice that can be heard, and Allen had such a voice.

"If you will be kind enough to be quiet while I present the attitude of the progressives in this convention," Allen boomed, "then I pledge you that no effort will be made during the remainder of the Convention to put any sand in the gasoline or do any mischief whatever to your sparkplug. . . ." (LAUGHTER)

The first thing he wanted to do, he said, was to read a statement from Roosevelt, just handed to him. His mention of Roosevelt's name started a twenty-one-minute demonstration. Then Allen read the Roosevelt statement:

"The Convention has now declined to purge the roll of the fraudulent delegates placed thereon by the defunct National Committee, and the majority which thus endorsed fraud was made a majority only because it included the fraudulent delegates themselves, who all sat as judges on one another's cases. . . .

"I hope the men elected as Roosevelt delegates will now decline to vote on any matter before the Convention. I do not release any delegate from his honorable obligation to vote for me if he votes at all, but under the actual conditions I hope that he will not vote at all."

In reading the rest of the Roosevelt statement, Allen hit hard on the line, ". . . It would be deeply discreditable to any man to accept the Convention's nomination under these circumstances."

A delegate then threw the convention into disorder when he yelled, "If a man does not know when he is dead, his friends ought to know. . . ."

When the noise subsided, Allen continued with his own statement but Taft delegates broke in repeatedly with caustic comments that ranged from "Sit down" to "Get out." Allen finally concluded:

". . . We do not bolt. We merely insist that you, not we, are making the record. And we refuse to be bound by it. We have pleaded with you ten days. We have fought with you five days for a square deal. We fight no more, we plead no longer. We shall sit in protest, and the people who sent us here shall judge us.

"Gentlemen, you accuse us of being radical. Let me tell you that no radical in the ranks of radicalism ever did so radical a thing as come to a National Convention of the great Republican Party and secure through fraud the nomination of a man whom they knew could not be elected."

Amid the applause came the unasked questions. Why did Allen substitute for Hadley in presenting the Roosevelt statement? Was

BALLOTS & BANDWAGONS

Roosevelt worried about a final break to Hadley as a compromise candidate? Nobody would say. But Allen's statement, which William Allen White had helped fill with amiable sarcasm, proved effective enough so that many Roosevelt delegates marched out of the hall "with as much dignity as men of wrath can assume in defeat."

Other convention committees now reported: Among other things, the Rules Committee recommended that future delegates-at-large continue to be selected by state conventions. Reporting on a proposed platform, Resolutions Committee Chairman, Senator Charles Fairbanks, followed a liberal trend, in an attempt to please as many progressives as possible, while still maintaining conservative support. The platform avoided the Payne Aldrich Tariff except to mention that some duties were too high; it opposed recall of judges, but suggested a simplified process of removing judges from office; it dodged the central bank plan, favored a clarified antitrust law, proposed a federal trade commission, advocated easier credit facilities for farmers, continued conservation of natural resources, and the establishment of a parcel post system.

La Follette representative Walter Houser of Wisconsin, referring to the convention's refusal to accept the La Follette platform proposals—including a national presidential primary—said that "whether nominated or not, he [La Follette] cannot consent to accept or support a platform that is not thoroughly progressive."

The convention adopted the majority platform with Yeas, 666; nays, 53; present and not voting, 343; absent 21.

It was a dramatic convention moment when the first Roosevelt delegate responded, "Present, but not voting."

Nominations for the Presidency began at six that evening and Warren G. Harding started off much on the wordy side ("glorying in retrospection, exalted by the contemplation and exulting in anticipation") and then describing Taft as "the greatest progressive of the age." Further describing Taft, Harding called him "as wise and patient as Abraham Lincoln, as modest and dauntless as Ulysses S. Grant, as temperate and peace-loving as Rutherford B.

Hayes, as patriotic and intellectual as James A. Garfield, as courtly and generous as Chester A. Arthur, as learned in the law as Benjamin Harrison, as sympathetic and brave as William McKinley, as progressive as his predecessor."

Harding had not mentioned Roosevelt's name for fear it would set off another demonstration. At his first mention of Taft, the convention gave its first and only tribute to Taft in a thirteen-minute demonstration.

Whenever Harding paused for breath throughout his speech, Roosevelt delegates tooted their whistles, or rubbed sandpaper together for an effective imitation of steam escaping from a steam-roller engine.

At one point in his speech, Harding said, "The people will rule . . ." and a delegate stood up and shouted, "You bet they will—next November."

"Why the people do rule now," persisted Harding.

"Where? . . . Where? . . ." yelled the Roosevelt delegates.

Following the Harding speech, another Taft demonstration tried to start, but only lasted a moment. Among the several seconding speeches for Taft, former Roosevelt man, Nicholas Murray Butler was careful to say, "I have in my heart no unkind or ungenerous thought toward any man who aspires to the nomination. . . ." Then he added a note that had all the flavor of prophecy, "Remember," he said, "that Presidents are not elected in these crowded halls, with cheering thousands. They are elected by the fireside in November. . . ."

Roosevelt had requested nobody to nominate him, and nobody did. The only other official nominee was La Follette.

In the crucial roll call, Root ruled that if a delegate did not answer, the secretary should call the alternate. One delegate protested, and Taft men said, "Shut up and take your medicine."

"I will not shut up and I will not take your medicine," said the delegate.

"I refuse to vote where the cards are stacked," added an Oregon delegate.

For every rap from a Root gavel came a blow from a tin whistle and delegates screaming, "Let the roller roll . . . more gasoline . . . more gasoline. . . . Draw your fires, Root, she'll go without steam now. . . ." Hoots, toots, groans, cheers, and the strange, almost-hysterical sound of laughter.

Reporting the mood, William Allen White wrote, "Slowly, motion by motion, phase by phase, the steamroller crushed its way toward the nomination of Taft. And here is a funny American expression: in the midst of all the rancor and wormwood pumping into the hearts of the delegates, every time a motion was offered by the Taft people, a thousand toots and imitation whistles of the steamroller engine pierced the air sharply, to be greeted with laughter that swept the galleries. An American crowd will have a terrible time behind barricades, or surging up Pennsylvania Avenue to overwhelm the White House. It will probably laugh itself to death on the way."

One-third of the Roosevelt delegates had stayed on to vote—for Roosevelt.

One Roosevelt man lowered a huge sign from the balcony that read: WHAT ROOT SAID OF THE PENROSE MACHINE: "A CORRUPT AND CRIMINAL COMBINATION MASQUERADING UNDER THE NAME OF THE REPUBLICAN PARTY." Police grabbed the man and the sign. Taft picked up three New York votes from Roosevelt, when Root recognized their alternatives, who were Taft men.

Then it was all over. The partly-filled hall was a wilderness of empty seats. The final vote: Taft, 561; Roosevelt, 107; La Follette, 41; Cummins, 17; Hughes, 2; Present and not voting, 344; absent, 6.

Somebody noted afterward how unprecedented it was that no delegate had the nerve to move that the nomination be made unanimous. This was the first time this had ever happened in a Republican convention.

The mood greeting the results featured gloom, confusion, bitterness. Some few Republicans saw the split as a godsend since they said it finally took radicalism out of the Republican party. But the more general and more meaningful note came from a man with a megaphone in the balcony, screeching:

> VICTIM: THE REPUBLICAN PARTY
> FUNERAL ORATOR: WARREN G. HARDING
> UNDERTAKER: ELIHU ROOT

And dapper delegate Chauncey Depew told reporters, "The only question now is which corpse gets the flowers."

There was still a Vice-President to pick and it was 9:45 P.M. and so speakers were advised to keep it short. Taft had indicated no choice of a running mate, but had requested "some man known as a progressive." Cummins had sent word that he would not permit his name in nomination for the Vice-Presidency. Hadley said the same. Regular Republicans anyway decided on a straight conservative, and John Van Vechten Olcott of New York nominated James Schoolcraft Sherman in a one paragraph nominating speech. Sherman, better known as "Sunny Jim," who had been a Congressman for twenty years, already had served four years as Taft's Vice-President (and died before Election Day). Seconding Sherman in a single sentence, was Harding's Ohio compatriot and friend, Harry M. Daugherty (who would prove providential to Harding in the 1920 convention).

Also nominated by Illinois delegate R. R. McCormick was Howard F. Gillette.

When asked who Gillette was, McCormick answered, "He's a friend of mine."

Sherman got 596 votes (thirty-five more votes than Taft), Borah with twenty-one votes led a string of others including Hadley with fourteen votes, Beveridge with two, and one vote for Howard F. Gillette.

As the convention crowd disappeared at 10:30, the band played, "Praise God From Whom All Blessings Flow."

Back at the Congress Hotel, the closer he came to final defeat, the more deadly Roosevelt became, pacing his room in a kind of impotent rage.

Borah came to say goodby, told Roosevelt he had no taste for third parties. Back in 1900, Roosevelt had written, "At times a man must cut loose from his associates and stand alone for a great cause; but the necessity for such action is almost as rare as the necessity for revolution."

Now he told Borah, "What would you have me do? These men are in earnest. If they do not nominate me, they will nominate La Follette."

"Colonel," insisted Borah, "Those men will do just what you tell them. . . . Call in some of the leaders and tell them that you do not want any such action and they will not take any such action."

Just then some Roosevelt aides broke into the room with piles of telegrams and said excitedly, "The country is on fire; you must lead us."

Borah eased out of the room, feeling that if the matter could have rested a day or so longer, the Progressive party might never have been born. Roosevelt himself wrote, about a week later, "I wish to Heaven I was not in this fight, and I am in it only on the principle, in the long run a sound one, that I would rather take a thrashing than be quiet under such a kicking." To have quit then, he felt, would have been "an avowal of weakness." In his own mind, he had long before framed his future course. Writing to his daughter in the first week of June he had mentioned the possibility of an "independent candidacy" if he lost the nomination to Taft.

O. K. Davis reports that Bryan also talked to Roosevelt, intimated that he expected the possibility of a similar split at the Democratic party convention two weeks later. Bryan added that if the Democrats nominated a conservative, he personally might support Roosevelt and there could be a realignment of parties resulting in a Roosevelt victory.

All this was problematical, and future Roosevelt success seemed slim indeed. Senator Albert Beveridge tried to talk Roosevelt out of holding a rump convention:

"No, no Colonel," Beveridge said, "that will be just as bad a mistake in tactics as the series of mistakes we have made throughout this convention. . . . To hold a rump convention is not the way to act if we are going to stay in the party, and it is certainly not the way to act if you intend to start a new party."

Roosevelt seemed weary, but not resentful. "You may be right," he said, "but it is too late to change things now. The matter has been determined."

But the real moment of the birth of the Progressive party, according to both Beveridge and Amos Pinchot, took place in the northeast corner of the Roosevelt suite where Perkins and Munsey stood apart, talking in whispers. "The others in the room," said Beveridge, "and there were but few—were merely spectators. Somehow they knew that great events hung on the whispered conference, and all eyes were turned on the two participants. Munsey was the more agitated of the two. Suddenly the whispering ceased when he made a decisive gesture. The two men straightened up, and moved together toward Roosevelt, meeting him in the middle of the room. Each placed a hand on one of Roosevelt's shoulders, and Perkins said:

"Colonel, we'll see you through."

"My fortune, my magazines, my newspapers are with you," said Munsey.

(The Perkins-Munsey effect on the Progressive party platform was to soften the antitrust plank, a plank Roosevelt regarded as "utterly unimportant.")

A huge crowd already had collected at Orchestra Hall, waiting for Roosevelt.

"To those of us who had rushed from the Coliseum straight to Orchestra Hall," wrote Richard Harding Davis, "the effect was like stepping from a board meeting of railroad directors, from a post-mortem in a coroner's office on a corpse into a Zuni snake-dance."

Governor Hiram Johnson presided and there were several short, sincere speeches before Roosevelt spoke. He told them the fight was between right and wrong, and that they should go home, stir up support and return in two months to formally organize their party and nominate their candidate for President. "If you wish me to make the fight," he told them, "I will make it, even if only one state should support me."

> "We will follow Roosevelt,
> Follow! Follow!
> Anywhere! Everywhere!
> We will follow on!"

"What made him great," said Medill McCormick of Roosevelt, "was that he understood the 'psychology of the mutt.'"

William Allen White saw Roosevelt soon after the Orchestra Hall meeting, and described him: "He was not downcast; indeed he was triumphant, full of jokes and quips as though the teakettle of his heart were humming and rattling the lid of his merry countenance. But rage was bubbling inside him."

If Roosevelt had few illusions of his political future that night, Mrs. Taft felt similarly about her husband. Told of his renomination, she listened to an old friend add, ". . . mark my word, the President will be re-elected in November!"

"Well," said Mrs. Taft, "you may be right, but just the same I intend to pack everything up when I leave Beverly, and I shall take the linen and silver home."

For Roosevelt and Taft, the political end had begun.

ACCORDING TO THE Carnegie Endowment for International Peace, the cash cost of the Great War was $337,946,179,657. Over-all loss of life was listed at 9,998,771, more than twice the loss of all wars of the nineteenth century since Napoleon.

More and more, the song "Over There" had changed into a new mood: Over Here.

And there was a fresh slang phrase everybody used: the cock-eyed world.

It was one of the big reasons President Woodrow Wilson couldn't pull enough American support for membership in the League of Nations—too many Americans now saw it as a cock-eyed world and wanted to stay away from it.

The price of the cock-eyed world was made fresh again in the beginning of 1920 when the first batch of some 20,000 American soldiers buried in France started arriving home for reburial.

The American people had passed a Prohibition Amendment, the Eighteenth, and William Jennings Bryan told an audience, "The liquor issue is as dead as slavery." But if Prohibition closed saloons, it opened speakeasies.

"Bootleg" became a big word. W. E. "Pussyfoot" Johnson had a short run as a known name. "Pussyfoot" Johnson was a professional "dry" who wanted to spread prohibition all over the world. But he stopped evangelizing when a resentful crowd manhandled him near a pub in England and he lost an eye.

As America entered the Twenties, a whole generation was waiting to be "lost."

REPUBLICAN NATIONAL CONVENTION OF 1920

"I BELIEVE THAT THE PEOPLE WANT AN ORDI-
nary man as President, being a little tired of supermen. . . . I believe that they want a little peace and quiet and rest from agitation
and sensationalism and loud talk and back talk . . . and they sort
of believe I want these reliefs myself. Make no mistake, the people
of this country are as sound at heart as a good red apple, and always
after a little emotionalism, they come back to the same, sane ways
of business and government. You won't think I'm indulging in big
talk, will you, if I say that is where I believe I fit in."

It was an interview with an old newspaper friend of his, a *New
York Herald* reporter, and the man talking was a strikingly handsome United States Senator about whom somebody had aptly said,
"he was the only man in the United States who might have worn
a toga and got away with it." He was Warren Gamaliel Harding
and he had summed up the tune of his times.

There was one man who could have changed that tune.

At a meeting in his apartment in Washington's Willard Hotel
late in 1918, United States Senator Boies Penrose, Pennsylvania's

political boss, was asked about his presidential preference. "There is but one candidate," said Penrose. "He is the only candidate. I mean Theodore Roosevelt." Asked if Roosevelt was his personal choice, Penrose said: "No, I don't like him. I once despised him. But that doesn't alter the fact that Theodore Roosevelt is now the one and only possible Republican candidate in 1920. He will surely receive the nomination."

Roosevelt himself acted coy. "If the Republican Party wants me, and I can advance the ideals for which I stand, I will be a candidate," he said. "But I will not lift a finger for the nomination."

This time, he never had the chance. Theodore Roosevelt died several months later, early in 1919.

With Wilson paralyzed, the Democrats demoralized, and the war fever cooled into a computation of hard cost, Republican presidential chances seemed almost gloatingly good. The country *did* seem to want less sensationalism, *did* seem to want more national normalcy. As Penrose later put it: "Any good Republican can be nominated for President and can defeat any Democrat."

Political Axiom Number One says that the brighter the presidential prospect of victory, the greater the crop of available candidates.

Favorite sons sprouted everywhere, shining up the smile on their promises, searching for key phrases that fit best into newspaper headlines, combing the country for wavering delegates to waver their way. And all of them tried to step as swiftly as possible into the ghostly shadow and onto the coattails of Theodore Roosevelt. All claimed his political kinship, his personal friendship, and openly named themselves as his heirs.

Nobody doubted the political strength of the Roosevelt image with the American people, but nobody knew how much decal quality the image had and nobody knew which candidate would rub it off best.

Of the two dozen candidates crowding for attention, the field of favorites narrowed to three: Lowden, Wood, and Johnson.

Frank Lowden was a handsome, forceful, fifty-nine-year-old

multi-millionaire who had gone in as Governor of Illinois and converted a political mess into a model administration. Illinois had 125 floundering state agencies and bureaus and Lowden consolidated them into nine efficient departments, replaced a cumbersome twenty-five-man Board of Equalization with a three-man Tax Commission, set up such a simplified budget system that political scientists long afterward referred to his whole state setup as the model "Illinois Plan."

Reporters wrote of Lowden that "he looks far more like a business executive than a politician." When he swept into state office by 150,000 votes, somebody wrote, "He will challenge the interest of the entire nation."

Politically Lowden had been a man of metamorphosis. Walter Lippmann summed it up best:

"His political associations, from the Republican Convention of 1900 through the gubernatorial contest of 1904, when he was defeated for the nomination, through three terms in Congress, through the Convention of 1912, to his election as Governor in 1916, are without evidence of independence of the dark forces of American politics. Lowden went to the top through the usual channels, a rich man and a favored man, accepting the standards of his time.

"The change came after his election as Governor. Lowden braced up. Lowden reformed. Lowden made himself one of the best governors in America. Again and again I was told in Chicago by friends and opponents that they had expected nothing and he had done extremely well."

Lippmann later added: "There's a logic to Lowden, once you grant the premises. He comes from the middle of the country, he stands in the middle of the road, in the middle of the party, about midway between Wood of New Hampshire and Johnson of California. He has risen from a farm to an estate, from obscurity to moderate fame, perhaps not quite the darling of the gods, but surely one of their favorite sons. . . ."

Lowden's campaign approach was the business-in-government

theme. Somebody described Lowden as "the noiseless candidate" who talks only about prosaic things, but Lowden hit a popular note when he attacked rising prices and taxes and insisted that he could and would reduce the high cost of living. "Now you cannot do that until you reduce the high cost of government," Lowden said. "Why not apply modern business principles to governmental methods?" Lowden supporters widely publicized a dramatic fact: at the time of Lowden's election as governor, Illinois had only $500 in the state treasury plus a fat pile of unpaid bills. Lowden not only cleared up the debts but gave the state treasury a surplus of several million dollars.

As for the Roosevelt mantle, Lowden found it hard to make a good fit because he had stuck with Taft against Roosevelt at the 1912 convention. However, Lowden quickly revealed a telegram of congratuations he had received from Roosevelt: "We want leadership!" Roosevelt had wired. "What I most desire is that you shall help bring the Republicans far enough forward to enable us to hold the Progressives far enough back to keep a substantial alignment."

Lowden was against the League of Nations, saw it as an unwanted super-state. On the Red scare, Lowden was "for 100 per cent Americanism."

His money and his marriage were his twin political handicaps. Not so much his possession of money, but his show of it—his favorite posed picture showed him in riding breeches and boots mounted on one of his full-blooded Arabian horses. Lowden's marriage to the daughter of George Pullman hurt him with American labor whose memory was still vivid of the bitter, bloody Pullman strike which state and federal troops were called in to quell. But Lowden's own labor record received this generally favorable reaction from the president of the Illinois Federation of Labor who said: "He has not always given us what we wanted, but he has always given us a hearing and said he would do such-and-such and what he would not do. We could always find out where he was."

Most colorful of the top three candidates was General Leonard Wood. Theodore Roosevelt and his Rough Riders served under

Wood in Cuba during the Spanish-American War, and Wood later became Governor General of Cuba, clearing the island of malaria. Wood was also one of the first to advocate military preparedness in 1914 after the outbreak of war in Europe. He was Army Chief of Staff then, and had set up an Officers Training Program. President Wilson made Wood a martyr when he refused to allow him to go overseas with one of the early American divisions.

Wood's friendship with Roosevelt had been deep and personal, but the two men did not share the same political philosophy. Wood was primarily a conservative. On some basic ideas, such as the Red Scare in America, one magazine quoted Wood as saying: "My motto for the Reds is SOS—Ship or Shoot. I believe we should place them all on a ship of stone, with sails of lead, and their first stopping place should be Hell."

Wood's handicap was major—the glamor of war was gone. His campaign advocacy of universal military training for all Americans was twenty years ahead of his time, and hardly a popular postwar issue. Still, the hero personality had lingered long enough so that Wood led all the public opinion polls.

Least likely of the three leading candidates was Senator Hiram Johnson of California. Johnson's greatest public appeal was his close political ties to Theodore Roosevelt. When Roosevelt bolted the Republican party to become presidential candidate of the Progressive party in 1912, Johnson also bolted and became the vice-presidential nominee. When Roosevelt returned to the Republican party before the next election, Johnson also returned. If Johnson's public appeal was as great or greater than the other two, his appeal to the political leaders was minus zero. Despite his successful term in the United States Senate and his notable two terms as California governor, the pros simply saw him as a bolter. Still, in a deadlocked convention between Wood and Lowden, Johnson held the balance of power and it was not a balance that could be discounted. In a stand-off between two leading candidates, Johnson conceivably could push in.

Johnson's handicap was his absolute inflexibility on international issues: he absolutely opposed the League of Nations, he absolutely hated the British and Japanese, he absolutely thought that America should stay isolationist.

The string of other presidential possibilities included Senator Philander Knox of Pennsylvania, too conservative for most independent voters, and his health was poor; Senator James Watson of Indiana whose conservatism was even more stand-pat than Knox; Senator Henry Cabot Lodge of Massachusetts, whose position against the League of Nations was too extreme to be popular; Charles Evans Hughes, with the stigma of presidential defeat in 1916; Nicholas Murray Butler, president of Columbia University with the huge hurdle of trying to succeed another former college president; Governor Calvin Coolidge of Massachusetts who had his eastern geography working against him; Will Hays, Chairman of the Republican National Committee, rated as a strong dark horse; and an assorted handful of others including Herbert Hoover and Senator Warren Harding.

Hoover was certainly the more popular of the two. A highly successful mining engineer, Hoover made a brilliant record as head of the United States Relief Campaign for Belgium and suddenly found himself a world figure. "May his spectre penetrate to the darkest corners of the closets where kitchen cabinets plot destiny," editorialized the *Grand Rapids Herald*. And the *New York World* took more than two columns to openly endorse Hoover for the presidential nomination.

What hurt Hoover most was that he had kept his politics so quiet that neither party knew if it could claim him. In his memoirs later, Hoover confessed, "Soon after I returned from Europe, September 1919, a host of politically-amateur friends began to work for my nomination as President for the election of 1920.

"I had been so non-partisan during the war, both in word and deed, that I had no standing in either political party. In serving under a Democratic President, I had given him the full loyalties he deserved in his gigantic task. Some thought, because of this service, I had a Democratic complexion.

"They felt more so, because of a letter I had written during the Congressional campaign of 1918, urging the election of Congressmen and Senators who would support the President, irrespective of political party. I was convinced that if a majority opposed to his foreign policies were elected, his position would be weakened in the impending peace negotiations. This happened and his influence was weakened."

Hoover then described himself as "an independent progressive." He said he objected as much "to the reactionary group in the Republican party as I do to the radical group in the Democratic party." He carefully noted, however, that he had two generations of Republican blood in his veins, that he had been a registered Republican since his twenty-first birthday, and that he had ardently supported Theodore Roosevelt in 1912.

Without equivocation, Hoover declared himself fully for support of the League of Nations. He would accept the Republican presidential nomination, he then said, but only if the party would adopt "a forward-looking, liberal, constructive platform on the Treaty and on our economic issues."

Listed as low man on the presidential totem pole—especially by himself—was the freshman senator from Ohio, Warren Gamaliel Harding.

Strong Wood supporter Henry L. Stimson (who later became Hoover's Secretary of State and Franklin Roosevelt's Secretary of War) heard a political rustle in the Washington wind and warned Wood in December, 1919: "Keep your eye on Harding. The gossip I get here is that his candidacy is more dangerous than you evidently anticipated, and is being aimed directly at you."

Stimson was right. But the man doing the aiming was not Harding himself but Harding's self-appointed political manager, Harry Micajah Daugherty.

Daugherty's political theory about the Presidency in 1920 could have come out of Lippmann, who said: "The people are tired, tired of noise, tired of politics, tired of inconvenience, tired of greatness, and longing for a place where the world is quiet and where all trouble seems dead leaves, and spent waves riot in doubtful dreams of dreams. . . ."

If Lippmann was right, if 1920 was not the time for greatness, then Daugherty felt sure he had the perfect presidential candidate in Warren G. Harding.

Daugherty was a tall, broad, bald man, with one blue eye and one brown, but both keen enough to size up people quickly. Five years older than Harding, Daugherty was a small-town lawyer in Washington Court House, Ohio, and had served two terms in the state legislature.

"Harry Daugherty was what we used to call a fringe politician," said Harry F. Busey of Columbus, who knew him well. "He was the fly on the rim of the wheel. You'd always find him on the outside looking in. When a good office was to be filled, Harry would always be among those mentioned—he'd see to that—and that let him out. He kept himself surrounded by we-men, but they couldn't deliver the vote."

At the state Capitol, Daugherty was best known as a political fixer, a lobbyist whose customers included American Tobacco Company, Western Union, Armour and Company, American Gas and Electric and others.

Defeated in his race for state attorney general, defeated in his attempt to get nominated for governor, defeated twice in seeking nomination for Congress, defeated in his race for the United States Senate in 1916 (he carried only three of Ohio's eighty-eight counties), Daugherty was even defeated in his attempt to get selected as a delegate-at-large to the Republican National Convention of 1920.

A *New York Times* reporter likened Daugherty to a disillusioned boxer, punch-drunk from too many knockouts, who wisely decides that his future lies in management.

Daugherty first saw the man he managed in Richwood, Ohio, when Harding was thirty-five years old. He saw him at a shoe stand. Here is Daugherty's description of Harding then:

"As he stepped down from the stand, his legs bore out the

striking and agreeable proportions of his body; and his lightness on his feet, his erectness, his easy bearing, added to the impression of physical grace and virility. His suppleness combined with his bigness of frame, and his large, wide-set, rather glowing eyes, heavy black hair and remarkably bronzed complexion, gave him some of the handsomeness of an Indian. His courtesy, as he surrendered his seat to another customer, suggested genuine friendliness towards all mankind. His voice was noticeably resonant, masculine, warm."

Daugherty then turned to Jess Smith, his closest confidant, and said, "Gee, what a President he'd make!"

The year was 1900 and Harding was a member of the Ohio State Senate, his first try in politics.

Harding described himself and his early life in a later interview in which he said:

"I'm just an ordinary man. I haven't any false notions about my own makeup. I lack some of the fancy trimmings that some other public men can display. But I do say that no man could have come up from the stock I came from and have worked up as I have worked, farmhand, blacksmith apprentice, newsboy, reporter, editor, publisher, and so on without getting the feel of the people. It's an instinctive thing, an unconscious thing, but it's a mighty good guide in political life."

In their *Rise of American Civilization*, the Beards say of Harding, "No one loved the common people more sincerely or understood them better or had less of Wilson's penchant for the moral overstrain."

Speaking before the National Press Club, Harding himself told the story of a conversation between him and his father, who was a country doctor:

"Warren," said his father, "it's a good thing you wasn't born a gal."

"Why?" Warren asked.

"Because you'd be in a family way all the time," said his father. "You can't say no."

That story is almost the story of his life.

Harding "took program" easily. He bowed quickly and completely to the voice of authority, the voices of his friends, the voice of his political party. Add to this the voice of his wife. She was five years older than he was, previously divorced, daughter of the town's richest man. Harding had sold insurance during the day, played the tuba in the town band at night, finally saved enough money to make a down payment on a rundown newspaper in his home town of Marion, Ohio. One of its newsboys was Norman Thomas (who later ran regularly for President on the Socialist party ticket). Thomas remembered:

"Mrs. Harding in those days ran the show. She was a woman of very narrow mentality and range of interests or understanding, but of strong will, and within a certain area, of genuine kindliness. . . . She was for years nearly the whole show on the business side—Advertising manager, Circulation Manager and what-have-you . . . ."

"Her husband was the front," Thomas continued. "He was, as you know, very affable; very much of a joiner and personally popular. He was a fine small town or city booster, and wrote editorials telling how Marion, Ohio had more miles of Beria sandstone sidewalks than any town of its size in the United States. Nay, he ventured to say, in the whole world. This was his best line."

After a detailed study of the editorial content of the *Marion Star*, Dr. H. F. Alderfer of Pennsylvania State College wrote: "Harding gave very little attention to the issues of the day. Very few of his editorials in this period dealt with the subjects upon which the people were debating. Now and then he would quote the comment of one of the leading Republican journals, and endorse it, but when he himself made any excursion into the field of tariff, regulation of railroads, or money, the result was conventional, naive or superficial."

Kansas editor and Republican William Allen White wrote of Ohio editor Harding, "He has never written a line that has been quoted beyond the confines of a state."

Interviewing a Harding neighbor, a reporter quoted him:

"Warren is the best fellow in the world. He has wonderful tact. He knows how to make men work with him and how to get the best out of them. He is politically adroit. He is conscientious. He has a keen sense of his responsibilities. He has unusual common sense."

"Well," aked the reporter, "what is his defect?"

"Oh," said the man, "the only trouble with Warren is that he lacks mentality."

Another Harding neighbor described him as "the best fellow in the world to play poker with all Saturday night."

The dominant feature of Harding's personality was his easygoing amiability. Somebody said he had an actor's mouth, and knew how to use it. When he smiled, he was highly conscious of that smile. He kept eyeglasses elegantly pinned to his coat and used them mostly in gesturing. His main vanities were his personal appearance and his literary style. "Of course I can make better speeches than these," he told a friend during a campaign, "but I have to be careful."

His voice could carry far, and it had a silvery quality which he could convert into a trumpet sound to still any crowd. He had his own word for speechmaking; he said he liked to go around the state and "bloviate."

But his bloviations were mostly polished platitudes. H. L. Mencken said ". . . it reminds me of a string of wet sponges; it is so bad that a sort of grandeur creeps into it."

William G. McAdoo, then a Democratic presidential contender, also criticized Harding's speaking style: "He spoke in a big bow-bow style of oratory," said McAdoo. "His speeches left the impression of an army of pompous phrases moving over the landscape in search of an idea; sometimes these meandering words would actually capture a straggling thought and bear it triumphantly, a prisoner in their midst, until it died of servitude and overwork."

Still, the people liked it and liked him. Ohio elected him lieutenant governor in 1903; (elected governor was Myron T. Herrick, whom Harding later appointed as Ambassador to France). As presiding officer of the State Senate, Harding made friends in both parties. A reporter described his effect there as "a tranquilizer."

President Theodore Roosevelt liked him, supported him when he ran for governor in 1909 (but he didn't make it). President William Howard Taft liked him, said of him, "A man of clean life, of great force as a public speaker, and attractive in many ways." Taft picked Harding to make the nominating speech for him at the 1912 Republican National Convention. To do this, Harding had to turn on Roosevelt, vilify him as "a Benedict Arnold." But again, Harding "took program" easily.

Daugherty meanwhile had swept completely into Harding's life, managing his political campaigns, seeking the political opportunities. It was Daugherty who wired Harding to cut short a Florida vacation and see him in Columbus. Harding came quickly. Daugherty outlined the political scene in the state then in regard to the upcoming race for the United States Senate in 1914 and urged that Harding run, that his chances looked good. Harding hesitated. He had lost two attempts at the governorship, and he didn't like to lose at anything, even a friendly game of billiards. Daugherty continued to press him. Harding finally agreed.

Something Harding said often in his campaigning, something he really believed in, and something people liked to hear was:

"What is the greatest thing in life, my countrymen? Happiness. And there is more happiness in the American village than in any other place on the face of the earth."

But during this particular campaign, the weather was bad, the travel tiring, and the happiness minimal. In fact, after two weeks of stump-speaking, a discouraged Harding told Daugherty he planned to quit the race because he knew he could not win.

Daugherty simply told him, "Oh, go out and get your shoes shined, get your clothes pressed, get a good meal and take a little rest."

Daugherty said Harding did just that, then came back to campaign, and win.

Harding was happiest as a Senator, although his secretary, George

BALLOTS & BANDWAGONS

B. Christian, Jr., later analyzed it more specifically: "Harding didn't like being a Senator; he liked being in the Senate."

"I like the fraternity of this body," he once told his fellow Senators.

The feeling was mutual.

His Senate record, however, was on the sorry side. One cynic sadly observed, "Perhaps his looks did him a disservice—nobody could be as great a Senator as Harding looked." *New York Times* editor, Charles Miller, took a tougher line, labeled Harding "an undistinguished and undistinguishable unit in the ruck of Republican Senators." And another critic called him "negligent, negligible, almost null."

As the Senate's "ranking slacker" Harding answered less than half of the 245 roll calls, failed to vote on 35 per cent of the motions. Nobody ever heard of a "Harding bill" or a "Harding amendment." Of the 134 bills he did introduce while in the Senate, 122 were better known as "private measures"—86 of them pension bills and 17 for relief of various Ohio financial and commercial institutions. His few public bills included an act to grant discarded rifles to the sons of veterans, encourage the teaching of Spanish, authorize the loan of Army tents for the relief of the postwar housing shortage, and a suggested change in the law protecting fur-bearing animals in Alaska.

On all controversial questions—whether it was prohibition or women's suffrage—Harding seesawed while he watched the way of the political wind. Interviewed on the women's suffrage question in November, 1915, Harding said he would leave the question to his party. Two months later, he said, "I am not sure how I will vote, but I think I will vote against suffrage. I don't see how I can vote for suffrage and against prohibition."

In other later interviews, he zigzagged twice again, finally voted for the suffrage amendment, along with the rest of the Republican party, (and voted for prohibition).

Harding friends have noted that Harding could hardly have initiated an important bill since the Democrats were in control of the Senate. They also claim that Harding made some impressive Senate speeches particularly on the event of America's entry into the World War. And they point out that it was Harding who led the attempt, however unsuccessful, to pressure President Wilson to permit Theodore Roosevelt to lead an army division into France.

Harding turned on Roosevelt when Roosevelt turned on Taft; rooted for Roosevelt when Roosevelt returned to the party. "Be for Roosevelt if you must; I don't care a rap," he told the Ohio State Convention in 1912. "But I warn you that you are urging your Titanic full speed on and there is ice ahead." He then called Roosevelt "utterly without conscience and truth, and the greatest faker of all time." But when Roosevelt returned to the Republicans, Harding said: "If Theodore Roosevelt would have been President, the Lusitania would never have been sunk, and we should today be living under the guarantees of peace."

With Daugherty's help, Harding acted as Temporary Chairman of the 1916 Republican Convention, made the keynote speech and Will Hays remembered it well:

"It was important as an item in developing a national acquaintance among those who go to conventions," Hays wrote. "There is no doubt about the impression that speech made on everyone who was in that convention. I never forgot that speech."

A large number of those who saw and heard Harding make that opening speech in the 1916 convention would also be delegates to the 1920 convention.

The Daugherty dream of the Presidency for Harding must have been dwelt on often in the Harding home but the dream took on a sharper focus in the summer of 1919. The first preliminary outside approach came from the key figure of Senator Boies Penrose, the Pennsylvania boss. Penrose's private secretary, Leighton C. Taylor, later wrote about what took place on a hot afternoon when the Senator did not go to the Capitol. "He asked me to call Harding," said Taylor. "When Harding came in, Penrose said, 'Take off your coat, Senator, and sit down.' The next thing from Penrose was, 'Harding, how would you like to be President?' I don't think any-

one could have registered more surprise than Harding. He said:
'Why, Penrose, I haven't any money and I have my own troubles
in Ohio. In fact, I will be mighty glad if I can go back to the
Senate.'

"Penrose said, 'You don't need any money. I'll look after that.
You will make the McKinley type of candidate. You look the part.
You can make a front-porch campaign like McKinley's and we'll
do the rest.' "

Penrose then invited Harding to address the Manufacturer's
Association in Philadelphia. Harding's speech there disenchanted
Penrose and he said, "Harding isn't as big a man as I thought he
was. He should have talked more about tariff and not so much
about playing the cymbals in the Marion Brass Band."

Daugherty also made the direct pitch on the Presidency to
Harding about this time. Daugherty's carefully angled approach to
the reluctant Harding tied up the Ohio political situation with
Harding's upcoming race for re-election to the Senate. Harding
had said often that his highest ambition was to return to the
Senate "a position far more to my liking than the Presidency possibly could be." He saw the Senate as a place of dignity and distinction with time for plenty of friendly leisure ranging from poker
to golf and vacations in Florida.

What Daugherty emphasized, that caught Harding, was that
there was a growing rival group in Ohio politics, gaining strength
fast, and they planned to control and declare the state delegation
for Wood—who was highly popular in Ohio. If they did this, and
especially if Wood won, this group would have a critical control
later that year in selecting the state nominee for the United States
Senate, and they would hardly pick Harding—they would have
their own man.

This made sharp political sense. But Harding still hedged when
Daugherty insisted that the only way to smother this rival group
was for Harding to declare himself into the presidential race, and
the state delegation would have to declare for him as a favorite
son.

Harding hedged because he hated the turmoil of being a presidential campaigner. But, finally, he called Daugherty one night, went over to his house and the two men spent six hours in Daugherty's library reviewing all the angles.

"What would you do in my place?" Harding asked Daugherty.

"I'd go into the big circus," said Daugherty.

"And maybe lose the Senate?"

"You'll know in time to file your papers as a candidate for the Senate—if you can't win the nomination for the Presidency," said Daugherty.

"And you think I have a fighting chance?"

"I think you have the best chance."

"How do you figure it?" asked Harding.

"Neither one of the leading candidates can win," said Daugherty. "General Wood is backed by a powerful group of rich men who wish a military man in the White House. They are nervous over the social disorders following the World War. They are nervous over the growing demands of Labor. They wish to entrench themselves behind the invincible force of the bayonet and the machine gun. The scheme won't work. People are sick of war. The boys who saw it in France have begun to tell tales out of school. They hate war to a man. They'll not vote for a general. The women will vote in the next election. It will be suicide on that account to name a general. The Republican convention will not do it."

"Money is a powerful force in our primaries," said Harding.

"That's so, too, but there's not enough money in the world to buy the nomination for a man who wears epaulettes in 1920."

The two men then discussed Lowden. Daugherty said he liked him, said he would make a fine President, but he wouldn't make it because he was too rich and because he had married Pullman's daughter.

"He and Wood will fight each other to the finish," said Daugherty, "and deadlock the convention."

Harding then said that Johnson might then slip in.

"Never," said Daugherty. "They'll say he defeated Hughes in

California, and the real Republicans will never forgive him."

"Come down to brass tacks," said Harding. "Am I a big enough man for the race?"

"Don't make me laugh," said Daugherty. "The day of giants in the presidential chair is past."

Daugherty said that the great Presidents were made by the conditions of the times, that such greatness was largely an illusion of people, and that he personally agreed with the poetess who had said: "The truest greatness lies in being kind."

"To my mind," said Daugherty, "you are the man of the hour. We must name a candidate who can carry Ohio. This year of all years, our state will be the battleground. But one man has been elected President in a half century without the vote of Ohio. The national leaders know this. They must carry Ohio. Governor Cox [James Cox of Ohio] is a formidable opponent for the Democratic nomination. You are the man who can beat him. That fact will be a big thing in your favor."

Daugherty finally added, "The nation, I tell you, is sick of war. You're a man of peace, human, friendly, genial, and popular. Our strength lies in your personality, your position in a great pivotal state, and the bitter antagonism of the three leading candidates, Wood, Lowden, and Johnson."

Harding retreated to Florida to think it over.

"I found him sunning himself like a turtle on a log," said Daugherty who went down there after him, "and I pushed him into the water."

Back in the Senate, a fellow Senator reacted typically to Harding's announced race for the Presidency.

"Harding," said this Senator, "I'm a good Democrat, and so, as a disinterested observer, I can talk pretty much as I please about the Republican situation." Then he added, "I certainly do hope that the Republicans nominate you at Chicago. I'd like to see somebody in the White House whom I could go up to and slap on the back and talk with as if he were a human being."

Daugherty's plan called for national exposure, then some selected primaries. A constant objective everywhere was to keep as noncontroversial as possible. In his speech before the Ohio Society in New York, Harding presented his noncontroversial six-point program:

> To stabilize America first
> To safeguard America first
> To prosper America first
> To think of America first
> To exalt America first
> To live for and revere America first.

Expanding on his political philosophy to a reporter, Harding said: "I do not want to confess literally to being a stand-patter. I do not know what a stand-patter is in American life. But if one who sometimes elects to go back to an old and efficient method and retain it is a stand patter, then I am going to choose to be one."

Harding talked tenderly to another reporter of "the good old times when the Republican protective tariff policy filled the treasury and at the same time gave that protection to American industry which stimulated the development which made our record a matchless one in the story of the world."

Speaking in Boston, Harding amplified this thinking, saying that what our country needed was "not heroism but healing, not nostrums but normalcy, not revolution but restoration, not agitation but adjustment, not surgery but serenity, not the dramatic but the dispassionate, not experiment but equipoise, not submergence in internationality but sustainment in triumphant nationality."

The key word that later became the campaign word was: "normalcy."

Harding tried to keep out of the primaries, but Daugherty insisted on it as a necessity. Otherwise, he said, the rival Ohio groups would claim that he really wasn't a presidential candidate and would move again for Wood.

Sixteen states had adopted the presidential primary by 1920, and most leading candidates felt forced to enter the majority of them. Refusal to do so indicated a public confession of weakness. Besides it made good political sense to meet important people, create some national headlines, possibly even pick up some delegates. These were important factors especially to this crop of candidates, none of whom were nationally known, except possibly Hoover.

As the candidates edged closer to the primaries, caustic critic H. L. Mencken summed them up in his inimitable way:

"All the great patriots now engaged in edging and squirming their way towards the presidency of the Republic run true to form. This is to say they are all extremely wary, and all more or less palpable frauds. What they want, primarily, is the job; the necessary equipment of unescapable issues, immutable principles and soaring ideals can wait until it becomes more certain which way the mob will be whooping.

"Of the whole crowd at present in the ring, it is probable that only Hoover would make a respectable President. General Wood is a simple-minded old dodo with a delusion of persecution; Palmer is a political mountebank of the first water; Harding is a second-rate provincial; Johnson is allowing himself to be lost in the shuffle; Borah is steadily diminishing in size as he gets closer to the fight; Gerard and the rest are simply bad jokes. Only Hoover stands out as a man of any genuine sense or dignity. He lacks an intelligible platform and is even without a definite party but he at least shows a strong personality, and a great deal of elemental competence. But can he be elected? I doubt it."

Mencken added that he saw no emotional push in Wood's candidacy although "one somehow warms to the old boy." Mencken saw Johnson as shrewd and far-reaching "with a very accurate understanding of the popular mind . . . and a conscience with as much stretch in it as a wad of chewing gum. From Roosevelt, he borrowed an excellent political formula, to wit, first scare Wall Street half to death by stirring up the boobery, and then make convenient terms behind the door. Johnson is almost the ideal candidate—an accomplished boob-bumper, full of sough and gush of the tin-horn messiah, and yet safely practical. He will give a good show if he is elected."

Harding's first test came in the Ohio primary, and he campaigned hard, spoke everywhere. He talked in terms that people understood. His favorite theme went like this:

"If I had a policy to put over," he said, "I should go about it this way. You all know the town meeting . . . now if I had a program that I wanted to have adopted by a town meeting, I should go to the three or four most influential men in my community. I should talk it out with them. I should make concessions to them until I had got them to agree with me. Then I should go into the town meeting feeling perfectly confident that my plan would go through. Well, it's the same in a nation as in the town meeting, or the whole world, if you will. I should always go first to the three or four leading men."

Or he would tell them: "It will help if we have a revival of religion . . . I don't think any government can be just if it does not somehow have a contact with the Omnipotent God."

When he said all this, again and again, his neighbors knew his deep sincerity. Sometimes he would stretch his images and often his phrases seemed too flowery. The *Cleveland Plain Dealer* once analyzed Harding's campaign speeches: "A speech by Mr. Harding knows neither time nor circumstance. It would have been applicable at the time of Benjamin Harrison or James G. Blaine as to that of Theodore Roosevelt and Woodrow Wilson. It has not the slightest relation to current problems. . . . No one need doubt his sincerity, for he himself is a relic of the good old days which were assuredly good to the Republican beneficiaries. Time and conditions change, but not Harding."

Harding could catch a crowd with simple honesty. Once when he stumbled over a sentence in a speech, he frankly told the crowd, "Well, I never saw this before. I didn't write this speech and I don't believe what I just read."

He still almost lost Ohio. His margin over Wood was less than 15,000 votes and meant a split delegation, thirty-nine for Harding and nine for Wood. (Lowden, who contested in fewer primaries, and concentrated on speeches in large cities of pivotal states, also came to the convention with a split delegation from his home state.)

Daugherty described Harding's face after the primary results as "a yard long." And Harding told Daugherty, "It looks like we're done for."

Daugherty talked him out of it, then discussed the upcoming Indiana primary. "There is a law in Indiana," Daugherty told Harding, "that delegates elected to a convention by a clear majority must vote for their candidate until he releases them. We can split Indiana's vote, prevent Wood from getting a majority, and release his delegates in time to vote for you. Senator New will be with us."

Indiana's Senator Harry New, who had served as Chairman of the Republican National Committee a dozen years before, did campaign hard for Harding, and it was at New's house that Harding heard the primary results.

As the results poured in, it became increasingly obvious that Harding would not get a single Indiana delegate. Harding finally put in a telephone call to Daugherty, but his wife, better known as the Duchess, raced swiftly across the living room, snatched the phone from him, and yelled into it, "This is Mrs. Harding, yes, Mrs. Harding. You tell Harry Daugherty that we're in this fight until hell freezes over." She then slammed the receiver and somebody in the room whistled and somebody else laughed and Harding silently took a seat with an utter look of resignation. Afterwards one of the guests told Mr. New, "It looks as if the Senator were in the race to stay." And New said, "You mean, Mrs. Harding is."

Daugherty, however, painted a different picture of Mrs. Harding's interest in the Presidency. At one time, Daugherty quoted her as saying, "We are happy in our home in Washington. He likes the Senate. I like being a Senator's wife. No strain. No pressure.

No nerve-wracking anxieties. We have charming friends. Warren is making a fine record. He can stay here as long as he likes."

"And you have no desire to become the First Lady of the Land?" Daugherty insisted he asked her.

"None," she said. "I have seen the inside of the White House. I have a vivid picture of President Wilson harried and beaten by the cares of the office. The office is killing him as if he'd been stabbed at his desk."

"She paused again and looked at me," Daugherty said, then told him, "I've a presentiment against this thing. Don't ask him to run."

The presentiment came from a crystal-gazer in Washington named Madame Marcia, who described herself as a "president-maker and president-ruler." Mrs. Harding went to see her, along with the wives of three other Senators. For Mrs. Harding, supposedly unknown to her, Madame Marcia rather remarkably described her husband as "sympathetic, kindly, intuitive, free of promises and trustful of friends, enthusiastic, impulsive, perplexed over financial affairs. Many clandestine love affairs; inclined to recurrent moods of melancholia."

Madame Marcia then reported that she also saw disaster hovering over the Presidency of "a man born on November 2, 1865 at 2 P.M."

That, of course, was Harding's birth date. As for the "clandestine love affairs," one later became a whispering campaign issue.

The story of what Mrs. Harding really wanted for her husband must be twisted somewhere between the presentiment story, which has been checked out, and the story at the New home, which happened in front of many other people as Ralph V. Sollitt testified. It must be twisted within Mrs. Harding herself because Daugherty elsewhere reported her support against Harding's reluctance by saying, "the two of us backed him against the wall, and made him stick."

Certainly, Daugherty needed everybody's support to make Harding stick, especially after the Montana primary. Out of 40,000 votes cast there, Harding received only 723.

BALLOTS & BANDWAGONS

But then came Harding's big break, one of those unpredictables in politics that can catapult a campaign in unrealized directions.

Early in the spring of 1920, Senator Hiram Johnson made a campaign speech in which he charged his two wealthy opponents Lowden and Wood with pouring enormous sums of money into their primary campaigns.

Daugherty claims he had somebody in Washington whisper these facts into Senator Borah's ear and demand a Senate investigation. Whether or not this is true, it is a fact that Louis Siebold, political reporter for the New York World, saw a report of Johnson's speech, suggested a follow-up story to his editor, Charles Lincoln, who then called Senator Borah about the possibility of a Congressional inquiry.

"The idea is all right," Borah told Lincoln, "but I'd have to have something more specific to go on before I could move an investigation."

Siebold then told Lincoln, "Tell him I'll get it for him."

That began it. Siebold then talked to John King, disgruntled because he had been supplanted as Wood's campaign manager. King gave Siebold a list of Wood "fat cats" and the New York World splashed it on their front page this way:

> Millionaire oil-man E. L. Doheny
> Millionaire metal-man Ambrose Monel
> Millionaire utilities-man H. M. Byllesby
> Millionaire copper-man William Boyce Thompson
> Millionaire steel-man and banker Dan R. Hanna
> Millionaire sports promoter E. E. Smathers
> Millionaire grocer A. A. Sprague.

In their story, the World claimed that these men were supposed to raise a million dollars for Wood and that Colonel William Cooper Procter of Ivory Soap had "loaned" $710,000 to the Wood cause, was prepared to double it, if needed.

Borah hardly was nonpartisan in the matter. He had refused to seek the Temporary or Permanent Chairmanship of the convention because he openly said he planned to fight Wood's nomination. More than that, Borah was the close friend and campaign consultant of Governor Johnson. When the *World* story broke, Johnson came to Washington to talk it over with Borah, and the next day Borah presented his resolution to the Senate, asking for an investigation of precampaign expenditures of various presidential candidates.

With the convention only several weeks away, the Senate passed the Borah resolution in May, and empowered a subcommittee on Privileges and Elections to carry on an immediate investigation. Chairman of the subcommittee was Iowa's Senator Kenyon and it had two Democrats and three Republicans (two for Wood and one for Harding). From its preliminary makeup, the subcommittee seemed stacked against Lowden.

Disclosures still worried the Wood men. Counting the $710,000 from Colonel Procter, Wood listed campaign funds of almost two million dollars up to that time. Wood's eastern manager, Congressman Norman Gould warned other Wood leaders that their own money might beat them. "You can't wave a thousand dollar bill like a flag," he said. And, after the committee report, a reporter checked a Wood lieutenant who admitted to him that southern delegates, from hopelessly Democratic states, whose convention vote still counted equally, were priced as high as $5,000 each, and "I have seen the checks going over the desk myself."

However badly these disclosures damaged Wood, they crippled Lowden. Although Lowden's campaign total was a huge $414,984, it was still small compared to Wood's. But the crippling came from two checks to Missouri delegates, two unexplained checks for $2,500 each.

Testifying for Lowden, Louis Emmerson accounted for $38,000 spent in Missouri, but could not account for these two checks found in his books. Called to testify, one of the delegates admitted he had said he would refund the money if he did not vote for Lowden at the convention. The inference was that $5,000 had bought two votes. Lowden maintained complete ignorance and innocence of the matter, but the dirt stuck and the mud smeared.

Johnson listed his expenses as $194,393; Hoover, $173,542; and Harding, $113,000. Of this Harding total, Wall Street financier Harry Payne Whitney supplied $7,500, oilman Harry Sinclair an equal sum, and Harding himself had put up $1,000. Daugherty testified that he had contributed $50,000 of his money to the Harding cause, "every cent I had in the world."

Commenting afterwards on his testimony, Daugherty said, "I answered all questions with great caution and made no bitter accusations against our opponents. In fact, I refused to make any accusations whatever."

He didn't have to—everybody else did. Hearst's *Chicago Herald and Examiner*, backing Johnson, headlined: "YOU DON'T HAVE TO HIRE 'EM FOR HIRAM."

The ripples widened. Leading Republican Edward Foristel, scheduled to nominate Lowden, publicly disassociated himself from him, and announced that he would support Senator Philander Knox.

Wood still had the greatest strength in delegates, and the popular *Literary Digest* poll ranked him first. The poll:

	First Choice	Second Choice
Wood	277,486	186,946
Johnson	263,087	161,670
Hoover	240,468	120,430
Lowden	120,391	129,992
Hughes	54,719	88,787
Harding	36,795	42,212
Coolidge	33,621	67,041
Taft	32,740	62,871

In the popular poll vote, Wood even beat Harding in his home state of Ohio. Even if the poll's figures were open to question, there was little doubt about Harding's low hopes.

Betting odds quoted even money on Johnson, eight to five on Wood, seven to five on Lowden, and only one to five on Harding. Harding came in last in every primary he had entered.

So despairing was Harding a month before the convention, after the disastrous Indiana primary, that he told Wisconsin Senator Irvine L. Lenroot that "he considered himself entirely out of the race and was glad of it." The two men were heading for the Home Market Club in Boston as featured speakers. In his speech, Harding predicted that Governor Coolidge of Massachusetts might get the nomination, "but that he himself had no expectation of receiving it."

Compared to whole floors rented by Wood and Lowden for Washington, D.C., headquarters, Daugherty still kept only two dingy rooms and an early realistic view of his possibilities. Long before the convention, he told reporter Mark Sullivan:

"I won't try to fool you; you can see what we've got here, it's only a shoestring. I'll tell you, in confidence, what's in my mind. All I'm doing is getting in touch with the leaders and delegates who are for Wood and Lowden, being friendly with them. When the convention comes, those two armies will battle each other to a standstill. When both realize they can't win, when they're tired and hot and sweaty and discouraged, both the armies will remember me and this little headquarters. They'll be like soldiers after a battle who recall a shady spring along a country road, where they got a drink as they marched to the front. When they remember me that way, maybe both sides will turn to Harding—I don't know —it's just a chance."

Weeks later, after the campaign revelations, Daugherty made a more startling, dramatic, and prophetic prediction to reporters:

"Well, there will be no nomination on the early ballots. After the other candidates have failed, after they have gone their limit, the leaders worn out and wishing to do the very best thing, will get together in some hotel about 2:11 in the morning. Some fifteen men, bleary-eyed with lack of sleep, and perspiring profusely with the excessive heat, will sit down around the big table. I will be with them and present the name of Senator Harding."

"Harding will be selected," Daugherty continued, "Because he fits in perfectly with every need of the party and nation. He is the logical choice, and the leaders will determine to throw their support to him."

This was the printed quote in the *New York Times*, but reporter Charles D. Hilles, who was also there during the prophecy, insists that the interview did not quite come out that way. Daugherty, according to Hilles, was quickly packing his bags in his room at New York's Waldorf Astoria when the two reporters arrived. Daugherty said he was sorry but had no time for an interview. One reporter persisted, but Daugherty said little, and started for the elevator. The reporter followed, tried to provoke him with questions, saying that since Daugherty didn't have the delegates to put over Harding, he supposed Daugherty planned to do it by manipulation, probably in some back room of a convention hotel by a small group of political managers reduced to pulp "by the inevitable vigil and travail," and that he presumed the confreres would be expected to surrender at 2:00 A.M. in a smoke-filled room." Daugherty replied, "Make it 2:11."

Whatever was really said, and no matter how freely Daugherty predicted, the horizon of the Harding cause seemed indeed remote. Even his friendly fellow Senators seriously doubted the Harding hope.

A group of these Senators, sometime shortly before the convention, gathered at the home of Senator Jonathan Bourne in Washington for a game of poker. Sitting in his chair, Harding fell asleep and Bourne gave him a quizzical look, and another Senator caught it as an accusation and answered it, saying, "Anyhow, you could talk to him, he would 'go along.'" As a President, he might sleep on the job, but he would go along with the wishes of his friends.

On the other hand, Hoover had an unquestioned popularity, especially with the American people. This showed clearly in the California primary where he ran against the strongly entrenched Johnson mainly on the League of Nations issue. Without making a single speech or statement, Hoover had 210,000 votes to Johnson's 370,000.

Hoover's organization, however, was largely amateurish, his supporting delegates thinly scattered, his principal support coming from the press.

"We're not going to make the mistake this time that we made four years ago," said Senator Penrose of Pennsylvania. "Our fellows are going to put in a man who will listen."

Four years before, Republicans had picked Charles Evans Hughes as their presidential nominee and he had insisted on running his own campaign in his own way on his own issues.

Penrose also predicted that the Senators would control this convention since they controlled some 400 of the 984 delegates.

Few Senators could match Harding's willingness "to listen." His record of party regularity was 100 per cent. Senator Lodge was so confident of Harding's consistent party line support that he even put him on his Foreign Relations Committee to insure his committee vote against our admission to the League of Nations.

Harding himself had clearly spelled out his political philosophy in specifics:

"Believing as I do in political parties and governments through political parties," he said, "I had rather that the party to which I belong should, in its conferences, make a declaration than to assume a leadership or take an individual position on the question."

His closest friends insisted Harding deeply wanted no part of the Presidency. Senator Joseph France of Maryland remembered such a conversation when Harding repeated he would rather be senator from Ohio than anything else in the world and "I knew he was sincere."

Close friend Senator Harry S. New of Indiana agreed, ". . . He did not want to be President . . . but his friends having prevailed on him to permit the use of his name, he most reluctantly withheld withdrawing it. Of course . . . he did stand up and fight a little because he was goaded into doing so."

"I was on the train with Mr. and Mrs. Harding, Justice of the Supreme Court George H. Sutherland, and Senator Frank Brandegee when they went from Washington to the convention in

Chicago," said Senator Charles Curtis of Kansas (who later became Vice-President under Hoover). "Harding said he had no show for the nomination, was extremely reluctant to be in it; said he felt like withdrawing even if his withdrawal left Daugherty on the limb."

Presidency or no Presidency, Harding had no intention of sacrificing his secure Senate seat for the glimmer of a Daugherty dream.

Years later, George B. Harris, a Harding aide, revealed how strongly Harding felt about it:

"On Thursday evening of the week of the Chicago convention in 1920, at the request of Senator Harding, I left Chicago for Ohio, bringing with me a declaration of candidacy for the office of United States Senator. My instructions from him were to go to the Deshler Hotel, be there the evening of Friday, which was the last day for filing such declaration, and await instructions from him. He called me between eight and nine o'clock and directed me to file the declaration. I did before midnight. At the same time, I paid the filing fee. Why this does not appear on the records of the Secretary of State, I am of course unable to state, but the information above set forth is correct."

Daugherty meanwhile moved ahead at the prescribed speed with his intended tactic. This tactic was best described with the phrase: don't get anybody mad.

Using the precision of technical terminology, political scientists have analyzed that alliances at political conventions come through the presence of shared goals such as issues, group affinities, and party regularity; attractions and repulsions of candidate personality and bargaining considerations; sanctions with its prospects of reward and dangers of reprisals.

Parts and pieces of all these textbook axioms cropped up in the course of the convention for Daugherty:

The shared goal:

"General Wood must be beaten first and Lowden's the man to beat him," said Lowden manager Louis Emmerson to Daugherty.

"Agreed," said Daugherty. "We'll form an alliance then to first beat Wood . . . we can't allow Harding's vote to be too small, but we'll loan you every vote we can until you pass Wood. The minute you do this, Wood is out of the race and all friendship on the floor ceases between us. You understand that?"

Attractions and repulsions of candidate personality:

Chicago Mayor and political boss William Hale Thompson hated Illinois Governor Lowden who refused to cater to him. Because of this hate, Thompson had split the Illinois delegation and held twenty-one delegate votes. Thompson tentatively approached Daugherty on a deal. To accept these votes, Daugherty would counter his prime tactic of not getting anybody mad at him, endanger his preliminary deal with Lowden to beat Wood. Daugherty side-stepped the Thompson offer but parted friends by saying, "I'll tell you what I'll do. I'll take off your hands the expensive rooms you've engaged in the Congress Hotel. I need them for my women's headquarters."

Prospects of reward:

Jake Hamon, "a combination of fat and force," was an Oklahoma oilman worth an estimated $20 million, much of which he made getting oil properties cheap from gullible Indians. A public benefactor to his hometown, Hamon was also a drunkard and a lecher; (he was finally killed by his eighteen-year-old mistress). But most importantly, Hamon and his money controlled a block of fifty delegates, and Hamon was for Hamon. He had offered to supply enough political and financial support to insure Wood's nomination in return for a Cabinet job and a free hand on oil leases, and Wood had thrown him out.

Daugherty wasn't that finicky. "We kept our eyes on Jake Hamon," he wrote. "He had more influence among the delegates than any other man in the convention."

Daugherty arranged to meet Hamon through a mutual friend, circus man John Ringling, impressed him slightly by duplicating his breakfast order of three eggs with plenty of ham, then impressed him more by talking tough political turkey.

BALLOTS & BANDWAGONS

Afterward Hamon let it be known that he expected to be made Secretary of the Interior if Harding won, that he had spent $25,000 to pay for Harding's Chicago hotel bill, or as he put it, "I signed the check which enabled Warren Harding to run for President." Hamon also boasted that he had spent $105,000 to elect a dutiful delegation from Oklahoma and was ready to spend a million dollars that year to bring Oklahoma into the Republican column.

Though Hamon and Daugherty were both single-minded in their ambition for power, they were hardly of a cut and kind—Hamon cared more for the cash, and Daugherty cared more for the control of the game.

The deal set was that if Lowden couldn't win, and if Harding seemed to have a chance, Hamon would switch to Harding.

This was Daugherty's fifth national convention, and he made the fullest use of past friendships. Still, of the 1,031 delegates seated (having either a full vote or a fraction), only 232 had been delegates or alternates at the previous convention, and only 102 had been delegates in 1912. This fact, plus the obvious lack of a single hard hand like Mark Hanna, resulted in many divided delegations. Because of all this, there was considerable editorial comment that here was a convention comparatively free from boss control.

It certainly looked like that. And if it wasn't, then there might have been no Daugherty and no Harding.

Daugherty kept his sell soft but persistent. To everybody he stressed that Ohio was pivotal. In ten of the seventeen Republican national conventions, Ohio men had been presidential nominees. Hayes, Garfield, McKinley (twice), and Taft actually lived in Ohio at the time of nomination; Grant and Harrison, each nominated twice, had come from Ohio. Four of the vice-presidential nominees were also Ohio men. Senator C. C. Dill said it more flatly, "Every Republican President who has entered the White House by the votes of the people since the Civil War has come directly from Ohio or been born in Ohio."

Daugherty's solicitation from delegates was simply for second and third choice votes. His main hope was that nobody really disliked Harding, nobody identified him with any specific cause or group. Here at the convention, Harding's inconspicuous record as a freshman Senator seemed to work for him rather than against him. But the Wall Street odds on Harding's chances still slipped against him eight to one (the same as Coolidge).

Holding firmly to his small block of southern delegates, Daugherty went to work to create "a sweet atmosphere" for his candidate.

He had brought in the Columbus Glee Club, a nationally-known group of singers, some seventy-five men in full evening dress, and sent them to serenade the headquarters of every other candidate. The group made no appeals for Harding, sang no Harding campaign songs and "their good humor and fine singing made a hit wherever they appeared."

He started with a staff of some five-hundred people recruited from Harding headquarters in Columbus, Washington, D.C., New York, and Indianapolis "and there wasn't a traitor among them." However, they did put "one or more of our representatives into the headquarters of every rival."

Every Harding worker was instructed to "smile, keep in good humor and make no enemies." As the staff grew, they met every train, shook hands with every incoming delegate they could find, got the addresses and room numbers of all of them, and made follow-up appointments to see them later.

"We had, I believe," said Daugherty, "the most complete poll of delegates from the first choice to the fourth."

Daugherty claimed that Harding's hometown of Marion and his hometown of Columbus provided most of the money to pay for the sixty rooms at the Harding headquarters in the Congress Hotel. The group also took over an assembly room, and part of the first floor arranged with movable partitions for $750 a day and the fresh cash from Hamon certainly helped.

National Committeeman R. B. Creager of Texas turned over his two-room suite at the Auditorium Hotel for Harding conferences

208

BALLOTS & BANDWAGONS

because the Auditorium Hotel had a convenient underground passage connecting it to the Congress. The Harding family and friends stayed at the nearby La Salle Hotel.

But if the Harding people had sufficient space, they did not seem to attract sufficient customers.

A *New York World* reporter found the Harding headquarters in the Florentine Room of the Congress Hotel "a vast vacancy into which had been thrown a mass of decorations." In an early check on campaign activity there, the same reporter noted "the conspicuous features were three young couples, apparently here on their honeymoon and apparently thinking of other things than the high cost of living. As a spoon-room, it was a success."

The Wood and Lowden headquarters were much more successful in attracting crowds. The so-called Wood "stable" was the opulent Elizabethan Room at the Congress with eight-foot partitions at the entrance featuring an impressive suit of armor with the sign, "LEONARD WOOD FOR PRESIDENT" and a host of pretty girls handing out red and green turkey feathers, symbols of allegiance to Wood. The Wood staff even prepared a daily newspaper for the delegates.

Lowden also had his headquarters at the Congress, in the $1,000 a day Gold Room. There was a Young Men's Lowden Club, the Lowden Women's Hospitality Room (where corsages of sweet peas and roses were given to delegates's wives), a Lowden Center at the Hamilton Club, and there were also Lowden cigars, Lowden arm bands, Lowden buttons, plus the usual badges, banners, stickers for cars, and two bands to make Lowden music.

Competing with Harding headquarters as the loneliest rooms in the convention were the headquarters of Nicholas Murray Butler and Calvin Coolidge.

As the convention host, as well as a leading candidate, Lowden was given a small psychological edge by many. The big preconvention question concerned the second choice strength once the favorite sons dropped out. This was also one convention that broke precedent because the coyness of the candidates had completely disappeared. They no longer waited at home next to their long distance telephones—they were all present, and working hard for themselves.

Then it began. The seventeenth Republican National Convention opened on Tuesday, June 8, with a prayer by a Kentucky Episcopal bishop asking for insight so that the delegates could make "a wise choice." Everybody sang "The Star-Spangled Banner" and convention cheerleader Albert Edmund Brown tried to pep things up by asking the crowd, "Now please give three cheers and a tiger for the greatest country on earth, the United States of America. Hurrah! Hurrah! Hurrah for the United States! Tiger!"

Republican National Committee Chairman Will H. Hays who then opened the convention, spoke from a point of considerable prestige. For the past two years, he had done such a first-class job of restoring Republican party power at a local level, that there was a considerable undercurrent that Hays himself might either be the candidate, or make him. No less a person than former President Taft charged that there was "a serious effort to prevent Harding's nomination by 'bitter-ender' Senators, that the candidate who was to be sprung on the convention to head off Harding was Chairman Hays."

Aside from Daugherty, Taft was a lonely eminence in this hope for Harding and the fear for his future. Anyway, to put a quietus on this Taft rumor, Hays announced, "In Indiana, we have a tradition that no man buys at his own auction." And, since it was no secret that Hays was a close friend of Colonel Procter, and that this therefore might mean Hays' support for Wood, Hays also publicly said, his job was "to elect, not select the candidate."

Later it was also revealed that Hays had handed Senator Lodge a strong letter of declination to be read to the convention if any attempt was made to put his name in nomination. This did not stop Hays' friends from pursuing their own private campaign for him and from proudly promoting his friendship with Theodore Roosevelt. The morning after Roosevelt died in his sleep, a note was found at his bedside: "Hays—see him; he must go to Washington for ten days; see Senate and House; prevent split on domestic policies."

But, at this convention, Hays moved in a different direction from the Roosevelt memory when he told the delegates, "There will be no bolt from this convention." (Applause was loud and prolonged.)

Unanimously elected Temporary Chairman was white-haired, goateed, Republican elder statesman, Senator Henry Cabot Lodge who brought with him, in his keynote speech, his unabated bitterness against President Woodrow Wilson. ". . . Mr. Wilson and his dynasty, his heirs and assigns," said Lodge, "or anybody that is his, anybody who with bent knee has served his purposes, must be driven from all control, from all influence upon the government of the United States. They must be driven from office and power not because they are Democrats but because Mr. Wilson stands for a theory of administration and government which is not American."

Lodge continued: "We must be now and forever for Americanism and Nationalism and against Internationalism."

When reporter Talcott Williams asked Penrose in Pennsylvania to define the term "Americanism," Penrose replied, "Damned if I know, but you will find it a damn good issue to get votes in an election."

But the New York Evening Post called the Lodge speech "a hymn of hate." And a Boston correspondent wired his newspaper, "Senator Lodge has made the issue of the coming campaign and it can be summed up in one word—Wilson."

Since the speech was the sole message of the convention, many felt it was disappointing, "the bromidic uninspired utterance of a cynic." But at the convention itself, the delegates all rose to give three cheers for this man who had attended every Republican convention since Blaine was nominated in 1884—three cheers for Lodge and the Grand Old Party.

With the keynote address completed, and the committees appointed, the first day's work was done and the Secretary of the

Convention announced that the mayor's entertainment committee would have 1,000 automobiles outside the Coliseum to take delegates for a ride to the stockyards for lunch.

Maneuvering for votes that evening had two inhibiting factors: not enough liquor and too many women. Commenting on the attempted enforcement of the prohibition amendment, newsman H. L. Mencken wrote, "How could you wring anything properly describable as enthusiasm out of delegates whose carburetors were filled with lake water?"

The growing presence of women delegates, seen everywhere, was simply because this was to be the first presidential election in which all women in the country could vote. The Nineteenth Amendment granting women suffrage needed only one more state to ratify it into law. (Tennessee did it that summer.) Political leaders therefore bent as far back as they could in giving women proper representation as delegates and alternates.

On the convention's second day, the Credentials Committee reported its recommendations on contested cases. The story behind the simple naming of names was that eighty-eight of the selected delegates were for Lowden, thirty-four for Wood and seven for Johnson. According to one report, this was part of a planned build-up for Lowden—who had the most support on the committee.

Once the permanent roll of delegates was set, Lodge was made Permanent Chairman, and told the delegates, "The best way and I think the most practical way to show my gratitude is to tell you that there will be no speech by the Permanent Chairman."

Adjournment came shortly after noon, but Chicago was having an insufferable heat wave and everybody was happy to call it quits for the day.

The ones who couldn't call it quits were the small group sweating out the League of Nations plank of the platform. One of them was William Allen White of Kansas, who wrote about it: "There were a dozen of us active and determined in the Committee who favored the League of Nations covenant as it was amended by the reservationists—tried all sorts of formulas, some frankly compro-

mising phrases, others slick and greasy which might get by. But
Borah's eye caught our subterfuges and finally we asked Senator
Lodge to take the matter up with Elihu Root, who was sailing for
Europe.

"Root was an internationalist; but he realized that the problem
before him was to get any formula into the Republican platform
that would not close the door absolutely to negotiations to join the
League. He sent back a plank. It was fearfully and wonderfully
made. It meant nothing except that it frankly did mean nothing,
and we accepted it. It was that, or defeat on the floor."

On domestic issues, Borah joined the White group to "slip into
the platform five demands of the National League of Women
Voters, most of which have been granted. But we were over-
whelmed on most of our suggested planks," said White, and
added, "For two whole nights and a day and parts of two other
days, we worked on the platform."

The new involvement of women delegates caused a fresh concentration of interviews with the various wives of candidates. One
of them was Mrs. Harding, who said, "You know, my husband
ought to win this fight. He has a winning way about him that has
always disarmed enmity. He can differ sharply with a man—but
always without offending him."

Asked by the reporter whether she thought Hiram Johnson
would bolt the convention if he wasn't nominated, she said, "Of
course not. I know Senator Johnson well. He is a fine fellow,
though he does make a great noise at times. His bark is much
worse than his bite. He's just trying to scare the delegates into
voting for him."

And, in another interview, Mrs. Harding said, "I can't see why
anybody should want to be President during the next four years."

Johnson's position of power was that he had enough votes to
turn the nomination to either of the two leading candidates—even
though he might not be able to pull it off for himself. Activity
in the Johnson area therefore reached an increasing frenzy of
maneuver.

Senator Joseph Frelinghuysen of New Jersey approached Wood along with Harold Ickes (who later became Secretary of the Interior for President Franklin D. Roosevelt). Frelinghuysen suggested a Wood-Johnson ticket.

"He threw us out of the room," said Frelinghuysen.

Senator Boies Penrose, so seriously ill that he couldn't come to the convention, had a private telephone and telegraph wire installed from his bedside to his Congress Hotel headquarters. Penrose contact man was John King of Connecticut.

Penrose, who had been disenchanted with Harding, personally favored Senator James Watson of Indiana, but saw small hope of putting him over. He then switched to his own man, Senator Philander Knox of Pennsylvania, discussed this some months before with New York boss William Barnes, but fell ill before he could follow it up.

From his sickbed, Penrose sent King a message: "Tell Johnson that the ideal ticket is Philander Knox for President and Hiram Johnson for Vice-President. Tell Johnson, too, that Knox is a very sick man."

Johnson had a curt answer of dismissal for King: "You would put a heart-beat between me and the White House?"

The third day's morning session at the convention featured a report from the Resolutions Committee that they had agreed upon a platform "including the paragraph dealing with the treaty of peace and the League of Nations" and that some of the details had to be revised before submission to the delegations. The convention then recessed.

It was now fifty hours before the nomination for the Presidency. New York banker Fred W. Allen gave a luncheon at the Blackstone Hotel that day for fourteen Republican leaders. These were the men who supposedly should have known the name of the upcoming nominee, and a guessing game was proposed—each guest to make a guess on the presidential nominee's name and deposit it with a five dollar bill into a pool. After it was all over, the money was returned. Not one of the fourteen had guessed.

The afternoon session wanted a political pep talk and yelled for their old faithful, eighty-four-year-old "Uncle Joe" Cannon, and they gave him three cheers when he finally agreed. He opened his talk in dramatic Cannon fashion by holding a glass of water above his head, imitating the Statue of Liberty enlightening the world, and said, "Water brewed in the clouds and filtered through the eternal hills, I drink to your health and to that of the delegates and the alternates and guests of the Convention as well as other good Republicans elsewhere. . . ."

"Can such a country fail?" he continued. "Can such a people fail? Can the sons and grandsons and great-grandsons of those men who won our independence, under the leadership of George Washington, the men who have made and are making the great progress; can they fail? There is no such word as 'fail.' "

("Right" yelled somebody from the gallery.)

It was old oratorical style and they loved it, especially when he ended his speech and again held the glass of water high above his head and drank his toast to them, as he had originally proposed.

"Hurrah for Uncle Joe" they shouted and then sang "Long Long Trail."

Now came business, the reading of the proposed platform. The Committee on Resolutions favored cutting the public debt, advocated taxes on the wealthy, government reorganization of protective tariffs, favored collective bargaining and child labor legislation, but ignored the burning issue of Prohibition and the dangerous issue of the soldier's bonus. The watered plank on the League of Nations seemed to please almost everybody except a Wisconsin delegate. He stood up to make a minority report and one delegate said, "Why take up our time with this?"

The Wisconsin delegate said, "We are opposed to the League of Nations as a standing menace to peace."

Another delegate roared, "Tell him to hurry up and get through. We have heard enough of that."

The platform quickly approved, the convention recessed until the following morning when presidential nominations would begin.

On every campaign manager's mind was the single great political rule of the bandwagon.

The unwritten rule of the bandwagon is simply that a front runner must always keep the front runner position, always make some gain, great or slight, on each succeeding ballot. To slip back even slightly is generally fatal. And, once a bandwagon front runner gets passed by another candidate, he is almost always out. It is just about that simple and that deadly. Why?

Some political scientists such as Polsby and Wildavsky suggest that it's mainly a matter of information: since few of the delegates really know what's going on during the balloting, the reading of the votes at the end of each roll call is almost like a broadcast prediction of what will happen. A leader's loss of votes then means that a man is a loser, and nobody likes a loser—everybody wants to be with the winner.

Of course, this unwritten law primarily applies to the front runner. Those straggling behind can seesaw slightly in their votes, or stand still, but once they lead, they must always lead.

Knowing this bandwagon psychology—even though his candidate was still a dark, dark horse—Daugherty tried to arrange his small group of scattered delegates with a sense of military logistics. Of course, most of his pledged delegates would have to keep continuously with Harding, but Daugherty planned for some to go with Lowden and a few other candidates, and then to move them back into the Harding column in later ballots to show a small growing strength for Harding.

But Daugherty was no longer making predictions.

At Wood headquarters, Mark Sullivan saw Wood's manager, Frank H. Hitchcock, and asked, "Frank, do you expect Wood to gain on the first ballot tomorrow?" Hitchcock said he did, and outlined in great detail, exactly what delegates he expected from which states on the succeeding ballots.

Harding himself was deeply discouraged. The next morning, while the convention was convening for its fourth day, the nominating speeches ready to begin, Nicholas Murray Butler sat alone with Harding. "The weather was very hot," said Butler, "and he had taken off his coat and waistcoat and was fanning himself vigorously. In the course of our conversation, he said, 'I cannot afford to keep these rooms any longer; and I have sent word downstairs to say that I am giving them up this evening. This convention will never nominate me. I do not propose to go back to the Senate. I'm going to quit politics and devote myself to my newspaper.'"

Ohio State Journal reporter Jacob A. Meckstroth also interviewed Harding about that time. "He showed great mental distress," said Meckstroth. "Harding had a trick of holding his right hand to the side of his head as if to rest a tired brain. That was his posture when I saw him. Discouragement hung about him like a cloud. He was not interested in anything."

Meanwhile the parade of presidential nominations had begun. Arizona yielded to Governor Henry Allen of Kansas to nominate General Leonard Wood.

William Allen White and Henry Allen were close friends and White later told how hard Allen worked on that speech. "Henry was working on the speech day and night," said White. "He wrote at least two, and if I am not mistaken, three, speeches, which were inevitably rejected by the Wood forces. I say inevitably, because any board of political strategy supporting a candidate wants nothing forthright, no commitments. They desire circumlocutions. One of the troubles with Governor Allen's orations was that they were too eloquent.

"A story began to creep among the delegates that the reactionary forces in control of the Convention would like to nominate Allen for Vice-President to appease the Progressives; so the Wood people watched every syllable of his speech to see that he did not glow and lure the delegates. It was a funny proceeding which I watched out of the corners of my eyes from time to time as I worked in the committee room and on my stories.

"Henry and I were dear and close friends and could laugh at the tragedy of his position; temptation glittering before his eyes, the suspicion of the Wood supporters clouding every moment. . . ."

In his nominating speech, Allen told the delegates: "While other men were preaching the need of keeping out of war, he sounded the reveille that awoke a slumbering nation and made victory possible. He insisted; he *demanded*, 'We must prepare.' . . .

"We watched him go away to the point of embarkation and then at the last moment we read with consternation that his great desire to take a division to the field was not to be granted. . . ."

("And what a shame it was . . ." interrupted a voice from the gallery.)

"Some men pretend to object to the fact that he wears the uniform of his country. Since when has this uniform become an emblem of disqualification?"

Allen then described Wood as "a plain, blunt man, with blunt belief in facts, he is today the best known American."

(And somebody else bellowed, "He is not a buck-passer.")

Concluding, Allen said, "If we make a mistake today, the great party may lose its major importance to the public. . . . With full appreciation of the challenge of the hour, I present the name of the man who fits the hour—Leonard Wood."

The final mention of the candidate's name was the standard signal for the convention demonstration, this one led by the Kansas delegation carrying flags and pictures while thousands of blue and red feathers marked "WOOD" rained from the roof onto the delegates. It all lasted forty-two minutes.

Despite these few highlights, the Allen speech had not been a bell-ringer. In fact, it had fallen flat. Allen's friend White said, "It was a terrible speech, as edited down by Wood's board of strategy."

It reminded one critic of a Disraeli comment on a revised speech: ". . . so altered, remolded, remodeled, patched, cobbled, painted, veneered and varnished that at last no trace is left of the original."

Lowden's nomination came next. Again came an attempted tie-in with a Roosevelt image.

"His work as a member of Congress and as governor of a great industrial state," said William Rodenberg, "with all its complex and diversified interests stamps him as the living embodiment of the 'square deal.' ["Square Deal" had been Roosevelt's famous phrase.]

"In the crucial and critical period upon which we have now entered, the nation demands as its chief, an executive of clear brain and steady nerve," said Rodenberg, "a man of visions but not a visionary, a man of ideals but not an idealist, a man of works but not of words.

"Illinois has such a man.

"We present him to you as our candidate for President.

"We present the patriotic governor of a patriotic state, Frank Orren Lowden."

Since the length of a convention demonstration is a small tick of supposed psychological importance, it is always carefully and officially timed. The Lowden demonstration was stretched out four minutes longer than Wood's, timed at forty-six minutes. It featured a huge banner carried by the Kentucky delegation: "Every traveling man wants a business man for President—LOWDEN."

Nominating Hiram Johnson next, Charles Stetson Wheeler of California got even more dramatic: "Do you want another four years of economic chaos?" he cried out. (Voices: "No! No!")

"Do you want another four years of the Wilson family in the White House?" (Voices: "No! No!")

"If you insist that the father of the dynasty shall abdicate, do you want the people then to take up the Crown Prince?" (Laughter and Voices: "No! No!")

"If you do not, then why gamble with chance?" he went on. "I am here to say for the rank and file of the Republican Party that

> The plain Yanks
> Who fill the ranks
> That have the votes
> Are calling for the son of California!"

Wheeler then referred to Theodore Roosevelt as the "greatest American of our generation" and added that the country now needed "another great-hearted, two-fisted leader." He was then interrupted by delegates exclaiming, "No! No! Wood! Wood!"

Wheeler then shouted, "Where is the man that cried 'No.' . . . Does he know what he is talking about? . . . Theodore Roosevelt, in the presence of 15,000 of his fellow countrymen said of California's son, 'He is at the moment fit to be President of the United States.' And, on the 26th day of January, 1917, Theodore Roosevelt said of California's son these unmistakable words: 'Of all the public men in the country today, he is the one with whom I find myself most in sympathy.' "

The Johnson demonstration lasted thirty-seven minutes, and its placards announced, "AMERICA WINS IN THE FIRST ROUND" and "JOHNSON A SURE WINNER" and "HIRAM, WE WANT HIRAM." From the far galleries, facing the platform, a huge portrait of Johnson was let down over the railing, and another one displayed near the back of the platform.

In nominating Calvin Coolidge, the speaker said, "Our candidate is a man of few words, and in that respect I shall imitate him." And the woman who seconded him noted that Coolidge was born the fourth of July "and every mother thinks of him as the first Governor in America to demand the establishment of a system of maternity benefits for mothers and care for their children. . . ."

Judge Jeter C. Pritchard, a favorite son rather than a candidate, was nominated by a man who promised that "he will carry not only North Carolina, his native state, which he has carried twice before, but he will carry his own state of Tennessee, where he first saw the light."

Nicholas Murray Butler was described by his nominator as "an American to the bone. Twice he has been urged to become Republican candidate for the Mayor of New York; he has been urged twice to become Governor of New York, and twice he has declined. That is what we think of him as an executive and leader. . . ."

Hoover's nomination got some audience reaction, the greatest applause from the gallery and some sharp questions from the delegates. When Judge Nathan Miller of New York said, rhetorically, "What is the record of my candidate on the peace treaty?" a delegate queried, "Yes, what is it?" Miller answered, "I say to you that if you take the official record and lay it side by side with the platform which we have adopted, you would think they were drawn by the same author."

After Hoover's nomination, the gallery kept cheering and chanting Hoover's name until Chairman Lodge finally silenced them.

To nominate Harding, Daugherty had picked an Ohio Congressman named Frank V. Willis whose speech was described as combining "the enjoyments of oratory, grand opera and hog-calling." Another critic described it as "one of the most orotund voices in contemporary America." Willis seemed to know which sounds seemed to stir what emotions. He could give the word "glory" a ring and a rhythm that stirred souls.

The Willis speech only lasted eight minutes and its tone was the Daugherty tone of spreading sunshine, sweetness and light. Willis said, ". . . these . . . great men, any one of whom is entitled to receive the votes of the people of the United States."

Willis noted that out of seven Republican Presidents elected since Lincoln "six of them came from Ohio." He called Harding, "Ohio's second McKinley." He reaffirmed that "for fifteen years, the record of this man has been coincident and synonymous with the record of the party." He reminded the convention that Harding had been a friend of both Taft and Roosevelt. And he added, "What we want is not brilliant maneuvers, but safe and sane seamanship by a captain who knows the way, by a captain, who, as he walks the deck working with officers and men in these troublous times can say, 'Steady, boys, steady.'"

But the highlight of the Willis speech came when he leaned over the rostrum railing and said, almost confidentially, "Say boys —and girls too—why not name as the party's candidate. . . ."

Laughter was loud and spontaneous throughout the hall and

voices were heard saying, "That's right, we are all boys and girls," and "The girls are in politics as well as the boys. . . ."

Coming down from the roof on the demonstration this time were pictures of Harding, and Harding delegates stood on their chairs waving flags, giving three cheers for their candidate. The demonstration, though, was brief—only ten minutes.

Other candidates nominated included Governor William Cameron Sproul of Pennsylvania who was described as "in good health . . . physically fit . . . mixes with the people and knows their hopes and ambitions"; Senator Miles Poindexter of Washington, "no clanging militarist"; Senator Howard Sutherland of West Virginia, "In selecting a candidate for the high office of President, we should not measure his worth and fitness by the size of his state."

Most of the seconding speeches were flowing and flowery, more for the record than for the result. Each candidate had a woman speaker, insisting that her candidate would get the newly-granted votes of all the women. And each candidate had at least one speaker making some kind of identification with either the friendship, the principles, or the personality of Theodore Roosevelt.

The nominations done, the balloting began, with 492 needed to nominate.

First ballot results showed Wood with 287½; Lowden, 211½; Johnson, 133½; Sproul, 84; Butler, 69½; Harding, 65½; Coolidge, 34; Poindexter, 20; La Follette, 24; Pritchard, 21; Sutherland, 17; du Pont, 7; Hoover, 5½; Borah, 2; Warren, 1; and one delegate not voting.

Wood only added 2 votes in the second ballot and Lowden picked up the most, 48 more. Johnson also added 12½, and both Sproul and Harding lost votes. Sproul dropped 5½ and Harding lost 6½, putting him down to 59. Daugherty's carefully collected votes seemed to be dribbling away.

A voice vote denied a move to recess and the third ballot showed Wood now with a total of 303; Lowden with 282½; Johnson, 148; Sproul, 79½; and Harding losing another half of a delegate vote, down to 58½.

Again, a move to adjourn was denied, this time by a roll call vote. The fourth ballot again showed Wood edging up, now with 314½; Lowden also gaining a little, up to 289; Johnson dropping slightly to 140¼; Sproul staying firm with 79½; and Harding finally picking up again to 61½.

The situation increasingly took on the look of a deadlock. Wood had gained only 27 votes in the first four ballots, showed little second-choice strength. Lowden had picked up the most votes, 77½, but seemed to be slowing down. Johnson had added the least among the leaders, only seven extra votes. From the first to the fourth ballot, Harding had dropped four votes. No dark horse had appeared.

It was seven in the evening and Republican leaders now decided to recess and reconsider.

Senator Smoot stepped up to the platform and moved for adjournment until the next morning. Lodge quickly put the motion, "Those in favor of a motion to adjourn will signify it by saying 'Aye.'" There were a few scattered "Ayes."

"Those opposed, 'No,'" added Lodge perfunctorily.

Mark Sullivan reported there was a roar of "No's." and Lodge turned away, almost looking bored, saying, "The Ayes have it."

"As Senator Smoot left," said reporter Sullivan, "I went with him. We rode downtown together. I asked him, 'Why did you and Lodge force that adjournment?' He replied, 'Oh, there is going to be a deadlock and we'll have to work out some solution; we wanted the night to think it over.'"

William Allen White saw Harding that afternoon, described him: "His clothes were wrinkled, his soft hat was crushed awry, he had a 36-hours' beard on his dark skin, which gave him a forbidding look. His eyes were tired, as though he'd been playing too much poker with whiskey obbligato. . . . His was the weary disillusioned countenance, not heartbroken at all, but just cynically dubious of the goodness of man and the purpose of God . . . the model I saw there at the elevator door looked like the Wreck of the Hesperus."

Ill as he was back in Philadelphia, Penrose had called Wood, Wood wouldn't take the call, and so his campaign aide James L. Himrod answered. Penrose offered a deal: The Pennsylvania delegation could switch from Sproul to Wood and insure his nomination. Would Wood give "us" three cabinet members if he was nominated the next morning?

One of Wood's managers, General E. F. Drenn was in the room then and told his candidate, "Now General, one word will make you President of the United States."

Without hesitation, Wood turned to Himrod and said, "Tell Senator Penrose that I have made no promises and am making none." The military man of principle refused to play politics.

Ohio's delegation caucused that night. Nine Ohio delegates, won by Wood in the primary now tried hard to shake the whole delegation away from Harding to Wood. Harding, however, picked up some spirit from somewhere, came to the caucus, made an impassioned pitch for continued support, insisted that neither Wood nor Lowden could break the deadlock and if he could maintain his own strength, and possibly increase it a little, his chances might be bright. The delegation considered carefully and agreed to stick with Harding.

Senator Albert Beveridge wrote home to Indiana of the confusion of the delegates at that time. "The things that went on, on the inside, were perfectly amazing," he wrote. Alice Roosevelt Longworth described the situation as "wormy with politicians, riddled with intrigue." Senator Hiram Johnson later described it bitterly, "1912 was a Sunday school convention compared to this."

But the intrigue had not really started yet. However, it was soon scheduled to begin.

About 8:00 P.M. in the Blackstone Hotel lobby, ex-Senator Murray Crane of Massachusetts, delegate-at-large to every Republican convention since 1888, saw Senator Frank Kellogg of Minnesota (later Secretary of State under Coolidge). "Frank," said Crane, "you better come up tonight. We're getting this thing up for the finale."

Kellogg didn't come. His was a lifetime habit of retiring for the night punctually at 9:30 P.M., and he had no intention of breaking it that night.

But most other key Senators did come. In fact, the sight of Senators everywhere prompted Governor Beechman of Rhode Island to ask a newsman whether this was "a Republican Convention or just a Senatorial caucus."

Still the man who maneuvered the smoke-filled room was not a Senator, and barely a Republican.

His name was George Harvey and his story ranges on the remarkable.

An intense-looking man with thin hair parted almost in the middle, thick glasses and high stiff collar, Harvey was a one-time brilliant newspaperman who was Managing Editor of the New York World before he was thirty. Highly active in the Democratic party in the Cleveland days, Harvey grew close to the party's financial backers, Thomas Ryan and William Whitney. Through them, he met J. P. Morgan. Morgan had just bought Harper's Weekly and put Harvey in charge.

It was George Harvey who helped pull Woodrow Wilson from Princeton University into politics; it was George Harvey who helped persuade New Jersey political bosses to accept Wilson as their candidate for governor; and when Wilson broke with him, it was George Harvey who helped raise a $100,000 fund to organize a nationwide Speaker's Bureau to fight Wilson's proposed American membership in the League of Nations.

Now it was George Harvey—who had cast his first Republican vote only four years before—who would play a major part in helping pinpoint the Republican nominee for President.

Somebody who knew him well, described Harvey this way: "Harvey plays the game of politics according to his own rules, the underlying principle of which is audacity. He knows very well the weak spot in the armor of nearly all politicians of the old school is their assumption of superiority, a sort of mask of benignant political venerability. They dread satire; they shrink from ridicule.

A well-directed critical outburst freezes them. Such has been the Harvey method of approach. Having reduced his subject to a state of terror, he flatters them, cajoles them, and finally makes terms with them; but he always remains more or less an unstable and uncertain quantity, potentially explosive."

When Republican National Chairman Will Hays made a speech during World War I, praising the virtues of the Republican party, Harvey denounced him: "As for Mr. Hays with his insufferable clap-trap about absolute unity as a blanket under which to gather votes, while the very existence of the nation is threatened . . . the sooner he goes home and takes his damn old party with him, the better it will be for all creation."

And yet, here was Harvey, two years later, giving a small dinner party in Suite 404-6 on the thirteenth floor of the Blackstone Hotel. And who did the suite belong to? Will Hays. And who seldom made a major political move without Harvey's advice and approval? Will Hays. And who was Harvey's own personal choice for the presidential nomination? Will Hays.

Such are the strange ways and wonders of politics.

Harvey's dinner guests that night included Senator Henry Cabot Lodge, the convention chairman; Senator Frank B. Brandegee of Connecticut, and Senator Charles Curtis of Kansas.

Just before coming to dinner, Lodge talked to his friend, New York publisher Henry Stoddard. Said Stoddard, "Lodge made no concealment to me or to others that he hoped to have the deadlock ended next day, and that it would be broken with Harding." Lodge gave no details.

Brandegee was pushing no private candidate. In the Senate since 1905 and a prime mover in the Senate fight against the League of Nations, he was still at his peak of Senate power (but committed suicide a few years later because of financial difficulties).

Curtis, described as "pink, pudgy and pompous" was not only the Republican whip in the Senate, but reportedly close to oilmen Harry Sinclair, Edward Doheny, and Albert Fall. Curtis was also for Harding.

After dinner, Lodge opened the discussion by saying that, as presiding officer of the convention, he could not hold the delegates in Chicago over the weekend, and it was up to them to decide on a candidate that night.

Lodge then said that it seemed to him that Harding might be the best bet. He emphasized that the Republican party never had elected a President without Ohio's vote and that it looked increasingly as if the Democrats would nominate Governor Cox of Ohio, and it was essential to get that state's electoral vote.

Backing up Lodge, Curtis also pointed out the fact that Harding had many friends and no enemies.

Other delegates were now dropping in including such Senators as McCormick, Watson, Smoot, Calder, and Wadsworth. One of them gave his own concept of the desired candidate: "the man in the White House must not think he is bigger than the Senators." These Senators wanted a man in the White House who would seek their counsel, defer to the party leaders. "They think that the President should not send legislation to Congress to be passed, but Congress should send legislation to the President."

Now came the discussion of other potential candidates:

Harvey strongly proposed Will Hays, but most of the rest felt that Hays had too little national reputation with the voters. Charles Evans Hughes? A once-defeated candidate who hadn't listened to party elders before and couldn't be trusted to do it again. Besides, he didn't even have the support of his own New York State delegation. Senator Philander Knox? He had voted against the Eighteenth and Nineteenth amendments and that would cost too many votes. In addition, he was supposed to have a bad heart. Herbert Hoover? Wasn't he the man who wasn't sure whether he was a Republican or a Democrat, and even permitted his name to be used in Democratic primaries? A string of others were mentioned without stirring any special enthusiasm.

"It was a sort of continuous performance," wrote Senator Wadsworth afterward. "I was in and out of the room several times that night. They were like a lot of chickens with their heads off. They had no program and no definite affirmative decision was reached. If they came to any decision at all, it was a decision to let the Harding suggestion go through, the fact being that they did not have anyone else to propose."

Throughout the evening, almost all the important Republican leaders had dropped in to listen and discuss. Most energetic of the original dinner group, Curtis did most of the corralling of key delegates. Smoot of Utah stayed a long time, and he was another strong Harding man. Everybody else was tired and hot and unenthusiastic. Brandegee summed up the mood: "There ain't any first-raters this year," he said. "This ain't any 1880 or any 1904. We haven't any John Shermans or Theodore Roosevelts. We've got a lot of second-raters and Warren Harding is the best of the second-raters."

As John Morley had once put it, "Politics is the science of the second best."

What happened later that evening is a matter of high contradiction in memory and testimony.

Ohio State Journal reporter Meckstroth, who had seen Harding earlier, passed Ohio headquarters and saw Harding and Myron T. Herrick coming out arm-in-arm, both beaming and both jaunty. (Herrick had been Ohio governor when Harding was lieutenant governor.) Meckstroth could hardly believe that this was the same Harding whom he had interviewed only a few hours before, glum and gloomy.

Herrick waved at Meckstroth and said, "You can say that Senator Harding will be nominated on the first ballot tomorrow." Harding and Merrick then piled into a car and left. Meckstroth specifically looked at the time—it was just 11:00 P.M.

Senator Smoot was also reported as telling a *New York Telegram* reporter what had happened in the upstairs conference room, sometime after midnight, "We decided on Harding and he will be nominated this afternoon after we have balloted long enough to give Lowden a run for his money."

Senator Wadsworth insists however that he saw Harding a little later, perhaps about 1:00 A.M., and Harding had said, "There is no new development," and added that if he could show some gain in strength, his friends felt the convention would break its deadlock and turn to him.

Except for one man, everybody, including Daugherty, has testified that Daugherty never did go to Harvey's room during that meeting. The exception was a fat, tall, pigeon-toed man named Jess Smith, Daugherty's closest confidant, also known as "Harry Daugherty's bumper," who long afterward testified under oath before a Senate Investigating Committee that Daugherty went to Harvey's room about 2:00 A.M. to set the final deal that gave Harding the nomination.

What is not in question is that Harvey sent for Harding close enough to 2:11 A.M. to make the Daugherty prophecy even more dramatic. That prophecy, again, had predicted to reporter Charles Hilles, almost a month before, that after all the other candidates had failed, "the leaders . . . will get together in some hotel room about 2:11 in the morning . . . sit around the big table . . . and present the name of Senator Harding."

Harding came quickly.

Harvey received him alone in another room and said solemnly, "We think you may be nominated. Before acting, finally, we think you should tell us, on your conscience and before God, whether there is anything that might be brought up against you that would embarrass the Party, an impediment that might disqualify you or make you inexpedient either as a candidate or as President."

The stunned Harding said he would like to have a little time to think it over and Harvey took him to an empty room.

Ten minutes later, Harding returned and said he saw no impediment to his nomination.

During those ten minutes, Harding must have thought about two people who were both in Chicago at that time: Nan Britton and Professor William Estabrook Chancellor.

Nan Britton was a pretty, vivacious girl from Harding's home town of Marion. Nan had a crush on him when she was twelve, became Harding's mistress when she was twenty and he was fifty. Whenever she had traveled with him, he had introduced her as his niece. Harding's friends loaned him their apartments so he and Nan could be together at different times; and another Harding friend, Judge Gary, president of United States Steel gave Nan a job in New York. Their illegitimate daughter was born on October 22, 1919.

During the Chicago convention, Nan worked at Republican headquarters, and later revealed that Harding visited her at her apartment several times during the convention. She also later wrote that she had whispered to their infant daughter, "Your Daddy is going to be President of the United States."

Professor William Estabrook Chancellor of Wooster College, had a seamier story to tell. Describing himself as "an anthropologist, ethnologist and genealogist," Chancellor had made a diagrammatic sketch of Harding ancestry dating back to the seventeenth century which claimed that Harding had Negro blood. A full page ad on this had been printed in a previous state campaign in an Ohio newspaper which was promptly bought up and suppressed. Using Chancellor's research, including supposed affadavits from various members of the Harding family and friends, a pamphlet was printed during the presidential campaign and circulated saying, "Warren Gamaliel Harding is not a white man. May God save America from international shame and domestic ruin."

While Harding never had formally denied this, he did call a press conference long afterward to make the denial, then canceled it without explanation. Still, during those ten lonely minutes, Harding decided that neither of these two situations was strong enough to prevent his nomination.

After leaving Harvey, Harding headed for the hotel suite of Senator Hiram Johnson. Harding had once called Johnson "not only a faker, but a blackguard." Now, however, he woke up Johnson, and reportedly said, "Hiram, the boys have just agreed to give me my run tomorrow, and I am going to be nominated. I want you for my vice-presidential candidate."

"I don't care to consider it," Johnson answered, turned to the wall and tried to go back to sleep.

The word spread. "Senator Curtis came to the Kansas delegation (just before the convention began its final day) and told us frankly that it had been decided (the phrase was his) to give Harding a play after trying for a ballot or two to name Wood," said Kansas delegate William Allen White. "The delegation was for the most part glad to take orders. I sat in the meeting of the delegation in our hotel that morning, and when Curtis' orders came, I blew off. I cried:

" 'If you nominate Harding, you will disgrace the Republican Party. You will bring shame to your country.'

"James Stewart of Wichita, who more than anyone else represented property—I'd met him in Paris trying to raise funds to build a railroad—sneered across the room:

" 'Ah White, you are a dreamer. Try to be practical once.' "

In the end, White did get practical, told the delegation chairman that he would go along to make it unanimous for Harding if the delegation would promise to switch with him to Herbert Hoover if Harding couldn't make it. They agreed.

Sometime between the dark and dawn, another message had come from the Penrose sickbed to his Chicago headquarters. Penrose's doctor H. W. Carpenter later documented it in the *New York Times*.

"He [Penrose] was a very sick man," said Dr. Carpenter. "He had been unconscious for hours. But even in that condition, his mind was subconsciously turning over the problem at Chicago. He came to at last . . . turned to Leighton C. Taylor, his secretary, and asked what they were doing in Chicago. It was the first question he asked after regaining consciousness.

"Taylor answered that they had been doing nothing, that a deadlock had been reached. The Senator lay a moment, thinking 'Call up King,' he said at last to Taylor, 'and tell him to throw it to Harding.' "

Penrose had even passed on a campaign suggestion for Harding, and told King, "Keep Warren at home. He might be asked questions if he went out on a speaking tour and Warren's the kind of a damned fool who'd try to answer them."

Daugherty also claims that Penrose called him later to confirm everything.

The conversation, according to Daugherty, went like this:

Penrose: "You think Harding will be nominated?"

Daugherty: "Beyond a question."

Penrose: "I do not see myself how he can be defeated now, if you have the organization I think you have. I am just about to issue a statement."

Daugherty: "Got it ready?"

Penrose: "Yes. And the newspapers are waiting for me to give it out."

Penrose then read the statement to Daugherty who had a stenographer take it down. It was a strong appeal for Harding. Concerned that a Penrose statement released then would raise a cry about a boss-controlled convention, Daugherty asked Penrose, "Now Senator, when you are running things, you don't let anyone interfere with you. I am in that position now. I don't want you to give out that statement in Philadelphia. I have it here and I'll give it out in conformity with my plans a little later."

"All right," said Penrose.

In the dining room of the LaSalle Hotel that morning, Harding breakfasted with his wife, his brother Dr. George T. Harding, Jr., and the two young sons of Dr. Harding.

Referring to a story in the newspaper, Dr. Harding asked his brother if it were true that he had filed his declaration for candidacy for the United States Senate, since the previous midnight had been the deadline. Harding said he had given instructions by telephone, and assumed it had been done.

Dr. Harding then asked, "Warren, is it really true you are likely to receive the presidential nomination, or does your filing for the Senate mean that you intend to drop out as a candidate at this convention?"

To this, Senator Harding replied with a quiet conviction that surprised his brother, "Deac, it looks as though I might be nominated on about the eighth ballot."

Mrs. Harding then expressed her opinion so emphatically that everyone at that table, even the small boys, remembered it vividly:

"It's utter nonsense. Warren hasn't a chance to get the presidential nomination, and he knows it as well as I do. He's happy in the Senate. He can stay there as long as he wishes to remain. If he hadn't filed for the Senate last night, he'd have lost that, too. It's a waste of time and money for him to be here as a presidential candidate."

There were no fun-loving frills on this final convention day, no pep talks, no cheers. The hall heat had pushed past 100 degrees "and the multitudes sweated, stank, and lifted from the floor sheeplike faces which fell under the hypnosis of the American madness of the hour."

After the opening prayer, the fifth ballot started immediately. During the roll call, a delegate challenged the Ohio vote and the delegation was polled, thirty-nine for Harding and nine for Wood. One Wood man, Thomas Turner of Canton, Ohio, shouted, "Mr. Chairman, Senator Harding having retired from the race for the presidential nomination and filed his name as a candidate to succeed himself as senator from the state of Ohio, I do not see why we should vote for him. I vote for General Wood."

(Other Ohio delegates shouted during all this, "No, No . . ." and "Shame" and "Hurrah for Harding.")

Final vote of the fifth ballot: Wood, 299; Lowden, 303; Johnson, 133½; Sproul, 82½; Harding, 78; and the rest scattered.

This was the first time Lowden led Wood.

On the sixth ballot, Wood and Lowden were exactly 311½ each and Harding had jumped to 89, picking up scattered single votes from Colorado, Indiana, Utah, North Carolina, with a couple from West Virginia and Texas, and 6½ from Missouri.

On the seventh ballot, Wood edged a half vote ahead of Lowden, 312 to 311½, and Johnson was out of it. Harding picked up from 89 to 105. But where did Harding's fresh votes come from?

Two from Delaware, but not from Senator Ball; three from Indiana, but not from Senators Watson and New; three from Missouri, but not from Senator Spencer; three from New York, but not from Senators Wadsworth or Calder.

The Senators had not yet made their move.

The preliminary to the break began on the eighth ballot, when even the four Ohio delegates pledged to Wood deserted to the Harding column. "On the eighth, we handed the Wood forces a surprise," said Daugherty. "We took a few of his votes. We also drew out four votes from Lowden and slipped them to Harding. The eighth ballot showed Lowden, 307; Wood, 299; and Harding, 133½. The Wood camp was thrown in a panic. Lowden had again passed him and Harding's name was on every lip."

Just before the eighth ballot count was released, Missouri waved for recognition and announced, "Mr. Chairman, Missouri asks permission to change the vote of Missouri before the result of the ballot is announced, desiring now to record same as thirty-six for Harding."

With that announcement came convention disorder and there were cries of "No, No!" followed by "Yes, Yes!"

But the Permanent Chairman ruled it was too late, and that the new Missouri vote should be recorded on the next ballot.

From the gallery now came shouts of, "We want Harding . . ."

Lowden floor leader, Alvin Tobe Hert of Kentucky, quickly made a motion that the convention recess until four o'clock that afternoon. A New York delegate seconded it, and Lodge called for a voice vote and a standing vote and adjourned at 1:40 P.M.

Just as he did it, a man on the rostrum told the crowd, "And the Ohio delegates have agreed to an adjournment."

"They have not," shouted Willis, the man who had nominated Harding.

Daugherty rushed to the platform. "I stood in front of Chairman Lodge and shouted, 'You can't beat this man by any such tactics! You ought to be ashamed of yourself! This is an outrage!'"

Why was Lodge doing this? Whose side was he on anyway? Did this old man with the cold mind still shelter a glimmering dream that the presidential lightning might still strike him—if the deadlock was prolonged enough? Daugherty saw the recess as an attempt to cool the heat off Harding and unite the opposition. Lodge's explanation sounded more like an excuse.

To the protesting Willis, Herrick and Daugherty, Lodge quietly suggested that the recess might be beneficial to Harding. To Daugherty alone, later, Lodge said, "We all want a harmonious finish with a solid enthusiastic party. They are going to offer Johnson the Vice-Presidency and swing his stubborn followers over to Harding."

"Senator Johnson will insult your messengers," Daugherty said. "They are on a fool's errand."

And so they were. When Walter F. Brown (who later became Postmaster General in Hoover's Cabinet) sought out Johnson and told him the second place was still open, he added, "Remember, Hiram, only a thin thread of life stands between the Vice-President and the Presidency." (He could also have added that one out of every seven vice-presidents had become President.)

"Walter," Hiram Johnson answered, "go sing your siren songs to somebody else."

Former President William Howard Taft later claimed he had "incontrovertible evidence" that the final day recess was an attempt by certain Senators to head off the Harding nomination, and substitute Will Hays. Taft, however, never presented this evidence.

A known attempt to head off Harding was made during the recess, but not by Senators, and not for Hays. It took place in a taxi along Chicago's lovely lake front and the two passengers were Leonard Wood and Frank Lowden.

Main current of conversation during that ride: each trying to persuade the other to accept the vice-presidential nomination.

Together the two men had polled more than 600 votes on every ballot, nearly two-thirds of the convention. Together these two men still could have named the ticket during that taxi ride.

"If one or the other of those men could have subordinated himself," said Wood's floor manager Frank Knox, himself later a vice-presidential nominee in 1932, "the one selected would have been nominated without a bit of trouble. I had a promise from Sproul, who was manager on the ground of the Pennsylvania delegation, that Pennsylvania would go for Wood whenever we could show a real prospect for success, and an agreement between Lowden and Wood would have brought the Pennsylvania delegation into line hot-foot."

The rumor later was that Wood's financial backer, Colonel Procter, had urged the meeting. But the two men could not persuade each other, and their only agreement was to try for a week-end recess during which time they would have more conversations. Selected to make this new motion for the recess was Lowden's floor manager, Hert. It was a bad choice.

For some reason, Lodge prolonged the afternoon recess for forty-six minutes. One version claims that Lodge was waiting for Hert to arrive and make the motion for adjournment. But Daugherty later wrote, "The time was short. I sent word to Chairman Lodge that I would be late and not to call the convention to order until I could reach the Coliseum, that Senator Harding would be nominated on the next ballot. This was a courtesy to which we were entitled."

Lowden later wrote, "I could not understand then, and I have never learned since why the motion to adjourn was not made."

It was not made because Hert was nowhere to be found. He deliberately absented himself from the hall until the ninth ballot was fully under way. Wood's man, Norman Gould had charged that Hert was working "hand in glove" with John King. King had his orders from Penrose to switch to Harding. Harold Ickes, who had recommended Hert to Lowden, afterward wrote, "It was alleged that the piece of silver offered him was the promise of a place in Harding's Cabinet."

Hert, who was not given a Cabinet job, and died a year later, publicly rationalized that the nomination would have gone to

Wood, if Lowden had stayed in the race, and he was bent on beating Wood.

Hert was bent enough on this to deepen the doublecross when he started the convention stampede by switching Kentucky's vote from Lowden to Harding on the ninth ballot. Lowden had said that if the weekend recess failed, he would release his delegates to go wherever they wanted.

The time had come for the Senators to make their move. The word went out.

"Curtis came to our delegation," said Kansas delegate White, "and told us that now was the time to break for Harding. Kansas was to lead the break, and I was up against it. I remember sitting there sweating, fanning myself with my new $25 panama, with my coat over the back of my chair, in a blue-and-white striped silk shirt of great pride, red-faced, perturbed, and the most miserable in body and spirit. I didn't want to vote for Harding. . . ."

On the alphabetical roll call, however, the beginning break came when Senator Brandegee's Connecticut delegation switched to Harding with thirteen of its fourteen votes. That started a floor demonstration. Then, when Kansas voted its full twenty votes for Harding, the demonstration renewed itself, and a Kansas delegate put Harding's picture on the state standard and started the march around the hall.

"And so in the heat and confusion and insanity of that afternoon," said White, ". . . I toddled along, followed the Kansas banner in the parade, ashamed, disheveled in body and spirit, making a sad fat figure while the bands played, the trumpets brayed, and the crowd howled for Harding; and in that hour the Republican Party bade farewell to the twenty years of liberalism which had grown up under the leadership of Theodore Roosevelt. . . .

"I marched . . . hoping in my heart that Harding would fail in a ballot or two and that I would collect my promise . . . I kept thinking, 'Is the long chance of Hoover worth this?' . . . I was torn, as I often am in politics, between the desire to jump in the fiery furnace as a martyr, and the instinct to save my hide and go along on the broad way that leadeth to destruction . . . and the crowd yelled and danced on the grave of the Colonel who had been my leader and my friend for a quarter of a century."

Harding passed both Wood and Lowden in the ninth ballot with 374½. Wood dropped from 299 to 249 and Lowden from 307 to 121½. Watching from the gallery was Harding's mistress, Nan Britton. Harding had given her a ticket a few days before.

"My eyes swam," Nan Britton later wrote, describing her reactions at the convention, "and I recalled my freshman school year at Marion, when, in the margins of all my books, I, then but thirteen years old, had written a prophecy of my heart-longing, 'Warren Gamaliel Harding—he's a darling—Warren Gamaliel Harding—President of the United States.' "

Another woman watching with equal eagerness was Mrs. Harding.

Daugherty went to see her just before the beginning of the tenth ballot because he knew Mrs. Harding had a weak heart and he wanted to prepare her for the upcoming nomination.

"She had removed her hat in the sweltering heat, and sat humped forward in her chair, her arms tightly folded," wrote Daugherty. "In her right hand, she gripped two enormous hatpins, in vogue at the time. . . . A deep frown shattered her face. 'It's terrible, isn't it? . . . All this wild excitement, all this yelling and bawling and cat-calling. I can't follow it . . .' "

Daugherty then told her that her husband would be nominated on the next ballot. "She gave a sudden start," said Daugherty, "fairly leaped from her chair; the movements drove both hatpins deep into my side." Daugherty thought the blood was running down into his shoe, and felt faint. Later he discovered his shoe was filled, not with blood, but with sweat.

Nicholas Murray Butler had commented before the tenth ballot began, "They're going to nominate a golf-player for President." Butler then joined Lowden and Harding in one of the small rooms behind the convention hall platform.

"We three were alone," Butler wrote. "Suddenly there was a

tremendous roar from the convention hall. In an instant, the door
of the room in which we were sitting burst open, and Charles B.
Warren of Michigan leaped into the room shouting, 'Pennsylvania's voted for you, Harding, and you are nominated!'

"Harding rose, and with one hand in Lowden's and one in mine,
he said, with choking voice, 'The great honor of the presidency
has come to me; I shall need all the help that you two friends can
give me.'

"Frank Lowden said, 'I congratulate you on your nomination,'
and Harding answered, 'I am not sure that I would not feel happier, Frank, if I were congratulating you.'"

(Four years later, Lowden was nominated for Vice-President,
and declined; and in 1928, Lowden won the Illinois presidential
primary but not the nomination).

Daugherty swept into the room immediately afterward to get
Harding out of there, back to his hotel, before a crowd could
assemble.

Pennsylvania had given Harding sixty of its seventy-six votes at
6:05 P.M. and it was enough to ensure the nomination. In the
fracas that followed with delegations screaming for recognition
to switch, a voice rang out in the hall, "Mr. Chairman, don't let
them all get on the bandwagon."

Almost everybody did. Every state except California, Montana,
Maine, New Hampshire, Vermont, and the Philippine Islands gave
Harding either its full or partial vote. Harding's total was 692⅕,
almost 200 more than the number needed for nomination.

Senator Joseph Frelinghuyson of New Jersey, strong Wood
backer, asked that the nomination be made unanimous. Some
Wisconsin delegates yelled "No," and were hissed, and Chairman
Lodge declared it unanimous anyway.

"Of all the candidates, Wood was the more gallant in defeat,"
wrote reporter Mark Sullivan in the New York Evening Post. "He
met defeat standing squarely in his solid military boots in the
middle of the entrance to his headquarters, giving every comer
smiles of almost jovial composure in return for condolences. This

is what duty and taste call for at such a time, and that is what Wood would always do. He is one of the most completely self-disciplined men."

George Harvey, who soon became United States Ambassador to Great Britain, later said of the Harding nomination, "He was nominated because there was nothing against him and because the delegates wanted to go home."

And how did that "cabal" of Senators vote? An analysis by Ray Baker Harris showed that Senator Wadsworth voted for Lowden until the ninth ballot, when Lowden released his delegates and Wadsworth then voted for Harding; Senator Calder had supported Butler, then threw New York delegation support to Lowden until the ninth ballot vote for Harding; Senator Smoot voted consistently for Harding, but was not able to sway his Utah delegation until the final ballot when five of the eight delegates joined him; Senator Watson favored Wood on every ballot including the last; Senator New stayed with Wood until the eighth ballot, then switched to Harding with a small slice of the Indiana delegation; Senator Lodge's Massachusetts delegation only gave Harding one vote on the ninth ballot, only seventeen of its thirty-five on the final ballot; Senator Sherman voted consistently for Lowden and his Illinois delegation didn't give Harding any votes until the last ballot; Senator McCormick followed the Sherman pattern; Senator Brandegee and his Connecticut delegation cast their first votes for Harding in the ninth; Senator Frelinghuysen fought for Wood until the final moments; Senator Knox and Pennsylvania didn't give Harding a single vote until the tenth ballot; Senator Phipps voted for Harding on all ten ballots but could not swing his Colorado delegation with him until the end; Senator Spencer stayed with Lowden until released, and then moved with Missouri for Harding; and Senator Ball's Delaware delegation gave Harding two votes in the early balloting, and all six in the tenth.

Of course, this might have been the preset plan, as Senators Curtis and Smoot had told reporters—give Wood and Lowden a few more ballots and then break for Harding. We know that Curtis did tell this to the Kansas delegation. We also know that the Brandegee break did start the stampede with the Connecticut switch.

Talking to a friendly *New York Herald* reporter, Harding later gave his own version of why he won:

"Let me tell you something that I've never told a living soul," Harding said. "Let me tell you why I think I was nominated at Chicago. You know all the talk that has been going around about me having been picked by the Senate oligarchy and having been meant from the first. Hell, that's all darned nonsense. I give you my word as a man that I had little real hope of winning the nomination until the very last days of the Convention.

"Then, as you know, came the deadlock of General Wood and Frank Lowden and Hiram Johnson. Then it became apparent to anybody with the least political acumen that neither would give way to the other, and therefore that none would win.

"That's an ancient story now. But the point is that when the deadlock was shown to be actual and unbreakable, the first real hope of winning came to me. I said to myself, 'Now what's going to happen?' I was dining alone away up on the roof of the Pullman Building on Michigan Avenue the Thursday night before the nomination, when I figured out I had a chance and a good one. There was not a soul that paid much attention to me. Even you newspapermen on your way to dinner, passed me with merely a nod and a careless, friendly 'Hello Senator!' I was not cutting much ice with the crop in sight up to then. I knew it and you did.

"But up there in the restaurant, surrounded by folks that didn't know me from Adam and wouldn't have had a thrill if they'd been told who I was, I tried to dope it out. I figured down to this: With Wood, Johnson and Lowden out of it, as had to come, I knew I could count on friends in every one of their delegations. Why? Because I found in my pre-convention campaigning the rule that has got me all through my political career, which was not to hurt feelings or step on anybody's toes if I could find foot-room elsewhere.

"I figured that if politeness and an honest desire not to humiliate any rival, just for the sake of winning a few votes, were ever going to produce anything, now was the time. Other fellows, just as competent as I or more so, had made enemies, and it looked to me that there wasn't one in sight that the convention could unite on, except myself.

"Now, Hill [reporter Edwin Hill], don't misunderstand me. What I mean is that I had built up a reputation for being able to bring men together, for creating a better understanding of men in my own party. I hoped and believed that when the leaders of the delegations got to talking things over, they would not fail to remember this. That's just what happened. When the leaders met that Friday night in a dozen places, and threshed over the situation, the result in every instance was that they said: 'Well, there's one thing about Harding—nobody seems to have it in for him. He's a great fellow for getting us together. Maybe he'll work that smile of his on all of us clear up to Election Day.'"

"There's the whole story," said Harding. "So-called Senate oligarchy that Jim Cox talks about followed along as much as they led, for the notion that 'Harding is a great fellow to get the party to pull together' got all through the Convention.

"Then they gave me the nomination. A bunch of you boys met me in my rooms right after the tenth ballot, you remember, and what I said impulsively, I meant, that I felt like a man who had drawn a pair of eights and caught a full house."

Another man who caught a full house at the convention was Calvin Coolidge.

Toward the middle of the tenth ballot, Republican leaders suddenly seemed to realize that they had not yet picked a vice-presidential nominee. Six Senators suddenly collected in a space under the platform, concealed by timbers and dimly lit. So much of a pawn was Harding that he was not even asked for his vice-presidential preference.

The small group held a quick conference and decided that Senator Irvine L. Lenroot, a progressive from Wisconsin would balance the conservative Harding. Lenroot seemed hesitant and Hays put on some pressure and finally Lenroot said he would consult his wife.

Picked to nominate Lenroot was Senator Medill McCormick. As he hurried to the platform, McCormick shouted to his friend Henry Stoddard, "We're going to put Lenroot in with Harding."

"The hell you are," shouted a surprised, indignant correspondent at Stoddard's side.

"Watch me and see," said McCormick, as he went up the ladder steps to the platform.

It would be a Senator's ticket, top and bottom.

"You have adopted a great and constructive program," McCormick told the convention delegates. "You have nominated for the Presidency of the United States a man of ripe experience, of deep learning, of great power . . . it is your duty to nominate and to present to the voters of the country a candidate for the Vice-Presidency whose experience, whose learning, whose ability, whose sterling Americanism will stand by that of the candidate for the Presidency."

From the rear of the delegate seats, a voice broke out, "Coolidge! Coolidge!" It was not a heavy voice, but the whole hall heard it.

McCormick continued and concluded, ". . . Therefore I present the name of Irvine L. Lenroot of Wisconsin."

Mixed with the applause came the same penetrating voice of the delegate in the rear, "Coolidge! Coolidge!"

Recognized in swift succession for seconding speeches were Alvin T. Hert of Kentucky, H. L. Remmel of Arkansas, Myron T. Herrick of Ohio, and Senator William L. Calder of New York. During Calder's seconding speech for Lenroot, a voice interrupted, "Not on your life."

The presiding officer then recognized Wallace McCamant of Oregon, presumably as another seconding speaker for Lenroot. But McCamant said: "When the Oregon delegation came here instructed by the people of our State to present to this convention as the candidate for the office of Vice-President a distinguished son of Massachusetts, he requested that we refrain from presenting his name. But there is another son of Massachusetts who has been much in the public eye in the last year, a man who is sterling in his Americanism and stands for all that the Republican Party holds dear . . . Governor Calvin Coolidge of Massachusetts."

Outbursts of applause had such sudden power that it put a feeling of electricity into the hot hall. Within short minutes, delegates from Michigan, Maryland, and North Dakota all seconded Coolidge.

Even though two thirds of the Republican Senators were delegates and most of them stood to shout for Lenroot, they were drowned out by the cheers for Coolidge. Not since Garfield's nomination in 1880 had there been such an uprising "from the floor."

For the second time in ten minutes, heavy-set elder statesman H. L. Remmel of Arkansas was recognized. Remmel probably made the quickest bandwagon about-face in political history. Said Remmel: "I had consulted with the chairman of the Massachusetts delegation and told him that Arkansas wanted to vote for Coolidge for Vice-President and he said he did not want his name presented. But in view of the fact that another state has placed in nomination the name of Governor Coolidge, I now wish to withdraw my second of the nomination of Senator Lenroot and to second the nomination of Governor Coolidge."

Delegates from Kansas, Connecticut, Pennsylvania, Colorado, all quickly followed.

How had it happened? Wallace McCamant later backgrounded it in a letter:

"A notice to the effect that Lenroot was the program choice for Vice-President was handed to the Chairman of the Oregon delegation, Hon. John L. Rand, by, I presume, one of the scouts in the group of party elders who had so decided. Mr. Rand passed the notice around to the other seven delegates then remaining in the Convention. None of the delegates was pleased by the Lenroot suggestion. The suggestion that Coolidge's name be put before the

Convention was made by Hon. Charles H. Carey of Portland. He also suggested that I speak for the delegation in so doing. I asked the others whether the suggestion met with their approval. They nodded yes."

Coolidge had come to the country's attention nine months before when a large part of Boston's police force formed a union and went on strike. Coolidge called out the state guard and sent the American Federation of Labor a telegram that caught the nation's imagination, "There is no right to strike against the public safety, by anybody, anywhere, anytime."

Also nominated for the Vice-Presidency were Henry W. Anderson of Virginia, a man who had headed up the Red Cross in the Balkans, and Governor Henry Allen of Kansas, the man who had nominated Wood.

Allen's possible nomination for the Vice-Presidency had been buzzed about before, and White later filled in some of the behind-the-scenes activity. "One day Henry Allen came to me," said White, "and said that he had been called to a room in a business block and taken out to a high mountain by a group representing oil who questioned him closely on his views on foreign policy, and particularly Mexico.

"This was in relation to his possibly being a candidate for Vice-President," said White. "That candidacy was one of those things that he did not encourage, and so far as he could, he let it alone. But his name was buzzed about in high places, so that all felt it worthwhile to probe him. Every delegation that I knew much about was loaded with one, two, or a half a dozen representatives of national commodity interests—oil, railroads, telephones, steel, coal and textiles."

On the single ballot, Coolidge swept in with 674½ to only 164½ for Lenroot, 68½ for Allen, 28 for Anderson, and a small scattering for others.

The convention greeted Coolidge's nomination "with tumultuous applause and cheers." It had been their one spontaneous act.

"I have been present at every Republican Convention beginning with 1856," said eighty-six-year-old Chauncey M. DePew to Coolidge, "and I have never seen such a spontaneous and enthusiastic tribute as the vote for you for Vice-President."

It was about 8 P.M. Saturday night, and Coolidge and his wife were in their simple two-room apartment in the Old Adams House, when the telephone rang. Coolidge listened, put down the receiver, and told his wife, "I have been nominated for Vice President."

"You are not going to accept, are you?" asked Mrs. Coolidge.

Without changing his facial expression, Coolidge said, "I suppose I shall have to."

Commenting on the Coolidge nomination at the convention right after the vote count, Robert L. O'Brien of the *Boston Herald* turned to his friend Richard Hooker of the *Springfield Republican*, and said, "Richard, I will bet thee a dinner that Harding will die and Coolidge become President."

Political writers afterward played their favorite game of what might have happened if the winner had not won. Henry Stoddard expressed a general consensus that if Harding had not made it on the Saturday ballots, then there would have been only three candidates on the likely list in the coming week: Coolidge, Hoover, and Wood. With a Sunday to negotiate and pressure, Wood might have won.

But Harding was the man, and Frederick Davenport in *The Outlook* magazine reported the mood: "Moral issues and idealism are going to wait a while. The country has had its fill of them. Just now it doesn't give a rap about these things, compared with its desire to get industry back on a sound basis and to have economic livelihood made more secure. And the country, including large numbers of conservative Democrats, is going to take to Harding and the Republican policies, like a duck to water.

"Harding stands for a kind of candid and unpretentious reaction that everyone can respect and that a great many people desire."

Stoddard called the ticket a combination of the small-town newspaperman and the small-town lawyer.

White, still rankled over his parade marching for Harding, wrote, "I think it is a great mistake to elect the President from the Senate, by the Senate and for the Senate." And he said of Harding, ". . . a mere bass drum, beating the time of the hour, carrying no tune, making no music, promoting no deep harmony; just a strident, rhythmic noise."

H. L. Mencken wrote: "Harding, intellectually, seems to be merely a benign blank—a decent, harmless, laborious, hollow-headed mediocrity."

The Nation called Harding, "colorless and platitudinous, uninspired and an uninspiring nobody . . . an amiable, faithful, obedient errand-boy for the Old Guard politicians and the business interests they serve, nominated on a platform that means absolutely nothing, Harding is put forward like a cigar-store Indian to attract trade. Very likely, he will do it."

The New York Times remarked editorially, "The nomination of Harding, for whose counterpart we must go back to Franklin Pierce if we would seek a President who measures down to his political stature, is the fine and perfect flower of the cowardice and imbecility of the senatorial cabal that charged itself with the management of the Republican nomination."

On the other hand, the New York Times in its Sunday Magazine had an article which read: "Harding has a far keener mind than McKinley. He is quite capable of thinking his own thoughts. He has personal magnetism, which McKinley had not. He can be dignified without being solemn. And he smokes cigarettes. That small fact tells a world of difference between him and McKinley."

"McKinley was not a great man," the article said, "Neither is Harding. But aren't you, the people, getting tired of great men? Wouldn't you like to rest up a bit with Dobbin after riding at breakneck speed for 19 years. . . ?"

The Boston News saw in Harding's nomination a new era of co-operative action between the executive and legislative branches of government; the New York Evening Mail also emphasized the legislative experience of the two men and the ability of Harding to get along with people; the *Minneapolis Journal* saw Harding as "a constructive conservative" and offered a slogan of "Harding and harmony."

The *New York Sun* said, "Everyone agrees that Warren G. Harding looks as though he ought to be President of the United States. He possesses a certain dignity, grace of manner and commanding stature that seem to go with the office." And the *New York Herald Tribune* wrote: "We had hoped that a man of undoubted courage, vision and executive ability would be chosen, but we have instead Warren Gamaliel Harding."

A magazine called *The Independent* ventured a prediction:

"As a party man—one incidentally with the cleanest of personal lives and with no skeletons in his closet anywhere—it is to be doubted if Senator Harding will on one hand entirely grant that to the victors belong the spoils."

A much more successful prophet, Harry Daugherty (who would help make *The Independent's* prophecy prove untrue) was in his gloating glory. Returning home to Columbus, the day after the convention ended, Daugherty had his chauffeur drive past the office of the *Columbus Evening Dispatch*—whose editor and cartoonist had scoffed openly at the idea that Daugherty could "put Harding over." *Dispatch* cartoonist William Ireland was at work by an open window when Daugherty drove past and jeered at him. Arriving at his own office, Daugherty immediately sent his secretary to buy an alarm clock, set the hands at 2:11 and deliver it to cartoonist Ireland precisely at 2:11. And then Daugherty had friends of his call Ireland at 2:11 and ask him what time it was.

If the nomination bloated Daugherty, it humbled Harding. He told an audience, "It might interest you to know that I have always been a great reader of the Bible. I have never read it as closely as in the last weeks. . . . I have obtained a good deal of inspiration from the Psalms of David and from many passages of the Four Gospels, and there is still wisdom in the sayings of Old Solomon. . . . I don't mind saying that I gladly go to God Almighty for guidance and strength. . . ."

Interviewed shortly after her husband's nomination, Mrs. Harding said: "I have faith in my husband; I know that he is equal to facing . . . anything that can possibly come to him." To close relatives, Mrs. Harding wrote, "Warren is wonderful. I believe in my soul he will measure up to the opportunities, because I know him. Even I have seen him grow from day to day during these weeks. I am glad for what has come to him and to us."

In the privacy of her own room, though, speaking to her close friend, Mrs. Malcom Jennings, Mrs. Harding said quietly, but with obvious emotion, "Warren will be a great President. But I see only tragedy ahead."

Shortly afterward, in the Letter to the Editor column of the *New York Sun*, a reader passed on some of the early Harding family history he had found. Mostly he described the massacre of a large group of the Harding family at a place called Forty Fort in Pennsylvania's Susquehanna Valley. The letter-writer mentioned a battle cry that grew out of that massacre: "Remember the Fate of the Hardings! . . ."

The fate of Warren Gamaliel Harding would soon be a fact of history.

THESE WERE THE YEARS of fear and the years of hunger.
These were the years when hate was an easy thing.
These were the years when an apple was a symbol, not a fruit.
These were the years of empty promises and slippery courage.
These were the years of values without money
   and money without values.
These were the years of shadow and the years of ghosts.
These were the years "when a crippled man was asked to teach
   a crippled nation how to walk again."

DEMOCRATIC NATIONAL CONVENTION OF 1932

WHEN WARREN G. HARDING RAN AGAINST JAMES
M. Cox in the 1920 presidential campaign, the Democratic vice-
presidential nominee with Cox was a young, handsome man of
remarkable energy, the former Assistant Secretary of the Navy,
Franklin Delano Roosevelt. In that losing campaign, Roosevelt
had toured almost every state in the union, made fifty-eight
speeches in fifty-three days, most of which put the crusading emphasis on support for Woodrow Wilson's concept of the League
of Nations. He was then a man with a deep, burning ambition.
After the Democratic defeat, Roosevelt and John W. Davis discussed the next presidential campaign of 1924, and Roosevelt predicted that Davis would be the nominee (as he was). But Davis
reportedly told Roosevelt, "You might get it yourself."

Roosevelt replied, "No, I won't be ready until 1932."

Roosevelt was ready in 1932, but the intermittent time had taken
a tortuous twist he had not foreseen.

Roosevelt once told a London *Times* reporter, "For twenty years
I had a perfectly natural and laudable ambition to become Presi-

dent, and was obliged to behave like a man who wants to be elected President."

To a *New York Times* reporter, however, Roosevelt said, "I told you I don't know why any man should want to be President. I didn't grow up burning to go to the White House like the American boy of legend. I have read history and known presidents; it's a terrible job. But somebody has to do it."

And, to still another reporter, Roosevelt leaned forward and said, "Wouldn't you be President if you could? Wouldn't anybody?"

Back in 1907, when he was still a working lawyer in New York, Roosevelt told a friend of his that he thought someday he might have "a real chance" to be President. In 1912, when Roosevelt was a State Senator fighting Tammany control of the legislature and heading a New York committee pushing for the presidential nomination of Woodrow Wilson, Louis Howe wrote Roosevelt a letter, addressing him, "Beloved and Revered Future President."

If fate converted Theodore Roosevelt into a quick President, Theodore's cousin Franklin reached the same station mainly because of Howe's persistent dream, and his own terrible nightmare.

The Franklin D. Roosevelt nightmare was polio, and it not only crippled his legs but crippled his ambition.

It was Louis Howe, together with Eleanor Roosevelt, who massaged his legs and his ego and brought his ambition back to life.

Louis Howe was a small, gnomelike, ugly man, a political reporter in Albany who had originally sized up Roosevelt as "a spoiled silk-pants sort of guy." But when State Senator Roosevelt fought Tammany Hall, Howe changed his mind, and said, "Mein Gawd, the boy's got courage." It was Howe who singlehandedly and successfully ran Roosevelt's campaign for re-election when Roosevelt was in bed with typhoid fever. Howe went along with Roosevelt into the Navy Department, helped run Roosevelt's unsuccessful primary race in New York for the Democratic nomination for United States Senator, and the equally unsuccessful vice-presidential campaign. After that defeat Roosevelt had written a friend, "Thank the Lord we are both comparatively youthful."

252

A year later, Roosevelt had polio.

"There are times," said Howe, "when I think that Franklin might never have been President if he had not been stricken. You see, he had a thousand interests. You couldn't pin him down. He rode, he swam, he played golf, tennis, he sailed, he collected stamps, he politicked, he did everything under the sun a man could think of doing. Then, suddenly, there he was, flat on his back with nothing to do but think. He began to read, he talked, he gathered people around him—his thoughts expanded. He began to see the other fellow's point of view. He thought of others who were ill and afflicted and in want. He dwelt on many things that had not bothered him much before. Lying there, he grew bigger, day by day."

Howe and Eleanor Roosevelt then offered him a choice:

"Look, you can go up to Hyde Park and write books and things, or you can try to conquer this crippling. The odds are against you and it may be a long grueling future of pain without real result."

And Roosevelt flashed his biggest Roosevelt smile and said, "Well, when do we start?"

The Presidency is seldom packaged and delivered to a man who does not push for it with all his political strength. Roosevelt and Howe pushed hard.

During his three months' campaign for the Vice-Presidency in 1920, Roosevelt wrote, "I think I spent eighty-nine out of ninety-two days on a sleeping car. I went to forty-two states in the union. I drove literally thousands of miles by automobile and got to know the country as only a candidate for national office or a travelling salesman can get to know it."

Most important of all, Roosevelt made many political friends, and throughout his later illness, Roosevelt and Howe kept those friendships fresh by continual correspondence.

Roosevelt's first political step back into the national limelight was his nominating speech for New York Governor Alfred E. Smith, the presidential candidate, at the Democratic National Convention of 1924 in Madison Square Garden. Leaning on his son's arm, adjusting his crutches, Roosevelt moved to the platform before a silent crowd and said of Smith, "He is the Happy Warrior of the political battlefield, this leader whose whole career gives convincing proof of his power to lead; this warrior whose record shows him to be invincible . . . this man beloved by all, trusted by all, this man of destiny. . . ."

Delegate reaction was tumultuous and the New York World reported: "No matter whether Governor Smith wins or loses, Franklin D. Roosevelt stands out as the real hero of this Democratic Convention."

Roosevelt nominated Smith again at the Democratic National Convention in Houston in 1928, and this time Smith did become the nominee. But Smith now had another request to make of Roosevelt. He wanted Roosevelt to run for governor of New York, because he felt this would help him carry the state in his presidential campaign. Roosevelt refused. "No, not until I can throw away my props, not until I can stand on my own two legs," he said. Howe agreed. Howe's timetable called for Roosevelt to run for Governor in 1932.

Roosevelt had taken a few steps without support of any kind, the first in seven years. "It probably means getting rid of leg braces during the next two winters," he wrote Smith, "and that would be impossible if I had to remain in Albany."

Smith persisted, finally telephoned Roosevelt and said, "Frank, I told you I wasn't going to put this on a personal basis, but I've got to." Roosevelt reluctantly accepted. On election night, Roosevelt and Howe stayed up until 4.00 A.M. to learn he had squeaked in by 25,564 votes, less than 1 per cent of the electorate. Smith lost both the state and the election.

"Anyone who is Governor of New York," he once told his friend Granville Clark, "has a good chance to be President with any luck." According to his son James, Roosevelt's heady reception at the 1928 Democratic National Convention convinced F.D.R. that his presidential ambition was again really possible, polio or no polio.

Roosevelt's record as Governor was hardly a new frontier. Political columnists noted how cautious Roosevelt was about getting involved in any program that had political risk. They also noted his relationship with Tammany, however cool, was still a working arrangement. His record did have some highlights: creation of a State Power Authority, a reforestration program, a social security setup with old age pensions. But most Albany newsmen felt his liberalism was based on impulse rather than intelligence. They felt he was indecisive, indiscreet, and lacked balance. They liked him but they didn't trust him. Walter Lippmann later said of him, "Franklin D. Roosevelt is no crusader. He is no tribune of the people. He is no enemy of entrenched privilege. He is a pleasant man, who, with no important qualifications for the office, would very much like to be President."

Or, as another critic put it, "All Roosevelt had was a good name, a winning smile and nice diction."

But the name was more than good—it was magic. The presidential years of Theodore Roosevelt still had the lingering quality of exciting legend. For the American generation who had given Theodore Roosevelt his political power, his vivid ghost was their living history. And for the new generation, Theodore Roosevelt was more than a man; he was a model. Some of the political pros reasoned: if Republican Theodore could pull wavering Democratic votes, perhaps the magic of that Roosevelt name and fame could help cousin Franklin pull in Republican votes.

Roosevelt's concern for the prize of the Presidency became increasingly obvious to close friends. One of his closest, Henry Morgenthau, Jr., who became his Secretary of the Treasury, wrote of a visit on June 4, 1930, to attend James Roosevelt's wedding. "I went up to Franklin's room at nine o'clock and spent one-and-a-half-hours with him," said Morganthau. "He told me in the strictest confidence that . . . he was beginning to be suspicious of the fact that Alfred E. Smith was working for the nomination as President in 1932."

The presidential picture entered a fresh phase when Roosevelt was overwhelmingly re-elected Governor in 1930 by 700,000 votes.

The day after that election, Will Rogers publicly quipped, "The Democrats nominated their President yesterday."

"The next day I was among those who rode up to Albany with him on the noonday train from New York City," said his speech-writer and friend Samuel Rosenman. "There was a lot of joking about the Presidency. Roosevelt only laughed. He was with inti-mate friends on this trip—O'Connor, Howe, Missy, Grace Tully, me—and yet I do not recall his saying seriously even once that he was interested in 1932—or that he was not. We all took it for granted that he was, and I am certain that by that morning, if not before, he had concluded that he would become a candidate for the nomination of the Democratic Party."

That assumption was sound. Later that day, the new Democratic State Committee chairman James A. Farley issued a statement that Louis Howe had helped prepare. "I fully expect," said Farley, "that the call will come to Roosevelt when the first presidential primary is held, which will be late next year."

"The Democrats in the nation naturally want as their candidate for President the man who has shown himself capable of carrying the most important state in the country by a record-breaking ma-jority," the Farley statement continued. "I do not see how Mr. Roosevelt can escape becoming the next presidential nominee of his party, even if no one should raise a finger to bring it about."

After issuing the statement to the press, Farley called Roosevelt in Albany to tell him about it. "Believe it or not," said Farley, "that was the first time that a word about his possible candidacy for the highest office in the land had ever passed between us, and I was in doubt as to how he would take it. He laughed and replied, 'Whatever you said, Jim, is all right with me.'"

It was more than all right. The Howe plans for the Presidency were already in high gear. Roosevelt invited Edward Flynn, the powerful political boss of the Bronx for an overnight visit at the Albany state mansion.

"No one was present at dinner but Roosevelt, Howe and myself," wrote Flynn. "In the library after dinner, the Governor turned to me and said, 'Eddie, my reason for asking you to stay overnight is that I believe I can be nominated for the Presidency in 1932 on the Democratic ticket.' "

Flynn afterward wrote that Roosevelt made the preliminary offer of campaign manager, but that he refused because he insisted he was not "an easy mixer," and preferred to remain in the background. Flynn said he also noted for Roosevelt that the name of Ed Flynn, Bronx boss, would be a political liability in the South and West where he would be labeled as a Tammany boss, simply because he was from New York. Also, Flynn said, he was personally and politically a Wet on the prohibition issue and this would similarly hurt in many areas.

It was afterward that Roosevelt wrote Farley his only letter of appreciation. "As I went through the state," wrote Roosevelt, "I got expressions everywhere showing that no man since the days of David B. Hill, has such hearty backing and enthusiastic co-operation from the organizations as you have. I have an idea that you and I make a combination which has not existed since Cleveland and [State Chairman Daniel S.] Lamont."

Big, bald, friendly Farley had been a Democratic Town Clerk in Republican Stony Point, 35 miles upstate in New York. He was then a building materials salesman who went to work selling Al Smith to the voters, and Smith made him State Boxing Commissioner, then Secretary of the Democratic State Committee in 1928.

"I became the front man or the sales manager or whatever you want to call it," said Farley, "and I would bring everything to Howe."

Here was Louis Howe, this slightly-built man (barely over a hundred pounds), almost sixty-years old, wearing oversize, stiff, white collars, and trousers that constantly had the burlap look. Here was this pale man with uncombed hair and the furrowed face who smoked incessantly and "whose desk looked as though the charwoman had used it to dump the accumulated wastepapers of the night before." Here was this strangely dedicated man who

freely sacrificed his own future, his fun, and even his family—
("They took away my father," said his son bitterly)—all for the
destiny of a crippled man whom he believed would one day be
President. Here was a man whose whole life was channeled into a
single code of action: How will this help or hurt Franklin D.
Roosevelt?

Roosevelt called Louis Howe, "my old side-kick," and nobody
came closer. Howe was the only man who could call Roosevelt and
tell him, "Franklin, you damned fool, you can't do it," or "Can't
you get anything through that thick Dutch head of yours?" One
time, Howe's assistant, Lela Stiles, overheard him phone Roosevelt,
who was just about to go for a swim, and say finally, "Well, go
ahead, damn it, and I hope to God you drown."

Yet inside this ugly, caustic, profane little man was not only this
enormous driving dream, but something else. Once, he wrote of
himself, "At heart, I am a minstrel, singing outside the window of
beauty."

"The reason Louis had faith in me and trusted me," said Farley,
"was that he knew I didn't want to get between him and Roosevelt. In other words, Louis didn't have anything that I wanted,
see?"

Howe and Farley set up some working space in a small office on
Madison Avenue and it became the funnel and the fountainhead
for a steady mass of mail, pamphlets, and a small growing group
who called themselves "Friends of Roosevelt."

One of the early friends was financier Joseph P. Kennedy, whose
own son would one day become President. Farley remembers
Frank Walker pleading with Howe to be nice to Kennedy because
he was a wealthy potential backer. Howe grumpily agreed, but
when Kennedy came in with Walker, Howe sat with his head in
his arms behind his desk, his eyes closed. Walker coughed for
attention and Howe opened one eye, glared through it. It took
several minutes before he even contributed to the conversation.
But Kennedy still made a most liberal contribution.

Howe's habit of favorably sizing up a volunteer was to say,

"You make a good appearance and you seem to know something about politics and to have some influence. I think you can be useful to Franklin."

Roosevelt soon needed all the useful volunteers he could get. With the country at the peak of prosperity, Hoover's renomination and re-election for a second term seemed assured and few Democrats were anxious to contest him; but when the prosperity bubble burst into a depression of growing disaster after 1929, the presidential crop of Democrats suddenly rushed into blossom. The prize now had a reach to it.

A much mentioned candidate was Governor Albert C. Ritchie who had been re-elected for an unprecedented fourth term in Maryland. Ritchie was ripe. He was 56, white-haired and handsome, a highly successful governor who mouthed Jeffersonian principles with the slogan, "People who are least governed are best governed." Ritchie recognized unemployment as "the strongest challenge to our social order and the strongest argument in favor of communism" but he steered away from unemployment insurance as a federal invasion of private enterprise. He felt that Americans were already too regimented. On prohibition, Ritchie was a frank "wet." On tariff, he wanted it lower, believed that high tariffs were "bringing retaliations from other nations whose trade we ought to have, and whose good will should be an American asset." Ritchie supporters claimed delegate strength in Illinois and several other states in the north and east. Ritchie himself had no coy quality about wanting the presidential job. "Who wouldn't?" he said.

Owen D. Young was another eastern candidate. His reputation in trade was world-wide. He had drafted both the Dawes Plan of wartime reparations and a plan identified by his own name. Despite his national prestige, his handicap was his corporation connection —Chairman of the Board of General Electric Company. Besides he had openly and loudly discouraged any boom for him. Still, he had been a strong Smith man in 1928 and his backing came from many influential party conservatives.

One of the most colorful and least likely candidates was Oklahoma Governor W. H. "Alfalfa Bill" Murray. Murray's varied background included service as a lawyer for the Chickasaw Indians, two terms in Congress, a long stretch in Bolivia. He described himself as "Born in a cotton patch during a November snowstorm" and "rocked in the cradle of adversity; chastened by hardship and poverty." While he was highly educated and could quote Lycurgus, he played it politically uncouth with an old frock coat, wrinkled white socks, unpressed trousers, and his much-repeated belief that some crops grow better if planted under a ripe moon. His campaign slogan: "Bread, Butter, Bacon, Beans."

Another Governor, only slightly more likely, was Harry Byrd of Virginia. Byrd, however, had quietly declared himself for Roosevelt. His brother, Admiral Richard E. Byrd, the famous arctic and antarctic explorer, was a close friend of Roosevelt's.

Senator Cordell Hull of Tennessee and Senator Ham Lewis of Illinois, also discussed as nominees, were for Roosevelt. Both were old friends of his.

Certainly one of the most discussed candidates was Ohio's "little great man," Newton D. Baker. Small and intense and a fiery speaker, Baker began his political career as a reform mayor of Cleveland, served as Secretary of War in President Wilson's cabinet, spoke up as one of the first advocates of American membership in the League of Nations and the World Court, sided with the progressive wing of his party on social legislation, and yet was one of the most successful corporation lawyers in the country.

Political reporter Gould Lincoln of the *Washington Star* also noted that Baker had the full support of former Ohio governor and Democratic presidential nominee in 1920, James Cox. Lincoln also wrote that Baker's stand on the prohibition issue would not be as offensive to the southern "dry" Democrats as "wet" Ritchie would.

Roosevelt himself analyzed Baker's presidential prospects in a letter to Josephus Daniels, his Navy boss and an old friend:

"He [Baker] labors under very definite political handicaps," wrote Roosevelt. "Because of, or rather in spite of, his perfectly legitimate law practice, he is labelled by many progressives as the attorney for J. P. Morgan and the Van Schweringens; he is opposed by labor; he would be opposed by the German-Americans; and also by the bulk of the Irish because of his consistent League of Nations attitude up to this year. As they say, 'Dem are the sad facts!' All this seems a pity because New would make a better President than I would!'"

Four years before, Roosevelt had tried to press Baker into greater political activity, but Baker had excused himself, referring to a heart ailment. In any event, Baker's greatest handicap was his refusal to seek delegates. Jouett Shouse, Chairman of the Democratic Executive Committee, who admired Baker, told a friend, "In these days, no one can hope for the nomination without an active fight."

Among the lesser-mentioned candidates in the early stages were Senator James A. Reed of Missouri, Governor George White of Ohio, Senator Joseph Robinson of Arkansas (who had been vice-presidential nominee in 1928), and Speaker of the House, John N. Garner of Texas.

But Roosevelt's huge concern, which he had mentioned to Morgenthau some months before, was the enormous political question mark of the man he had twice nominated for President, former governor of New York, Alfred E. Smith.

In a strange way, the Smith-Roosevelt feud paralleled the Roosevelt-Taft feud of a previous generation. Both sets of men had started as close friends. Just as Theodore Roosevelt had picked Taft to succeed him as President, so did Al Smith pick Franklin D. Roosevelt for the New York governorship.

In each case, the rift began when the selected successors refused to play the continuous roles of protege. In each case, the rift began with the growing jealousy of the man out of power for the man in power. In each case, a binding friendship broke up into deep bitterness.

At the Albany Legislative Correspondents Dinner in 1931, the program featured this poem:

> "Franklin D., Alfred E.
> One for each and each for one.
> Till the presidential run;
> Franklin D., Alfred E.
> Love no longer—Hope is stronger
> Each for ME."

Smith had kept clear of any political activity after his 1928 defeat. He was no longer interested in the Presidency, he said. He pointed out also that only two defeated candidates for President had been renominated in the Democratic party, Grover Cleveland in 1892 and William Jennings Bryan in 1900 and 1908. Smith did make several speeches criticizing the Hoover administration, particularly on its inadequate unemployment relief, its failure to repeal the Eighteenth Amendment on prohibition, and its enactment of a tariff law "unfair to the American people and discriminatory to our foreign market."

But to his friend, Bronx boss Ed Flynn, Smith insisted he was through with politics and never could be persuaded to get into it again. "He opened a drawer in his desk," said Flynn, "pulled out and spread before him a number of papers, and said, 'Ed, these are all debts that I must clear up. Financially I am in a very bad position.' "

He told Farley much the same thing and he was even more specific with Nebraska Democratic leader Arthur Mullen, who had worked hard for Smith in previous campaigns.

"There's no chance for a Catholic to be President. Not in my lifetime or in yours, Arthur," said Smith.

"I know it," said Mullen. "I knew it in '24. I knew it in '28. I knew we couldn't carry Nebraska for you, and I knew then, just as in '24, that you couldn't win; but you almost read me out of the Catholic Church in '24 because I knew it."

"Well, you were right," Smith said. "I can't win against bigots."

Smith's daughter, Emily Smith Warner, wrote that the Smith-Roosevelt rift started when Roosevelt fired or refused to reappoint

good Smith men to important state jobs—much the same complaint Theodore Roosevelt first had of Taft.

"Roosevelt, without consulting Father, or even informing him,"
wrote Smith's daughter, "called a meeting of the State Committee
of the party. The Governor had been re-elected only five months
earlier on a platform that had contained a Wet plank. Father had
favored it and Roosevelt himself had finally accepted it. Now, however, without Father's knowledge, he pushed through the State
Committee a resolution requesting the New York State members
of the National Committee to oppose the adoption of a Wet plank
in the Democratic national platform and Robert Moses has told
me that there was a very obvious feeling among Governor Roosevelt's supporters, even during his first term, 'to leave Smith out of
the picture.' "

The Roosevelt side of that story was this:

Democratic National Committee Chairman, John J. Raskob
called a special meeting of the National Committee for March,
1931. Raskob was a strong Smith man. Before announcing the
meeting, he had sent all committeemen a letter saying that he
hoped they would adopt a resolution recommending repeal of the
Eighteenth Amendment. The general political feeling was that this
Raskob move was made primarily to embarrass Roosevelt. Roosevelt's acceptability in the "dry" south was because he was known
as a mild "Wet" rather than a "dripping Wet." But if Raskob
pushed through a "dripping Wet" plank at this early stage, and
Roosevelt felt forced to accept it, his southern popularity would
diminish.

"The theory was that the Raskob crowd did not care for whom
the South voted," wrote Charlie Michelson, "as long as it was kept
out of the Roosevelt column."

Roosevelt people claim F.D.R. tried to call Raskob and Smith,
without success, then sent letters of protest to both men, and
finally called a meeting of the New York State Committee to be
held in Albany three days before the National Committee met in
Washington. The morning of the state meeting, Roosevelt met

with Howe, Farley, and Flynn in his bedroom at the Executive Mansion and the quartet drafted a resolution saying that the National Committee had no authority to pledge or advise the party on any issues arising between national conventions. Farley then got on the phone to committeemen all over the country, and filled them in on what was happening. As soon as the Democratic State Committee in New York passed his resolution, Roosevelt sent Farley to the Washington meeting with a copy of it, and he and Howe contacted key people such as Senator Cordell Hull, Governor Byrd, and Senator Joseph Robinson to organize the fight against Raskob.

"I made a count of noses before the meeting got under way," said Farley. "It disclosed the fact that we could defeat the Raskob proposal by at least two to one."

Despite a speech at the National Committee by Al Smith, Raskob's wet bomb fizzled.

Roosevelt wrote about this first victory to New York committeeman Norman Mack, "I think on the whole that, largely thanks to you and Jim Farley, that meeting did no harm—and indeed I am inclined to think that in the long run, the result will be beneficial to the party. . . . The thing we must avoid now is no harsh words and no sulking in tents."

With that danger averted, Roosevelt turned to face fresh danger from New York's Tammany Hall. Tammany graft and corruption had started to seep to the surface. *Time Magazine* had said of Tammany: "First in war, first in peace, and first in the pockets of its countrymen."

In March, 1931, the City Affairs Committee presented its charges against Mayor James J. Walker, requesting his removal. Roosevelt ruled that he had not found "sufficient justification in these documents, as submitted, to remove the Mayor of the City of New York."

The time was ticklish. If Roosevelt clamped too quickly and too hard on Tammany, he might not only lose most of the ninety-four New York delegates at the upcoming convention, but he might cut his vote in New York City alone by a hundred thousand. In a tight race, this could cost him the state. On the other hand, he could not seem too subservient in a Tammany investigation, or it might stamp him as a Tammany man throughout the rest of the country, with even more damaging effect.

Roosevelt tried to steer zigzag down the sensitive middle, and made nobody happy. The *New York World*, which had supported Roosevelt for Governor, now denounced him, saying he had "lost a respect for which no victory can compensate."

Attending the Woodrow Wilson Foundation meeting early that year, Henry Morgenthau, Sr., saw a picture on the wall of Franklin D. Roosevelt in the 1920 campaign. "That's my candidate," he told Bernard Baruch. After some silence, Baruch said, "Uncle Henry, if Frank is nominated, I won't give one cent to the Democratic Party."

"But Bernie," said Morgenthau, Sr., "hasn't he been a good Governor?"

"Yes," said Baruch, "but he's so wishy-washy."

The wishy-washiness continued, especially in the Tammany situation. Roosevelt refused to take the initiative in pressing for any further investigation. However, the State Senate and Assembly passed their own resolution for a joint legislative committee to investigate New York City affairs and appointed Judge Samuel Seabury as its chief counsel. Seabury stretched the investigation deep into the following year.

Nationally, the Roosevelt picture kept brightening.

The Howe-Farley office at 331 Madison Avenue, New York City, was now on a full-time campaign basis. Roosevelt completely dropped the occasional coy, uncandid quality he had shown only a few months before on December 8, 1930, when he wrote a Mrs. Casper Whitney, "I have seen so much of the White House ever since 1892 that I have no hankering, secret or otherwise, to be a candidate."

Roosevelt scouts were busy everywhere: Lester Dillingham of Idaho working the southwestern states; Joseph Guffey of Pennsylvania, concentrating on Ohio and Kentucky; Robert Jackson of New Hampshire, in the New England area. "While they were not on salary," said Farley, "we paid their expenses. Frank C. Walker, the committee treasurer, was able to scratch up the cash just when it was needed most. We were on a hand-to-mouth basis, and on more than one occasion it actually happened that we didn't have enough money in the till to buy postage stamps from Uncle Sam."

About fifty Roosevelt-for-President Clubs sprang up—some spontaneously, some assisted—throughout the country by March, 1931, including fifteen hundred members of the "Warm Springs and Merryweather Roosevelt-for-President Club." Howe-Farley widely publicized the Warm Springs Club plus the announcement by Governor Russell who said, "Georgia is happy to have a favorite son to present to the next Democratic National Convention."

In the parade of pamphlets, out of the Howe-Farley office, one of the most effective was a statistical study of Roosevelt's phenomenal vote pull in upstate New York compared to previous candidates. Another good one was called, "Roosevelt and Human Welfare." Separate pamphlets touched on the Roosevelt record in labor, unemployment, care for the aged. Meanwhile Howe kept up a flow of advisory memos to his staff: one warned of special care in answering letters from Negroes. Another warned those in Texas and Arizona to make sure "that the wet Catholics do not leap on the bandwagon first. . . . If that happens, we will not get any of the Independent and Republican Drys, who are at present most kindly disposed. . . ."

Somebody else most kindly disposed was Colonel Edward M. House, who had figured so prominently as Woodrow Wilson's confidant. Roosevelt suggested that Howe and House get together. At their first meeting, which began with a long silence, Howe asked House, "What about Texas?"

"You can count on Texas," said Colonel House.

"Why?" Howe wanted to know.

"Because I will send word to my friends there that Roosevelt is our best bet," said House.

BALLOTS & BANDWAGONS

House did send friends to the annual Texas Round-Up at Austin to boom Roosevelt, later sent to Howe the names of his collected recruits. House and Howe later got along so well that House wrote Roosevelt, "It is a joy to co-operate with him for the reason that he is so able and yet so yielding to suggestions. We never have any arguments, and have no difficulty in reaching conclusions satisfactory to us both. I congratulate you on having such a "loyal and efficient lieutenant.""

Something that grabbed the headlines at the end of March was the first of five presidential polls by Jesse Straus, president of R. H. Macy and Company, and one of the original "Friends of Roosevelt." The first Straus poll of delegates and alternates to the 1928 Democratic National Convention put Roosevelt far in the lead.

Of approximately 2,000 queries, 942 replied and 844 expressed a preference. Of these, 478 voted for Roosevelt, 125 for Smith, 73 for Young, 39 for Ritchie, 38 for Robinson, 35 for Baker, 15 for Reed, 8 for former nominee Cox, 6 for Hull, 6 for White, and a scattering for such candidates as William G. McAdoo of California, Woodrow Wilson's son-in-law, who deadlocked Smith in the 1924 convention to give the nomination to John Davis; Governor Murray of Oklahoma; Governor Joseph B. Ely of Massachusetts, and others. Undecided: 98.

Most of those voting for Roosevelt expressed high regard for Smith, but believed his nomination might cause a revival of the religious issue. New York was not canvassed. No returns came from Oregon, Wisconsin, Wyoming, only two replies from California, and one from Virginia.

Straus estimated that two-thirds of the polled delegates and alternates would also attend the 1932 convention. Roosevelt led in all but three states—Massachusetts where Smith led; Maryland where Ritchie was a majority choice; and Arkansas, home of Senator Robinson. Roosevelt and Smith tied in Connecticut and Delaware, and Roosevelt led in Ohio which had four of its own favorite-son candidates. Roosevelt also led in every southern state, except Arkansas.

Two weeks later, Straus took another poll, this one of Democratic business and professional men, a total of twelve hundred, representing ever state but New York. Roosevelt led Smith five to one, and even beat Owen D. Young, supposedly the candidate of big business, by a two to one margin.

Commenting on the polls, and on its own survey of the situation, the New York Times editorialized: "Whether it is an advantage to lead the field a year in advance of the conventions, most political observers believe that Governor Roosevelt of New York holds this position at the present time. His prestige as Governor of the most populous state, the wide margin of his victory in last year's election and his long association in the National Council of the Democratic Party have combined to give him this position."

Roosevelt's good friend Robert W. Wooley had written him about the perils of being the front-runner so early:

"Herein lies the danger," wrote Wooley, "a very serious danger. Automatically you become the target of other candidates, real and potential. There isn't a single favorite son whose delegation won't be held out of the Roosevelt column so long as there is a reasonable chance of getting something for that favorite son, even at your expense."

Wooley also passed on the whispered word that a good friend of Governor Byrd had told him, "The ticket is Baker and Byrd—B. and B. They were born in adjoining houses in Martinsburg. Baker's nomination assures Virginia of the Vice-Presidency. If Roosevelt is nominated, the vice-presidential nomination will inevitably go to the West."

"No blame attaches to Byrd or Virginia," added Wooley. "You and I know that human nature gets on the job in a political convention. It is quite true that you can't beat somebody with everybody, but by offering the Vice-Presidency, Cabinet posts, ambassadorships, etc., it is a simple enough trick to combine the opposition and vanquish the lead horse, meaning you. Now that the 'tumult and shouting' has died . . . Roper and I took stock this morning as to the possibility of your being made an 'ancient sacrifice.' Frankly, we are very apprehensive—I might say alarmed. We saw McAdoo far out in the lead at this stage, stopped in 1924."

Roosevelt was similarly concerned. The Stop-Roosevelt movement had picked up speed and strength. Heading it was the Raskob-Shouse group—who ran Smith's previous presidential campaign—now with all the money and authority they needed. Their great handicap was that they were playing the field against the favorite and seemed unable to focus on any single strong candidate.

As the Democratic National Committee Chairman, John J. Raskob had also given more money to the Democratic party than anyone else. A converted Republican and a prominent industrialist, he was a Catholic, a Wet, a millionaire, and the author of a magazine article entitled, "Everybody Ought To Be Rich." When Smith chose Raskob to run his presidential campaign in 1928, Roosevelt regarded it as "a grave mistake," and the two disliked each other ever since. A deceptively bashful man with a quiet voice, Chairman Raskob was still the logical focus of a united force to stop Roosevelt.

While Chairman Raskob found politics "difficult and unattractive," his full-time, high-salaried director, dapper Jouett Shouse, with his spats and walking stick, enjoyed the full play of politics. Raskob planned to use Shouse as his front man to control the upcoming Democratic National Convention. Anyway, together, they made a powerful team.

But they still didn't have a candidate.

At the Governor's conference that year, Roosevelt made a serious impression on other state leaders by his expressed willingness to experiment economically to end the depression. Coming back home through Ohio, Roosevelt talked with every politically powerful leader in the state, except Newton Baker, and very carefully avoided offending all the state's favorite sons.

Roosevelt returned full of political ideas and passed some of them on to Howe in a memo: "*Oregon:* Scott Bullitt. Should he govern Washington, Idaho and Colorado as well? *Southern California:* Dockweiler. Who for Northern California? *Nevada:* We have Key Pittman here, but his loyalty is doubtful. Whom shall we get? *Montana:* J. Bruce Kremer and Walker's brother, who is State Senator. Should we ask J. Bruce Kremer to cover generally Montana, Idaho, Washington, Wyoming and possibly Nevada and North Dakota? If Bruce says so, matters exclusively pertaining to Montana can be referred to State Senator Walker, and other states to such persons as Bruce recommends. *New Mexico:* Somebody to be dug up from the Straus poll, unless Colonel House knows somebody. *Oklahoma:* Shall we play with Farley's friend, Lorton, of the *Tulsa World? North Carolina:* Try and get in touch with Byrnes. *Kentucky:* This should be decided—several people possible. *Michigan:* G. Hall Roosevelt. *Maine:* Ask Henry Morgenthau, Sr., to let us know. *Delaware:* leave alone. *New Hampshire:* Ask Colonel House. *Georgia:* F.D.R."

It was about this time that Jim Farley scheduled his annual trip to the national convention of the Benevolent and Protective Order of Elks, this one set for Seattle. "I had made plans many months in advance to be there," said Farley, "solely with the thought of attending the convention and enjoying a bit of scenery en route. But Louis had other thoughts. He saw an opportunity to mix a little politics with good-comradeship."

Roosevelt liked the idea. "At his suggestion," said Farley, "I was equipped with a Rand McNally map of the United States, a flock of train schedules, the latest available list of Democratic National Committee members and state chairmen. We ate lunch and then adjourned to his [Roosevelt's] tiny office in Hyde Park, off in a wing of the house where we spread out the documents and went to work. . . . The itinerary was decided upon in large measure by the Governor, who had a keen sense of selection, determining what states it was wise to visit and what states it was wise to shun."

In nineteen days, Farley covered eighteen states. "I was a kind of roving political 'listening post,'" wrote Farley, "whose purpose was to gather up every available scrap of information. . . ."

"If I got to a city," wrote Farley, "and found as many as five-hundred people waiting to look me over, I shook hands with each one personally. I was extremely careful to get first and last names correctly, and of course never disputed the views of others if it was at all possible to agree. It always creates a bad impression to start off with an argument."

Roosevelt's friend, noted author and Ambassador Claude G. Bowers, later told of attending a political rally in Terre Haute, Indiana, and hearing constant references to "Jim."

"Assuming the reference was to some local politician," said Bowers, "I asked, 'What Jim?' Evidently astonished by my ignorance, they replied in a chorus, 'Jim Farley.' He had spent a few hours in this Hoosier city and was already established as a sort of next-door neighbor."

Indiana's state chairman, Earl Peters, was overly optimistic about being able to capture the state delegation for Roosevelt, and he transferred this overoptimism to Farley.

Farley's contact in Nebraska was Arthur Mullen. At the special National Committee meeting in March, when Raskob tried to promote a repeal plank, Mullen was quoted in the *New York Times* as saying that the Raskob plan took away the genuine electoral prerogative of the delegates, and that wasn't democracy.

"Farley asked me point-blank if I was for Roosevelt," wrote Mullen. "I said I wasn't interested yet in any one candidate, but that I wouldn't be for anyone who'd contributed in any way to defeat Smith in 1928. I passed Farley on to Governor Charles W. Bryan. Bryan had told me a little while earlier, that he thought the way to win the election was having as candidate a progressive Democratic governor of a middle western state who, like himself, was being pressed to run. I don't know who was pressing him—but I thought it wise to have Farley see him."

In Aberdeen, South Dakota, Farley sat in a hot lunchroom with National Committeeman William Howes. "We sat there for some time, exchanging generalities," wrote Farley, "without discussing what either of us really had in mind. Just before it was time to go, Bill decided to let me know what he really thought. He plumped his fat fist on the table and growled in a deep voice, "Farley I'm damned tired of backing losers. In my opinion, Roosevelt can sweep the country, and I'm going to support him."

Reporting to Roosevelt and Howe during his trip, Farley wrote: "Since I left New York, I have visited Indiana, Wisconsin, Minnesota, North and South Dakota, Montana and am now in Seattle. There is apparently an almost unanimous sentiment for you in every one of these states, and the organization in every instance is for you wholeheartedly. Here and there, and not very frequently, is sentiment for Smith. To be frank with you, that comes mostly from ardent Catholic admirers, and in some instances, from strong Wet advocates. On one or two occasions, I have heard Baker's name mentioned, but that is all.

"In my talks with the different leaders, they indicated that there crops up occasionally a boost for Ritchie or Young; and in nearly every instance, it comes from the power group (Raskob-Shouse). They apparently are trying to get back of either one or the other in the hope that they may be able to tie up some votes for Young and Ritchie, to be used later on when they decide what candidate they are going to try to support, to try to keep you from getting the nomination. . . ."

In another report, Farley said, "It has been brought to my attention that the reason a number of these senators and governors want their names presented to the convention as presidential candidates is because they feel it is the only way they can be considered for the Vice-Presidency. . . ."

Elsewhere in the report, he added, "If I continue to find the same sentiment in the other states that I have found already, my statement on reaching New York will be so enthusiastic that those who read it will think I'm a fit candidate for an insane asylum."

He had a parting word in one report on the growing crop of rival candidates: "Governor, the presidential job must be a great one, judging from the way they are all anxious to have it. . . ."

Howe passed on some of the Farley enthusiasm to field worker Daniel C. Roper. "The situation north of the Mason and Dixon line is on the face of it too good to be true," he wrote. "In practically every state we have received very definite assurance from the heads of the state organizations as well as from their Senators and Congressmen that they are in favor of Franklin's nomination and that their state will instruct for him.

"The only two exceptions of importance are Illinois, which will probably give Lewis a complimentary vote. Here Lewis called in person on the Governor and assured him that he was for him and only wanted a complimentary vote, and the Chairman of the State Committee has assured us that the state organization will be for Roosevelt. The other state is Missouri, which will probably give Reed a complimentary vote, but he has gone out of his way to express his friendliness toward Franklin, and confidentially I learn that he is in very bad health and becoming mentally uncertain, and that there is great doubt of his being physically a presidential possibility by primary day."

To an Illinois friend, Buell Brake, Howe said, "It is a long way to convention time, and many things may happen; but at the present moment, I think all the Governor's friends who have been in touch with the various state leaders feel that, were the convention to be held tomorrow, the Governor would be elected on the first ballot, with not more than three states out of line."

A private Kiplinger Letter sent only to Roosevelt in mid-July agreed with all this high hope.

"The gossip during the last thirty days is that your chances for the Democratic nomination have been greatly strengthened," Kiplinger wrote Roosevelt on July 10, "and that there is no other candidate who compares with you in availability. Most of the dark horses have dropped out of the gossip but Mr. Smith and Mr. Young are still mentioned frequently by shrewd commentators as pretty fair possibilities. . . ."

Shortly after his return from the Elks tour, Farley announced that Roosevelt already could count on 678 certain votes on the first ballot, only 92 short of the required 770 needed to nominate. Farley then predicted a bandwagon swing that would put F.D.R. over on that first ballot.

"I was amazed that a campaign manager could be so frank and open," later wrote prominent historian Claude Bowers, whom Roosevelt much admired. "Farley said that 'while some people think me crazy' he could not figure the possibility of a combination that could prevent Roosevelt's nomination. Taking a pencil and paper, he wrote down for the opposition, Massachusetts, Connecticut, New Jersey, part of Pennsylvania, Ohio, Illinois, California, Maryland, Virginia, Texas, and Missouri—much more than necessary to prevent Roosevelt's nomination; but he did not think these opposition votes could be held, and he was sure that if Roosevelt went into the convention with 600 votes, he would be nominated."

The *New York Herald Tribune* deprecated Farley and his predictions. In an editorial entitled "Roosevelt's Farley," they said that while Farley made friends quickly, the old party warhorses would never let such a newcomer select the nominee.

The Farley talk disturbed Colonel House and he called Howe about it. Howe wrote House:

"My dear Colonel:

"Indeed I am only too pleased to have you call me Louis, instead of the formidable Mr. Howe; and I am really flattered, and feel that you consider me a well-established member of your wide circle of acquaintances. You spoke to me over the phone about the possible danger of using Mr. Farley as our representative for Field. I have of course kept that in mind, but I am anxious to have you meet Farley, and have you talk with him yourself, in order that you may gain an idea of his virtues as well as his faults. I doubt if Mr. Farley would be a good man to send anywhere in the South, and I want to talk to you sometime soon about where we can find a man familiar with Southern ways to use for that purpose this fall. But my judgment has been that Farley is temperamentally and physically the ideal man to use in the Western states. He has a wholesome breeziness of manner and a frank and open character which is characteristic of all westerners. In addition, I think he gives a distinct impression of being a very practical and business-like politician, as well; and the reactions I have received from many letters which came to the Governor after his trip, have been exceedingly complimentary and favorable to him."

Farley saw House, and the two got along well (even though House had hoped to see his friend Homer Cummings of Connecticut get Farley's job).

"Colonel House said that his idea of an ideal candidate for Vice-President was Senator Cordell Hull of Tennessee," Farley wrote afterward, "I agreed with him. The Colonel said further that, although he could not conceive of Governor Roosevelt being stopped, his next choice for President was also Hull. I agreed that no better choice could be made."

One of Farley's recruits, Arthur Mullen of Nebraska, came to New York, and Farley took him to F.D.R.'s town house.

"I told Roosevelt that Charlie Bryan was a candidate," said Mullen. "You want to start out with the theory that Nebraska will be against you if Bryan can run it," Mullen told F.D.R. and added, "He thinks that since he was defeated as candidate for Vice-President in 1924, he should have been the candidate in '28. He'll be against you now because he'll be for himself."

Roosevelt had a direct question for Mullen. "What about you?" he asked. "Will you take charge of the fight for me in Nebraska?"

"I'm friendly to you and your candidacy," Mullen told him, "but I want assurance that my feet won't be pulled out from under me, as they were by McAdoo in 1924."

"I'll give you that assurance," said Roosevelt.

"Write it," said Mullen.

Roosevelt wrote it.

Back in Nebraska, sometime later, McAdoo visited Mullen, talked at length about Roosevelt's ill health and inability to campaign and added, "We don't want a dead man on the ticket, Arthur."

"You won't have one," said Mullen.

The health issue cropped up more constantly now. Even Kiplinger mentioned it in one of his letters to Roosevelt, ". . . there was a wave of gossip among newspaper men that your health would be a very strong deterrent—not in itself but in the public doubt which the opposition could build up about it."

Howe decided to hit the issue full face, contrived a challenge from F.D.R.'s Republican friend Earl Looker who asked Roosevelt to submit to a physical examination to assure the country of his fitness for the Presidency.

The Director of the New York Academy of Medicine then selected a committee of prominent doctors, including a brain specialist. "We believe," they said of Roosevelt after the examination, "that his health and powers of endurance are such as to allow him to meet any demands of private and public life."

Writing about the medical report and his own observations, Looker said in *Liberty Magazine*, "I had come to the conclusion that he seemed able to take more punishment than many men ten years younger."

Howe ordered 50,000 reprints of the article, sent them to key people all over the country.

Still unsettled was the hovering question of the Smith candidacy.

The *Washington Star* reported that Smith had declined to come out in favor of Roosevelt when he was asked the pointblank question. He also declined again to say that he would not be a candidate for the Presidency. Then the *Star* added:

"If he is to oppose the nomination of Governor Roosevelt, as has been insisted in certain Democratic quarters, he has given no public indication of that intention. Furthermore, unless he himself is to be a candidate, he will have to find some very good reasons for opposing the man who three times placed him in nomination for the Presidency, or else be considered an ingrate."

Feeding the simmering feud was the steady gossip. Roosevelt heard that Smith had called him "a crackpot," and Smith heard that Roosevelt had called him "a rotten governor."

Louis Howe confided to a friendly reporter that Roosevelt had been told he could have the presidential nomination if he would make Al Smith his manager and accept his guidance while in the

White House. Howe reported that Roosevelt had pounded his desk with fury and said, "I'll be damned if I do it!"

Smith's daughter later wrote that her father had a growing feeling of distrust that Governor Roosevelt acted sometimes without proper consideration for the public welfare, that Roosevelt's great personal charm was marred by "a capacity for vindictiveness."

The vindictiveness worked both ways.

Acting as a peacemaking mutual friend, Clark Howell, publisher of the *Atlanta Constitution*, went to see Smith, and told him, "Governor, you hold in the palm of your hand the assurance of an overwhelming Democratic victory next year, or you are in a position where you could jeopardize the present prospect of sure success."

"How?" said Smith.

"By your attitude toward Franklin Roosevelt," Howell said. "With your support of him, all opposition to him will vanish, and his nomination will be a mere formality. The country expects you to support him, and it will not believe that you can possibly do otherwise."

"The hell I can't!" said Smith.

Smith then went on to say that he was for the party first, above any man, and would support the man who seemed best for the party.

"Governor," said Howell, "is there any ground for personal hostility on your part against Roosevelt?"

'No," said Smith. "Socially, we are friends. He has always been kind to me and my family, and has gone out of his way to be agreeable to us at the Mansion in Albany."

Then Smith rose, stamped his foot, and said, "Do you know, by God, that he has never consulted me about a damn thing since he has been Governor? He has taken bad advice, and from sources not friendly to me. He ignored me!" Smith then slammed his fist on the table and added, "By God, he invited me to his house before he recently went to Georgia, and he did not even mention to me the subject of his candidacy."

Smith added a parting slam at Roosevelt's "dodging" the repeal issue. "Why the hell didn't he speak out," said Smith to Howell. "He has been more outspoken on the subject than even I had been, and now ain't the time for trimming."

Howell wrote all this to Roosevelt in specific detail.

It was still a long jump from vindictiveness to open revolt. The Stop-Roosevelt leaders now more persistently courted Smith to lead their movement.

"I asked him about it," said Smith's daughter, "and found him reluctant to head the movement."

". . . What are your objections?" she asked.

"Well," said Smith slowly, "in order to build up any great amount of support for me, somebody would have to go all over the country. It would take a lot of money—more than I could put up. I don't want to ask my friends to do it. I just don't want to do that any more. In 1920, my name was offered to the convention, though it was just a gesture. In 1924, I made a fight for the nomination. In 1928, I was actually nominated. So I don't want to go looking for it again in 1932. I don't want to be the Bryan of the party."

Still, on December 28, 1931, the New York Times front-paged the story that Smith again would be a candidate for President. It was somewhat premature.

For Roosevelt, the possible Smith candidacy and the Tammany corruption scandal had an obvious political connection: as long as Smith stayed out of the race, F.D.R. still had a possible chance to get the Tammany-controlled New York delegates. As long as that possibility existed, Roosevelt tried to soft-pedal his own participation in the Seabury investigation.

The deeper Judge Samuel Seabury dug, the more Tammany corruption he exposed. The biggest initial target was New York County Sheriff Thomas M. Farley (no relation to James A.). Newspapers soon nicknamed Farley as 'Tin Box" Tim because he had managed to deposit $396,000 over a seven-year period when his total salary had been $87,000, and had insisted that all this extra money came from a tin box. Seabury sent Roosevelt a transcript of the Farley testimony and Roosevelt's only answer was continued silence.

Seabury, whose sensational investigation now gave him a national prominence, and even some pretensions for a presidential nomination, took an obvious cut at Roosevelt in a speech at Cincinnati, in which he said of the Tammany menace: "It drives public men, whose instincts would lead them to speak out in protest against the corruption that has been revealed, to a solemn silence. . . . Where they hold public office and are forced on given occasions to rule adversely to Tammany Hall, they soften their opposition so that while the public will not regard them as pro-Tammany, Tammany Hall will not regard them as opposed to it."

After Seabury's Cincinnati speech, Irwin Steingut, the Democratic leader of the New York State Assembly said of Seabury, "He hopes the Democratic Convention next June will nominate him for President or Vice President." Various newspapers around the country echoed this. One paper wrote, "Tammany foe to be candidate for Presidency." Another Indiana paper said, "Judge Seabury, controlling genius behind New York investigations, does not deny aspirations." And, in a series on presidential possibilities, Walter Chambers wrote in *Forum* magazine of Seabury, "He combines the virtues of Franklin Roosevelt, Newton D. Baker, Owen Young, Albert Ritchie and Alfred E. Smith."

This same Chambers, who wrote a book on Seabury, was reported to Howe as approaching some people on Capitol Hill, "especially Wheeler of Montana, to get his viewpoint on Seabury as a presidential possibility."

But if Seabury's political oar was out, he still kept his prow pointed straight at Roosevelt's inaction with Tammany corruption.

As if to give life to the Seabury charge, Roosevelt maintained his official silence until Smith finally announced himself as a presidential candidate in February. Two weeks afterward, with the Tammany delegates firmly switched to Smith, Roosevelt finally fired Sheriff Farley.

Once the Tammany cord was completely cut, Roosevelt men

then milked it for all the national political value they could get.

Daniel Roper, an old friend of both Roosevelt and McAdoo, in a letter to Henry Morgenthau, Jr., earlier had summed up the situation:

"I doubt whether conditions have radically changed from those to which General Bragg of the Iron Brigade of Wisconsin referred when he said in the Democratic Convention of 1884 with regard to Cleveland, 'we love him for the enemies he has made.' Cleveland was nominated and Tammany voted for him in the General Election of that year. In 1892, Tammany was still bitterly opposed to Cleveland in the Convention, voting solidly against him on every ballot, but he was nominated, and again Tammany voted for him in November. The New York delegation walked out of the Baltimore Convention in 1912 for a conference and came back to switch their vote from Underwood to Champ Clark, hoping to defeat Woodrow Wilson, yet Tammany voted for Wilson in the election.

". . . If Governor Roosevelt goes to the Convention of 1932 as the idol of Tammany, he may be nominated but would not likely be elected. On the other hand, if the Governor, in the near future by word and act makes the American people understand that he is not and will not be controlled by Tammany, I believe he can both be nominated and elected in 1932."

Roosevelt became an openly declared candidate on January 23, 1932. North Dakota's State Democratic Convention already had endorsed him but under state law it was necessary for Roosevelt himself to announce his candidacy in his own handwriting in order to have a slate of delegates in the primary. In his letter to F. W. MacLean, secretary of North Dakota's Democratic State Committee, Roosevelt said, "As Governor of a State containing nearly thirteen million people, I am, especially at this time, obligated to a still higher duty. . . ."

On that same day of January 23, six Alaska delegates were pledged to Roosevelt at its Democratic Territorial Convention, the first delegates actually pledged to him. Howe and Farley had laid that groundwork with a flow of letters. United States territories and possessions totaled thirty-eight delegates, and Roosevelt got thirty of them.

Chairman of the Democratic Executive Committee Jouett Shouse was a Smith-Raskob man, an anxious candidate for the job of Temporary Chairman of the upcoming convention. When Shouse toured the South, stirring up whatever favorite-son sentiment he could, Howe wrote him a stern letter of disapproval. Shouse wrote Roosevelt, denying partisanship, and Roosevelt answered:

". . . I think that these situations arise in large part because a great many people who are very enthusiastic friends of mine, in different states, have jumped to the conclusion that, while you and John [Raskob] have very properly not come out in favor of any candidate for nomination next year, you are going into different states to 'block Roosevelt' by encouraging uninstructed delegations or favorite sons. They feel, of course, that this would be just as unethical as if you and John were to come out definitely for an individual, and, of course, they are right in this point of view."

"What many of them fail to realize," continued Roosevelt, "is that I have in good faith lived up to my declaration, and that I am taking absolutely no part in any movement in my behalf. I feel confident that, just as Governor Smith is maintaining an absolutely correct attitude as titular leader of the party, that it would not be correct for him to endorse any individual candidate, so you and John will, as Executive Officers of the National Committee, maintain the same position."

This, of course, preceded the Smith statement on his own candidacy.

The *New York Herald Tribune* had predicted, "If Smith should actively and publicly oppose Roosevelt, Roosevelt would not have a chance in the world." The *Tribune* added that if Smith did fight F.D.R., "the prize would go almost certainly to someone not a party to the quarrel, such as Newton D. Baker," and then the *Tribune* put in a political parenthesis, "it may go to him anyhow."

Smith made his statement on February 8:

"So many inquiries have come to me from friends throughout the country who worked for and believed in me, as to my attitude in the present political situation, that I feel that I owe it to my friends and to the millions of men and women who supported me so loyally in 1928, to make my position clear.

"If the Democratic National Convention, after careful consideration, should decide that it wants me to lead, I will make the fight; but I will not make a pre-convention campaign to secure the support of delegates.

"By action of the Democratic National Convention of 1928, I am leader of my party in the nation. With a full sense of the responsibility thereby imposed, I shall not, in advance of the convention, either support or oppose the candidacy of any aspirant for the nomination."

Commenting on the Smith statement, the *New York Times* editorialized, "What promised at one time to be a rather tame contest for the Democratic nomination, will hereafter be bristling with excitement. When one of the contestants is named Al Smith, none of the others can afford for an instant to be off their guard."

The day after Smith's announcement, Shouse told newsmen, "I have repeatedly expressed the opinion that, from the standpoint of party welfare, it was unwise to foreclose the nomination months in advance of the convention. . . . I have not hesitated to voice the belief that it would be wiser, from the standpoint of party and country alike, not to instruct delegates to the convention in favor of any candidate, save where such instruction is necessary under the Primary Laws of some of the states."

Roosevelt answered this statement sharply in a press interview several days later: "His suggestion that all delegations go to the National Convention uninstructed is unfortunately contrary to the principles of a party, and the intent of the laws and party rules of almost every state. More than a generation ago, there existed widespread disapproval of the kind of national convention which became merely a trading post for a handful of powerful leaders, and where the nomination itself had nothing to do with the popular choice of the rank and file of the party itself.

"As a result, and in keeping with the historic tradition of the party, primary laws and party rules were enacted in practically every state for the purpose of permitting the party voters to express a choice for candidates. Mr. Shouse's suggestion would nullify and destroy this fundamental principle. The rank and file of the party should be heard."

Strip away the words, and the loud insistence on principles, the final fact was much more basic: Shouse wanted Smith and Roosevelt wanted Roosevelt.

This conflict was scheduled to come to a head on April 4 in Chicago when the convention's Arrangements Committee was to meet and pick the Temporary Chairman and decide other convention preliminaries.

To counter the Shouse move, Roosevelt wrote his friend, Governor Harry Byrd of Virginia:

"Dear Harry: John Raskob spoke to me about Jouett Shouse for Temporary Chairman. My hesitation to agree with this has nothing to do with personal politics; but frankly, as I told Raskob, I am inclined to think that Shouse has become rather an old story throughout the country because of his many speeches, propaganda statements, etc. etc. In other words, by the average voter, Republican and Democrat, he is regarded as a propagandist. . . . On the other hand, if we can get some comparatively new name, which is free from this, might it not be a very excellent idea? . . .

"I have no candidate for the temporary chairmanship; that is something we should talk over."

At the Arrangements Committee meeting, Farley went as an observer and the Roosevelt forces proposed Senator Alben Barkley of Kentucky as Temporary Chairman. Shouse, however, had campaigned hard. "Not realizing what was going on," wrote Farley, "many members favorable to us had already promised to give him their support. It was an awkward situation; and little time remained to do anything."

Byrd suggested a compromise: Barkley for Temporary Chairman, Shouse for Permanent Chairman. Shouse agreed, but only if Roosevelt personally approved it.

"We went upstairs to the suite occupied by Bob Jackson and myself," wrote Farley, "and telephoned Albany. Jackson read the proposed compromise resolution to the Governor, who promptly pointed out that the Arrangements Committee had no authority to recommend a Permanent Chairman, and never had done so in the party history. What Roosevelt said he would do was to 'recommend' Barkley and 'commend' Shouse. It was a kind of weaseled semantics but the Arrangements Committee accepted it."

The Smith statement of candidacy also pushed Roosevelt into a sharper stand on the wet-dry issue. The *New York Times* headline of February 21, read:

'REPEAL THE DRY LAW'
ROOSEVELT DEMANDS
IN BUFFALO SPEECH

It was his first declaration on the issue since the gubernatorial campaign of 1930.

For mutual friends of Smith and Roosevelt, it was the difficult time for decision. Senator Key Pittman of Nevada, a Senate veteran of four terms, and a close personal friend of Smith who had served on his inner council in 1928, told *New York Times* reporter Arthur Krock: "They should no longer expect this great leader, who will always have a powerful influence in our party, further to contest when he is not a candidate for the nomination and will make no campaign . . . the thoughtless action of some of his [Smith's] friends in placing him in a humiliating position which I deeply deplore."

"There are times for all things and all men," Pittman continued. "Sometime the man and the issue meet, as they did in Governor Smith in 1928. Another time the junction does not seem to be made, as in Governor Smith's candidacy this year."

Besides Smith, the presidential picture suddenly featured a new face, John Nance Garner of Texas, the picturesque Speaker of the House with the white hair and the heavy, white eyebrows, the ruddy face and the piercing eyes, the high voice, and the disheveled suit.

Back in 1930, after Roosevelt's overwhelming re-election, Garner had said, "I think the Democrats have a real political catch in this fellow Roosevelt. He looks like the man for us in 1932." And, when a Garner friend had discussed Roosevelt's physical handicap, Garner had said, "For the Presidency, you run on a record and not on your legs."

About his own candidacy, Garner had said, "No Democrat from Texas is going to have availability for his party's presidential nomination except under extraordinary circumstances." Then he told his friend, Bascom Timmons, "I have been Speaker less than 60 days. I have got a tender majority of three. If I can stay close to the gavel, I can get along all right. The biggest single bloc of votes in there is controlled by Tammany. It's more than a tenth of all the Democratic votes in the House. They have got a Roosevelt-Smith split among themselves already. Smith has got support among Congressmen from other states. The Maryland fellows are lined up for Ritchie. There are Roosevelt people in nearly all the delegations. I don't want to jeopardize our cohesion and the legislative program by a presidential candidacy of my own."

But the Garner boom was not of Garner's making—it was the private campaign of the powerful figure of sixty-nine-year-old William Randolph Hearst, publisher of a national chain of important newspapers, and a key figure in California politics.

Hearst had a firm hate for Woodrow Wilson "internationalists" and the League of Nations. He saw Baker as the leader of this group, closely followed by Young, Roosevelt, and Smith. With Smith, his feud was even more personal.

When Smith first ran for Governor, and was elected, Hearst was a rival candidate. At the next New York State Democratic Convention in 1922, in his room at the Onondaga Hotel, Smith listened to a parade of pleaders that he accept Hearst as a candidate for United States Senator—and Smith finally refused. Ever since then, Hearst papers had barraged Smith with constant attack.

Hearst and Garner had served together as freshmen Congressmen but the two men had not seen each other since 1907. Before declaring himself for Garner, Hearst sent his representative and Washington political analyst, George Rothwell Brown, to interview Garner on international issues. Garner told Brown he opposed foreign entanglements, opposed canceling the war debts. Brown also found him sound on finance and tariff.

Then on New Year's Day, 1932, Hearst took over the N.B.C. radio network and specifically denounced Baker, Roosevelt, Smith, and Young as "internationalists," and added, "Unless we Americans are willing to go on laboring indefinitely, merely to provide loot for Europe, we should personally see to it that a man is elected as President this year whose guiding motto is, 'America First.'"

Hearst then described Garner as "a loyal American citizen, a plain man of the plain people, a sound and sincere Democrat; in fact, another Champ Clark."

Despite the Hearst speech, Garner refused to declare himself for reporters, "There are no presidential bees buzzing around my office," he said.

But the presidential bees were buzzing for Baker and Roosevelt.

Baker always had personified the Woodrow Wilson concept of the League of Nations. But, within a few weeks of the Hearst speech, Baker learned the political maneuver of the sudden sidestep, the quick backtrack, the fast doubletalk. Baker announced that he had changed his position on the League of Nations, that he now would only take the United States into the League of Nations "if an enlightened majority of the people favored the step."

Roosevelt was also ready to crawl and eat crow, but tried to do it privately. Farley talked to the editor of Hearst's *New York American*, persuading him to pass on the word to Hearst that Roosevelt really wasn't an internationalist. Then Colonel House made a direct pitch to Hearst himself, and Hearst demanded specific proof. Hearst had been front-paging strong pro-League statements made by Roosevelt when he was running for the Vice-Presidency in 1920. "This is bad ball," Howe had told Roosevelt, and warned him that he might have to make a statement if Hearst got any rougher.

Hearst did get rougher. "He [Roosevelt] made his numerous declarations publicly when he said he WAS an internationalist," Hearst editorialized. "He should make the declaration publicly that he has changed his mind and that he is NOW in favor of keeping the national independence which our forefathers won for us; that he is NOW in favor of not joining the League or the League Court. . . ."

"I must say, frankly," Hearst continued, "that if Mr. Roosevelt is not willing to make public declaration of his change of heart, and wants only to make his statement to me privately, I would not believe him. . . ."

Roosevelt then ate his public crow quickly. Two days later, at a meeting of the New York State Grange, Roosevelt meekly said, ". . . The League of Nations today is not the League conceived by Woodrow Wilson. . . . Too often through these years, its major function has been not the broad overwhelming purpose of world peace but rather a mere meeting place for the political discussion of strictly European political national difficulties. In these, the United States should have no part. . . ."

Hearst's attacks on Roosevelt diminished suddenly, but many of F.D.R.'s supporters were saddened and some of them bitter. Josephus Daniels complained to Senator Hull that Roosevelt had gone too far, and F.D.R.'s family friend, Mrs. Charles Hamlin said, "I am devoted to Franklin but he ought to be spanked."

Liberal radio commentator Elmer Davis then saw Roosevelt as "a man who thinks that the shortest distance between two points is not a straight line, but a corkscrew." Heywood Broun later picked up the same note by saying, "If Franklin D. Roosevelt is nominated, he will go before the country as the corkscrew candidate of a convoluting convention," and added, "I'd rather be right, than Roosevelt." And Oswald Garrison Villard, editor of The

Nation, editorialized that if the nomination were to be awarded "on the grounds of great intellectual capacity, approved boldness is grasping issues and problems, of courage and originality in finding solutions"—it would never go to Roosevelt.

Roosevelt later told *New York Times* reporter Anne O'Hare McCormick, "Let's put it this way . . . say that civilization is a tree, which, as it grows, continually produces rot and deadwood. The Radical says, 'Cut it down.' The Conservative says, 'Don't touch it.' The Liberal compromises, 'Let's prune, so that we lose neither the old trunk nor the new branches.'"

On this issue, F.D.R.'s friends complained that he had pruned too deeply.

F.D.R. continued to prune deeply on the Tammany issue too. Judge Seabury revealed increasing details of huge sums of money easing into the pockets and expenses of Mayor James J. Walker, who seemed to give no adequate explanation. New York City newspapers continually headlined for action and Roosevelt merely stretched out his silence. Walter Lippman took a different tack: "Governor Roosevelt has lost his moral freedom. He is so heavily mortgaged to Tammany that he must prove his independence of it. Yet, at this late date, there is no way of proving his independence except by a procedure which must outrage everyone's sense of justice; for to try James J. Walker before a man who stands to profit enormously by convicting him, is a revolting spectacle."

Roosevelt again hesitated. He now saw no enormous profit in a Walker conviction. He seriously worried about an outraged Tammany not only holding firm against him at the convention, but helping him lose New York State in the election.

Mounting pressure so intensified that Roosevelt felt compelled to say of the Seabury investigation, "It is time to stop talking and do something. It is not the time for political sniping or buck-passing."

Just about this time, an important, highly secret lunch took place at New York's Waldorf between the politically ambitious Judge Seabury and the politically powerful William McAdoo. The two men talked of presidential possibilities. Seabury left that lunch with the firm impression that they both would back Newton D. Baker for President and Samuel Seabury for Vice-President.

It was shortly after that when Seabury put increased fire into his Tammany fight.

Seabury sent Roosevelt a fifteen-count indictment against Mayor Walker's corruption—and Seabury made no suggestion of action. The choice was now Roosevelt's.

Despite all the Roosevelt backtracking and side-stepping, his national political strength kept growing. Howe and Farley kept Roosevelt busy writing letters everywhere.

Typical memos from Farley to F.D.R.:

"Would you send a letter to Governor Ross of Idaho. A letter from you would flatter him, Governor, and he would probably get busy to see that his delegation is positively instructed to you. . . ."

". . . Please write to John H. Wilson of Honolulu who is Democratic National Committeeman and thank him for the part he played in trying to secure an instructed delegation in Hawaii. Just send him a short note. . . ."

". . . McLean is a solid and substantial fellow, and can be of great help to us. Drop him a line. It won't do any harm. . . ."

Reporting to McAdoo in California early in 1932, Breckinridge Long, onetime Secretary of State for Wilson, said, "Roosevelt is way out in front again. When I saw you, it was my impression that he lost some ground, but when the men met here from all over the United States at the Jackson Day dinner, I talked to a good many of them from everywhere, and almost every one of them were for Franklin Roosevelt. I was quite astonished at the unanimity of opinion."

McAdoo, however, soon declared for Garner. McAdoo's close friend, Thomas Storke, editor of the *Santa Barbara News-Press*, later explained why: "McAdoo confided then that William Randolph Hearst had asked him personally to head a delegation for Garner. Hearst had promised all-out support and had also promised McAdoo the same support if he should run for the U.S. Senate."

Announcing for Garner, McAdoo said, "He is beyond the reach of those sinister and subtle influences which work unceasingly against the interests of the masses of the people. He will know how to use the executive power to promote the common good. Under Garner, all elements of the party should be able to unite."

The *Philadelphia Public Ledger* joined the Garner parade by calling him a "Democratic Old Hickory." Texas, which had been expected otherwise to go for Roosevelt, now activated itself for Garner, and appointed Garner's friend, Representative Sam Rayburn, as its national representative. Not many weeks earlier, Rayburn had written a letter to his friend, Lewis Carpenter in Dallas, saying, "It appears to me that Franklin Roosevelt is far and away in the lead of all probable Democratic nominees. There is quite a movement throughout the country, however, designated to be a 'Stop-Roosevelt' campaign. Roosevelt, with his position in New York has appealed to the popular imagination of the American people as no other man does at this particular time. However, within the next two months there will be developments that will show us all, I think, a clear road, whether it leads to Roosevelt or another direction."

Soon afterward, in another letter to another friend, Rayburn explained that he was not against Roosevelt, but that he was for Garner as a favorite son. "In other words, our attitude should be that we will not fight any candidate; but if neither of those most prominently spoken of now is satisfactory to the convention, then we offer a man that everybody can, and should, get together on."

But when a Texas delegation visited Garner in Washington, he told them that he appreciated the honor but that he was not a damned fool, he wasn't kidding himself, and "he was just a country fellow who knew his own limitations and he didn't expect to be nominated."

"He growls like an old bear when you mention it," said Garner's friend Representative John McDuffie of Alabama. "If he is not interested, why should his friends be?"

Garner tried to cool off his candidacy still further by telling reporters, after coming out of a conference with President Hoover, "I always thought of the White House as a prison, but I never noticed until today, how much the shiny latch on the Executive office door looks like the handle on a casket."

Meanwhile Hearst kept the Garner campaign stirring by ordering his political analyst George Rothwell Brown to write a glowing biography of Garner, which he published in installments in all his newspapers. Brown did not mention that, although every Speaker of the House had been mentioned as a presidential possibility, only one Speaker, James Polk, ever became President.

But the presidential bug began to bite even Garner, just a little. He confided to Claude Bowers, "I'm wondering if my conservatism has been exaggerated."

However, Roosevelt's more immediate worry was Al Smith.

Despite Smith's announcement of availability, there had still been no open break between the two men. Smith had sent Roosevelt a congratulatory telegram on his fiftieth birthday, and the two men met and shook hands at the funeral for Tammany Hall head, John Voorhis. Roosevelt suggested a meeting at his 65th Street home in New York City afterward. He later said that Smith then had told him the only reason he had allowed his name to be entered in the Massachusetts primary was that his friends there were very bitter about his 1928 defeat.

To meet the growing need for more speeches and background papers on national issues, Roosevelt had collected a small "brain trust" (a phrase Louis Howe coined and New York Times reporter James Kieran popularized). F.D.R. advisor Samuel Rosenman assembled the group, headed by Raymond Moley, Columbia University professor of public law. It was Moley who had said of Roosevelt, "One thing is sure, that the idea people get from his charming manner—that he is soft or flabby in disposition or character—is far from true. When he wants something a lot, he can be formidable. When crossed, he is hard, stubborn, resourceful, relentless."

It was also Moley who used that "forgotten man" phrase in a Roosevelt speech. Moley had picked it up from William Sumner who had used it to refer to the middle class. Moley used it to describe the aged and the jobless. In a speech on April 7, Roosevelt talked of restoration of farm purchasing power, more favorable loans to small banks and homeowners, the need for more employment and reciprocal trade, all important political subjects at the start of the national primaries. Moley described Roosevelt's grasp of these issues as an intelligence "that skips and bounces through seemingly intricate subjects."

Less than a week later, at the Jefferson Day dinner in Washington, which F.D.R. did not attend, Al Smith ripped into the Roosevelt "forgotten man" speech.

The *New York Times* reported:

"Weighing his words to lend each its full emphasis, Mr. Smith, his eyes flashing and his face red with anger, hurled his denunciation at demagogic appeal:

'This is no time for demagogues,' said Smith. 'At a time like this, when millions of men, women and children are starving throughout the land, there is always a temptation to some men to stir up class prejudice, to stir up the bitterness of the rich against the poor, and the poor against the rich. Against that effort I set myself uncompromisingly.

'I have recently stated that, while I would accept the nomination for the presidency if it were tendered me by the Convention, that before the Convention assembled, I would not be for or against any candidate. I announce tonight an exception to that statement. I will take off my coat and vest and fight to the end against any candidate who persists in any demagogic appeal to the masses of the working people of this country, to destroy themselves by setting class against class and rich against poor.' "

Before that speech, Louis Howe had insisted that the Smith boom was "largely a fake." Roosevelt also had made a reference to "Governor Smith's active or inactive candidacy." But now the wraps were off, the Smith candidacy had been clarified.

About two weeks later, Roosevelt journeyed slowly to a Jefferson Day rally at St. Paul, Minnesota.

At La Crosse, Wisconsin, flags and bunting decorated Main Street, where Roosevelt's Burlington Railroad special train stopped long enough for him to talk to the crowd. After they cheered him as "the next President," a grimy-faced man in overalls yelled, "Governor, are you Wet or Dry?"

"Wet," he said, smiling.

"Then when you come back as President, I'll see that you get a good glass of foaming lager," said the workman.

"Don't forget that," said Roosevelt.

"If we get beer, we'll all be better off," said an elderly farmer.

"We'll see what we can do about it," said the Governor.

Stopping off in Oregon, Illinois, Roosevelt conferred with former Governor Frank Lowden, a presidential candidate in 1920 and 1928. Republican Lowden had refused to support President Hoover, and F.D.R. hoped to win him over, but Lowden wasn't yet ready to bolt his party.

During his speech at the Minnesota Jefferson Day rally, Roosevelt paid the usual tributes to Jefferson and Jackson, but political reporters noticed that Roosevelt devoted a greater space and time to a lengthy quote from his Republican cousin, President Theodore Roosevelt. It was an obvious political pressing of the magic Roosevelt name all over again, and it spelled smart politics.

By May, Roosevelt had collected slightly more than 300 delegates, needed 470 more to win, and Smith—with the considerable handicap of the late start—claimed some 225 delegates.

The state of Washington instructed sixteen delegates at its state convention on February 6 to vote for Roosevelt on the unit rule. Two weeks later, the Democratic State Committee of Louisiana gave its "Kingfish," Senator Huey P. Long, an uninstructed delegation to move with his will. Long and Roosevelt had had a publicized friendly debate on the pages of the *Atlanta Constitution* on whether or not corn pone should be crumbled into potlikker, but Long had a general hesitancy about the Roosevelt candidacy. Plugging hard for Roosevelt was one of Long's best friends in the Senate, Burton K. Wheeler of Montana. Wheeler had been the first Democrat of national reputation to openly support Roosevelt.

Wheeler had been La Follette's running mate on the Progressive party ticket in 1924, and he had named Roosevelt as his presidential preference back in 1930 in New York at a Jefferson Day dinner. When he talked with Huey Long in favor of Roosevelt, it was no secret that Wheeler had hopes of being the vice-presidential nominee.

Oklahoma had its state convention at the end of February, with its twenty-two delegates, of course, all wrapped up for its Governor "Alfalfa Bill" Murray.

The first serious test was the nation's first primary, New Hampshire on March 8. Because of its psychological importance of being first, Howe poured in $12,000 to his state campaign manager, Bob Jackson (no relation to the Supreme Court Justice). State newspapers favored Smith, but Jackson had picked his slate of delegates carefully based on geography and religion, to give it proper balance, and also secured support from the state organization. Despite a heavy snowstorm, which cut down his rural vote, Roosevelt beat Smith 14,500 to 9,000, capturing all eight delegates.

The next day, a Minnesota state convention set its twenty-four delegates for F.D.R., but a Smith group held a rump convention thereby putting the result in question temporarily.

Roosevelt faced another test, an easier one, in mid-March when he took on "Alfalfa Bill" Murray in the North Dakota primary. Murray tried to tie up Roosevelt with the Klu Klux Klan, claiming that some of the Roosevelt Clubs in the area were Klan-financed. Murray stumped the state for three days, pushing his populist program which supposedly had strong farmer appeal. Senator Wheeler moved in from Montana to talk for F.D.R., and F.D.R. sent a wire stressing his belief in farm relief. Roosevelt won 52,000 to 32,000. With a lot of Republicans—worried about Murray— crossing over to vote for him, he took all ten delegates.

Roosevelt had made his winter home in Georgia because of his visits to Warm Springs for his polio treatments. "I am at least an adopted Georgian," he said when Georgia accepted him as its favorite son, even paying his filing fee at the primary. Hearst wanted to enter Garner in the Georgia primary, but Garner's manager Sam Rayburn wasn't interested. However, Hearst's Atlanta newspaper thought that Garner could pick up some rural delegates and backed a Garner proxy. Roosevelt not only won all twenty-eight delegates on March 23, but he crushed Garner by eight to one.

Missouri had its own favorite son, the venerable Senator James Reed, but Roosevelt had a friend in Missouri's state political boss, Tom Pendergast, the only big city boss to declare for Roosevelt. "Pendergast has assured me," a field worker reported to Roosevelt, "that he has informed Senator Reed that he might have the Missouri delegation as a complimentary vote until it was needed by Roosevelt." This meant an F.D.R. reserve strength of thirty-six votes.

That same day, March 27, Maine and Iowa held their state conventions. Bob Jackson had maneuvered Maine politicians somewhat, but ran into trouble. After listening to various reports, F.D.R. felt it unwise to antagonize too many elements there and called Jackson to stop trying for an instructed delegation, and settle for a friendly one.

"Later that night," said Farley, "Jackson telephoned me in Iowa and said that he still wanted to try for an instructed delegation, despite the Governor's instruction. I advised him to follow his own hunch. He did, and as a result succeeded in swinging the convention his way. According to pre-arranged instructions, Bob telephoned me the minute the Maine delegation was definitely pledged. Shortly afterwards, I related this information in a speech to the Iowa convention and the Democrats in attendance seemed duly impressed."

Farley returned to Iowa on the eve of its state convention, only at the insistence of Louis Howe. Farley had been in Iowa on his Elks tour and felt the state was sewed up for F.D.R. But Howe had heard rumblings of an intensified effort to have the state delegation uninstructed. Farley's efforts on that final day, plus the

Maine results, turned the tide for F.D.R. This gave Roosevelt twelve more from Maine, twenty-six from Iowa. It also gave the voters a sudden picture that Roosevelt, pulling in these widely separated states, had national appeal.

On his own private prediction list, Roosevelt had given himself a zero in Arkansas, because of the state's favorite son, Senator Joseph Robinson. But Robinson withdrew his name on the eve of the state convention. That left the eighteen delegates uninstructed, but generally considered favorable to F.D.R.

Four days later, on April 5, in Wisconsin, Smith was expected to pick up five of the twenty-six delegates in the primary, but F.D.R. not only had the state party organization but all the support of the strong Progressive party and so swept in all the delegates.

New York had its primary contest that same day for two district delegates in Buffalo, and Roosevelt men won, but Tammany leaders at its state convention decided on an uninstructed delegation. This meant that an estimated fifty-four of its ninety-four votes would stay with Smith. Roosevelt strength came from upstate and from Ed Flynn's Bronx County. Tammany still held out a tease of a possible deal and a New York politician said, "Tell me about Walker and Seabury and I'll tell you about Roosevelt and Hoover."

Translated, this meant that if F.D.R. would go easy on Walker, Tammany might go along on a Roosevelt bandwagon. Otherwise F.D.R. might not only lose the nomination, but Hoover might win the state.

Governor Charles Bryan of Nebraska, whose brother had been a presidential nominee three times, had his own deep ambition and asked F.D.R. to stay out of the state's April 12 primary. F.D.R. agreed, if no other presidential rivals ran. But the Hearst newspaper, the *Omaha Bee* filed Garner's name and Governor Murray also decided to try his luck. "In order to fix Bryan," said F.D.R.'s campaign man, Arthur Mullen, "I waited till the closing hour to file Roosevelt petitions at the State Capitol." Mullen also had been working the Midwest, and wrote, ". . . they were hot as horseradish for the Governor of New York. We were old-timers, every one of us. We knew the short cuts, and we knew the coulees. We knew that we were working toward a majority, but we also knew that we needed every vote we could get."

Roosevelt not only got Nebraska's sixteen delegates, but his total popular vote was twice as much as the combined votes of Garner and Murray.

That same day Kentucky and Illinois also decided on its delegates. "I was on the political merry-go-round almost constantly during the spring months," said Farley. Illinois had its favorite son, the slightly eccentric Senator James Hamilton "Ham" Lewis. Farley had a long talk with Lewis in Washington, and felt Lewis was friendly enough to F.D.R. to shift to him at an early moment in the convention. However, Lewis was the Illinois front-man, not the Illinois power. Illinois political control rested with the Nash-Cermak machine. "I think that Cermak [Mayor Anton Cermak of Chicago] had been tied in with a sort of agreement with Walker [Mayor James J. Walker of New York]," said Farley. "Cermak wasn't too keen for Smith, but he was against Roosevelt and also with Hague [Mayor Frank Hague of Jersey City, the Jersey state boss and Smith's campaign manager]."

"We found out that Pat Nash also had some sort of commitment to Smith," said Farley.

The fifty-eight votes of Illinois formed a huge question mark.

If Illinois was a question mark, Kentucky was a small comma of uncertainty. Governor Ruby Laffoon wanted its twenty-six votes for favorite son, Senator Alben Barkley, and a minority group headed by *Louisville Courier-Journal* publisher Judge Robert Bingham favored F.D.R. Barkley himself was unsure about being a favorite son, and liked F.D.R. A Louis Howe deal, operated by his representative Homer Cummings, compromised with an F.D.R. offer to make Barkley the convention keynote speaker and Temporary Chairman. Governor Laffoon was so pleased with the deal that he made Howe an honorary Kentucky Colonel. Barkley issued a statement: "Instead of attempting to confuse and clutter up the situation and waste our energy and opportunity, we ought to be uniting all our forces behind a man who can appeal to the imagination of the people."

Working for Roosevelt in Michigan were his brother-in-law, G. Hall Roosevelt, City Controller of Detroit, and Detroit's Mayor Frank Murphy (who would one day become a Supreme Court Justice). After Murphy won the mayoralty in 1931, Howe had wired Murphy and Hall Roosevelt, "Now that you fellows have won, isn't it time for us to get busy delegate collecting?"

Murphy and Roosevelt collected all thirty-eight Michigan delegates at the state convention.

A day of disaster for Roosevelt was April 26, the day that both Massachusetts and Pennsylvania held their primaries.

Back on March 1, Roosevelt had received an urgent warning letter from Massachusetts contact Patricia Van Dorn who wrote: "In view of the Honorable Alfred E. Smith consent in Massachusetts, we strongly advise against any entry in primary there. It would be political suicide to oppose Smith there. New Hampshire and Vermont will be carried by you and would minimize Massachusetts outcome, and furthermore escape bitter conflict and leave no scars. Curley could not carry Boston by a sufficient margin to offset upstate vote."

Attached to the Van Dorn warning was an F.D.R. memo to Howe: "Please prepare a soft answer for this lady."

But the lady was right. Many months before the Van Dorn warning, Colonel House had set up a luncheon for Roosevelt and Massachusetts Democratic leaders "to discourage Smith and his followers and to show how hopeless it was to oppose our man." Massachusetts had been a Smith stronghold and House felt that if Smith saw that his Massachusetts cause was lost, then he would give up the presidential fight.

Complicating the situation was the power feud between Governor Joseph Ely and James Michael Curley, Boston political boss and former mayor. Since Ely was a Smith man, Curley saw a clear hope in regaining political power by jumping early on the Roosevelt bandwagon. According to Farley, Curley repeatedly urged

Roosevelt to enter the Massachusetts primary, although Curley later denied this, and wrote, "I made it clear to the New York chief executive that Al Smith owned Massachusetts."

Uninvited to the "love feast," promoted by Colonel House, Curley not only showed up with Roosevelt, but invited his own press and newsreel people for whom he made the public announcement, "We have been making history here today," he said. "Franklin Delano Roosevelt is the hope of the nation. His splendid administration of the affairs of the Empire State make him outstanding as the man to nominate for the Presidency."

F.D.R. and House beamed, but there was no smile on the face of Senator David Walsh. "If Al Smith desires to have the nomination," said Walsh, "then of course Massachusetts will be for him, and none can prevent such a development."

Walsh was right and so was Patricia Van Dorn. Curley's crusade for Roosevelt attracted the support of only a few mayors of small cities. F.D.R.'s son James, then a Boston insurance man (and later a California Congressman) worked with Curley, and was recalled by Howe for a bawling out because he had been prematurely promising flat repeal of the prohibition amendment.

Told by supporters that he would not get a single Massachusetts delegate, Roosevelt authorized them to seek a compromise. Walsh said, "Next to Smith, of course, I am for Roosevelt." Brown also conferred with Governor Ely and Walsh about getting second-choice commitments from some of the delegates-at-large and district delegates, who might go to Roosevelt after several ballots.

"We were making progress," said F.D.R. man, La Rue Brown "when the newspapermen sent in word that Mr. Curley had chosen that particular afternoon to make a bitter assault on Al Smith, charging him with deceit and other improprieties. That 'tore it,' as the English say. Whether Mr. Curley's timing was fortuitous or intentional, I cannot say. It was effective."

Smith swept the state slate and even caused Curley's defeat as a delegate.

"We felt we had to contest," said Farley, "because if we didn't contest in Massachusetts, it would look as if we were afraid, see? But we went in with our eyes open, knowing what the consequences would be."

Despite this loss of thirty-six delegates, F.D.R. wrote Curley, "I am not the least bit downhearted." Neither was Curley. He got himself made a delegate, and then chairman of the Puerto Rican delegation where he was known as "Alcalde Jaime Miguel Curleo."

The psychological importance of going into the Massachusetts primary was politically tied up with its possible effect on the Pennsylvania primary, held that same day for seventy-eight delegates. Former National Committeeman Joseph Guffey had freely predicted that F.D.R. would win sixty-six of them. But the Smith men controlled the state organization as well as the big cities, and F.D.R. only picked up forty-four delegates.

Rhode Island was expected to give its ten delegates to Smith, and did, overwhelmingly. Then the critical California test with forty-four delegates, and California was another Massachusetts. It had started out as a Smith-Roosevelt race, but when Hearst moved in with McAdoo for Garner, he not only supplied the primary financing and the full support of his four powerful state newspapers, but also helped get the support of the Texas Society of California with its 100,000 members.

Also circulating everywhere was the slogan:

> "If you are Wet, vote for Smith,
> If you are Dry, vote for Garner,
> —If you don't know what you are,
> Vote for Roosevelt."

The Associated Press story said:

"California democracy swept John N. Garner from the gallery of favorite sons in today's presidential primaries, giving him a sweeping victory over Franklin D. Roosevelt and Alfred E. Smith in the contest for the state's 44 votes in the National Convention." The final tabulation shower Garner, 211,913; Roosevelt, 167,117; Smith, 135,981. F.D.R. had led in thirty-six of California's fifty-eight counties but Smith had swept San Francisco and Garner had carried Los Angeles. Said McAdoo hopefully, "It is a serious and perhaps irreparable blow to the Roosevelt candidacy."

Walter Lippmann agreed. "When one remembers that he [Roosevelt] has been in sight of the nomination for months, that he alone among the candidates has a nation-wide organization, that his name is Roosevelt, that he has sought to identify himself with the discontent of the people, his failure to show popular strength is remarkable. . . . The truth is that he has not a good enough grasp of issues nor the power of quick and firm decision to withstand the withering fire which the Republicans would subject him to."

Some sunnier news came to F.D.R. from the South and Southwest. Alabama gave him its twenty-four delegates and he wired them, "As TR would have said, 'Delighted!'" He was especially delighted because Alabama leads off the presidential roll call and might have a psychological impact. Hawaii gave him its six delegates and so did Arizona. Leading the fight in Arizona was Mrs. John Greenway, a girlhood friend of Mrs. Roosevelt, whom one politician described as "a political phenomenon, if not a political genius." The Wyoming state convention also gave F.D.R. six delegates, thanks to the support of National Committeeman (and later Senator) Joseph C. O'Mahoney.

One of the F.D.R. field workers during May in the Midwest and South was Henry Morgenthau, Jr., who surveyed the opinions of farmers, editors, agricultural experts, milk producers, and reported, "Our New York story on agriculture has reached them, and they all admit New York has done more for the farmer than any other state."

Roosevelt stayed out of the Ohio primary, which declared for Governor White with its fifty-two votes, adding that these votes would switch to Baker if White failed to move. Roosevelt here had unsuccessfully tried to court publisher Roy Howard of the Scripps-Howard newspapers who was openly for Smith, but secretly for Baker.

West Virginia also held its primary that same day, May 10, with "Alfalfa Bill" Murray again contesting F.D.R., again losing by a 9 to 1 majority. F.D.R. took all sixteen delegates, helped by the full support of the state organization and Senator Matthew Neely.

Two days later, Maryland expectedly gave its sixteen votes to favorite son and governor, Ritchie. That same week, New Jersey boss Frank Hague, Smith's campaign manager, easily collected the state's thirty-two votes. Hague predicted to the press that F.D.R. "could not carry a single state west of the Mississippi, and very few in the far West." He added, "It is only fair, as the leader of the party in New Jersey, to predict that if Governor Roosevelt is nominated, our state will be in the Republican column."

Kansas had shown strong pro-Baker tendencies, and Jouett Shouse's law partner was especially active there for Baker, but Roosevelt had the backing of Governor Harry H. Woodring and won the state's twenty votes on the unit rule. That meant that Jouett Shouse, an elected delegate, was forced to vote for F.D.R. The political pill was bitter.

In mid-May, New Mexico's state convention handed its six votes to its governor as political trading stamps; Connecticut gave its sixteen votes to Smith; Montana, with both of its Senators, Walsh and Wheeler working for F.D.R., gave him their eight votes; and Vermont gave F.D.R. another eight votes the next day, bucking the Smith tide in New England.

"Dixie is with you!" a South Carolinian yelled at F.D.R. when he passed through that state heading home from Warm Springs. "That's right," Roosevelt yelled, "I'll have every state below the Mason-Dixon Line except Texas and Virginia." He should have added Maryland, but he was otherwise right. He got South Carolina's eighteen, the twenty-four votes of Tennessee—thanks to the combined control of Boss Edward Crump of Memphis and Senator Cordell Hull. Boss Crump saw in Roosevelt the strong hope of federal patronage, which he then needed badly.

Up in Oregon, there was "Alfalfa Bill" again, but F.D.R. easily won by four to one to get the state's ten votes. He also, just as

easily, got Delaware's six. Texas, of course, held its forty-six votes
for Garner, screening out most of the pro-Roosevelt delegates from
the slate. Colorado came to Roosevelt with twelve at the end of
May, and Utah provided another eight. Utah's governor, George
H. Dern was much mentioned as a Roosevelt running-mate.

In charge of the Florida primary for F.D.R. was the state highway commissioner George B. Hills whom F.D.R. had hand-picked
in a memo to Howe: "This Mr. Hills is the man in Florida to run
things for us," F.D.R. wrote. "He is active and one of the best
known and best liked citizens of Florida." Later Hills had written
Howe: "I will carry the State for him in the preferential primary.
Conventions in the past have ruled that delegates from the state
were not definitely bound by the results of such a primary. Baker
has a number of warm admirers in Florida, who will probably run
as delegates in our primary. For that reason it will be necessary for
me to organize the State through the medium of Roosevelt Clubs.
Unless I can control, by my organization, the selection of delegates,
we might have a number of Baker delegates nominated and have
plenty of trouble from them in the Convention."

Hills' control was complete and F.D.R. took Florida's fourteen
delegates in the primary.

Control over Mississippi was much more skittish, and its state
convention provided for an uninstructed delegation for its twenty
votes. F.D.R.'s hope in handling them was the delegation chairman, Pat Harrison, but this hope was on a seesaw.

Virginia reserved its twenty-four votes for its Governor Byrd.
Earlier, F.D.R. had received a letter from a mutual friend who
wrote, "The Governor is very friendly disposed towards you, and
his opinion is that you will receive the nomination. I believe that
Governor Byrd would like to come out and openly support you,
but his friends in Virginia have placed him in a position where
he does not feel at liberty to do so at this time."

With Nevada's six delegates, and Idaho's eight, Roosevelt completed his sweep of ten Southwestern states—but all of them only
added up to eighty-six votes.

When North Carolina came to him with twenty-six votes on June 16, Roosevelt wired Josephus Daniels, "Perfectly delighted with good old North Carolina's action."

That left Indiana, on June 20, as the last state to decide on its delegates, and Indiana did not delight F.D.R.

"The Hoosier State was entitled to thirty votes in the National Convention, and how I wanted those votes!" wrote Farley afterward. "On my earlier stop, I'd reported the leaders were all friendly, but somebody'd gone in there, giving us the foot."

"I visited Earl Peters at Fort Wayne," Farley continued, "and again urged on him the necessity of a delegation definitely pledged to Roosevelt, not forgetting to mention that the leaders who gave us the votes needed to clinch the nomination would be very pleasantly remembered. As a further inducement, I promised that, if Indiana instructed its delegates, I would make certain that any man named by the delegation would be made Chairman of the Committee on Permanent Organization at the Chicago convention. He suggested that Paul V. McNutt, who was expected to be the party nominee for Governor, could fill the post with distinction, and the place was left open, to await the latter's decision."

Colonel McNutt decided the price was not right, and wrote Farley, "While Governor Roosevelt has many staunch supporters in this state, I find that an overwhelming majority of the Democratic leaders feel that they should not be hampered by instructions. Undoubtedly this feeling will be reflected by the delegates."

Later Farley learned that the Scripps-Howard publisher had made a deal with McNutt that called for a minimum of eight Indiana votes for Baker on the first three ballots in exchange for Scripps-Howard support of McNutt's state ticket. McNutt supposedly also had vice-presidential ambitions.

Roosevelt had counted on all thirty Indiana votes in his private tally sheet made on April 15 that year, on which he wrote, "My Guess." His guess called for 665 votes, and included twenty-three of the thirty-eight territorial votes. Farley now claimed delegates from thirty-four states and six territories, with a total of 690 votes on the first ballot—a huge jump from the 300 delegates at the end of April.

Examining the overall result, F.D.R. made a shrewd, quick calculation to Josephus Daniels that the key was the California-Texas bloc of Garner, that this "would cinch the matter."

Garner had his own estimate of the situation. "I have felt for several weeks that we have this election in our hands," he told his friend Timmons. "But we had the same kind of situation in 1924. Public confidence is sometimes a delicate and fragile thing. It did not survive the rough handling we gave it by making a spectacle of ourselves in the Smith-McAdoo deadlock. It may not this time. An ugly situation can develop in Chicago.

"I am not going to deadlock the Convention against the leader. Roosevelt is the leader in delegates. He will have a majority, but not two-thirds. Al Smith will have around 200 delegates, and they will hold out till the last against Roosevelt. Ritchie will have some, and they will be against Roosevelt all the way. Senator Lewis will not be a candidate, and Cermak will hide out his anti-Roosevelt votes behind Melvin Traylor." Garner saw Traylor, a Chicago banker, as F.D.R.'s vice-presidential nominee. As for Baker's potential, Garner said, "Compromise candidates don't win presidential elections. Garfield was the last one who did, and he won in a very close popular vote. . . . Besides Governor White controls the Ohio delegation and I don't think he favors Baker."

"Roosevelt is both strong and weak," continued Garner. "He seems to have practically no second-choice delegates. . . . The Stop-Roosevelt men could, with little help, deadlock the Convention."

Two weeks before the end of the primaries, on June 5, F.D.R. called for a Sunday strategy meeting at his Hyde Park home. Louis Howe prepared the agenda. It was a highly detailed subject list topped by a discussion of the Permanent Chairman—whether or not to retain Jouett Shouse; a selection of convention committee chairmen; the decision on who would make the nominating and seconding speeches; the advisability of introducing the proposed change in the two-thirds rule; selection of a working floor leader and assistants, and the seating of delegations; local arrangements of bands, galleries, crowds, police, demonstrations; the time, place, and staff of the advance headquarters; and an assortment of general topics for discussion such as the method of financing a national campaign, advisability of a low tariff statement at this time, proper recognition of women delegates, the need now for a Farley statement, and a final item labeled, "Paying expenses of delegates."

There were seventeen men at that meeting.

"In the first place, it was definitely decided that we should back Senator Walsh for the permanent chairmanship," said Farley. "The Montana Senator was present, agreed to enter the contest, and I was authorized to make the announcement." Farley nominated Arthur Mullen of Nebraska for floor leader; Hull was decided on for Chairman of the Resolutions Committee, and J. Bruce Kremer as head of the Rules Committee. Several committee chairmanships were left open for trading purposes.

The choice of their own permanent chairman was of primary importance. The power of recognition, the ability to cut short debate, and the authority to adjourn a meeting at a critical point, made the permanent chairman a key influence in the convention.

"The choice of a man to nominate Governor Roosevelt was more difficult," Farley said. "Senator Robert F. Wagner of New York had been approached some time earlier, but it was my impression that ex-Governor Smith had requested him not to do it. His position was difficult, as he had been associated with both men intimately for many years, and had no wish to offend either. The next man, tentatively agreed upon was Claude G. Bowers, author and newspaperman, who had electrified Democratic gatherings on previous occasions by his superb oratorical powers."

Invited to the Roosevelt home, Bowers explained his hesitancy over some bottles of beer.

"Nothing could have been more embarrassing," Bowers later wrote. "I was writing a political column for all the Hearst papers, and it would appear daily during the Convention in Chicago. At that time, Hearst was supporting the candidacy of Speaker Jack Garner. While my contract left me free in such matters, I could see that the delivery of the speech might be embarrassing to the paper in Chicago."

After listening to this, Roosevelt said, "Is there anything I can do? Can I get Hearst on the telephone?"

Bowers suggested that the best way to handle it was through the Hearst office. The next day a telegram from Hearst came to the *New York Journal* editor saying, "While I would not think of interfering in any way with Mr. Bowers' personal and political views and preferences, I think it would be less embarrassing for the papers if he did not too intimately identify himself with any one candidate."

Even more embarrassing for Bowers is that the Tammany leaders let him attend the convention as a New York delegate and he felt forced to vote with them for Smith.

Roosevelt finally settled on John Mack of Poughkeepsie, New York, who had nominated him for his first public office twenty years before. One item, not on the Hyde Park meeting agenda was Roosevelt's announcement that if he were nominated, he planned to break tradition and fly to Chicago to address the convention.

Working hours now went into overtime for the wheelers and dealers. The head of the Georgia delegation got a letter saying: "We are extremely anxious that the men and women selected in your state for appointment on Rules, Permanent Organization, Credentials, and Resolutions Committees be delegates who will absolutely go along with the Roosevelt program 100 per cent after we decide upon our policy. There may be certain matters that will have to be handled by these Committees that will be of great importance to the Governor's nomination and the ultimate result so we want to be certain that the delegates nominated for these particular committees are men and women in whom you have implicit confidence, and regardless of their personal opinions, will go through for Governor Roosevelt on the program that may be outlined before these Committees."

Another letter to labor leader William Johnson, said, "By the way and very confidentially, if things go unexpectedly wrong and there is a chance to block the Governor's nomination, I understand the financial crowd are planning to frame a stampede to Baker. It would do no harm, as a matter of precaution, if the delegates to the Convention from the different states were informed as to Labor's attitude on this matter.

"Personally I do not believe that Baker intends to allow his name to be used and of course, we are very old friends, but at the same time my first allegiance is to the Governor and I would rather hate to see him nosed out due to anything which could have been avoided had we let our good friends in the Federation know about it in advance."

To Louis Howe, Daniel Roper wrote: "My investigation of the Baker-Byrd ticket convinces me that the suggestion is being talked more in Virginia and the East than in Ohio. The friends of Mr. Baker in Ohio do not believe that there is any such movement being approved by Baker. They do say, though, that Raskob has been asking some questions about Byrd for the first place and I do find some talk among Virginians of a Baker-Byrd ticket."

Roosevelt himself wrote to Robert W. Bingham a week before the convention began, "The drive against me seems to be on. All I can hope is that it will not develop into the kind of row which will mean the re-election of Brother Hoover."

Talking to Al Smith before the convention opened, Ed Flynn reported Smith saying that Roosevelt delegates would start deserting him even before the first ballot, and certainly afterward. Smith's confidence had been freshened by a meeting of minds with his old political rival McAdoo who shared their common wish to stop Roosevelt. Their combined voting bloc needed little else to help deadlock the convention. McAdoo still hoarded his own presidential ambition as a compromise candidate, had even sounded out Hearst on the idea.

Hearst, however, kept his own counsel. In a post-election analysis, though, the New York Times quoted a Tammany leader who had said that Hearst had told him a year before that if it looked like Baker might make it, he would swing his support to Roosevelt.

Farley and Ed Flynn arrived in Chicago eight days before the convention opened. Just a week before, Farley had predicted to the press that Roosevelt could be nominated and elected even without New York State. Hopping hard on this statement, the *Times* called Farley "an architect of disaster" and suggested that if Roosevelt was going to be stopped, Farley was the man to do it.

Farley repeated his first ballot victory prediction to the newsmen in Chicago, and Al Smith referred to the Farley predictions as "Farley's Fairy Stories," and "Boxing Baloney." The last remark swiped at Farley's former job as New York State Boxing Commissioner—a job to which Smith had appointed him.

"Smith was telling people like Bob Jackson that I had run out on him," said Farley. "I had gone to him and he had told me he wasn't going to run, but he didn't see it that way now. I think the reason he didn't stop me, or try to stop me, from working for Roosevelt is that he thought I wasn't going to get anywhere going around the country for Roosevelt. He thought I was a New Yorker and didn't know the country. He didn't think I knew anybody."

But Farley's memory was phenomenal, his mind accurately card-indexed with first and last names of all the political hands he shook on his Elks tour and his other zigzags across the country. To supplement the Farley memory was the painfully detailed Louis Howe file on three-by-five pink cards, with a concentration on the wavering ones and their weak spots. Typical entry: "Tom Connally . . . Politician . . . no conviction . . . Friendly, but non-committal . . . delegate at large . . . Fears New York situation. . . ." (Connally later headed the Senate Committee on Foreign Relations.)

As to the question of who sat, and who sat where, Farley dumped that problem on Bruce Kremer and Arthur Mullen. "The ticket job brought nothing but a row," said Mullen, "for Shouse took the tickets and traded them for votes for himself as Permanent Chairman. He filled the galleries with anti-Roosevelt rooters. He dealt with Tony Cermak, Mayor of Chicago, giving him blocks of tickets. I got no tickets at all until one day when I stormed into Shouse's office, found a little Pittsburgher who was his secretary, and threatened him with such violence that he handed me over 100 bits of pasteboard."

Mullen and Kremer had better luck in arranging delegate seating. "Remembering the adage of the one bad apple in a barrel, we put California behind New York, and both of them a half-mile away from Texas. We left New York and New Jersey together, but took Illinois away from them both. We put the District of Columbia with Dan Roper, who was a Roosevelt man, right under our noses. Texas, with its four delegates to every vote, we put in splendid isolation."

Mullen also picked the guards for the two stairways to the platform, and no one got by without his approval. "My son had charge of one of the stairways," said Mullen, "and Neil Vanderbilt of New York and Dan McGrath of Texas had the other."

For convention hall conferences, the ever-suspicious Howe had Farley pick three rooms, so that they could meet in the center room without being overheard by any opposition in a side room. At the Congress Hotel, in Room 1702, Howe had his son and secretary act as doorkeepers, brought in his own faithful switchboard operator to handle the private telephone lines to F.D.R., had Farley and Flynn maintain widely separated suites with a system of confidential liaison messengers routed through stairways and special elevators.

Secretaries were even warned of the dangers of dating men from rival political camps, and Howe had his own secret list of amateur agents on his side, as well as suspected spies from the other sides.

At Roosevelt's suggestion, Farley put up a huge map in a corridor of the Congress Hotel, for conspicuous consumption by all available delegates. The map was brightly colored, indicating the different states pledged to the different candidates. Newsmen kidded about "Field Marshal Farley's map," and its purpose was to show that Roosevelt had more support than all his opponents combined. The Roosevelt sections of the map had the psychological impor-

tance of including the vast states of the West (even though these
states had the fewest delegates). Smith saw it and wrote on the
map, "People vote, not land."

Howe adopted all kinds of gimmicks. To every incoming delegate went this message: "A wish expressed by Governor Roosevelt
that he could personally talk to the friends who have been selected
by their various states to attend the Democratic National Convention, rather than to send a letter, brought out the suggestion that
he take advantage of the newly devised paper phonographic records to convey his actual spoken words to those whom he wished
to thank for their support. . . . If by any chance you have neither
a phonograph in your own family or access to that of a friend and
will let me know, I will send you the message in writing."

As a follow-up on this, Howe had a voice amplifier rigged onto
the private switchboard for F.D.R. conversations with the delegates.
Farley would interview delegates first, send them up to the Howe
suite, and introduce them over the loudspeaker to Roosevelt in
Albany.

"I would get on the phone first," said Farley, "and I'd say,
'Governor, we have in this room the delegate from Iowa. And the
first man I'll introduce to you is that chap from Twin Falls, Ned
Chapman, who knows you and you met him,' and then I'd mention the names of the other fellows who were there, and then
Roosevelt would come on the loudspeaker and talk to these fellows, calling them by their first names, and thanking them for what
they were doing."

"Those chats became so popular," said Farley, "that one or two
delegations complained when they thought they were being left
out."

Incoming newsmen, still filled with impressions of the Republican convention two weeks before, noted generally that Democratic delegates seemed to be younger and dressier than Republican
delegates, and also seemed to spend more money. George Creel
also wrote in the *Women's Home Companion*, "With the Republicans, politics is a business; with the Democrats, it is an emotional

experience . . . a combination of Christmas and the Fourth of July." Anne O'Hare McCormick of the *New York Times* summed it up even more succinctly: "To the Republicans, politics is a business," she said, "while to the Democrats, it's a pleasure."

Presenting a front of obvious pleasure, Al Smith arrived in Chicago wearing a jaunty-looking straw hat, full of high style and quick confidence.

Asked by reporters what the Democratic party should do to assure victory, Smith grinned, rolled his cigar in his mouth, seemed to bite his words when he answered, "Write an honest, concise, clear platform and nominate me."

Told that he was being regarded merely as part of a Stop-Roosevelt movement, Smith growled, "Nothing to it. I'm combating a 'stop Smith' movement that commenced a year and a half ago."

He had no second choice, he said.

"I'm for myself alone."

Smith not only claimed six northeastern states, and two-thirds of the Pennsylvania delegation, but felt he also had a second call on the Garner bloc. His conversation with McAdoo had convinced him not only that they could deadlock Roosevelt but that McAdoo then might also come over to Smith. Of course, McAdoo similarly felt that Smith support might come to *him*.

But the deadlock seemed certain, and the Stop-Roosevelt group was in high gear. Farley referred to its High Command as "The Owls," and they met in utmost secrecy, with Hague or Shouse representing Smith, and other candidates also represented. Favorite meeting place was a penthouse three miles from headquarters, but the Farley-Howe spies kept the meeting under close tabs.

"Sam Rayburn later told me an amusing episode in connection with these meetings," said Farley. "He had returned to the Congress Hotel in the same taxicab with John Raskob. Upon getting out, they separated immediately and they thought no one had seen them together. Ten minutes later, he was in his headquarters when the telephone rang and someone said, 'Jim Farley wants to speak to Sam Rayburn.' The fact that he had been seen with Raskob was already known at our headquarters. No doubt, the opposition was just as cagey in checking our movements."

Ed Flynn paid a social visit to his old boss, Al Smith and Smith said, "Ed, you are not representing the people of Bronx County in your support of Roosevelt. You know the people of Bronx County want you to support me."

Flynn admitted this, but pointed out that he, and others, had made their commitment to Roosevelt when Smith had seemingly eliminated himself from the running, and that they could not renounce their original pledge just because Smith had changed his mind.

Smith still didn't seem to be worried. He expected that Roosevelt delegates would desert Roosevelt even before the first ballot, and certainly afterward.

Smith also got the front page editorial support of all the Scripps-Howard newspapers:

"As Roosevelt generalizes," the editorial said, "Smith is specific. As Roosevelt loves to delay, Smith loves action. Irresolution is ingrained in one. Boldness in the other. . . . In Franklin Roosevelt we have another Hoover."

Among the pros was the sure feeling that Smith was simply a Scripps-Howard stalking horse—that Roy Howard's private preference was Newton D. Baker. Walter Lippmann seemed to agree with Howard on Baker. "My impression," wrote Lippmann, "is that he [Baker] is the real first choice of more responsible Democrats than any other man, and that he is an acceptable second choice to almost everyone. Although there is not a single delegate instructed to vote for him, he is the man, who, once pre-convention pledges have been fulfilled, could most easily be nominated. The strength of Baker derives from an almost universal confidence in his ability and in his character. He is profoundly trusted."

Ostensibly Baker was keeping aloof from delegate-hunting, but actually Colonel Leonard P. Ayres of Cleveland had set up a Baker headquarters in Chicago, and delegates had started to receive telegrams urging them to vote for Baker.

First of the unexpected preconvention breaks seemed to be for Roosevelt: "I was in the hotel apartment, putting on my clothes," said Farley, "when Vincent Y. Dallman, of Springfield, Illinois, came rushing into the room, breathless with excitement and exhibiting a telegram in which Senator Lewis withdrew his name and released the Illinois delegates. Louis Howe was in the room. Carried away with happiness and enthusiasm I exclaimed, '. . . This is the beginning of the end. Roosevelt will be nominated on the first ballot.' "

Howe refused to get excited, and he was right.

"We muffed the ball badly on the Lewis telegram," said Farley. "It was released far too early . . . and the result was that the opposition had plenty of time to muster their forces."

Former presidential candidate Judge Alton B. Parker had once described Illinois as "a commonwealth for sale." If it then was, the Nash-Cermak machine had settled neither on the buyer nor the price. Instead, they produced another favorite son, Chicago banker Melvin A. Traylor who they tried to publicize as the barefoot boy who became a millionaire. Traylor's own bank was in a state of crisis during the convention.

Roosevelt leaders muffed another ball in their fight against the two-thirds rule.

This rule threatened to deadlock the convention, just as it had in 1924 when Smith blocked McAdoo's nomination for 102 ballots, with John W. Davis finally winning on the 103rd ballot.

". . . About the two-thirds rule," Roosevelt had written his friend Justus Wardell in California months before, "my thought is that it is an anachronism anyway, and, as you know, particularly in our conventions. Nevertheless, I hesitate to have Jim Farley say anything about it, because it might sound like a confession of weakness at this particular moment."

The question had cropped up again at the Hyde Park strategy conference that June, and was temporarily set aside. Farley and Flynn, however, had discussed it with Roosevelt from Chicago, and F.D.R. agreed that perhaps the time was right. It wasn't. Far-

ley called a meeting of sixty-five pro-Roosevelt leaders on June 24.
Before Farley knew it, the friendly get-together turned into a free-
for-all. Describing Farley, Molly Dewson said, "He looked be-
wildered, confused and pathetic, like a terrier pup being reproached
for knocking over a table holding a vase of flowers." Farley himself
admitted, "My confidence was badly shaken for the first time . . .
the incident hit me like a blow on the nose."

The man who seemed to take over the frenzied meeting was
Senator Huey P. Long, who seconded the motion to fight the two-
thirds rule, took off his coat and made such a stem-winding stump
speech that the group swept in the motion.

Had this motion been made at convention time, Farley felt he
had enough votes to win it. But, coming so early, the announcement again gave opposition forces strength-gathering time.

"The day after," said Ed Flynn, "Senator Josiah W. Bailey of
North Carolina stormed into our headquarters, told us that we
would not only lose the votes of North Carolina, but we would
alienate every other southern state if we persisted in raising the
question of the two-thirds rule. Farley and I took a lesson in
national politics then and there."

"Some of our strongest supporters came from the south," said
Farley, "and so things got a little bit rugged."

This had happened before Howe came to Chicago, and Farley-
Flynn temporarily lost contact with Roosevelt because a storm in
upstate New York had downed the wires. In the meanwhile, the
opposition closed in: Smith said F.D.R. was trying to change the
rules in the middle of the game. Senator Carter Glass of Virginia
called the move "a short-cut" and "gambler's trick" that should
not be tolerated. Former presidential candidates Cox and Davis,
both denounced the move. And Newton D. Baker, deciding to be
heard, announced that a nomination won by changing the rules
would have a "moral flaw" in its title. The New York delegation
voted sixty-five to twenty-five to keep the rule. The whole thing
had picked up too much dangerous heat, and Howe persuaded
Roosevelt to issue this statement:

"I believe, and always have believed, that the two-thirds rule should no longer be adopted. It is undemocratic. . . . Nevertheless, it is true that the issue was not raised until after the delegates to the convention had been selected and I decline to permit either myself or my friends to be open to the accusation of poor sportsmanship, or to use the methods which could be called, even falsely, those of a steamroller. . . ."

Accordingly, he said, he was asking his friends to stop the fight for it now.

Commenting on it editorially, the New York Times said, "While about it, it is rather a wonder that he did not abandon Chairman Farley, too. . . . It was almost the crowning mismanagement of his mismanaged campaign."

Farley later described the whole thing as "a rather foolish gesture on our part." Lippmann called it "a small stampede led by hotheaded and inexperienced men."

Coolest reaction came from Garner: "The power it gives the South is a negative one," he said. "If the South would stand up for its rights affirmatively, support a southern man for President when that man is more competent than the others, instead of merely trying to veto, there might be a time when capability, rather than a place of residence, would be a test of availability."

One of these nationally ambitious southern leaders—and could he have been thinking of this when he fought the two-thirds rule? —was Senator Huey P. Long. Long's friend Senator Wheeler had helped lean him toward Roosevelt, but Long still had been shopping around.

It was the night before the convention began and Ed Flynn returned to his hotel room about 2:00 A.M. Shortly afterward, there was a loud knock on the door.

"Wearily, I asked who it was," said Flynn. "A trumpet-like voice informed me it was Huey Long. I opened the door, and there, to be sure, stood the Kingfish, somewhat the worse for wear and completely surrounded by bodyguards. Long and his little army marched into the room, and, after the briefest of preliminaries,

Huey announced that he thought he would support Roosevelt."

Long said he had visited each of the candidates, and would have none of them. He had no intention of calling on Roosevelt, he said, because should he do so and be disappointed, he would have no one to support in the convention. Therefore he would support Roosevelt, 'sight unseen.'

For once, the timing for Roosevelt was perfect.

That same night, Farley held a more carefully-controlled meeting to introduce his key men to key delegates with these instructions, "Accept whatever orders these men bring you on the floor."

Ed Flynn had a preconvention estimate that figured 663 votes for Roosevelt out of the 1,154, with 768 needed to nominate.

Trying to pick up steam for Smith, Frank Hague was indignant about bandwagon jumpers for Roosevelt, such as Huey Long, who had "no other thought but patronage." He also told newsmen that F.D.R. "must be promising cabinet offices—there's no other way to explain some of the switching of votes." He also repeated that F.D.R. was the weakest possible candidate and could not carry a single state east of Mississippi "and very few in the far West."

Farley answered Hague softly, "Governor Roosevelt's friends have not come to Chicago to criticize, cry down or defame any Democrat from any part of the country."

Colorado delegate Philip Hornbein also revealed a plot to deluge convention delegates with 100,000 telegrams protesting Roosevelt's nomination and demanding Al Smith. And McAdoo cornered his friend Dan Roper and said, "Don't you know he'll Tammanize the United States."

While Roper kept close to McAdoo, Farley searched for the votes that might cinch F.D.R.'s nomination. "I was cautiously tendering support for the vice-presidential candidacy in return for delegations," Farley said. "I offered to support Ritchie for the second place, if he would withdraw his name for the Presidency, which he refused to do through Mayor Howard W. Jackson of Baltimore. We offered the same post to Governor Byrd of Virginia, through his brother, Admiral Richard E. Byrd."

"Not until after the convention was over," said Farley, "did I learn that Ritchie had not expected Smith to take his own candidacy seriously. He had previously been given to understand that Smith's only interest was in stopping Roosevelt, and confidently expected to get Smith's strength and the nomination in the balloting. He felt he'd been double-crossed."·

The most important political move of the preconvention week didn't happen in Chicago, but in Washington.

On the Monday night of convention week, in the United States Senate office of Harry B. Hawes of Missouri, he and Senator Key Pittman of Nevada were talking about the upcoming convention, and they were worried. What worried them most was the possibility of a prolonged convention deadlock which might mean election defeat as it did in 1924. Out of their conversation came an idea for action. Hawes called Governor Roosevelt in Albany, asked if he would accept Garner as a vice-presidential running mate. "Senator, that would be fine," said Roosevelt, "the Governor from New York and the Speaker of the House from Texas—clear across the country." Roosevelt then told Hawes to contact Farley.

Hawes sent Farley this telegram:

"GROUP BELIEVE THAT WINNING TICKET WOULD BE ROOSEVELT AND GARNER STOP NINETY VOTES OF CALIFORNIA AND TEXAS WOULD ELIMINATE DISPUTE STOP AM ADVISED IT WOULD BE SATISFACTORY TO PARTY HERE STOP SEE SAM RAYBURN TOM CONNALLY AND CHECK MY OWN IMPRESSIONS STOP"

Then, while Farley hunted for Rayburn, Hawes sent hundreds of telegrams to Democratic leaders all over the country, including those collected in Chicago, urging a Roosevelt-Garner ticket.

At 7:30 the next morning, after reading the papers, Garner called Hawes, bawled him out in his high-pitched voice, making it plain he had authorized or wanted none of this. Hawes explained that he had merely suggested it as a good idea and seriously urged Garner to consider it for the good of Texas and the good of the party.

Farley couldn't find Rayburn, but he did find Silliman Evans, who promised to bring Rayburn to his hotel room that night.

Farley made his pitch to the two men that night and Rayburn answered slowly in measured words that Farley never forgot:

"We have come to Chicago to nominate Speaker Jack Garner for the Presidency, if we can. We are not against any other candidate and we are not for any other candidate. Governor Roosevelt is the leading candidate, and naturally he must be headed off if we are to win. But we don't intend to make it another Madison Square Garden."

That was it. Farley reported all this to Howe, and Howe emphasized that Garner was more than a favorite-son candidate, that Rayburn-Evans had made no commitment and further discussion was more to their benefit than to Roosevelt's.

Howe was busy pulling other strings, particularly solidifying the commitment of Byrd of Virginia.

A *New York American* reporter well described Howe in Room 1702 (the presidential suite):

"Hunched down within the depths of an overstuffed chair is the most singular personality in American politics.

"I defy anyone to find his counterpart outside the pages of Charles Dickens or Victor Hugo. A diminutive, incredibly thin, gnome-like individual who seems scarcely to belong to this day and age. There is something utterly medieval about him. His head, full-domed and thinly-patched is over-large for his body. His forehead is high and furrowed. His eyes are set back under heavy brows. His face is narrow and points from high cheekbones to subtle chin. The whole face is amazingly creased and wrinkled.

"This amazing man is Louis McHenry Howe, the closest man alive to Franklin Roosevelt; his alter-ego; the real head and directing mind of the Roosevelt drive for the Presidency.

"Every moment of his waking and sleeping hours has been spent in Room 1702, or in an adjoining room. Day or night, he has not stepped out of that place. I doubt if he has even glanced out of the window upon the stirring panorama of Michigan Avenue and Grant Park—the surging crowds, the marching bands, the squadron of Army airplanes . . . these spectacles leave him cold.

". . . The only thing that means anything is votes for Roosevelt.

". . . He is the rare bird in political life, this curious little man who serves his master with the unhesitating fidelity of a loyal dog; this remarkable Louis McHenry Howe who presides in this new throne room where history is in the making."

The difference between Louis McHenry Howe and Harry Daugherty was that Daugherty ran Harding, moved and maneuvered him at will; while Howe simply served Roosevelt, utterly and completely.

The drama of the Louis McHenry Howe dream formally began shortly after noon on June 27, 1932, in the Chicago Stadium.

In the opening prayer, Commander Evangeline Booth of the Salvation Army said, "In this tragic hour of world history, we wonder if there is an interpretation of Thy will written upon the walls of the nations in letters of want and sorrow which we have not caught . . . give us the light that will show the way."

After Madame Rose Zulalian sang the "Star-Spangled Banner," Democratic National Chairman Raskob introduced Mayor Anton Cermak, "He has not flattered. He has not wavered. He is doing his job well for the glory of the people of this city." The Cermak-packed galleries applauded as if he were a presidential candidate. Raskob then also paid tribute to the "master mind" of Jouett Shouse, adding, "The party has paid him not one penny for his services." Raskob then turned to the Republican charge that Democrats were smearing them. "Upon consulting the dictionary," said Raskob, "we found a definition of the word 'smear' to mean, 'to prepare a dead body with sacred oils before burial.'"

It sounded slightly strange, immediately afterward, when a Californian read Thomas Jefferson's first inaugural address in which he said, "We have called by different names brethren of the same principle. We are all Republicans. We are all Federalists."

Then onto the platform came the Temporary Chairman to make the keynote address, the witty Kentucky Senator, who would one day become Vice-President, Alben Barkley.

"Millions of able-bodied men who three years ago were usefully employed are today without work," he said. "And these millions of men are not responsible for this tragic change in their fortunes, unless they voted for Herbert Hoover as President of the United States."

Barkley detailed the depression: "stocks were manipulated, prices pyramided then split up, then distributed among innocent people under the influence of the opiate of fabulous financial hopes built up by the most gigantic campaign of official ballyhooing ever witnessed in the annals of American history."

Barkley mocked the Hoover promise made in 1928, that, "We in America are nearer the final triumph over poverty than ever before in the history of any land."

Moving on to the prohibition plank, Barkley said, "Two weeks ago in this place, the Republican party promulgated what it called a plank on the Eighteenth Amendment. It is not a plank. It is a promiscuous agglomeration of scrap-lumber. (APPLAUSE) Nicholas Murray Butler condemns it because it is dry, Senator Borah condemns it because it is wet, and the American people will condemn it because it is a fraud. . . . This convention should . . . recommend the passage by Congress of a resolution repealing the Eighteenth Amendment of the Constitution. . . ."

The convention broke loose at that point with a forty-five minute demonstration of parades and cheering, and the featured song was "How Dry I Am," in fast-time.

And, when he continued, Barkley said, "Allow me to repeat what I was saying when so delightfully interrupted. . . ." In repeating, Barkley added that the repeal issue should be submitted to the people of the states for their decision.

When Barkley was done, Senator James F. Byrnes of South Carolina (who would aim himself at the Presidency within a dozen years) asked the convention to give Barkley a rising vote of thanks. Will Rogers wrote of the speech: "This was no note . . . this was in three volumes. . . . But it had to be a long speech for when you start enumerating the things that the Republicans have got away with in the last twelve years you have cut yourself out a job."

Walter Lippmann was similarly appreciative: "A keynoter must never say that two and two make four," he wrote. "It is also the rule that the orator must never use one adjective if he can think of three adjectives, or make one statement except in superlative terms. Barkley did ask for freer trade by lowering of domestic tariffs and by international co-operation, and said that the convention should recommend to the Congress a passage of a resolution repealing the Eighteenth Amendment, and submitting it to the conventions elected by the people of the states. It is impossible to deal more simply or more straightforwardly with the issue."

The convention's first day was then over, with delegates invited to a preview of Chicago's World's Fair, the buses waiting on the south curb. "All good Democrats" were also invited to a dinner that night featuring Will Rogers and Admiral Richard E. Byrd.

It was only four in the afternoon, and for most of the delegates, the day's work was done—for the average delegate is a simple spoke on a wheel turned by a hundred hubs. If his state voted the unit rule, his main function was to attend and announce, to sit and listen, and to occasionally explode at the proper time. Only at an occasional state caucus, where the vote might be close, would his individual vote have special meaning. For the uninstructed delegates, of course, convention life touched on a thin high note of constant hysteria, all the candidates courting him for his vote, everybody respecting his judgment, weighing his whispers, reporting his movements, ringing his telephone.

But the men who move the convention, who know the twists and turns of the tangents, who can speak to each other almost in gestures, are the hundred hubs who move the spokes who turn the wheels who shape the platform and the party and the presidential nominee.

For the members of the various committees, the work had just begun.

Meeting in the Gold Room of the Congress Hotel, the big headache of the Credentials Committee was the seating of the

Louisiana delegation. There were other questions and contests before the committee, such as Minnesota, but Louisiana was the stinger. To burlesque the proceedings, Huey Long created a third slate of delegates, made up of his own henchmen, strictly for clowning purposes during the hearings. When the clowning in committee reached the farce stage, Arthur Mullen cornered Huey Long and told him, "I'll support your delegation on one condition —that you quit your clowning."

Long quickly sobered: "I'll quit," he said.

The committee then voted to seat the Long delegation, thirty-seven to seventeen, and also the pro-Roosevelt Minnesota delegation. Delegation recognition became the first order of business on the convention's second day.

Presenting the minority report against Huey Long's delegation, Senator Scott Lucas of Illinois claimed that Long had handpicked his delegates with his state Central Committee, instead of permitting the Louisiana state convention to pick them, as it had for the previous fifty years.

Then Huey Long presented his case before the convention and, when the delegates applauded him, said, "My friends, please don't take up my time. All your applause comes out of my time, and I haven't time to present these facts to you."

Long's main point was, "if you are going to put the state of Louisiana out of this hall, then you have got to put Arkansas out and several other states that have elected their delegates by the same process by which we have elected ours."

Describing the Long presentation, Claude Bowers wrote:

"When he appeared on the platform, nattily dressed, he looked serious and not at all like the comedian whom the public knew best. . . . Speaking rapidly, in excellent English and with closely knit logic, he made one of the strongest and most dignified speeches of the convention. It was a revelation to me that there was a Huey Long quite distinct from the frothing demagogue with whom the public was familiar."

(Bowers wrote that in his column, and Long called him in.

"Throwing back his shoulders," wrote Bowers, "and looking more belligerent than pleased, he roared, 'As a rule, I don't care a damn what any crooked newspaperman says about me, because they're mostly goddam liars; but you gave me a square deal and I want to thank you for it.'")

As per promise, Arthur Mullen spoke for the Long delegation, saying, "The question that is now before this convention was thrashed out both in the National Committee, the Credentials Committee and the National Convention in 1928 at Houston. . . ."

The issue was seen in the larger stage as a first Roosevelt test, and Long's delegation won 638¾ to 514¼.

"I sat behind Judge Joseph M. Proskauer, one of Smith's close friends," wrote Farley, "and when Mississippi cast its twenty votes for the Long delegation, Judge Proskauer was a bit surprised. He inquired, 'When did you win back that delegation?'"

"We never lost it," was Farley's reply.

When the convention gave its final count for Long's delegation, Farley observed, "The face of this long and faithful friend of Al Smith fell when the result was announced. As an astute political observer, he knew the Happy Warrior was in for another defeat."

The pro-Roosevelt Minnesota delegation was similarly seated, by an even larger majority.

Then came a critical contest of the convention, the selection of a Permanent Chairman. The issue had reached the sharp edge of bitterness. Jouett Shouse openly charged a double cross by Roosevelt on an arranged deal. Shouse had considerable press support, including liberal columnist Heywood Broun who charged, ". . . when Fearless Frank scents a moral issue, veracity, fair play and pledges all go overboard."

Shouse had campaigned across the country for the Permanent Chairmanship, and told Arthur Mullen, "If there was any decency in this convention, it'd elect me Permanent Chairman." And Mullen replied, "If there was any decency in you, you'd resign as a delegate from Kansas. You were elected as a Roosevelt man, and what are you doing?"

Roosevelt announced Senator Thomas J. Walsh of Montana as his candidate for Permanent Chairman. It was Walsh who had exposed the Teapot Dome scandal during the Harding regime, and who had acted as Permanent Chairman during the 103 ballots of the 1924 convention. Walsh had questioned his own selection in an earlier letter to Farley, but had added, that in no circumstances should Shouse's selection "be tolerated."

"We felt that we could put Walsh over," said Farley, "and it was a wise thing that we did because anything could have happened in that Convention if you had a Chairman who was not friendly disposed—I mean a chairman who was unfriendly. And in politics, those things happen—there's nothing wrong with that. The other side is fighting for their cause and their man and that's understandable. But the Chairman is so important because he must recognize the man who rises for recognition to offer a resolution, and it's up to him to decide yea or nay, and to decide when to adjourn."

The New York caucus the night before had voted to support Shouse, despite the approval of the Committee on Permanent Organization for Walsh by thirty-six to twelve. Smith and John W. Davis had both plugged for Shouse.

The convention debate began with Senator Clarence C. Dill saying, "This is not a contest between individuals. . . ."

Speaking for Shouse, Mrs. Bernice S. Pyke pinpointed the issue even more specifically, ". . . We learned that one of the most conspicuous candidates for the nomination at this convention approved through his friends and gave us the resolution that recommends to this convention for the Temporary Chairman, Senator Barkley, and for Permanent Chairman, Mr. Shouse. . . . I come to you in the interests of fair play. . . ."

Answering her, Senator James Byrnes read an affadavit from the convention secretary, Robert Jackson, describing the telephone conversation at the time on that question with Roosevelt. Stressing the semantic difference between "recommend" (which Roosevelt did for Barkley) and "commend" (which he agreed to do for

Shouse), Jackson added, "He [Roosevelt] said that the matter was entirely for the Committee to decide and that, while he did not favor Mr. Shouse, he would not stand in the way of the Committee's desire to make a generous gesture in his direction."

"We were most uneasy," said Farley. "Shouse was well-liked and had procured many pledges. In our own camp were many men who were determined to keep their word and vote for him. I have the yellow paper on which I followed the balloting . . . and its many markings and calculations show my deep concern over the outcome."

In the stream of speakers, everybody noted the clear absence of Al Smith who had been expected to speak for Shouse.

Why didn't he? Here was a chance to be the strong voice of the convention. Smith could have made the critical difference in a close vote. Here was a chance to plead for a man who had long supported him, a man nationally known and widely popular. Here was a chance to touch a sensitive Roosevelt nerve and twang it loudly enough so that it touched the convention conscience. Everybody at that convention knew of the Roosevelt deal on Barkley and Shouse. Everybody there knew that this ducking away from the deal was a weasling of semantics—and however wise it was politically, it was still wide open to general attack on the grounds of fair play.

A flamboyant, emotional, Smith speech, of which he was completely capable, could have stirred and carried the convention. It not only might have nominated Shouse, it could conceivably have nominated Smith. And, even if it didn't, it could have crippled Roosevelt's chances.

Smith underestimated the opportunity and the possibility of victory. Instead, he decided to make his main speech on prohibition in the hope that the repeal issue would swallow Roosevelt. Instead, Roosevelt easily swallowed the issue.

The Smith mistake on not speaking for Shouse was fatal.

The final vote, the closest of the convention, 626 for Walsh and 528 for Shouse.

Roosevelt called it the most exciting moment of the convention. Lippmann commented that if Roosevelt had been the leader of his forces, he would not have had to renege on his promise to let Shouse be Permanent Chairman. "The fight against Shouse was made in order to obliterate the memories of the campaign of 1928," wrote Lippmann, "when those Westerners and Southerners were compelled, at great risk to their own personal careers, to support Al Smith and to accept John Raskob. Mr. Shouse, being a Smith-Raskob man, was made a sacrificial victim to prove they had purged themselves of the sin of 1928. The rite was not performed in the interest of Governor Roosevelt. It was done at his expense, in the local interests of the politicians who are supporting him."

Heywood Broun's comment was much more caustic: "The Governor is not one who opposes swapping horses while crossing a stream. He will change a horse for a mule, a mule for a goat, and a goat for a shoat. If there is mane or tail to which to cling, Franklin D. Roosevelt will not scorn to take hold so long as the beast is travelling in his direction."

Slim and serious, Senator Thomas Walsh walked to the platform to the tune of "Happy Days Are Here Again."

The first Walsh note turned the convention memory back to the deadlocked 1924 convention, when he said he hoped that in this convention "the task will not prove so protracted, nor the labor of the place so arduous or delicate as those . . . that devolved upon me when I last undertook to meet a similar assignment. . . ."

A reporter wrote that you could almost hear the convention saying a silent amen.

With the convention now permanently organized, the Rules Committee presented its short report. It indicated none of the heat of the committee meeting in the Balloon Room where the fight on the two-thirds rule resolution had picked up a fresh fury, despite the Roosevelt letter trying to shelve it. Rules Committee Chairman Bruce Kremer, strongly in favor of killing the two-thirds rule, pushed through a recommendation that if the first six ballots failed to produce a presidential nominee under the two-thirds rule, then only a mere majority would be sufficient on the seventh ballot.

The opposition charged "bad faith, deceit and trickery" and it took a personal plea from Roosevelt for Kremer to kill his own resolution. In his report to the convention, Chairman Kremer merely said, "We recommend to the next National Convention that it shall consider the question of changing the two-thirds rule . . . so as to make the nomination by a majority vote of the delegates to the convention, with a further declaration that that convention is to be the sole judge of its own rules." (Farley finally did kill that two-thirds rule in the 1936 convention.)

That ended another day at the convention hall.

The focus now shifted to the Rose Room of the Congress Hotel where the Resolutions Committee was framing its party platform around the prohibition repeal issue.

Roosevelt forces originally had named Senator Cordell Hull as the Resolutions Committee chairman but Hull had backed out pointing out that he was a Dry from a dry state, and so was Chairman Walsh. "It overbalances," he said.

They then picked Senator Gilbert M. Hitchcock, a known Wet, from Nebraska. This also left Hull freer to fight the proposed repeal. "It would be a damnable outrage, bordering on treason," Hull told the press, "if this Democratic Convention, like the recent Republican National Convention, should meet and adjourn without serious thought or mention of the unprecedented panic." Any delegate, he said, who failed to recognize the depression as the key issue "should be kicked into Lake Michigan."

Hull said all this after Raskob testified before the committee that prohibition was the greatest economic and social question before the country. The committee went Wet by thirty-five to seventeen and the *New York Tribune* reported:

". . . The extreme wet proposal, wetter even than the minority plank defeated in the Republican Convention, and exceeding the expectations of the professional Wet leaders, had been forced through the Roosevelt-controlled committee as a substitute for a subcommittee proposal pledging the party merely to the submission of the question of the repeal. It called for party submission of a repeal amendment to state conventions elected strictly on that issue."

Roosevelt maintained a hands-off policy on the platform plank, told his supporters they could vote their convictions, and unsuccessfully and privately tried to persuade Hull to soft-pedal his Dry opposition. Forcing through the dripping Wet plank was the other Senator Walsh, David I., of Massachusetts, the Smith man, and E. Brook Lee of Maryland, the Ritchie man.

Besides repeal, there were other hot planks. "We wanted a bank deposit guarantee plank," said Arthur Mullen. "I had framed the first law for a bank deposit guarantee in Nebraska and had defended it all the way up and through the Supreme Court of the United States to win its right to existence. Keith Neville, former Governor of Nebraska, was ready to make a speech on the floor for the resolution, but Roosevelt telephoned me:

"These bankers here in New York think I'm a Communist now," Roosevelt told Mullen, "so let's leave that plank out of the platform. I'll take care of it later."

"I'd lived more than fifty years by trusting my fellow man a little," said Mullen, "so I said all right. We defeated in Committee the measure we all really approved."

To California editor and delegate Thomas Storke, close friend of McAdoo, this vote "indicated that possibly the money interests— or as some liked to refer to them, 'Wall Street'—were to exert a controlling force in the 1932 nominations."

The next day's convention meeting was postponed until the evening when the Resolutions Committee was finally finished with its prepared platform. Senator Hitchcock described it as "the shortest and one of the most impressive platforms ever adopted by a National Convention in the United States."

Hitchcock quickly ticked off the proposed planks and when he reached the repeal amendment, the convention hysteria started, delegates throwing hats and handkerchiefs and everything else in the air, parading with state standards while the great pipe organ pealed the popular tunes including the "Maine Stein Song." One group kept chanting:

"WHO DO WE WANT. . . . WE WANT SMITH. . . .
WHAT DO WE WANT. . . . WE WANT BEER. . . ."

H. L. Mencken looked at it all and called it "the death-bed of prohibition."

Determined Senator Hull made his Dry minority report after the convention quieted but he only stirred them up again into prolonged booing. "I ask you Democrats to be quiet and listen to this," he told them, "because we may realize later on that it is more important than we now think. . . ." Hull even quoted an earlier, more moderate view on repeal by Al Smith.

After the platform was reread for the benefit of the radio audience, who had just started to listen, an Iowa delegate urged the beer plank as part of a Democratic party pledge "to furnish immediate relief to the farmer in the middle west by providing a much needed market for his grains."

Then Al Smith walked to the platform and, again, the convention went wild. Chairman Walsh let the demonstration run its ten-minute course. "Even Smith seemed surprised by his reception," said Bowers, "and there was moisture in his eyes."

His face was almost as red as his necktie, and if his collar was wilted, his spirit was roaring.

"I desire to make a few corrections in some of the statements made by Senator Hull," he said. "Now the Senator made the statement that it was an innovation to have a party declare in favor of an amendment to the constitution. . . .

"What about the income tax, Senator? Didn't we declare as a party in favor of that? (APPLAUSE AND CHEERING)

"What about the direct election of United States Senators? Did we not as a party declare in favor of that? And, if I am not mistaken, the Senator was a delegate to one of the conventions and voted for that. (APPLAUSE AND CHEERING)

". . . The Senator quoted from my speech of acceptance. That was four years ago. (LAUGHTER) . . . did the Senator agree with me four years ago? He did not. (VIGOROUS APPLAUSE AND CHEERING) And, because I happened to be four years ahead of my time, just look at what happened to me." (LOUD APPLAUSE)

An attendant offered Smith a glass of water and Smith said loudly, "Drinking water is not in the time. . . ." and the gallery roared with laughter. If there was no allotted time for drinking water, there was time for hard words. With an obvious dig at Roosevelt, Smith said, ". . . if there is anything in the world today that people dislike, it is a dodger. That time has thoroughly passed when you can carry water on both shoulders, when you can be Wet when you are among the Wets and Dry when you are among the Drys, invoking always that quiet little subterranean passage whereby you hope to ease by when nobody was looking."

In the flow of speeches for repeal, Maury Hughes of Texas added the point, "I want to keep the records straight when I tell you that it was not on account of the Wet issue but they crucified that great American and Happy Warrior, Al Smith, on the cross of religious intolerance."

A feminine note for repeal came from Mrs. Jean Springstead Whittemore of Puerto Rico who said, "Just think, a woman is voting for repeal . . . but times have changed."

Times had not changed for T. A. Walters of Idaho who said bitterly, ". . . men outside this convention hall are begging for bread and we waste our time talking about booze. . . ."

Another Dry speaker, Alabama Fitts of Alabama made the mistake of attacking Smith, saying, "He made some delightful wisecracks . . . did he state any argument . . . ?" As the boos continued, Fitts finally said, ". . . if you would keep still, you would be rid of me in thirty seconds . . . you are not as smart as you think you are. . . ."

Governor Ritchie also spoke for repeal, reminding the delegates he had pushed for it a dozen years before "when it was not as fashionable as it is now."

The convention mood was obvious and so was the vote on the repeal plank, 934¾ to 213¾.

"In so doing," said Farley afterward, "the convention eliminated the biggest reason for nominating Ritchie or Smith."

Governor "Alfalfa Bill" Murray had also proposed a Bonus plank for World War I veterans with a moratorium on mortgage fore-closures, and he had a colorful argument:

"I say to you . . . that every law of this country, state or national, should have for its ultimate purpose getting one man in love with one woman and in a home owned by them, and every law that can be made to secure that home and protect the wife and the mother should be enacted; otherwise this civilization can-not live."

The convention voted down Murray's proposal and, after adjournment, Claude Bowers dropped in on Murray.

Murray was "standing in the deserted doorway of his head-quarters in his shirt-sleeves, without a collar, and with one sus-pender off his shoulder. Drawing me inside the room," said Bowers, "he astonished me with a penetrating analysis of my book, 'Jefferson and Hamilton,' and then introduced me to his wife, a charming and motherly woman."

Bowers also visited the Byrd headquarters, where Byrd's cam-paign manager, Major Reed, was loudly unhappy because "Smith had taken the center of the stage, creating the impression that the nomination had to go to Smith or Roosevelt."

At the Smith headquarters, on Presidential Row, Bowers found the rooms packed, and Smith seated by a window "cordial, jovial and without the slightest indication of nervous strain. One of his men entered the proposal that Smith make a demand on the entire New York delegation for its support, accompanied with a threat. Smith seemed startled. 'Oh no,' he said, 'I wouldn't do that. I *never* would do that. Every man is entitled to his opinion.' "

The convention's fourth day started with one of those fancy, flowery little flourishes. "Mr. Chairman, on behalf of Arizona," said National Committeeman Wirt G. Bowman, "the forty-eighth star in our flag, the baby state of the Union, the greatest copper-producing unit in this nation, I present to you . . . this gavel made of copper, the eternal metal, emblematic of the enduring principles of Democracy. . . ."

There was still some unfinished platform business: McAdoo's minority report on bank deposit guarantee, home rule for Hawaii, Congressional representation for the District of Columbia, and scrapping the monetary system to go back to a silver basis. ". . . the money of Washington, the money of Jefferson, the money of Jackson, the money that bought Louisiana, the money that bought Florida, the money that bought Alaska, the money that bought California. . . ."

Walsh slammed down his gavel and yelled "Time up" and the convention applauded. They also voted down all these minority reports, completely accepted the majority platform.

"The next order of business," boomed the voice of Chairman Walsh, "is the calling of the roll for nominations for President of the United States."

Alabama yielded to New York, and delegate John E. Mack, who had nominated Roosevelt for his first political office now told the convention that Roosevelt had picked him because "to his ears, the plodding hesitating utterances of one whose heart is filled with a friendship which has existed for a quarter of a century, would be to him a finer and more welcome tribute than that of the most gifted tongue."

"Plodding" was Mack's word, and he was right. It was a speech without stir, and then a huge portrait of Roosevelt unrolled from the galleries and the organist played "Anchors Aweigh."

Back in the presidential suite of the Congress, lying on the floor next to a radio, suffering seriously from asthma, Louis Howe reportedly whispered to Ed Flynn, "For God's sake, tell 'em to play something else. Oh tell 'em to play 'Happy Days Are Here Again.'"

(Ed Flynn and James Farley both remember that they were the ones to suggest "Happy Days.")

It was comparatively a short demonstration and H. L. Mencken commented, "I can recall no candidate of like importance who ever had so few fanatics whooping for him. His followers here are as silent as if they were up to something unpalatable to the police."

Seconding Roosevelt's nomination was the ubiquitous super-energetic delegate, Mrs. John C. Greenway of Arizona who noted, "I ask your special attention to the next sentence that is to follow. In his personal life," she said, in a quiet allusion to his polio, "he has gallantly waged and triumphantly won a battle against Fate such as few men are called upon to fight."

Nominating John Nance Garner, Senator Tom Connally called him "the Field Marshal of the Armies of Democracy . . . a democrat without prefix, suffix or qualifying phrases . . . John Garner did not spring from the plain people. John Garner is still of the plain people."

Rayburn had turned down the idea of having an old gray mare lead the Garner parade, but there was a Texas band and a woman singing "The Eyes of Texas Are Upon You," and Will Rogers carrying the Oklahoma flag for Garner and William McAdoo with the California Gold Bear flag. A few other states joined in, more in friendship than in support.

Probably the most stirring speech of the convention was Governor Joseph B. Ely's nominating speech for Smith. "Give us a man who dares!" he said.

"Shall we admit that education and prosperity have softened our muscles, drained our vitality and left us only speculating, doubting, equivocating, polite gentlemen? Thank God, no! There is a man who sits amongst us who is a modern Andrew Jackson. You know who he is."

"He thought, my friends," said Ely, "that he threw that future into the political wastebasket, but he found it again in the hearts and minds of his countrymen. . . . There is no reason of him to speak of the forgotten man because with him no class of men or women or children is forgotten. . . . In 1928, riding the crest of the wave, the Republican party was unbeatable, yet our candidate polled 15 million votes—more than any other Democrat ever received . . . 200,000 votes properly distributed would have made him President of the United States. Now when the tide has turned—when the tide has turned, my friends—should he be cast aside?"

A move was soon made for adjournment for three hours "since the radio is not open from six to nine, and for the benefit of those who are attending the convention and in the sake of humanity."

Those next three hours had the hectic quality of hysteria.

"The hotel corridors looked like the Main Street in a Texas oil town just before they're going to bring in the gusher," wrote Arthur Mullen. "Big shots, little shots, candidates, delegates, National Committeemen, reporters, photographers, lobbyists, gangsters, beer-runners, local politicians, curiosity-seekers, all milled around with bands blaring and banners waving, while in locked rooms, shirt-sleeved Warwicks labored with and on each other."

"We never knew when we went into Louis' room," said Lela Stiles, "whether we'd trip over a senator, a governor, a farm delegation, a labor group or a bunch of coils and wires."

Describing Howe then, braintruster Raymond Moley wrote, "Except that he threw his coat aside occasionally when he took a nap, I don't think he had his clothes off during the entire week. It was a moment when his fondest ambitions, the fruit of a lifetime of labor hung in the balance. And his nerves were raw with the strain, his body racked by illness."

While Howe headquartered in Room 1702, Farley was everywhere.

"I was working 18 or 19 hours a day," said Farley, "conversing with hundreds of people, constantly consulting with other leaders, receiving reports from every delegation, and meeting at least twice daily with several hundred newspapermen. I ate my meals, usually consisting of sandwiches and milk, off a tray, and slept a few hours just before dawn, if the opportunity offered. To add to my burdens, I was besieged on all sides for convention tickets, which I did not have."

The Stop-Roosevelt forces claimed a last-ditch block of 431

votes that they could hold out against Roosevelt "until Hell freezes over." Within this group, the Tammany opposition to F.D.R. was well known, and Farley and Flynn publicized that opposition with all Midwestern and Western delegates. "We wished to show," said Flynn, "that Tammany was rough-riding rough-shod over the plain people of New York . . . our tactics did more to hold the delegates together . . . toward the Roosevelt candidacy . . . than any other factor."

The strangeness of this political situation was that here was a New York governor who had most of the big cities and industrial states stacked up against him, while the farm states supported him.

One of his farm state supporters, Huey Long, called Roosevelt in Albany that night:

"Hello Franklin—this is the Kingfish," said Long.

"Hello Kingfish," said Roosevelt laughing, "how are you?"

"I'm fine and hope you are," said Long. "I have a suggestion for you which will clinch the nomination."

Roosevelt listened attentively.

"I think that you should issue a statement immediately," said Long, "saying that you are in favor of a Soldier's Bonus, to be paid as soon as you become President."

"Well," said Roosevelt, "I'm afraid I cannot do that because I am not in favor of the Soldier's Bonus."

"Well," said the Kingfish, "whether or not you believe in it, you'd better come out for it with a strong statement; otherwise you haven't got a chance for the nomination."

Roosevelt thanked Long for his interest, but said it was not possible for him to make any such statement.

"Well," said the Kingfish, "you are a gone goose."

Farley still saw it as a first ballot victory. He pinned his greatest hope on converting the Garner bloc. Garner had briefly testified before the Resolutions Committee on the need for repeal, reduced cost in government, and increased danger of socialism and communism—and then immediately returned to Washington, making himself incommunicado except to Rayburn. Farley's private contact with Rayburn was Swagger Shirley, a former Kentucky Congressman who kept constantly close to his good friend Rayburn, always talking up Roosevelt. "The frequent references to Roosevelt's ability and strength, Rayburn admitted, did have a certain conditioning effect upon his thinking."

Farley set another meeting with Rayburn and Evans and told them, "Now this time I know positively that we can bring about his [Garner's] nomination for second place on the ticket."

"Sam asked what I wanted him to do," wrote Farley.

"Have the Texas delegation record its vote for Garner on the first ballot," said Farley, "and then before the result is announced, switch to Roosevelt. I feel certain that some state will make the break after it becomes apparent that the Governor has a big majority, and Texas might as well be the first.

"Sam replied that he had more than 180 delegates, and the same number of alternates who had come up from the Lone Star State for the purpose of backing Jack Garner for the presidency, that it would be unfair to them and to the state to agree to any such arrangements. He said that Texas was bound to vote for the Speaker for two or three ballots at least, until it was shown whether he had a chance to be nominated. Then Sam asked me how many ballots we could hold our lines without breaking. After pondering for a second or two, I answered, 'Three ballots, four ballots, and maybe five.'

" 'Well,' said Sam, 'We just might let the convention go for a while, even if we are interested in the vice-presidency, and I'm not saying that we are.' "

With the start of the convention's evening session, Senator Carter Glass of Virginia presented the name of Harry Flood Byrd, "an experienced and successful farmer, the largest individual orchardist in the world with 175,000 trees on his various estates . . . has produced a surplus in his state treasury while Governor. . . . He united the warmth and kindly emotions of a tender heart. He is honest; he is courageous; he is fit."

An Illinois delegate nominated his state's favorite son, Melvin

T. Traylor ". . . a businessman, but he has been that kind of a businessman who believed that good government was essential to the welfare of the American people."

Nominating Albert C. Ritchie, Senator Millard Tydings described him as "a man who can appeal alike to all sections, who will inspire enthusiasm everywhere . . . a stalwart magnetic figure with a courageous heart, a sound vision, an inspiring personality. . . . Here is that man!"

During the Ritchie demonstration, Farley went over to the Maryland Governor, put his hand on his shoulder and said, "Bert, it's a great demonstration, but it doesn't mean a thing. We have the votes, and that's what counts."

Ritchie shrugged his shoulders, and smiled, "Maybe you're right."

Reporter Thomas Stokes described Ritchie looking "like a wax figure in a show window. His dress was elegant, as always. He was pleasantly reserved, seeming to hold himself in for fear he might disturb that bland equanimity which was his public self. His face was constantly alight with a benificent smile that never became openly joyous. His chuckle often was strained and artificial. He just wouldn't let himself go. He wouldn't emerge from the campaign photograph."

Putting the name of Senator James Reed in nomination, the Missouri delegate said of him, "even if he fought a duel with a rattlesnake, he would give the snake the first bite."

And William H. "Alfalfa Bill" Murray was nominated and detailed as "mentally equipped . . . a born leader . . . a child of destiny . . . organically qualified to bear the standard. He is a sun-crowned, God-gifted gigantic man. . . ."

The big question for the Roosevelt forces was whether to seek adjournment after the long stretch of speeches or else to move straight into the balloting.

"I was nearer the point of mental and physical exhaustion that night than at any time during the convention," said Farley. "Throwing myself on one of the cots in the tiny gallery headquarters, I decided upon a council of war; the leaders were called in; I remained on the cot too weary to get up and questioned each of them in turn as they came in. The verdict was that delay was dangerous; that time was bound to work for the opposition; that the only sensible course was to insist upon a ballot that night before adjournment."

Farley called Roosevelt in Albany, told him their decision, and he agreed, "Go to it, Jim."

Roosevelt kept close to the radio all night, sitting in his shirt-sleeves, chain-smoking cigarettes, so superstitious that he refused to change his seat at the dining room table that night, but later moved closer to the private wire to Chicago so that he wouldn't have to get up or move to get there.

"I would have given anything in the world to have been there, too," F.D.R. wrote a few days afterward. "It was the most difficult thing for me to sit here with the telephone and get everything second-hand."

Smith arrived at the convention hall that evening, dressed in evening clothes, to catch some of the excitement first-hand.

Smith spotted delegate John Sullivan, of Waterloo, Iowa, an old friend of his who now supported Roosevelt. "I was behind them," said Farley, "and neither saw me. John said to Al, 'Oh hello there!' and Al started to give him hell, see, saying 'what the hell is the matter with you?' And John said, 'Well, you have only yourself to blame . . . I went down to see Jimmy [Farley] and Jimmy told me you were not going to run; but Jimmy told me not to take his word, but to go down and see Al. I went down and saw you and talked to you and you told me you were not going to be a candidate, and then I came back and told Jimmy that I'd go along with Roosevelt. So don't be blaming me and don't be blaming Jimmy!'"

"I thought this was a good place to leave," said Farley, "so I ducked out."

"I was standing on the runway which admitted to the convention floor," wrote Thomas Stokes. "Overhead was the platform. Some orator was delivering a seconding speech for Roosevelt and he was doing it up with lavish and extravagant phrases. Al Smith came bustling in his erect and brisk manner, along the passageway. He was dressed in evening clothes. He stood beside me and inclined his ear upward toward the platform. I can see him now. He heard the name—Franklin Delano Roosevelt. His face twisted into ugly lines. He turned on his heel and stamped away snarling:

" 'I can go back to the hotel and listen to that over the rad-dio.' "

H. L. Mencken saw Smith then in evening dress and later wrote: "He had ceased to be the wonder and glory of the East Side, and became simply a minor figure of Park Avenue . . . his association with the rich has apparently wobbled him and changed him. He has become a golf-player."

For Farley, with the decision made to push for the ballot, the next step was to stop the speeches and get the vote started.

"There were a number of Roosevelt seconding speeches still scheduled to take place," wrote Farley, "and we felt they would do the cause more harm than good because by that time, it was after midnight and the delegates were getting restless. We felt that if our 'seconders' yielded their time, the speakers for other candidates might do likewise. So we sent messengers around suggesting that it was time to get down to business."

"I learned something on that occasion," Farley continued, "that perhaps we should have known before: a thorough-going Democrat will give you his support, his loyalty, his vote and his money— but never his radio time. When a Democratic orator has his throat cleared and ready, holds his manuscript in his hand, and knows the folks back home are there at the radio, it's too much to expect him to give way. Our appeal was in vain. The orators boomed away tirelessly."

Oklahoma delegate Henry Johnston got an appreciative laugh when he said, "Nothing in the kingdom could induce me to remain at large as late as three o'clock at night except a case of dyspepsia or a Democratic convention."

A seconding speaker for Byrd admitted, "We suffer under the disadvantage of speaking to you at four o'clock in the morning, but

what we say to you will be as true as if it were noonday and what
we say . . . will shine at midnight. . . ."

Some of the loudest applause and cheering went to a Utah
delegate who said, "Utah does not wish to impose a speech upon
this convention at this hour."

And, finally, delegate George P. Marshall of the District of
Columbia stood up and said, "Perspiring delegates, I am closing
the show. This is the finish. There is one thing I would like to
say to you. We haven't got a vote in the District of Columbia, but
there are certain people in the District who have ideas. We have
to do one thing that no one else in this convention has to do—we
have to live with the next President. We have to live with the
nominee, and we have lived next door to a man that we know is
worthwhile living with. I second the nomination of Albert
Ritchie."

"All the glamor and most of enthusiasm had gone out of the
hall by that hour," said Farley. "Galleries which had been whooping it up for Al and booing Roosevelt were yawningly empty. Delegates were napping in their seats. Clothes were wilted, collars were
askew, ties hung open and hats sagged at the brims. Aisles were
littered with the debris of demonstrations. The scene was one of
general dejection. Even the bunting drooped limply."

Chairman Walsh then had the job of waking up the delegates
and he called in "Alfalfa Bill" Murray's kilted band of pretty girls
to parade around the place. Then at 4:28 A.M., Walsh banged his
gavel and roared, "The clerk will call the roll for the nomination
for the first ballot for President of the United States."

The first ballot took almost two hours—the delay caused by
delegates demanding a poll of each member of their delegation,
mostly to show the specific strength of their candidates.

During the poll of the New York delegation, the convention
suddenly silenced when Chairman Walsh asked, "Is delegate
James J. Walker in the convention hall?"

Would Walker duck his vote for personal reasons?

All the delegates knew of the Tammany fight with Roosevelt,

and the fact that Mayor Walker's political fate rested in the decision on his corruption charges by Governor Roosevelt.

But just as daylight started streaming into the hall, a small man hurried down the aisle wearing his coat (without a shirt under it). He had obviously been waked out of a sound sleep. Now he stood by his state standard demanding recognition.

The tired hoarse voice of Chairman Walsh boomed again over the convention noise and said, "Who is it that desires recognition?"

"Walker of New York," said the man in the coat.

The convention hall hushed again. Here was drama at dawn.

"The Mayor of New York is recognized," said Walsh.

"Mr. Chairman, I hear that in my absence, an alternate voted on my name. May I ask the privilege of casting that vote myself at this time?"

"The delegate has that right," said Walsh. "The vote taken will be cancelled and the Chair will now receive the vote of the delegate. Let me remark that the alternate of the delegate did not vote. We will receive the vote of the delegate now."

"I desire," said Mayor Walker loudly and firmly, "that my vote be cast for Alfred E. Smith."

Here was a man mocking his fate, and the whole convention hall cheered his courage.

(In between ballots, Mayor Walker's attorney, John J. Curtin, sought out Roosevelt floor leader Arthur Mullen "with the proposition that, if I'd give him the promise that Roosevelt, as Governor of New York, would take care of Walker, they'd swing their votes in the New York delegation to Roosevelt. I didn't even take up the proposition with Roosevelt," said Mullen. "I figured that we were going to get through without New York and, in a national election, Jimmy Walker would be more of a liability than an asset to us. To the best of my knowledge, Curtin didn't propose the deal to anyone else, or take it up with the Governor. I told Curtin that I knew Roosevelt wouldn't touch it, and I knew I wouldn't touch it.")

The first ballot ended with 666¼ for Roosevelt; Smith, 201¼; Garner, 90¼; Byrd, 25; Traylor, 42½; Ritchie, 21; Reed, 24; White, 52; Murray, 23; Baker, 8½.

On this ballot Roosevelt was 465 votes ahead of his nearest rival, but still far short of the 770 needed to nominate on the two-thirds rule. Martin Van Buren and Champ Clark were the only other Democratic presidential nominees to have a majority of votes at the convention—and not get the nomination, and their majorities were not as large as Roosevelt's

Farley, who had forecast a Roosevelt first ballot strength of 679 votes, with enough bandwagon switches for a first ballot nomination, now waited for the break that would begin the bandwagon.

"I was so sure that the opposition lines would break," said Farley, "that the disappointment was almost more than I could bear. Nothing happened. Not a single delegate shifted. Two years of tireless work seemed headed for political oblivion. I closed my mind to such gloomy thoughts and charged into action."

"On the floor, I pleaded with Mayor Cermak to switch Illinois," said Farley, "knowing full well Indiana would follow his lead. Cermak was sympathetic, but regretful his delegation could not switch without a caucus. I knew better, but could do nothing. He had everything in his hands at that moment—national promise, possibly the Senate, which he had his eyes on, and life itself—but he postponed the decision, and political opportunity passed him by. Had he jumped to our bandwagon then, he would not have been in Miami a few months later seeking political favors, only to stop an assassin's wild bullet aimed at Roosevelt."

If Cermak had said the word then, "there is no doubt in my mind," said Farley, "that under the customary practice of political conventions, the vice-presidential nomination would have gone to that state."

"There is an old saying in poker," said Farley, "that a man frequently overplays his hand by staying too long. It happens in politics also."

Other incoming Roosevelt news was similarly bad. Dan Roper

reported that McAdoo had said that California could not change its vote without a caucus. McNutt of Indiana let it be known that he felt the Roosevelt first ballot vote had been disappointing, and that otherwise Indiana would have led the bandwagon for him. "Not only were we in a position to do Roosevelt some good with our votes," said McNutt, "but our action would have brought half a hundred more." And Governor White of the Ohio delegation announced that he would refuse to release his delegates because it would violate his understanding with Newton Baker and James Cox.

A Connecticut delegate had moved for adjournment, but Chairman Walsh already had moved into the roll call for the second ballot.

The second ballot result showed Roosevelt, 677¾; Smith, 194¼; Garner, 90¼; Byrd, 24; Traylor, 40¼; Ritchie, 23½; Reed, 18; White, 50½; Baker, 8; and 22 votes for comedian Will Rogers. "Alfalfa Bill" had turned over his votes in an honorary gesture to his friend Will Rogers.

Roosevelt had picked up a scant 12½ votes on this second ballot, some of them votes that Farley had carefully hoarded.

"Indiana gave us two of them," wrote Arthur Mullen. "That meant that young Tom Taggart had gone out. While he was in the hall, his state voted fourteen for Roosevelt, scattering the rest of its thirty votes. When he went out, we got sixteen. The problem was to keep him out. He solved it for us by failing to know how close was our figuring. He didn't come back for the third ballot; and we had sixteen on our side from the banks of the Wabash."

Farley credited the six Missouri votes to the friendly persuasion of Missouri political boss Tom Pendergast. "In moving about the convention," Farley wrote, "I pushed my way past Daniel Cohalen as he was talking with Reed and urging the latter to stay in the race. The latter needed no urging; Missouri was breaking away simply because he was unable to hold the delegates in line."

"When it came down to brass tacks," said Mullen, "all the Missouri delegation would vote for Roosevelt with the exception of Mrs. Donnelly, the woman who afterward married Senator Reed. She'd keep on voting for Jim, even if no one else in the stadium did. That was true love, but bad politics."

The first crack came in the Ohio delegation, but it was almost invisible—a half-vote for Roosevelt from delegate W. W. Durbin, a practicing magician. Durbin proved himself even more of a magician on the third ballot by bringing with him another two Ohio votes.

During the second ballot, Mullen visited the Texas delegation to talk to his old friend, Senator Tom Connally. "I asked him why they were holding out for Garner," said Mullen. "I told him that by one promise to New York I could get enough votes to put over Roosevelt." "Why don't you give it?" Connally asked. "You're promising everyone else."

"What do you mean?" asked Mullen.

"There are, I hear," said Connally, "a half dozen men to whom you promised the vice-presidential nomination."

Mullen insisted that no such promise had been made by anyone with the authority to make it. "I'm telling you now," said Mullen, "that you are the first man to whom I've said anything of the kind, that if Garner will take the vice-presidential nomination, an arrangement can be made to have him get it."

"I don't know that he'll take it," said Connally.

"I hear from men in Washington whom I believe," said Mullen "and whom you'd believe that Garner will take it. If he does that, will Texas come to Roosevelt?"

"I don't know. There are some men in the delegation who are pretty strong against Roosevelt. We'll have to know more about how Garner stands and what can be done for him before he can go ahead. Let's adjourn and see what we can do."

Mullen hurried back to the platform, and made a motion to adjourn. Sensing this as a sign of Roosevelt weakness, Smith manager Frank Hague, still wearing his high stiff collar, stood up and protested, "We desire here to nominate the next President of the United States. You have kept us here all night. . . ."

New York delegate Dudley Field Malone jumped up to say, "I wish to state the objection of the New York delegation to an adjournment at this time by those who control the proceedings; we have been here all night at great inconvenience and we are prepared to stay here all day."

Tammany man Daniel F. Cohalen then asked for a roll call on the motion.

Turning away from the microphone, Chairman Walsh warned Mullen he was afraid that if the motion went to a vote, it might be lost. Mullen quickly withdrew his motion to adjourn after convention parliamentarian Clarence Cannon said it was allowable.

Mullen checked with Farley on Garner's acceptability to Roosevelt as a vice-presidential nominee, then hurried back to Connally.

Walsh started the roll call for the third ballot.

"I knew I was face to face with disaster," said Farley. "I turned to Bob Jackson, and attempting a smile, said, 'Bob watch this one. It will show whether I can ever go back to New York or not.'"

A small crisis came within the Mississippi delegation, which had voted for Roosevelt on the previous ballots under the unit rule. The state's delegate vote was slimly held for Roosevelt by a single vote, ten and one-half to nine and one-half, and it was the delegation head, Senator Pat Harrison who provided the winning margin for Roosevelt. But Harrison had heard of Mullen's intention to ask for adjournment after the second ballot, took it for granted and headed back to his hotel, undressed for bed and turned on the radio only to hear the start of the third ballot. Knowing that Mississippi Governor Connor would take advantage of his absence to caucus the delegation and switch away from Roosevelt, Harrison put on some clothes, grabbed a cab and arrived at the convention hall, only partly dressed, but in time to prevent the switch.

There had been a dramatic electrical storm during the night, and the damp heat still hung heavy throughout the hall.

"Senator Connally and I went to a hot dog stand near one of the doors," said Mullen. "There on a wobbly stool, with no one but a sleepy, uninterested, dirty-aproned cook for an audience, we made Franklin Delano Roosevelt the Democratic candidate for thirty-second President of the United States.

"I told Connally that I could assure him of what I'd already said—that there were no promises to anyone, but that if Texas would come to Roosevelt, we'd do everything humanly possible to carry the vice-presidential nomination for John Garner, if he'd take it. . . . I said, 'I'll call the man in Washington who's closer to Garner than anyone else, and find out. I'll let you know.'"

"All right," Connally said, "It's a bargain. Let's adjourn now; we can iron out the details during the day. And will you pass the mustard?"

On the way back to the platform, Mullen asked McAdoo if he would make a motion to adjourn at the end of the third ballot.

"I'll second it, if you'll make it," said McAdoo.

By the time Mullen got to the platform, McAdoo changed his mind, sent up a note that he would like to make the adjournment motion. Mullen passed on the word to Walsh.

The third ballot had stretched out interminably with repeated polling of delegations and North Carolina fractionalizing its votes into one-hundredths of a vote to increase the difficulty of the final tabulation.

The third ballot result: Roosevelt, 682.79; Smith, 190¼; Garner, 101¼. Roosevelt had picked up only 4½ votes; Smith had lost some and Garner had picked up 11. The others stayed much the same.

That done, Walsh looked in McAdoo's direction for him to make the adjournment motion, but McAdoo was busy talking to somebody.

"For what purpose does the delegate from California rise?" boomed out Walsh to McAdoo who was still busy sitting and talking. McAdoo, hearing this, jumped up, made his motion for adjournment and Mullen instantly seconded it.

"Do what you did when they tried to nominate you for the Vice-Presidency in '24," Mullen whispered to Walsh. "Bring down that gavel so fast they can't challenge it."

Walsh banged his gavel and the session was adjourned until 8:30 P.M.

The importance of a friendly permanent chairman had now proved itself with multiplied meaning.

Walter Lippmann summed up the mood of delegates and newsmen that morning:

"The author of this dispatch is no more fit, at this moment, to write about the struggle to nominate a President than the delegates are to make a nomination.

"He is, as they are, so stupified by oratory, brass bands, bad air, perspiration, sleeplessness and soft drinks that the fate of mankind is as nothing compared to his longing for a bath, a breakfast and a bed. We have been through the third degree; and no man who has been through what we in Chicago have been through since about nine o'clock Wednesday evening, will ever again have difficulty in realizing how a blameless man, if he were tortured enough, might be persuaded to confess that he had stolen the crown jewels and eloped with Caesar's wife."

It was then 9:15 in the morning of July 1, and a bedraggled lot of delegates moved out into the street, many of the men still in evening clothes.

"Cabs were hard to get," said New York delegate Marion Dickerman, a close personal friend of the Roosevelts, "but I stepped into one and a man came in through the other door and we both refused to get out, so we introduced ourselves. He was Sumner Welles, (who later became Undersecretary of State) and the two of us were heading for the Congress Hotel, so we went together, and we had breakfast together in our wilted evening clothes."

Miss Dickerman checked with Louis Howe who told her to take a shower and come back to work with her friend Nancy Cook. The two of them also served as alternate door-watchers for Howe.

"When I came back," said Miss Dickerman, "there was Louis curled up on top of a chest of drawers, where he said the air was a little better. His son Hartley was stretched out on the floor, and so was Farley and I'll never forget Jim saying, 'We've got to get something to eat,' and he got on the phone and ordered a lot of chocolate ice cream."

Louis Howe finally got down from the top of the chest of drawers, stretched out on the floor, his shirt open, his head on a pillow, two electric fans blowing on him. His constant coughing from the unceasing asthma attack had left him weak and gasping for breath.

"I asked the others to step back," said Farley, "while I sprawled my long frame on the carpet to whisper in Louie's ear. We reviewed the situation rapidly; I told him that in my opinion Texas was the best bet . . . Louis wanted to concentrate on Byrd of Virginia. . . ."

Howe and Farley then got Roosevelt on the private wire and Roosevelt told them to work in both directions.

Howe's voice was so weak that Joseph Guffey whispered to Farley as they were leaving the room, "This is the end of Louie, isn't it Jim? He can't possibly last through the day, can he?"

But Howe was very much alive. He sent for Governor Harry Byrd, asked him bluntly what he wanted to swing into the Roosevelt column. Byrd said he wanted to be United States Senator from Virginia. Virginia already had two firmly entrenched Senators, Carter Glass and Claude Swanson.

"Is that your price?" asked Howe.

Byrd said yes.

"Very well," said Howe. "We'll put either Glass or Swanson in Franklin's cabinet."

(Roosevelt later offered Glass the job of Secretary of the Treasury, but Glass turned it down. Roosevelt then made Senator Claude Swanson his Secretary of the Navy and Governor Harry Byrd ran for Swanson's Senate seat, and was elected.)

Elsewhere the mood of Roosevelt men was much discouraged. Raymond Moley visited some of the New York delegation friendly to Roosevelt and remembered that "the air was blue" with cursing at Tammany. And Doc O'Connor told Moley, "Well, we'll have the governorship six more months anyway and, boy, we'll make those damn Tammany fellows wish they hadn't played this game!"

Rumors increased that there was serious trouble in the pro-Roosevelt delegations of Mississippi, Iowa, Michigan, Minnesota, and Arkansas. There also had been considerable anti-Roosevelt pressure put on Alabama Governor W. W. Brandon, who finally issued a statement that the country's Democrats "will not submit to the dictation of a few cities like Jersey City, Tammany New York and Boston."

The stew inside the Iowa delegation was the growing group who wanted to bolt to Baker. Thomas Stokes asked an Iowa delegate how the state happened to pledge to Roosevelt in the first place.

"Well," he said, "Jim Farley came out and asked us and nobody else did."

Mississippi was rumored ready to break to Baker, and Arkansas was similarly unsettled. The Arkansas situation was psychologically more serious since it came early on the roll call and could throw the whole convention into chaos.

"We got in touch with Huey Long," said Ed Flynn, "who went to work on the delegates. He threatened. He cajoled. He bullied the two Senators concerned—Robinson and Harrison. He shook his fist in Harrison's face and bellowed, 'If you break the rule, you so-and-so, I'll go into Mississippi and break you!'"

Arkansas and Mississippi held fast.

Two members of the California delegation, Thomas Storke and Ham Cotton, McAdoo's closest and most intimate personal advisers, headed back to their hotel from the convention hall, hoping for some sleep. Cornering Cotton at the hotel elevator were two prominent San Francisco bankers. Both were Republicans, both violently opposed to Roosevelt. "They said if the California delegation would switch to Newton Baker on the fourth ballot," Storke wrote later, "that Baker's nomination was assured. They promised all the money necessary for Baker's campaign, and McAdoo's if he ran for the Senate."

Up in their room, sleep was impossible. The phones never seemed to stop ringing, telegrams kept coming in a flood, and there was always somebody important knocking at their door.

"Perhaps the most insistent visitor we had, outside of the Georgia delegates," wrote Storke, "was Mrs. Isabella Greenway, who headed the Arizona contingent. She had formerly lived in Santa Barbara; her daughter Martha had attended school with my daughter Jean. Ham and I could hardly ignore the appeal when Mrs. Greenway begged us at least to consent to a meeting with Roosevelt's manager Jim Farley. Her tearful pleas, coupled to those of Major Cohen of Atlanta and various other friends, finally induced Ham and me to accept her invitation to confer with Farley."

Farley was then asleep in his hotel room. "I told my wife," he said, "that I wouldn't take any calls other than Rayburn or Pat Harrison. Pat was supposed to find Sam for me and set up a meeting. Finally the call came and I went down to Harrison's room, and Pat soon came with Silliman Evans."

"Once again I stated my positive opinion that we could swing the vice-presidential nomination for Speaker Garner if Texas threw in their lot with us," said Farley. "Neither Sam nor Silliman needed much convincing. They were both realists in politics and they saw the situation exactly as it was. The conference lasted only a few moments."

"And no matter what may have been said to the contrary," Farley said afterward, "there was no actual commitment to Garner for the vice-presidency." His stress was on the words "actual commitment."

As Rayburn left the room, he told Farley, "We'll see what can be done."

Farley rushed to Howe with the news and Howe was barely able to whisper, "That's fine."

Back in his castle at San Simeon, California, William Randolph Hearst was kept completely informed of the situation. Most of the incoming calls were from his good friend, Joseph P. Kennedy; his columnist, Damon Runyon; and Mayor James Michael Curley of Boston, all of whom repeatedly warned him of the blossoming Baker movement, and the increased talk of Baker as a compromise candidate. Earlier Hearst had thought that if Roosevelt were beaten at the convention "the worst he could get would be Governor Ritchie of Maryland."

It was true that Baker only had a small handful of delegates openly pledged to him. But this was similarly true of Harding in 1920, John W. Davis in 1924, and of a dozen other Presidents and nominees in our political history. Once the front runners are killed off in deadlock, the race is wide-open. In such a race, Baker had all the color of a compromise candidate. And, while his support was not obvious, it was deep. Most of the Roosevelt votes, for example, would prefer Baker to Ritchie or anyone else. In addition, Judge Seabury had come to Chicago with an energetic staff to plead hard for a Baker-Seabury ticket.

Baker would be too bitter a pill, and this finally pushed Hearst into further action. His secretary in Chicago, Joseph Willicombe, phoned him from Farley's room, and Farley spoke to him, emphasized the potential seriousness of the Baker threat. Hearst listened without comment. Then, after receiving via Willicombe, the assurance from Roosevelt forces that F.D.R. would not meddle in Europe, Hearst relayed the message to his Washington man, George Rothwell Brown. Brown was to see Garner, describe the situation, and ask if he would release his delegates to Roosevelt.

The message was: "Mr. Hearst is fearful that when Roosevelt's strength crumbles, it will bring about either the election of Smith or Baker. Either would be disastrous. Tell Garner that the Chief believes nothing can now save the country but for him to throw his delegates to Governor Roosevelt."

Arthur Mullen meanwhile had sent his own Washington contact man to see Garner. Mullen's man was Edgar Howard, a long-haired man in a white hat who was Garner's closest poker-playing crony. "Now Edgar," said Mullen, "go over and see Garner and ask him if he'll run for Vice-President if we nominate him. I've talked to the man who knows the temper of the Texas delegates. They're out now and he's with them. Tell Garner he'll have to decide in a hurry and notify them."

About this time, Storke and Cotton kept their appointment with Farley.

"Farley opened the conversation with the startling admission that the Roosevelt fight was lost and could only be saved by the swinging of the California delegation over to Roosevelt on the next ballot," said Storke.

"With a great show of emotion, emphasized by pounding on a chair with his closed fist, and with tears literally flooding his eyes, he [Farley] said: 'Boys, Roosevelt is lost unless California comes over to us on the next ballot. I am eighty-seven votes short and I cannot hope to get them unless you switch to Roosevelt on the fourth ballot.' "

Farley then told Storke and Cotton that he expected Minnesota, Iowa, the two Dakotas, and Mississippi to break and scatter on the fourth ballot, and that probably meant Baker would win.

Storke said that Farley continually kept asking, "What does Mac want? Will he go as Vice-President?"

"Mac wants nothing," Storke and Cotton said.

"Then how about Ambassador to the Court of St. James? Or Secretary of the Treasury?"

Storke and Cotton insisted that McAdoo wanted nothing.

"Who *will* he agree to then?" asked Farley. "Well, do you think he might be agreeable to John Nance Garner?"

Storke and Cotton said they thought he would.

"All right then," said Farley, "let's make it Roosevelt and Garner."

Storke and Cotton then grabbed a cab to the Sherman Hotel, caught McAdoo in his room coming out of the shower, explained everything to him quickly, then urged he call a caucus.

"But boys, it's too late now," McAdoo protested, but finally agreed to call his delegates together.

McAdoo already had received the word from Hearst, and he also had conferred with his two old friends, Dan Roper and Cordell Hull. Roper even tentatively offered the possibility of McAdoo as Secretary of State. McAdoo refused. He said he would see what he could do with his delegates, but that Roosevelt must agree to take Garner as Vice-President, consult him about federal patronage in California and about appointments to the Treasury and State Departments.

Meanwhile Edgar Howard called Mullen:

"I've seen our man," he said. "John told me he's received all the honors he's ever had through the Democratic Party, and that no man situated as he is can decline the honor of the vice-presidential nomination."

Mullen quickly called Connally. "That sets us," said Connally.

Garner also saw Hearst's man, George Brown in the Speaker's private room in the southeast corner of the Capitol. Brown gave him Hearst's message, and Garner maintained an expressionless face, then said slowly, "Say to Mr. Hearst that I fully agree with him. He is right. Tell him I will carry out his suggestion and release my delegates to Roosevelt."

Rumors of all this swiftly reached the Smith headquarters. "Father and McAdoo had agreed to hold another conference in the event of a deadlock materializing," wrote Smith's daughter later. But that conference was never held. Smith asked mutual friend Herbert Bayard Swope to call McAdoo, but McAdoo never answered the call. Then Smith asked Judge Proskauer to reach Garner in Washington, but the Judge similarly had no luck.

Smith's friend and associate, Mrs. Moskowitz knew the manager of the Washington hotel where Garner was staying, so she called him and explained that it was Smith who wanted to talk to Garner. "You may tell Governor Smith from me," said the manager, "that Speaker Garner is here. The reason you can't get him is that he refuses to answer the telephone."

Garner afterward explained why. "I meant no discourtesy to Smith," he said. "I knew he was in a bitter, last-ditch fight in which I did not intend to take part. I decided it was best for me to talk only to Sam Rayburn, Amon Carter or some other members of the Texas delegation. There was no reason to talk to outsiders. If Roosevelt had called, I would not have taken that one either."

Smith wanted to tell Garner that Texas and California were Roosevelt's only chance for the nomination, and that if Garner held fast, Roosevelt would shoot his bolt.

But the die was set. Garner called Rayburn. "I think it is time to break that thing up," he said. "This man Roosevelt is the choice of that convention. He has had a majority on three ballots. We don't want to be responsible for tying up this convention and bringing on another Madison Square Garden that might defeat the party candidate in November."

Rayburn earlier had outlined the situation to Garner.

"I do not remember exactly what Sam told me," said Garner, "but this is the impression it made on my mind . . . Smith's bloc was standing firm . . . Roosevelt could not break into all the delegations . . . and some states were about ready to desert him. Feelers showed that California would go to Roosevelt if I released the delegates. Texas would not unless I went on the ticket with the New York Governor. . . . They had to sell the Texas delegates on the idea. . . .

"If Texas and California did not go to Roosevelt on the fourth ballot, Rayburn thought the convention was in for a deadlock."

"All right," said Garner to Rayburn, "Release my delegates and see what you can do. Hell, I'll do anything to see the Democrats win one more election."

California and Texas held their caucus meetings in adjoining rooms of the Sherman Hotel. Just before the Texas meeting began, Rayburn decided to get the final official authorization from Garner. In the hallway, en route to the phone, Rayburn met McAdoo.

"Sam, we'll vote for Jack Garner until hell freezes over, if you say so," said McAdoo.

Rayburn briefly explained the setup, suggested he return to his caucus and release the California delegates. Then Rayburn called Garner.

"Do you authorize me to release the Texas delegation from voting for you for the presidential nomination?" asked Rayburn.

"Yes," said Garner.

"Do you release the Texas delegation from voting for you for the presidential nomination?"

"Yes."

That was it. But the fight was just beginning.

Inside the California caucus, the heat reached a fever. Without indicating his own preference, McAdoo had told his delegates that he wanted their view on California's policy in the event either Smith or Roosevelt made significant gains.

In the general discussion, many said they wanted to stay with Garner for at least two more ballots; one spoke for Smith as a second choice and another for Baker. Shouting angrily, Mrs. Grace Bryan Hargreaves, daughter of the late William Jennings Bryan, repeated over and over again, "We came here to nominate John Nance Garner and no one else! I am ready to stay right here in Chicago until we nominate John Nance Garner!"

Suddenly, a San Diego delegate yelled, "McAdoo, you are attempting to betray us!"

McAdoo turned white, clenched his fist, said nothing.

"Personally, I would estimate that more than half would have insisted on staying with Garner for at least one more ballot," said Storke. "Perhaps fifteen might have gone over to Smith. Possibly a majority favored Roosevelt. The only certain judgment of the situation was that unanimity was impossible."

During the meeting, Storke was called outside the caucus room by an urgent message from Mrs. Isabella Greenway. "I have never seen such an excited and nervous woman," said Storke, "as she begged, 'Please come over to our side, Tom! Let me tell Jim [Farley] that California is going to switch to Roosevelt on the next ballot. Please! Please!'"

There was no vote taken at the California caucus. Instead the highly respected Jack Elliott proposed a steering committee of three, adding McAdoo as chairman and spokesman, empowered "to determine when and to whom the vote of California should go in the event of a switch from John Nance Garner."

Surprisingly, the caucus agreed possibly because of their strong regard for Elliott's judgment. Besides McAdoo and Elliott, the committee consisted of National Committeewoman Nellie Donohue and C. C. McPike of San Francisco. Before leaving for the convention hall, the quartet met and instructed McAdoo to declare the delegation for Roosevelt on the next ballot.

If the California caucus was hot, the Texas caucus sizzled.

Garner had second choice strength in Alabama, and Representative John McDuffie hoped to swing it to Garner on the fifth ballot. Will Rogers had checked Arizona and Arkansas and saw the strong possibility that both might swing to Garner on the fourth ballot. With Alabama, Arkansas, and Arizona all on top of the roll call, a three-way swing to Garner conceivably could start a convention stampede. Besides Garner had picked up eleven votes on the third ballot, more than anyone else. Representative Lindsey Warren of North Carolina, a Roosevelt floor worker, felt that Roosevelt was finished if he didn't make it on the fourth ballot, and he already had canvassed North Carolina for Garner as a second choice. Warren picked up eighteen North Carolina pledges for Garner before he ran into his rival canvasser, Dr. Hugh Young, a famous Johns Hopkins Hospital surgeon, working frantically for Ritchie. Dr. Young had sewed up eleven North Carolina delegates firmly for Ritchie—very firmly because he had performed serious and successful operations on all eleven of them.

"I think Garner would make a great President," said delegate T. M. Washington to Warren, "but I might have to go back to Johns Hopkins, and if I did, Doc Young might not admit me. He's that strong for Ritchie."

The Texas delegates were that strong for Garner. The irony was that Rayburn had screened out the pro-Roosevelt Texas delegates in presenting the slate to the state convention back in the early spring. Now Rayburn himself was faced with the job of converting these "bitter-enders" back to Roosevelt.

Texas had forty-six convention votes, but had 180 men and women delegates, each with a fraction of a vote. Of these 180, 105 had been rounded up in time for the caucus.

As Rayburn told the story, he made the announcement that Garner had released his delegates and then "A good friend of ours jumped up and said, 'I'm gonna make a speech' and he began telling that Garner had said this, that and the other. He kept on going around and around saying, 'We don't want to run out on Mr. Garner,' and then some of the women around me began crying, and I said, 'We're not running out on Mr. Garner. He's not a candidate anymore.' We just argued and argued. I tried to tell them Garner was out of it."

Fort Worth publisher Amon G. Carter was the strongest voice urging the delegation to stay pat for Garner. Tom Connally talked just as hard for Roosevelt and the place was in an uproar. To make it worse, a couple of Illinois delegates had sneaked into the caucus, kept busy circulating the room, telling everybody that Garner would get thirty Illinois votes on the next ballot if they kept him in. "Finally, though," said Rayburn, "when they began to row, I had to squeeze down on them, and we voted fifty-four to fifty-one to go for Roosevelt."

Nobody knows what might have happened if the seventy-five absentee Texas delegates had also attended that caucus.

Rayburn then sent Silliman Evans to tell Farley what happened. Evans also met Pat Harrison of Mississippi and told him.

"Pat started on the run for the Mississippi delegation," said Farley, "then turned around and raced back to Silliman. He grabbed him by both shoulders and shouted, 'Are you sure?'" Again assured, Harrison double-timed it to his delegation, which had just before decided by a single vote to break away from Roosevelt. What Harrison didn't know was that this delegate with the deciding vote had been influenced to switch through the efforts of Silliman Evans the night before.

Farley then held a press conference, and said, "Mr. Roosevelt will be nominated on the first ballot tonight."

When reporters pressed him on where he would get the extra votes, Farley answered, "I am not prepared to say."

On his way to the convention that night, Farley stopped off at the Blackstone Hotel, dropped in on the Tammany headquarters.

"Mr. Curry and Mr. McCooey and Jimmy Walker were in Curry's apartment there, and John Delaney was also there and so was Dan Rhine, and Charlie Hand, Walker's secretary," said Farley, "and I told them what was going to happen; I didn't tell them where the break was coming from. Now I'll never forget Curry. He said to me, 'Now Hague has just left here, and he said they had Roosevelt stopped—there's not going to be any break.' And I said, 'Now I'm not here to question what Hague said to you, I'm merely here to tell you what *is* going to happen, and I don't want this to happen and have you say to me after the balloting is over, 'Why didn't you come and *tell* me, to tip us so that we could make our move?' "

"I'm not asking you to do anything," Farley told Curry, "I'm not trying to secure any pledge of support. He will be nominated on the next ballot whether or not any New York votes come to Mr. Roosevelt. My only reason for being here is to let you know what's going to happen."

"And I went on out," said Farley. "I know they didn't believe me."

Also on the way to the convention hall, Chairman Walsh met Daniel F. Cohalen, the Tammany man. "We have Roosevelt stopped," said Cohalen, "and I'd like to have authority to present your name to the convention as a compromise candidate."

Walsh coldly thanked Cohalen, explained that he had no presidential ambitions. Walsh already had received the word from Louis Howe about the upcoming switch from California and Texas.

Farley shared a cab to the convention hall with two friends of his, both strong Smith supporters, both arguing with him all the way to the hall that he should switch to Smith.

Inside the hall, Mayor James Curley of Boston, then officially known as "Alcalde Jaime Miguel Curleo" did a small jig-step as he walked past some Smith delegates from Massachusetts, and they glowered. Curley later said he had called his friend Hearst three times to tell him, "You have the opportunity to name the next President and Vice-President of the United States."

Delegate Marion Dickerman, who also knew what was going to happen, passed by Al Smith's box. Though Smith knew she was for Roosevelt, he and Miss Dickerman had always kept on friendly terms. "We've got this in the bag, Marion," Smith shouted at her.

Miss Dickerman tried to smile and said, "May the best man win. . . ."

It was the convention's fifth day, the seventh session and Dr. John Thompson, of Chicago's First Methodist Church, said in his opening prayer, "Great confidence hast Thou placed in us. We have made a bit of a mess of things. We have things all topsy-turvy. Help us to make a clear housecleaning. . . . And we pray Thee to guide these delegates. . . ."

But the guidance already had been firmly set by others.

The fourth and final ballot began shortly after Mrs. Ruby Bell, of Paducah, Kentucky, sang, "My Old Kentucky Home."

The roll call of the states started, but McAdoo had not yet arrived in the hall. McAdoo afterward said that he had realized the political danger of having him make the announcement of the switch, that he had offered to let Texas do it, but that Rayburn felt it would cause too much bitter feeling within the Texas delegation.

Alabama was called, declared again for Roosevelt.

Arizona was called. It stayed with Roosevelt.

"The roll call was resuming when our Chairman came rushing down the aisle to his seat," said Storke. "He was flushed and out of breath. He told me later that his limousine had gone about a mile from the hotel when the motor died and the chauffeur announced nonchalantly that they were out of gas. . . ."

McAdoo then hitchhiked on a policeman's motorcycle, but he had to get off because his legs were too gangly, and he finally stopped a passing taxi. The McAdoo suspicion was that his chauffeur had been too friendly with the Smith forces.

"As McAdoo slumped in his chair," said Storke, "he turned and showed me a note he had written in the taxi. He had already signaled for a runner to carry the slip up to Chairman Walsh. I read it:

"Please recognize me when California is called, Tom. You will not be disappointed. McAdoo."

As the clerk called California, Walsh recognized McAdoo. At first the Smith delegates and much of the gallery cheered McAdoo as he stood and said, "California asks the opportunity of explaining its vote to the convention."

They kept cheering him as he continued on to the platform.

"I learned later," said Storke, "that a few of our San Francisco delegates had given Al's forces the impression that they planned to vote for the Happy Warrior."

Up on the platform, McAdoo loudly announced, ". . . California came here to nominate a President of the United States. She did not come here to deadlock this convention or to engage in another disastrous contest like that of 1924 . . . when any man comes into a Democratic National Convention with the popular will behind him to the extent of almost 700 votes. . . ."

Now everybody knew; now the prolonged booing from the galleries seemed to swallow up the delegate applause.

So continuous was the booing that Chairman Walsh turned to Cermak and said, "I appeal to the Mayor of the City of Chicago and to the citizens thereof. If he or they have any regard for the honor of their city, he will silence this disturbance in the gallery."

"Let me appeal to my friends in the galleries," said Cermak. "The Democratic National Committee was kind enough to come to our city with this great wonderful convention. You are their host. Please act like their host. Please, I appeal to you, allow this great gathering to go home with nothing but pleasant memories of our city."

McAdoo had a canary-eating catlike smile on his face. Somebody later called it the "Payoff Pow-wow." Smith had killed his presidential chances in 1924 when McAdoo had the majority, and this was his payoff for Smith. It was also his revenge on the galleries, because it was the gallery in the upper tiers of Madison Square Garden eight years before who had shouted "Erl, erl, erl . . ." everytime McAdoo's name was mentioned on those continuous ballots. The "erl" was an allusion to a $150,000 law firm fee McAdoo had accepted from oil king E. H. Doheny who was tied up with the Teapot Dome scandal.

As the convention hall quieted after almost thirty minutes of booing, McAdoo continued coldly, "I want to thank the galleries for the compliment they have paid me. The convention wants to know, for the guidance of future Democratic conventions, whether or not this is the kind of hospitality Chicago accords to its guests."

"I intend to say what I propose to say without regard to what the galleries or anybody else think. . . ."

In a reference to Garner, McAdoo said, "He is worthy of the highest place you could give him, but he hasn't as many votes as Mr. Roosevelt. Mr. Garner himself is in accord to the position I take. . . . I want to cause no wounds. Those of 1924 were created against my wish . . . California casts forty-four votes for Franklin D. Roosevelt."

Sitting in front of the radio in his Executive Mansion in Albany, Governor Roosevelt exclaimed, "Good old McAdoo!"

Standing beside Claude Bowers in the hall, former presidential nominee John W. Davis said quietly, almost as if to himself, "What a pity!"

Farley jumped onto the platform to slap McAdoo on the back. On the floor, Arthur Mullen looked and listened, remembering McAdoo's expressed wish that he would be the presidential possibility in case of a deadlock. "I knew his ambition had been killed as surely as Al Smith's," said Mullen later. "As well as anyone there, he knew he was tolling the bell for his own funeral—and I'll hand it to him that he did it with valor."

Smith left the hall in an obvious rage. Ritchie marched out more rigidly, with a more impassive face, after adding Maryland's vote to Roosevelt. Cermak already had done the same for Illinois, loudly blaming Pat Nash for not letting him make the break earlier. Then came Minnesota, Missouri, and much later, Texas.

When Texas did it, Will Rogers quipped sourly, "Here I've been neutral all my life until now, and the first time I come out for a man, he throws his strength to a fellow with a Harvard accent. No good can come to a Texan who does a thing like that."

Counting the votes, Farley noted the moment the two-thirds majority was reached, raced for a phone on the gallery floor, called Albany through the private switchboard. "I then experienced the greatest thrill of a lifetime of politics," said Farley, "the privilege of congratulating Franklin D. Roosevelt on his nomination for the Presidency of the United States."

The final ballot result: Roosevelt received 945 votes. Smith, his nearest rival, had only 190½ votes. The New York delegation refused to make the nomination unanimous.

Senator Reed of Missouri sat on the platform, his face expressionless throughout the final ballot, and Chairman Walsh then asked him if he would address the convention. Reed refused.

Going over to him, Mullen said, "We're all Democrats, Jim."

"We are—yet," growled Reed, but stood up and started speaking to the noisy, angry crowd.

"At a time like this," Reed told them, "every man who claims to be a Democrat should banish from his heart all feeling of disappointment, all sense of chagrin, and like a good soldier, fall in line, salute the colors and face the enemy."

Chairman Walsh then read a message from Roosevelt thanking them for the nomination, and adding, "It is customary to hold formal notification ceremonies some weeks after the convention. This involves great expense and in these times I would prefer that this be not followed. Instead may I ask the convention to remain in session after the selection of the Vice-Presidential candidate tomorrow, that I may appear before you and be notified at that time. . . ." The convention accepted this and adjourned. It was an hour before midnight.

New Yorker magazine reporter Alva Johnston tore into the idea that the Roosevelt trip was to save "great expense" of the delayed notification ceremonies. Johnston noted that the Roosevelt arrival kept the convention in session for an extra day. "Roughly, he caused ten thousand persons to remain over in Chicago at an expense, conservatively, of ten dollars a head, or a total of one hundred thousand dollars," said Johnston.

On the other hand, said Johnston, a simple notification ceremony, which had often been held on a candidate's front porch, wouldn't cost more than a thousand dollars.

While it may not have been an economy measure, the proposed Roosevelt airplane flight to Chicago was a masterstroke of dramatic showmanship.

The next afternoon's convention session started with an anticlimax. Everybody knew it was Garner and the opening organ recital set the tone with "Eyes of Texas."

Garner had been the only rival candidate to wire congratulations to Roosevelt, saying "Your nomination means your election."

Shortly before, on the roof garden of the Washington Hotel in Washington, a reporter cornered Garner and asked him, unbelievingly, "You gone to Roosevelt?"

Garner slowly flicked away the ashes of his cigar and said, "That's right, son. . . . I'm a little older than you are, son. And politics is funny. . . ."

If Garner truly wasn't excited about the vice-presidential nomination, others were. Governor George Dern of Utah had campaigned hard for it. Senator Wheeler also wanted it, and the *Chicago Examiner* earlier had printed a story that Roosevelt had promised it to him. Roosevelt felt forced to send a telegram saying, "Story is not true."

"I know Dill was disappointed that his invaluable early organizational work went unrecognized by the vice-presidential nomination," said Farley. "I've suspected Hull, our pre-convention choice for second place was also a bit discontented, although I am sure he was more than satisfied later by his selection as Secretary of State."

Bernard Baruch called on Farley the morning after the Roosevelt nomination to find out if it was too late to consider Governor Ritchie for the vice-presidential nomination. "I replied that it was," said Farley.

The main opposition to Garner among Roosevelt leaders came from Ed Flynn. "I was not against him personally," said Flynn, "but I had my doubts because of the fact that he came from the south—from Texas in particular. My reason for this was that the main support in the convention for Smith was largely among Irish-Catholics. I felt it was necessary that this large group of people, who were by tradition mostly Democratic, should be brought back into the Party as quickly as possible. They felt keenly that Smith had been defeated in 1928 because of his religion. They knew also that Texas, which was normally overwhelmingly Democratic, had gone for President Hoover. I felt therefore, that if a candidate were named from Texas, the Catholic would use this as an excuse for opposing the national ticket."

But Roosevelt had agreed on Garner, and Alabama's John McDuffie was named to nominate him. "Let the country understand," said McDuffie optimistically, "there is happiness in the Democratic household. We have had our differences . . . Democrats often differ . . . but Democrats are good sports."

(Smith, at that moment, was preparing to leave Chicago, still in a huff, and refusing to tell reporters whether or not he would support the national ticket that November.)

Among the many seconding speeches, a Minnesota woman delegate said, "I know not if there is a precedent in a national convention . . . to pay tribute to the wife and helpmate of a candidate, but why care for precedent when joy is in our hearts and victory is perched upon our banners? . . . Mrs. John Garner is loved in Minnesota. . . ."

The only other vice-presidential nominee was General Matthew Tinley of Iowa. After the nominations ended at 3:25, out again came "Alfalfa Bill" Murray's Oklahoma Kiltie girls and brass band to start a parade while the organ played, "I've Been Working On the Railroad." Some of the parading delegates carried "GARNER FOR PRESIDENT" placards on which "PRESIDENT" had been crossed out and replaced by "VICE PRESIDENT."

Five minutes later, acting chairman Senator Tom Connally interrupted the procession to say that Governor Roosevelt's plane was only sixty miles out of Chicago.

Tinley then asked the convention to make Garner's nomination "by acclamation," and a gallery band played, "Turkey In The Straw," the Texas delegates sang "Dixie," and the organ followed up with "The Old Gray Mare."

Chairman Walsh later announced another bulletin on the plane arrival: "PLANE TEN MILES WEST OF SOUTH BEND. WILL BE IN IN FIFTEEN MINUTES."

Garner's telegram of acceptance was then read. "I am an Organization Democrat," said Garner. "I never in my life cast a vote against my own judgment, except I had to go along with the Democratic organization. I have done that. I will do it again. You must have organization."

To his friend Bascom Timmons, discussing the rumored deal of the Vice-Presidency for his delegates, Speaker of the House of Representatives Garner later said, "I have something of a reputation as a trader, and that reputation would not be helped any by trading the second most important office in the nation for one which, in itself, is almost wholly unimportant."

Then why did he do it, Timmons wanted to know.

"I'm a Democrat," said Garner. "I believe the country needs the Democratic Party in power at this time. . . . If Roosevelt's strength had begun to break on the fourth ballot, as it would have, I don't think any candidate would have got a two-thirds majority until after so bitter a contest that chances of winning an election would have ceased to exist."

The convention mood was happier now and the partisan quality of the gallery was gone. Delegates passed a resolution of appreciation to John J. Raskob, the band played "He's a Jolly Good Fellow," and Raskob bowed from his box. The convention clerk afterward read aloud from the afternoon newspapers, a Washington report that Nebraska Republican Senator George Norris, who had bolted Hoover in 1928, now announced his support of Roosevelt. Delegates cheered, the band played "Happy Days Are Here Again" and Oklahoma's blind Senator Thomas Gore proposed a resolution thanking Norris for his support and inviting support from all voters "without regard to previous political affiliation."

During the waiting period, reporters interviewed champion gate-crasher, Maurice ("One-eyed") Connally on how he had done it again. "It was nothing," said Connally. "I had saved the badge I got in Houston in 1928, and all I did was flash it and in I came. With this badge, I can go on the Speaker's Platform, but I am not using it now. The first day of the convention I got a Sergeant-at-Arms badge and have been helping the boys keep out gate-crashers. You'd be surprised at the number of people who are trying to get in for nothing. It's a shame."

At 4:27, Chairman Walsh asked the convention for quiet to listen to a radio report of the Roosevelt arrival at the Chicago airport: The tri-motored airplane had started from Albany at 8:30 that morning, with thirteen people, flew through some thunderstorm areas, stopped in Cleveland to refuel. Before leaving, Roosevelt told the press, "I'm glad to be going to Chicago. Everybody knows why I'm glad."

Sitting in the convention hall, the delegates heard the radio announcer: ". . . They are now entering the airport in Chicago. Ladies and gentlemen, I repeat, the plane bearing Governor Franklin D. Roosevelt has successfully outridden adverse weather conditions and is now circling the airport in Chicago, preparing to land . . . the most beautiful ship has glided down to the ground . . . you are going to hear those motors in about ten seconds . . . Governor Roosevelt is now being greeted by his son. . . ."

Farley was next to greet the Governor and Roosevelt said, "Jim, old pal, put 'er right there. Great work."

Roosevelt's glasses were knocked off in the quick crush around them, but somebody handed them back unbroken.

Cermak greeted him and Roosevelt answered, "Mr. Mayor, I am glad to be welcomed by you, my very old friend. . . ."

Somebody estimated a crowd of 15,000, and a motorcade of sixty cars led by screaming sirens headed for the convention hall some twenty miles away. Also among the welcoming committee at the airport was Tammany Hall leader John F. Curry.

Al Smith left the Congress Hotel by way of a side door at the moment when a crowd was assembling at the Michigan Boulevard entrance awaiting the arrival of Governor Roosevelt. Smith left the hotel an hour before train time, just to make sure he would not meet Roosevelt.

"The sad feature of the Convention for me," said Claude Bowers, "was the failure of Al Smith to avail himself of the opportunity to make himself the hero of the day. It was known that Roosevelt, on his way to the Convention, would stop at the hotel where Smith was staying. The defeated candidate was surrounded by men and women passionately devoted to his fortunes, but irreconcilable in their bitterness because of his defeat. These persuaded him to leave the hotel before Roosevelt's arrival. Had he been better advised, he would have remained to greet the victor, would have ridden with him to the Convention, and gone onto the platform with him, arm in arm, and have moved to make the motion by acclamation. An emotional reaction would have swept over the convention, and Smith would have gone forth, better loved than ever before."

But Roosevelt came, Smith was gone and it would be some three months before the two men would meet or greet each other. Knowing the Smith mood, Roosevelt had taken the precaution to arrange for their mutual friend, Judge Bernard Sheintag to meet Smith's train at Harmon, New York and persuade him not to blast the Democratic ticket to newsmen on his arrival at Grand Central Station. It was known that Smith had received several hundred telegrams that morning urging him to form a third party. Of the other candidates, Baker had no comment; Ritchie said he would follow the candidate; Traylor said he was happy with Roosevelt's nomination; "Alfalfa Bill" Murray said "It was my opinion that Roosevelt was not the best man, but now I sincerely wish I was mistaken"; and Governor White said, "We bow to the will of the Convention."

And Senator Huey P. Long, who had told Roosevelt he was a "gone goose," confided to the press, "There never was any doubt that we would put him over."

En route to the convention hall, Louis Howe sat in the back seat of the car with Roosevelt. Also in the car was Roosevelt's son James who later reported "one of the most incongruous perform-ances I ever have witnessed."

"Louis had strong objections to parts of Father's proposed Acceptance speech," wrote James, "and he began arguing with him even as the car was rolling in from the airport. Pa listened to him with one ear, argued back out of the side of his mouth—all the while smiling and waving at the wildly-cheering crowds. Finally— and it was one of the few times I ever heard him really get rough with Louis—Pa suddenly exploded: 'Damn it, Louis, *I'm* the nominee.' "

Louis Howe had written his own version of the Acceptance speech, and what Roosevelt finally did was to take the first page from Howe's speech and substitute it for the first page of his pre-pared speech, and then read the rest as planned.

Back in the hall, the waiting delegates were so excited by this variation in event, that they twice voted the same resolution of thanks to the radio broadcasting companies. One reporter credited the final show of convention harmony to the fact that delegates felt they had made a bad national impression over the radio during their bitter, night-long Thursday night session.

The carpenters had quickly put up a rail near the rostrum, on the extreme right of the small rectangular enclosure which was the speaker's rostrum. It also had an inner enclosure, an improvised stall similar to steamship gangplanks standing about a yard high.

After Madame Rose Zulalian again sang "The Star-Spangled Banner," Chairman Walsh quieted the crowd, made a short speech formally notifying Roosevelt of his nomination, then introduced him. Dressed in a blue sack suit, his eyes twitching nervously, Roosevelt moved into the inner enclosure, along the right rail, holding onto the arm of his son James, a happy grin on his face as he waved cheerily to the crowd. Mrs. Roosevelt moved up from the background and the crowd cheered louder as she stood alongside him and the great organ rolled out the heavy chords of "Happy Days Are Here Again."

Roosevelt started to speak shortly after 6:00 P.M.

"Then I first knew that characteristic toss of the head," said reporter Thomas Stokes. "Then I first knew that confidential look with the upraised eyebrow he gives his audience when he has delivered a thrust, succeeded by the slow grin as the audience catches it and tosses it around in laughter. Then I first knew the mockery which he touched off by popping his mouth open suddenly in the shape of a O. Then I first knew the tone of his voice as it drips with scorn. Then I first knew the emphatic rage as he lambasts his enemies. . . . I can see the tricks now, the tricks of gesture and of rhetoric, the tricks he plays with facts and figures often. Still I love to watch it."

"I regret that I am late," F.D.R. said, "but I have no control over the winds of heaven and could only be thankful for my Navy training."

He said he appreciated what had been done because he appreciated "the sleepless hours which you—and I—(LAUGHTER) have had."

"The appearance before a national convention of its nominee for President . . . is unprecedented and unusual," he said, "but these are unprecedented and unusual times. I have started out on the tasks that lie ahead by breaking the absurd tradition that the candidate should remain in professed ignorance of what has happened for weeks until he is formally notified. . . . You have nominated me and I know it, and I am here to thank you for the honor.

". . . That admirable document, the platform, which you have adopted is clear. I accept it one hundred percent. . . . This conven-

tion wants repeal. Your candidate wants repeal. . . ." Then, near
the end, Roosevelt said, ". . . I pledge you—I pledge myself to a
new deal for the American people. . . ."

It was a short speech of forty-seven minutes, the punctuating
applause brief and scattered, the biggest burst coming when he
mentioned repeal. Arthur Mullen quickly moved for adjournment
and the delegates rushed out for their trains, which were being
held for them.

Except for the cleaners, who had carted off sixty tons of waste
paper after the long meeting the day before, the convention now
belonged to the critics.

"It's a kangaroo ticket," said Archie Parr, veteran Texas political
leader, "stronger in the hind quarter than in the front."

A wise-cracking Republican Senator called Roosevelt, "God's
greatest gift to the Republican Party."

"The nomination was bought by as cold a political bargain as
our convention histories have known," said the New York Post.
"He is a slippery opportunist who will break the rules of the game
when it is his advantage to do so," wrote the Boston Herald.
". . . A shifter and an intellectual dodger . . . too timid to make
a last-ditch fight for anything at any time," said the Des Moines
Register.

"Very soon now the people will be given to know whether the
great Governor of New York is the timid, the irresolute, the
vacillating, the compromising, the self-seeking, the unprincipled
politician that his enemies in both parties have painted him to be,"
wrote the Omaha World-Herald. "They will find, before many
suns have risen and set, that they have raised for themselves a
brave and earnest leader, an unselfish and devoted champion. They
will find themselves with such a candidate for the presidency as
this dark period of distress and emergency imperatively requires;
and they will come, as was said of another great governor of New
York, to love him for the enemies he has made and for the enemies
he is certain yet to make."

Before everybody headed home, blind Senator Gore issued a

kind of challenge to Tammany Hall. "We have nominated a lame lion," he said. "The Tammany tiger must admit that only the lion could lick the tiger. We have nominated him without Tammany's help. We must plan to elect him without Tammany's help, although for one, I hope to have their help."

Whatever the future problems, Roosevelt seemed unfazed.

"I found Roosevelt in his room at the hotel, along with Louis Howe, seated by the window," wrote Claude Bowers. "When he saw me, Roosevelt threw back his head and laughed: 'We must razz you for voting for Smith,' he said."

"Almost immediately, he had a problem in his lap," said Bowers, "when somebody came to say that McAdoo was in the reception room and wanted to pose with him for a picture. Roosevelt's face fell. He asked my opinion. I thought it would be a mistake, since it would mean rubbing salt into the wounds of the Smith followers. He decided to say so frankly to McAdoo, and when the latter entered, I left. There was no picture."

Talking later about who arranged the final switch for Roosevelt's nomination, Basil O'Connor, an old friend, told F.D.R., "Of the 55,000 Democrats allegedly to have been in Chicago for the . . . convention, unquestionably 62,000 of them arranged that . . . shift." Roosevelt roared with laughter.

Garner also later had a private message for Roosevelt: "All you have to do is stay alive until election day. The people are not going to vote for you. They are going to vote against the depression."

Raymond Moley was even more prophetic when he wrote Louis Howe after the victory, "You and Jim have done more than elect a President—you have created a new party that ought to hold power for 25 years."

And Louis McHenry Howe, the little man with the large dream, wrote a poem called "Success" and put it on the Roosevelt breakfast plate. It began:

"Pity him most who gaineth most,
Who won all things for which his heart aspires. . . ."

THERE HAD BEEN a new generation of citizen-soldiers and the commanding general had become President of the United States.

Europe was shaking itself out of the shock, and rearranging itself; Communist Russia was regearing itself to again become a threat to the world; and the world itself had hopefully formed a United Nations to help weld instead of destroy. The atomic bomb, which only destroyed cities, had grown into hydrogen bombs, which now could destroy a civilization.

Still, it was a time of new babies, new houses, new hope in multiplied supply.

Hot jazz became cool, quiet writers became angry, double-breasted suits became single, and the small square box of television brought a strange new world into the American living room. Most of it was a world nobody ever made, a world of old movies and drama of incredible corn. But with it came a marvelous sense of intimacy, brought instantaneously to millions of people, that completely changed the face and feel of American politics.

Rising fast out of our politics was a whole new crop of fresh faces priming to take over. The time was not yet, but soon, very soon.

DEMOCRATIC NATIONAL CONVENTION OF 1956

IT ALL REALLY BEGAN ON A CRISP ST. VALENTINE'S afternoon, 1956, in the push and rush of a floor of offices in Chicago, housing the National Volunteers for Stevenson. A young law student, in charge of sending out letters and literature, had just finished a mass mailing to Minnesota, a prelude to the upcoming primary there, and now he took the afternoon off to worry.

He was worried about a lot of things. Advance incoming intelligence from Minnesota indicated a shoo-in for Stevenson. And the tone of most of the mail duplicated this shoo-in feeling all over the country.

This meant to the young man a dull series of primaries, with Stevenson sweeping them all, and an even duller convention, with Stevenson in big on the first ballot. His worry was how to pull in the American people and tie them up emotionally with the candidate and the convention. And then, suddenly, came an idea so simple, so flashing that the young man spent the rest of a frenetic day and night and next day putting it all into a memo for Stevenson's campaign manager, Jim Finnegan.

That memo gave such dramatic impact to the 1956 Democratic National Convention that—twenty years from now—many of the 120,000,000 people who watched it on TV will remember it as the single vividness of that convention.

That memo so transformed the political face of an unhopeful freshman senator named John Kennedy that it literally pushed him ahead ten political years in a single afternoon, transforming him from a vice-presidential dark horse in early 1956 to a presidential front runner in early 1960.

The idea that caused all this? Opening up the nomination of a vice-presidential candidate, letting the delegates themselves pick their man for the first time in modern history.

But one point must be made sharp and strong.

Even if that young man had never dreamed up that idea, never fought for it, never made it happen—most politicians now feel something similar would have had to happen.

Democratic National Convention vice-presidential politics had reached such a turn that there almost was no other out.

Somebody else would have had to dream up the idea.

Somebody else would have had to fight for it.

Somebody else would have had to make it happen.

Three months before the young man wrote his memo, a Kefauver delegate reported to Utah Democratic National Committeeman Calvin Rawlings on a secret meeting between Stevenson and Kefauver representatives in California at Pat Brown's office. (Rawlings then forwarded the report to Bill Blair, Stevenson's closest confidant, at the Stevenson office on December 9.)

". . . they believe also that Stevenson would welcome the Convention picking the Vice-President rather than hand-picking him, as has been done by previous candidates for the presidency. This is also pretty intelligent analysis, as I believe the people in 1956 will increasingly vote for the Vice-President, in view cf the recent sickness of the President. . . ."

Overconfidence infected Stevenson's headquarters. And one of the most overconfident was the dark-haired, medium-built, aggressively bright young law student from Washington, D.C., who reacted to politics with the enthusiasm of a volunteer fireman. His name was John Sharon and his previous political experience was helping to brain trust a losing United States Senate campaign in New Jersey.

There had been no staff talk of the Vice-Presidency. Finnegan felt this was a Stevenson decision. But Sharon felt the urgent need to counter the coming dullness of a cut-and-dried primary campaign.

"I recalled something that had been used to help nominate Franklin D. Roosevelt in 1932," said Sharon. "Phonographs were something very new then and F.D.R. sent a recorded personal message to the home of each delegate. Lots of delegates didn't have phonographs, but even if they didn't, they all knew somebody who did and hustled over to hear it. It was a fantastically successful gimmick."

At the same time, Sharon was also remembering the running mood of the mail—delegates all saying that they were for Adlai but they wanted to see this or that man for Vice-President.

Gimmick and Vice-Presidency, gimmick and Vice-Presidency, those were the two things whirling in Sharon's brain in the quiet of that February afternoon. And then came the idea:

As a contrast to the Republican "bossed" convention, give Democratic delegates a chance to voice their own minds on the Vice-Presidency.

The more Sharon thought about it, the more presumptuous it all seemed. "Where did I come off writing such a memo to the campaign manager?" said Sharon. "But I couldn't sleep that night. The more I thought of it, the more I felt the idea of an open convention was right.

"My wife Ruth is a tough critic. She grabbed this idea instinctively, said I had to push it, I just had to. So I sent a copy to Finnegan, and another copy to Bill Blair in Stevenson's office. I figured it would probably wind up in the bottom of their IN baskets."

Finnegan's reaction: "We don't know what Minnesota will show," he said. "And even if we do win, there are still a lot of primaries after that. It's just too early."

Brilliant James Aloysius Finnegan seldom wasted words. He was an idealist and a dedicated politician's politician. Chairman of the Democratic party in Philadelphia and later president of the City Council, he had learned his politics from the wards up. His hair had white in it and his eyes had wisdom, and both were set in a head that seemed almost too huge even for his chunky body.

In the months before the convention, when Finnegan said he had the vote of a given delegate, he didn't mean simply that the delegate had promised his undying support, crossed his heart, and signed the sworn pledge—he meant that he had the delegate almost manacled to the lamppost right outside his headquarters at 231 South La Salle Street. And every night, he was the mother hen going down the list, state by state, name by name.

He was this kind of professional:

Sitting with his state delegation at a previous convention, his protégé Joe Clark (now a senator from Pennsylvania) told Finnegan that he had talked to key people who all agreed that Stevenson would get thirty-nine Pennsylvania votes on that ballot. Finnegan simply said, "Thirty-nine and a half."

Speaking for Pennsylvania on the roll call, Democratic leader and Pittsburgh Mayor David Lawrence toted up his state's votes for the various candidates and said, "And thirty-nine for Stevenson." Clark smiled a cat's smile at his friend Finnegan and said, "See?" But just then some delegate demanded a poll of the delegation. With all the half votes, it took a tedious time, and Lawrence announced the new results which were almost the same except for one small change, "And thirty-nine and a half for Stevenson."

Friend Finnegan got up to go and had only a single smiling word for friend Clark, "Amateur."

The political seismograph reported strange rumblings just one week before the Minnesota primary. A primary can't always tie up positively, but it can kill absolutely. A Wisconsin primary killed Willkie's hopes; Nebraska did the same with Senator Robert Kerr; Oregon did it to Harold Stassen.

And now here were reports coming in from Minnesota, first flat and dribbling, now furiously, pieces of political mosaic, all disquieting. Back in January, Senator Hubert Humphrey had written Adlai Stevenson, "[The Republicans] are attempting to make an analogy between yourself and Dewey and the 1948 campaign with Kefauver carrying the Truman mantle. This is a strange fact, but the effort is under way."

A month later, former Minnesota Governor Harold Stassen was effectively busy telling Republicans to cross over and support Kefauver, thereby knocking out Democratic front runner Stevenson. Analyzing it afterward, a staff study revealed that 125,000 Republicans did just that, increasing the Democratic vote 261 per cent over 1952. Several weeks later, in a dinner at the Waldorf Astoria, Republican John R. "Tex" McCrary pointed to a group on the dais and said that those same people in one night raised all the Republican money to get Kefauver nominated over Stevenson in the Minnesota primary. Kefauver won handsomely.

"I was one red-faced cookie," said Sharon. "Now my idea was completely shelved, even in my own mind. Not dead, but shelved, definitely shelved."

Besides, there was too much else to do now. Finnegan had picked Sharon as one of his top assistants, and everywhere there were brush fires catching overnight, delegates getting doubtful again, the day-to-day emergencies preparing for the next primary in Florida, no time now for long-range perspective.

A slim Stevenson victory in the Florida primary, then a big win in California, and that same night Sharon pulled his idea out of cold storage.

He was close to Finnegan now, entrusted with more and more important jobs. No longer did Sharon have coy self-questions.

So again he asked Finnegan, that very night: "How about that open-convention idea now?"

Finnegan's answer was brisk: "Still too early."

This no longer stopped Sharon. He decided to test it on others.

He tried it on two bright campaign staff members, one of them Stevenson's young law partner, Newt Minow, and the other, also a Chicago lawyer, Bill Rivkin. Both had been politically seasoned by the 1952 campaign.

Sharon threw the idea at them and saw it fall flat.

But they had reasons for their reactions, strong reasons, and Sharon didn't know them then.

Both were busy pushing private candidates for the Vice-Presidency. Minow for Kennedy and Rivkin for Humphrey. Both thought they had a good chance, and for good reason. And so they both saw this open convention idea as an added confusion complicating their candidate's chances.

Stevenson was doing his own thinking on whom he wanted, and why.

"I guess it was right after the California primary," said Adlai Stevenson, "after Estes knew he had been licked, that we got the first overture from a lot of people about Estes and I getting together. I remember that even Drew Pearson called, trying to arrange a meeting between Estes and me at his home. Then lots of other people would approach me about my calling Estes on the phone or how would I feel if he called me on the phone. I guess the idea was that we might make a deal on the Vice-Presidency. But I would have none of that fiddling around. I was going to make no deal with Estes or anybody else. . . ."

Also on the political grapevine: Kefauver people were making overtures to Harriman people.

"I was geting into a plane and there was Estes Kefauver," said sharp, able Chicago Democratic boss Jack Arvey. "So we sat and talked about the upcoming convention and I told him then and there that I didn't think he had any right to the Democratic nomination for President. As long as Eisenhower was all right, neither he nor Harriman wanted any part of the nomination, but as soon as Eisenhower got real sick, both he and Harriman scrambled right into the race. I also added that by all the rules of the game, Adlai was entitled to it this time if he wanted it, and this time he wanted it.

"Then Estes said he knew none of the political bosses wanted him. I said I supposed he meant me and Dave Lawrence of Pennsylvania and people like that, and he said yes, and so I said, 'Look, I'm not for you and I'm not against you—it's just that I feel Adlai is entitled to it.'

"And then Estes said, 'What about the Number Two spot?' As far as that was concerned, I said, I thought he would be fine, but I couldn't be for him or against him because I didn't know what Adlai wanted to do. At that time, I don't think Adlai did either."

Adlai didn't.

"I knew of course that Estes did have considerable strength and friends in California," Stevenson comments, "and other places like Minnesota, where he did beat me. Estes did have this delegate strength and a good organization and I knew this could be an important help on the ticket.

"Then there was Hubert Humphrey. I knew Hubert well. I don't think I ever met Estes before the 1952 campaign, but Hubert and I have had a long and warm and friendly association and I have high respect for him. Hubert has a fine mind and an awful lot of ability. Besides, Hubert represented the farm vote of the Midwest, and I needed that. We had made mistakes in slighting the farm vote in 1952 and Hubert knew their needs and had their confidence and their votes. At least I thought he had their votes. His people talked about six states in the Southeast and some more in the Midwest as being solid for Hubert. I was really fooled by them and maybe Hubert was, too. But, anyway, at that time, Hubert was a top candidate.

"And then there was Jack Kennedy. Now I had never talked to Jack about the Vice-Presidency, but his father came to see me several times—he had contributed to my campaigns—and we talked about Jack in a general way. I have a personal fondness for Jack and I admired him, and I told his father that. Then, of course,

BALLOTS & BANDWAGONS

Jack's sister Eunice and her husband, Sarge Shriver, are good friends of mine. There was also our concern for the Catholic vote, which we had lost in 1952. Yes, we had thought seriously about Jack as a vice-presidential candidate.

"So there they were, all three of them, each with important qualifications for the job. And the pressures from each group kept mounting. The greater the pressures," said Stevenson, "the more difficult the decision, especially since you never want to leave any stones unturned."

The next time you go to a political dinner, carefully notice who sits next to whom on the dais and then find out who was in charge of the seating arrangements. It's often enlightening.

At the farewell dinner for Senator Walter George of Georgia in Washington, D.C., in February, 1956, it was no political accident that Adlai Stevenson and Hubert Humphrey sat next to each other—a Humphrey man was among those in charge of dinner arrangements. There was nothing wrong in this. Stevenson wanted to talk to Humphrey. Stevenson had called him from Chicago to talk about vice-presidential candidates, ("No, my name was not mentioned then," said Humphrey), and they had tried to get together that afternoon to talk more about it, but Humphrey had been tied up on the Senate floor. So, finally, there they were at dinner, talking about possible nominees for the Vice-Presidency. ("No, my name wasn't mentioned then, either.")

Afterward, both men went to the Mayflower Hotel—to different rooms. Humphrey went to a room with a Washington lawyer who is one of his closest political advisers. For an hour and a half, Humphrey presented all the reasons why he wasn't right for the vice-presidential nomination, and his companion kept busy knocking down every reason. He reminded Humphrey that reports had been coming in from all over the country that Stevenson had been conversationally eliminating all other vice-presidential possibilities except Humphrey. But the friend's clincher was: let's not be coy about it. Do you think any of the other candidates are more qualified than you are?

It was now long past midnight. Humphrey's man called Stevenson's suite and Bill Blair answered. "I know it's damn late," he said, "but do you still want to talk?"

"Sure we still want to talk," said Blair, "but there's a mob up here. I'll call you when we're ready."

Twenty minutes later, Humphrey and his adviser walked in to find a cozy group: Stevenson, Finnegan, Blair.

Before anything else, Humphrey had a quick complaint. He knew that a Democratic Convention Committee had selected him as keynote speaker on a first tentative vote, then rejected him on the final vote in favor of Governor Frank Clement of Tennessee.

"That was the one thing I always had in my craw," said Humphrey, "some day to be the keynote speaker of the Democratic National Convention."

Finnegan started to answer, saying they had nothing to do with those arrangements, but Stevenson interrupted rather impatiently and said, "Let's not worry about that, let's get to the point."

The point was the Vice-Presidency, and again they ran through every available candidate: Kefauver, Kennedy, Gore, Mansfield, Fulbright, Rayburn, Johnson, Monroney, Jackson, Wagner. Stevenson said he wanted a vice-presidential nominee who could ably succeed as President, if necessary, serve as an effective liaison with Congress, and help him win the election. Then he listed the liabilities and assets of all the candidates, with the stress on their liabilities.

"And then he leaned towards me like this," said Humphrey, edging forward, "and he said, 'Hubert, how about you?' "

Hubert was now ready with all the negatives but Stevenson brushed them all away and said, "Hubert, if you are acceptable to the leaders of the South, I could support you. But if you want the nomination you better go out and work for it."

"I don't feel he said anything more committal than that," said Humphrey.

Blair remembers only that Stevenson was delighted that Humphrey was going to make the vice-presidential race. Stevenson confirms this, adding, "But I never told him he was my candidate."

As the Humphrey aide remembers it, they had all said, in effect, "You're it." He also remembers Stevenson saying, "It's four o'clock and I have to get up at six-thirty," and then headed for bed, suggesting that the others discuss ways and means of building up Hubert's "acceptability" so "it won't come as a surprise."

Political reasons are seldom simple, but they're also seldom as subterranean as some politicians like to think.

Now why would Stevenson ask Humphrey to declare himself openly as a vice-presidential candidate, months before the convention? The surface reason is simple: he wants him.

The subterranean reason? Well, here was Kefauver, still in the race, still a threat at the convention despite his primary losses in Florida and California. How do you flush him out, get rid of him, lock up the convention? Well, now if there were an actual announced candidate for the Vice-Presidency, wouldn't it put pressure on Kefauver to make some kind of deal before others got too far ahead and while he still had a chance to get on the ticket?

Simple or subterranean, take your choice. Or perhaps you like a blend?

A growing number of important Democrats, worrying about the growing bitterness between two big parts of the party, now looked kindly on the healing force of a Stevenson-Kefauver ticket.

Finnegan was one of these people.

Meanwhile, Kefauver supporter Howard McGrath, former governor of Rhode Island and Truman's campaign manager in 1948, made preliminary contact and walked away with a general understanding that Dave Lawrence was inclined to give Kefauver his personal support for the vice-presidential nomination.

Then McGrath and Kefauver campaign manager Jiggs Donohue set up appointments with some thirty top Democratic leaders for Kefauver to discuss his political future. After sampling their views, Kefauver started to reconsider his candidacy.

The date: June 18. The place: Washington's Willard Hotel. The occasion: a wake.

Some seventy people had come from all over the country to drink cocktails without enthusiasm and listen to speeches without hope. Their candidate seemed dead, long live their candidate, and now came the talk they didn't like, the talk of deals.

Jiggs Donohue, once a special assistant to the Attorney General, took a lawyer's tone in offering three alternatives: a deal with Harriman, who might then take care of their $80,000 campaign debt (and also, according to a running rumor, make Jiggs Donohue the Democratic National Chairman, if he won); a deal with Stevenson people, intimating that conversations with top Stevenson aides had indicated Kefauver's acceptability as a possible running mate; no deal with anybody, running the race and definitely losing.

Some muttered that Kefauver had been sold out. Others reluctantly agreed that perhaps the Stevenson setup was the best. Most felt that the decision must be Kefauver's.

They held no vote. You don't vote at a wake.

Even then, Kefauver was still torn in his decision. "My people went through hell for me. I can't withdraw—they went through hell for me."

He could have come into the convention with several hundred votes, perhaps dragged out the contest a little, but it would also have dragged out the pain of losing because he didn't have a chance. If he stayed in, it could only tear apart both the convention and Kefauver.

"We worked on him every time he came to Washington," said Helen Fuller, managing editor of the *New Republic* and one of his close friends. "But then he would go out into the field and people there would unwork him. One day a mutual friend called me with the news, 'I've got him to do it. Come on over.' Estes was convinced all right, but I've never seen a man so down. What hurt him was that he was letting down all the people who had spilled their guts for him. He was finally agreeing to do this only because all the people whom he trusted best were insisting on it."

Kefauver recalls, "Many of our people thought Adlai would pick up Kennedy because of the close connections between the Kennedy family and some of the Stevenson staff, and because of their need for the Catholic vote."

And just when and where did Jack Kennedy's candidacy spring from?

Where was the beginning? Where was the first national push?

The first column item in which Kennedy saw himself mentioned as a newly discussed vice-presidential candidate was in *Newsweek's* Periscope. A curious Kennedy quickly called the Periscope editor, Debs Myers, wanting to know where the editor heard all this; who were these people discussing him? The editor, who wasn't telling, smiled over the phone and said, "Me."

"I don't know where it all started," said Senator John Kennedy. "I remember I was up in Rhode Island visiting my mother-in-law, and Governor Roberts talked to me about it. He's an old friend. And so is Governor Abe Ribicoff of Connecticut. Abe openly proposed me for the Vice-Presidency at the Governors' Conference that year. And I talked it over with Paul Dever, who was then governor of Massachusetts. But I didn't talk it over with all the New England governors; I didn't talk it over with Muskie."

However, Roberts proposed the idea of a New England bloc. "I felt that New England wasn't having enough influence at the convention any more because our votes were so scattered," he said. "If we could all get pledged together we might have impact."

So they brought together all the New England leaders—Democratic governors and state chairmen and national committeemen, and met at the Engineers' Club in Boston.

"We knew we had ninety per cent of them and the job was to bring in the other ten per cent," said Roberts. "It took some doing because all of them thought they should be in charge. So we gave some breakfasts, with a different man presiding at the head table each day. And poor Paul Dever had to pay the bill."

For once, a candidate's strongest asset to his national ticket was his religion.

A survey was circulated by Connecticut's Democratic boss John

Bailey, although Kennedy's Ted Sorensen wrote it. A printed copy went to each delegate and every important Democrat, as well as the press.

It said some startling things:

"The Al Smith myth is one of the falsest myths in politics. The year 1928 was a Republican year, regardless of who was on either ticket. It was the year for 'drys' like Hoover, not 'wets' like Smith."

The survey then listed fourteen states with 261 electoral votes: New York (32% Catholic); Pennsylvania (29%); Illinois (30%); New Jersey (39%); Massachusetts (50%); Connecticut (49%); Rhode Island (60%); California (22%); Michigan (24%); Minnesota (24%); Ohio (20%); Wisconsin (32%); Maryland (21%); and Montana (22%).

Then came the impact:

"In 1940, 13 of these states with 240 electoral votes went Democratic—without which the Democrats would have lost the election.

"In 1944, 12 of these states went Democratic—without which the Democrats would have lost the election.

"In 1948, 8 of these states went Democratic—without which the Democrats would have lost the election.

"In 1952, none of these states went Democratic, all 261 of their electoral votes went to Eisenhower—and the Democrats lost their first presidential election in 24 years."

The Bailey Report further added that 30 per cent of the national Catholic vote, normally Democratic, had shifted to Eisenhower, making up 7 per cent of his total vote. Without that vote, Eisenhower would have lost.

The prod was plain. A close friend quoted Bailey as then saying, "I just want a Catholic on the ticket," with no mention of Kennedy nor his record.

From other sources came the observation that the various statistics made no ethnic distinctions among Catholics. Some political scientists discredited the statistics. Nevertheless, men around Kennedy soon heard the word: the Bailey Report had hit Stevenson hard.

Back in Washington, Kennedy and Sorensen were driving to town in the same car, as they often did, and one said to the other: "You know, I'm getting a little interested in that Vice-Presidency."

Ted Sorensen smiled and said, "That's against our agreement. You weren't supposed to get interested in it so that if you wouldn't get it, you wouldn't be disappointed. Now you will."

Kennedy fingered his heavy mop of hair, thought a minute, and said, "Yes, I will, a little bit—from the end of the convention session on Friday to the time I head for Europe on Saturday."

And that's the way it was.

Then, as now, Stevenson's three law partners were politically divided on the vice-presidential candidates: Newt Minow for Kennedy, Bill Wirtz for Humphrey, and Bill Blair torn betweeen.

Now that Stevenson was way out in front, more and more delegates hurried to hop on the Stevenson bandwagon. "I'm for you, Governor . . . I always was. . . ." However, many of them still added the word ". . . but . . ." ". . . but I think you ought to have so-and-so as your Vice-President. . . ."

The mail then was strongly pro-Kefauver, no anti-Kefauver mail at all. With Kennedy it was the contrary—no pro mail at all, but strongly anti, and this mostly from the Midwest Bible Belt. Emphasizing the anti-Kennedy mail were the delegates themselves dropping in personally to tell Stevenson how strongly they were against Kennedy, and why they and others would never vote for him. To counter this came New England governors, Roberts, Ribicoff, and ex-Governor Dever, all stressing the need for a Kennedy candidacy.

In the background of all this conflict, Sharon waited for his moment, again at a quiet informal dinner with Finnegan, and then reopened the subject of the open convention. This time Finnegan was ready to talk, stacked with arguments against it.

"Nothing would make me happier than being responsible for getting a Catholic into such a national office," Finnegan told Kennedy-supporter Newt Minow, "but it just isn't politically smart. It will hurt."

Shortly before the convention, Kefauver came for a conference with Stevenson in his Hilton Hotel headquarters suite. The bedroom door wouldn't close very well and Finnegan asked an aide to lean against it, keep it closed, and keep visitors away. Inside that bedroom, Stevenson and Kefauver were in conference.

The man leaning against the door couldn't help overhearing some of the conversation snatches; they talked about the different delegations where Kefauver had influence, some specific individuals on these delegations who might be helpful, suggestions as to what to say to whom at appearances before the various caucuses.

And then Kefauver asked for Stevenson's support for the Vice-Presidency. Stevenson previously had sent Kefauver a note thanking him for his gracious gesture in withdrawing from the race and asking support for Stevenson. His written note then, however, was noncommittal. His vocal note now was equally noncommittal.

"Jim never once told me to stop fighting for my idea," said Sharon. "Jim always felt that goddammit, if a guy felt he had an idea, then to let him go ahead and fight for it. Never once did he try to dismiss or gag any idea just because he disagreed with it. Had Jim ever told me, 'Now lay off,' why I would have laid off, but he never did, he never did."

With the convention coming closer, all problems picked up pressure: the Maryland delegation was still not sewed up; Tom Finletter was calling to say, "Jim, you better call this New York delegate because I think he's leaning towards Stevenson." Democratic National Chairman Paul Butler, setting up the convention schedule, wanted the presidential nomination one day and the acceptance speech the following night. Finnegan thought this would be anticlimactic, but Butler was adamant. One of Stevenson's aides remarked, "You know, Adlai, I think Paul is trying to scuttle us."

Finnegan had other concerns. One of his Missouri correspondents, a man close to Truman, wrote to say, "Symington is holding some of these meetings and when they get together and mention him as a favorite son, he states that he is not a candidate. I suppose, however, he has a feeling that if there is a situation that might arise at the convention, he might want to keep himself in position as a dark horse."

Finnegan's major concern was the possibility of a last-minute maneuver by Truman's Number One candidate, Harriman. This finally spread to Stevenson, who walked in on him one day and asked, "Jim, you don't think there's any possibility of my not getting the nomination, do you?"

And Jim said, "No, but I want to make sure I touch all the bases."

Meanwhile, what about the open convention?

How do you keep something alive when the boss says no?

In politics, as in anything else, it depends on how strongly you believe in what you're doing, how much courage you've got to fight the odds. If you believe, if you have courage, you lobby.

John Sharon lobbied all over the place.

"I went to see Bill Blair. Bill was really open-minded about it, said the idea had a lot of potential, that it should not be dismissed. I tried it on Newt again and he was adamant against it, adamant. I told Stevenson's press secretary, Roger Tubby, about it. Roger thought that it was a fine idea but that it was a political decision, not a public relations decision. Then I tried it on two young researchers and both of them liked the idea. One of them said, 'Darn it all, you've got to fight for this idea. These things never happen unless you fight for them. This campaign needs a few more fighters and fewer people who think to death every fresh idea that comes up.'"

"I was so down at the time," said Sharon, "that if he hadn't buoyed me up with that pep talk, I might have dropped the whole thing then and there."

Next came Sharon's most critical convert: George Ball, Stevenson's old friend, a distinguished international lawyer who had been put in charge of all campaign public relations. Sharon worked for Ball in Washington, and Ball had recommended Sharon for Stevenson's staff.

"George was in and out of Chicago all the time and it was hard to catch him," said Sharon, "but I finally got to him and told him the idea. George was the only person totally favorable to the whole thing immediately. All the others needed convincing but George saw it at once and grabbed at it."

But Ball was too busy with other matters to fight for this one, and Finnegan was as opposed as ever. Who could Sharon talk to now? Stevenson? Why should Stevenson listen to Sharon instead of Finnegan? It made no sense. But then how could he get Stevenson intrigued with the idea, get everybody on the staff talking and thinking more about it?

"I called Stu Alsop and we had lunch and I told him we were thinking about his open convention idea, and what our reasons were, and, sure enough, he printed it in his column." Finnegan knew Sharon had leaked it, but he never said a word to Sharon about it. George Ball knew, too. He walked over to Sharon with a copy of the column and his eyes twinkled as he asked. "Have you read this?" And this time Sharon's eyes twinkled as he said yes. "Well, what do you think about it?" asked Ball, his eyes almost laughing. And all Sharon could safely say, without really laughing, was, "It's very interesting."

"We wanted no part of an open convention," said Sorensen, Kennedy's aid, "because we didn't think we had a chance that way, simply because we weren't organized for it and the convention was only a few days away."

"What Sorensen told me," said Sharon, "was that Kennedy definitely would not allow his name to be put before the convention because he was afraid all this anti-Catholic feeling would stir up on the floor and people would recall all that Al Smith bitterness, and this bad feeling would hurt the ticket rather than help it."

"I went to see Jack Kennedy during the convention week," said one of Stevenson's closest advisers. "I wanted to find out just how serious he was about the Vice-Presidency. And he told me he was very serious because he felt that the only way a Catholic could ever become President in our lifetime was if a Catholic could get on the national ticket in a low period of Democratic fortunes, when they were strongly concerned about the Catholic vote. And he felt that this was the year when Democrats were in real trouble and needed such help."

Sometime before the convention in Washington, Tennessee's Senator Albert Gore and Kennedy and their wives had dinner with friends. The Vice-Presidency came up in the conversation, and a bystander described it as a regular Alphonse and Gaston act. Kennedy was saying to Gore, "I think it ought to be you." And Gore was saying to Kennedy, "No, I think it ought to be you."

Of course that mood soon changed.

At a cocktail party in Chicago for the Connecticut delegation, Governor Ribicoff stood on a chair and made a fifteen-minute speech in which he didn't mention Stevenson once but was fulsome for Kennedy.

"Jack started going around talking to delegations soon after we got there," said his good friend, Senator George Smathers of Florida. "I thought he was wasting his time, and I told him so. I figured, like everybody else, that Stevenson would pick anybody he wanted to pick and it was pointless to campaign for it."

"Which just goes to show how wrong a guy can be."

Kefauver worked hard, too. He felt he had to earn his way into the vice-presidential nomination and so went from one caucus to another, urging all his delegates to vote straight down the line for Stevenson. And it wasn't easy. Many of the delegates wouldn't make this commitment unless they heard a commitment from Stevenson to make Kefauver his running mate.

Humphrey wasn't sure what to do. He had dinner with his close friend, Bill Rivkin, a remarkable campaign worker of eager energy, and John Sharon. Humphrey asked them what he should do.

Rivkin, knowing about the Mayflower meeting, urged him to do nothing, just lay low.

Sharon, feeling the possibility of an open convention, told Humphrey about it, advised him therefore to be more prepared.

It was now or never for Sharon. He decided to talk to the three men to whom Stevenson would and did listen: Wilson Wyatt, not only his able 1952 campaign manager but his close personal friend; Tom Finletter, former Air Force Secretary and another old friend; and George Ball, a friend who always had his ear.

"So I called Tom," said Sharon, "and asked him when he was coming to Chicago and we set up a breakfast for the four of us at the Blackstone Hotel Grill. In my book, this was the last move I was going to make on this."

It was a dangerous place to meet. Harry Truman was breakfasting two tables to the left and Jim Finnegan two tables away to their right.

Sharon started right in as soon as they sat down. "Tom said immediately that he was unalterably opposed to the idea," Sharon recalls. "George countered quickly that there was a lot to it and Tom should hear it out. And Wilson, the way he always does, said, "We should be willing to listen to all the ideas that can help."

Then Sharon made his full pitch.

Finletter was still dead set against it, gave most of the Finnegan arguments on how it might hurt the Party, that the old pros wouldn't like it, that the gamble was too great. Wyatt listened intently, asked probing questions, kept himself on the fence. Ball threw in full enthusiasm for it, said it would give a fresh breeze to the convention, a new dramatic lift. And then Ball battered down the Finletter arguments one by one.

"The wonderful thing about Tom is that he's a reasoned man. He states his position, but if the other arguments are better, he's always willing to change his position."

It was Finletter who finally said, "We must do it." And Wyatt phone and I remember he liked it."

"I really talked to very few people about the open convention," said Stevenson. "It was the kind of thing that I was most apt to talk to Wilson [Wyatt] about. I did discuss it with Dave Lawrence, and he was all for it, really strong for it, said it would dramatize the whole convention, and he was right.

"Jim Finnegan equivocated about it, he wasn't sure. If I would have settled on any one candidate, he would have been equally satisfied, maybe more so. I talked to Jack Arvey about it on the phone and I remember he liked it."

Word trickled down from somebody high in the Stevenson group that Kennedy had been counted out. "It was one of those highly unofficial things," said Sorensen, "but we figured it was true because it sounded true."

After all, Kennedy had been picked to narrate the movie film of Democratic history at the convention. When they photographed him at the old Chaplin studios in Hollywood, it was no secret that the Democratic National Committee had offered his name on a list because he wasn't figured in the vice-presidential thinking and they wanted to use him at the convention. (Dore Schary, who produced the film, said, "I picked Kennedy mainly because his book *Profiles in Courage* was such a best seller on the list, and because he was more nationally known than the others.")

TV changed the convention.

Somebody said there were more TV employees at the convention than there were delegates, and it was almost true. N.B.C. sent a 400-man staff with 10,000 pounds of electronic equipment. C.B.S. sent 335 people and spotted thirty television cameras in as many places. And of course there were the other networks—one of them even hired a man to wear its identifying button and move around into the TV pictures taken by rival networks. They had everything from hip-pocket wire recorders, wrist-watch microphones, walkie-talkies, to creepie-peepies (which looked like a coal miner's headlight and which one Missouri reporter described as "a country constable's spotlight on a dark lane"). Brassier interviewers took their TV with them as they climbed into Mrs. Truman's box, queried Mrs. Symington, and cornered Adlai Stevenson's sons, asking all kinds of questions, even the most impertinent.

The better commentators caught groups of leading figures and asked the sharpest questions, which the politicians couldn't easily duck because TV had put them into a smoke-filled room without walls. But TV now offered an audience of more than 100,000,000 Americans compared to an audience of only 10,000,000 in 1948.

For that price they could dictate terms, and did: streamline the schedule, cut speechmaking time, eliminate the middle aisle for parading purposes, sell candidates the way business sells boxtops—clearly, quickly, forcefully—organize demonstrations so they start on a side aisle, move up front past the rostrum, and swing up the other side aisle to complete the circle. And limit demonstrations to twenty minutes.

Newcomers said this was all for the best, but old-timers remembered the yesterdays and said, "How can you have spontaneity in a strait jacket?"

The C.B.S. producer quietly dropped the word to a Stevenson staff man: Eisenhower and Nixon, of course, would get complete TV coverage because of their elected positions. Stevenson would get similar treatment, but the Democratic vice-presidential nominee would get the light touch—unless it was Kennedy. Why? "Because Kennedy has box office."

The producer added a personal confidential footnote: Don't get him wrong, he said. Personally, he was anti-Kennedy, but politically he wanted Kennedy picked because that would double the Democrats' TV coverage. And he prided himself, first and above all, on being a good Democrat who placed Party above Person.

To control a convention, you must control the chairman, the galleries, the music, the procedures, the microphones.

Gray-haired Illinois Senator Paul Douglas had a convention observation on Speaker Sam Rayburn's tremendous authority; he had given twice as much time to the proponents of the mild civil rights plank as he gave the opponents, then had a voice vote instead of a roll call, and interpreted it as he pleased.

Douglas remembered the previous convention when Rayburn wanted to keep continuous session to break the back of the Kefauver presidential push, and Douglas privately protested to Rayburn, "Mr. Chairman, to keep this convention in session for thirty continuous hours is inhuman. Mr. Chairman, a motion to adjourn is always in order." And Rayburn answered, without expression, "Yes, it's always in order if the chairman recognizes you."

Afterward Douglas tried to get the man in the Illinois delegation to turn on the loudspeaker so that he could make this request to adjourn. The man said he would do this only if Rayburn first recognized him.

"You mean," said Douglas, "that I can't have the use of that microphone in order to get attention to be recognized?"

The man smiled, "That's right."

If the keynoter has a prime part full of political potential, the man who makes the main nominating speech runs a hot second.

Almost a week before the convention, John Sharon confided to Ted Sorensen that he hoped Kennedy would nominate Stevenson, mainly because of the appeal to Catholic voters. Sorensen said that would be fine but they better make up their minds fast because the speech was important and should be first-rate.

"But I made the mistake of telling Ted he needn't worry," said Sharon, "that all those speeches were being written."

"And I remembered those words later," said Sorensen ruefully.

Tuesday was Woman's Day at the convention, with the Democratic party's sparkling Katie Louchheim in control and Rayburn making a speech that night.

Word came to Kennedy Wednesday that Stevenson wanted to see him at noon. Based on the unofficial word from a Stevenson staff member, Kennedy had virtually counted himself out. Therefore, when Stevenson asked his opinion on the various candidates for the Vice-Presidency, Kennedy talked with full frankness about everybody else's qualifications.

Kennedy even made a recommendation of his own: Hubert Humphrey.

Then Stevenson told him that he was one of several being considered to make the nominating speech, that he, Stevenson, personally wanted Kennedy, but he would first have to clear it with a few people, so it wasn't yet absolutely definite.

"When the governor told me that," said Kennedy, "I asked him if that meant I was thereby being disqualified for the vice-presidential nomination and he said, no, not necessarily. So when Arthur [Schlesinger, Jr.] came to see me that day, I told him I felt I should know whether or not I was being eliminated before I made the nominating speech, or at least before it happened. And that's when Arthur told me that nobody yet had been picked."

But, then, later that afternoon Bill Wirtz, another Stevenson law partner, came down to talk to Ted Sorsensen about the nominating speech. It was more definite now, but it still wasn't set.

"So I tried to phrase it very carefully," said Sorensen, "I asked Bill, 'Does this mean that when the group meets in a room, the name Kennedy will not come out of it?' "

Wirtz answered, "Yes."

"Well, that was final enough for us," said Sorensen, "and so now all we had to do was to wait for word on the nominating speech." (Wirtz's explanation of what he meant was that no name would come out of any meeting.) Whatever Wirtz meant, Kennedy thought he understood, and accepted it.

They were just three friends, three senators attending a convention, and they sat around, all relaxed: Jack Kennedy, Hubert Humphrey, George Smathers.

They all knew that Jack had been tapped to make the Stevenson nominating speech and that this probably meant his elimination as a vice-presidential nominee. Humphrey got the word from a Stevenson staff member that this move now cleared the air. It looked good for Humphrey; it looked very good.

Kennedy's relaxed reaction was, "Well, I've had it for this convention." And he seemed to feel he had a pretty good play for one convention—narrating the film, being introduced from the floor, making the major nominating speech.

"Then Jack said to me, 'Hubert, I want you to know that I'm going to give you all the help and support I can for the Vice-Presidency.' And Smathers said the same thing. . . ."

The small core of able Stevenson speechwriters had their own quiet corner on a floor far away from the fast pace of the convention. The mood there was much more a library than a newspaper city room, and they were already working on Stevenson speeches on all kinds of issues deep into the campaign. But even their most finished product went into the special Stevenson blender to emerge as something purely personal.

This blending happened with the nominating speech, too.

"It was terrible," said Sorensen, "it was absolutely terrible. I tried to do what I could with it to work it over in a rough way and then I decided I better get to the senator. He was at the convention then and I couldn't get any car and my cab broke down so I ended up on the train. And when I got there, I couldn't find him. And when I finally did spot him, I couldn't get to him on the floor because someone had stolen my credentials."

But Sorensen passed the word to somebody who passed the word to somebody else and Kennedy finally came, looked over the speech, and agreed it was terrible. Arthur Schlesinger, Jr., also dropped in to read the rewrite, said it was an improvement over the original. Schlesinger was one of the small group of Stevenson speechwriters.

The absolutely final word on Kennedy's selection for the speech still hadn't come. It came, finally, at 1:30 A.M. And the nominating speech was the first order of business when the convention opened nine and a half hours later, Thursday morning.

"So the senator and I got into a room together," said Sorensen, "and he dictated the beginning and the general ideas and I said, 'I suppose I've got to do it,' and the senator said, 'That's right. Have it in my room by eight in the morning.'

"Then we got a sleep-in driver and a secretary to stay the night and I went to work on it, woke up the secretary at 6:30 A.M., and she typed it clean and I got in the car and brought it over to the senator. He looked it over, rewrote some of it, cut out some things and added a few paragraphs, and by then it was so chopped up that we had to have it retyped because the TelePrompTer people were screaming for it. We gave them one copy and sent another copy to be mimeographed for the press—we had a vice-president from the

Merchandise Mart acting as a messenger boy, taking down a page at a time right out of the typewriter, as soon as it was ready.

"When we all got into the car, we noticed that one page was missing, and I said, 'Well, the TelePrompTer will have it anyway,' and the senator said he wouldn't trust the TelePrompTer. So Tom Winship—he's with the *Boston Globe*—and I went over to the TelePrompTer guy and took back that one missing page and he started screaming again. Tom took it to the press room to get somebody to type it but by then the convention session already had started and they were having the Invocation and "The Star-Spangled Banner" and the typist wouldn't type during that. Then when the typing started, it was so slow that Tom took it to another typewriter and did it himself and then I grabbed it and pushed myself into the Amphitheater and shoved myself over to Jack and gave him a completed copy at fifteen minutes to eleven. And he made his speech. And it went over big."

The Harriman nomination was a formality. The votes had not been cast, but they had been counted.

Just as the Harriman balloon burst, so did the Symington.

The Symington nomination came at the end of a bedlam day of nominations and demonstrations that drove delegates and spectators home to their hotels. A *St. Louis Post-Dispatch* correspondent described the convention hall "almost as empty as a Missouri haybarn in March after a hard winter."

On the next day's first ballot, Adlai Stevenson got 905½ votes; Harriman, 210; Symington, 45½ out of the total 1372 votes. It took 686½ to win.

Stevenson's first comment on getting the news: "Trust that Finnegan."

During some of this, John Sharon was on the convention floor. "And I felt this emotional feeling among so many delegates, saying, 'Damn it, it's got to be our man for Vice-President. . . .'

"That so much impressed me that I toyed with the idea of calling Bill Blair and making one more pitch on my open convention idea and ask him to tell the governor, but then I said the hell with it, I already had made my decision, there were now three other guys carrying the ball."

The three other guys had pushed hard on the idea, and Stevenson was getting more and more intrigued by it.

The convention, meanwhile, was confusion. Nobody there knew whether Stevenson was going to come that night, accept the nomination that night, or what; nobody knew anything.

"I will say this," said Sharon, "that the decision itself was so delayed that our public relations with delegates was so bad as to be embarrassing. Governor Meyner saw me on the floor and said, 'Say, John, what the hell is going on anyway?' I was wearing a Stevenson staff badge. And I said, 'I don't know. I'll try to find out.' And I didn't know, I just didn't know."

Stevenson now liked the open convention idea enormously. He had tested it on such political intimates as Jack Arvey and David Lawrence, and their reaction was equally good. But the big obstacle was Jim Finnegan. So Stevenson called in his closest associates, including Finnegan, pointed to the room that adjoined his law office, and said, "It's your baby, get in there and thrash it out."

The thrashers included George Ball, Jim Finnegan, Wilson Wyatt, and Bill Blair. "And then Bill Wirtz was in and out and Tom Finletter came later and so did Newt Minow."

It was the kind of accidental meeting that might someday make a President.

Stevenson's law partner Newt Minow was on the run to somewhere, as he always seemed to be, when he bumped into Ted Sorensen.

"Newt thanked us for the nominating speech," said Ted, "and I said we were glad to do it and it was a nice gesture on Stevenson's part inasmuch as we had been counted out.

"And Newt said it wasn't all decided yet, that there had been a restirring of the open convention idea and that he was headed for a meeting right then and there to talk about it.

"So I came back quickly and said we had changed our minds on this and we were now for it. I figured we had nothing to lose since we already had been counted out. Newt said he would pass on the news."

But is wasn't simply a point of passing on the news. Newt was the strongest pro-Kennedy man inside the Stevenson circle—he had been against the open convention because Kennedy was against it. Now he would go to that meeting and fight for it.

"I came at the tail end of that meeting," said Minow, "when the only point of discussion was whether Stevenson should send a message to the convention opening it up, or whether he should personally address the convention."

Still, if Newt had come in stirred against it, he might have given fresh hope to Finnegan to renew the fight against it.

If Finnegan had not given in, there might have been no open convention and Kennedy's bid for the Presidency might have waited ten years.

Just an accidental meeting of two men in a hotel lobby.

Back at Stevenson's law office, the group had locked themselves in one of the rooms. They started talking about five o'clock in the afternoon. They didn't stop for two hours. While they argued, Stevenson worked on his convention speech in the next room.

"I was the most vocal for it," said George Ball, "and Wilson was pretty much on my side and so was Tom [Finletter]. My argument was that it would be a fresh breeze for the convention and Finnegan's main worry was that it might break up the convention."

"Finnegan kept listening more and more," said Ball, "and finally he said, 'All right, if you boys feel that strongly about it, let's do it.'

"So all of us went to Adlai and told him, 'O.K., you're going to open up the convention. You better call Mr. Sam right now.' "

The final decision was Stevenson's and he made it.

Stevenson picked up the phone and called Rayburn, asking him to leave the convention for a half-hour to have an important meeting at the Stock Yard Inn with Paul Butler and some others. He didn't tell Rayburn what it was all about. Mr. Sam exploded, didn't want to do it, argued, finally agreed.

"All of us then piled into cars," George Ball said, "fighting our way down to that convention, and Adlai and Bill Blair and Jim Finnegan went to that meeting with Butler, and the rest of us pushed our way into the convention floor, knowing what was about to happen, knowing that nobody else knew, knowing how exciting it would be. . . ."

Present at the meeting were Butler, Rayburn, Johnson, Blair, Mayor Daley of Chicago, Arvey, and Finnegan. Governor Ribicoff of Connecticut was a late arrival and had to be identified at the door before he could get in. Ribicoff was there because "I got one commitment out of Stevenson when I had seen him at his suite to make a pitch for Kennedy; he told me that if he did not pick Kennedy, he would notify me beforehand."

"Mr. Sam was really unhappy," remembered Stevenson. "He thought the open convention would cause friction, prolong the convention, and a lot of other things. Lyndon [Johnson] was startled but he tried to compromise things."

One of the arguments Rayburn and Johnson pitched was that if Stevenson opened the convention, people would say he lacked decisiveness, couldn't pick his own candidate, and "people would say that if you were President and there was a crisis in the Formosan straits, you wouldn't be able to make up your own mind some night on whether to send in the Seventh Fleet." Stevenson refused to buy that argument.

"Then," said Stevenson, "I remember Lyndon saying, 'Mr. Sam, it's the governor's decision. After all, he has to live with it, not us.' Arvey and Lawrence and Daley were for the idea, and so was Finnegan now."

"But Butler didn't even want me to go out on that convention floor at all that night to announce anything," said Stevenson.

"Butler was fuming," said one of Stevenson's close friends, "and he just wouldn't agree, and so I finally turned to him and said, 'Who won the nomination anyway?'"

And then Stevenson said, damn it, he had made his decision and he was going in to make his announcement.

Then it was that Sam Rayburn, with a Texan's defeated grace, said, "All right, if your mind's made up, give me your arm and I'll take you out there and introduce you to the convention."

As Stevenson walked toward the platform, Butler walked the other way, to the back of the hall. Not much later, a Kefauver staff man, walking in the back, saw a man there, standing between two trailers, crying. It was Paul Butler.

John Sharon and his wife, Ruth, were sitting with the Puerto Rican delegation when Stevenson was introduced and started speaking:

"I have presumed to ask this special favor that I could appear here for but a moment. My heart is full and I am deeply grateful, but I did not come here tonight to speak of the action you have just taken. That I shall do tomorrow night after you have chosen a Vice-President. Now it is in connection with that choice that I have taken this unusual step of asking to be heard briefly tonight. . . .

"I have decided that the selection of the vice-presidential nominee should be made through the free processes of this convention, so that the Democratic party's candidate for this office may join me before the nation, not as one man's selection but as one chosen by our great party even as I have been chosen."

"As soon as he started speaking, I knew what he was going to say," said Sharon, "and I looked over at Ruth and she was beaming from ear to ear and of course I was very thrilled. The long battle had won out.

"And do you know the three most important words in his speech? Three non-Hamlet words: 'I have decided . . .' They weren't in that original speech, but Wilson Wyatt inserted them. Those words were loud in their meaning because they showed real leadership, real presidential capacity for major critical decisions.

"As I walked out of the hall, I walked right into Hubert Humphrey. And while I was overjoyed with the result of this long personal campaign, there was Hubert, pale white. I've never seen a guy so white, almost as if he had just heard that his mother had died. The poor guy was in a terrible state of shock. I must say I was trembling when I met him because I knew what was on his mind. And still, he tried to smile, and said, 'Well, do you want to come and work for me now?' And I laughed weakly and said I couldn't do that because we all had to stay neutral, but that Bill Rivkin and I would be around later to see him."

(As soon as he had heard the Stevenson announcement, Humphrey said he knew the jig was up.)

"After I saw Hubert—and he really punctured my balloon," said Sharon, "Ruth and I walked towards the exit barrier and there was the Stevenson group leaving, and Ruth and I cheered, just like a couple of spectators, '. . . ray Governor, hooray. . . .' And Finnegan saw us and leaned out of his car window and yelled, 'C'mon you bastard, we're going to have a party. . . .'"

The party started out strictly social—just friends and staff—but Mr. Sam and Lyndon Johnson soon arrived on the scene, and Stevenson took them into a bedroom and they talked for almost an hour. This was Rayburn's last-minute effort to persuade Stevenson to reverse his decision.

Reporters caught Rayburn as he left and asked him what he thought of the open convention and he answered snappily, "That's it. It doesn't matter what I think."

"And when Stevenson walked out of that bedroom and saw me," said Sharon, "he said, 'John, I have either done the smartest thing in my life or I've done the dumbest thing in my life!' And he wasn't smiling, he was utterly serious."

Some of the political postscript was slightly sneering. Sure, the open convention was dramatic, got good publicity, but really, how open was it? Wasn't the deal really set with Estes Kefauver all the time? Didn't everybody know that? How open was it?

It was this open:

Up in Kefauver's hotel room at the Hilton, a group of his closest associates watched him furiously pack his bags. He was leaving for Tennessee that very night, he said. He had been double-crossed and the whole thing was loaded for Kennedy.

Kefauver's old friend, noted public opinion analyst and broadcaster Elmo Roper, had walked in, listened, then started arguing. He told Estes he didn't believe it, that he knew Adlai well and Adlai would never stoop to this kind of deception.

Howard McGrath, one of Kefauver's key supporters, violently disagreed. "You're being sucked in, Estes . . . they're using you for a sucker . . . don't let them do it. . . ."

For those few moments, McGrath looked angry enough to hit Roper.

Roper kept arguing: "At least talk to Adlai before you leave town, at least hear what he has to say. . . ."

Kefauver cooled a little. "I don't know why I should go over and see Adlai," he said, "unless he at least asks me."

Roper promised to see Adlai first and Kefauver promised to wait.

Roper walked across the street to Stevenson's victory party at the Blackstone, saw Stevenson, who said he'd be glad to reassure Estes, but didn't want deliberately to invite him there because that could create rumors. So why didn't Roper simply bring back Estes as *his* guest.

Roper reported this to Estes. McGrath kept saying, don't do it. Roper kept talking and Kefauver finally agreed to come. As they walked out of the elevator on Stevenson's floor, reporters quickly clustered with questions: What was the purpose of his visit? Was Kefauver actually Adlai's choice for Vice-President? Was some kind of deal going on?

Kefauver had readied the politician's perfect answer. "Of course not," he told them. "I've just come to congratulate the next President of the United States. Isn't everybody doing that?"

Backed up now by a flood of photographers and reporters, Kefauver knocked on the door of the Stevenson suite and walked in.

"Bill Blair then made a very smart move," says Sharon. "He wouldn't let Estes and the governor talk in a closed bedroom—he put them in a corner of the party room, formed a human wedge of staff people in front of them to keep away the curious.

"I saw what was happening," Sharon continued, "and I went over to Finnegan and said, 'Say, Jim, with all those reporters out there, this doesn't look too good.' And Jim said, 'Get Kennedy, Wagner, and Humphrey.'"

"I remember Jack Kennedy coming in," said Minow, "and telling Stevenson, 'It's a fixed convention. You've set it against me.'"

"And of course Humphrey felt the same way," said Wirtz. "I remember Hubert asking us if he could use our convention floor communications since he didn't have any, and we said no, because we had to stay impartial. I guess everybody found it hard to believe us."

"After the party was over, Bill Rivkin and I went to Humphrey's suite," said Sharon. "We saw Eugenie Anderson (former Ambassador and strong Humphrey supporter). She was very upset about the open convention and said that Hubert didn't have a chance, and I told her, 'Pardon my French, but that's a lot of bull.'"

Kefauver returned appeased from the Stevenson talk, but Mc-Grath still worked on him. Kefauver finally looked at McGrath and said, "Stop arguing with me . . . I've made up my mind . . . now let's get to work . . . contact my delegates and let's get going. . . ."

McGrath's first stop was Pennsylvania's political boss, David Lawrence. The last time he had talked to Lawrence was in Pittsburgh after the California primary.

"Lawrence made it clear then that he was not speaking for Stevenson," said McGrath, "and would make no commitment, but he indicated that he felt Kefauver would be the best man to run with Stevenson and I felt that he would support him."

Now McGrath again came to Lawrence.

"To my dying day, I'll never forget his words," said McGrath. "He said, 'Howard, don't worry about it. This isn't a double cross. You'll get a lot of our votes.'"

Roper was able to relay some additional intelligence of interest. He ran into Humphrey who told him, "I'm in this to try to be Vice-President. . . . I don't know now whether I have the votes to win, but I'm in it to win . . . if it turns out that it is deadlocked between Kefauver and Kennedy, I'll withdraw . . . if I have the wisdom to perceive the moment that I no longer have a chance to make it, I will swing my support to Estes."

"I was standing in back of the stadium with Governor J.P. Coleman of Mississippi," said former Democratic National Chairman Steve Mitchell, "when Stevenson made that startling statement about opening up the convention. We all couldn't have been more surprised and Coleman turned to me and said, 'Well, what do you think your boys are gonna do?'

"I said that I thought a lot of the Illinois delegation would be for Kennedy, especially the Chicago people, and that I would vote along with my delegation. By this time Senator Stennis and some people from North Carolina and a group of southern leaders had joined us and I asked Coleman what his people might do. Coleman thought a minute, then said his delegation might go for a favorite son as a kind of an honorary thing.

" 'Well, if you do,' I said, 'if there's a lot of that splitting up, it might put in Kefauver.' I saw that sink in, not only with Coleman but with all the other southern leaders there, and then one of them said, 'That's right, maybe we just oughta go for Paul Dever's young man, that Kennedy boy, right away.' In a way, this was their kind of payoff for the way Dever and McCormack had helped the South compromise the civil rights plank.

"Then Coleman asked me if I could help them and I said I couldn't solicit for Kennedy because then delegates could claim that I was acting for Stevenson and that the whole thing was rigged. I started walking away then and when I looked back, there they all were, all huddled together."

(The background on the Coleman-Mitchell conversation was this: Mitchell had been cultivating the South ever since February, 1953, when he toured there as the party's national chairman, trying to smooth sectional differences. The influential Coleman met him, liked him, trusted him.)

"It couldn't have been more than five minutes after I left Coleman," said Mitchell, "when this Illinois bailiff I know comes run-at me to say that Jack Kennedy was just rounding the curve coming to see me, and would I talk to him? And, sure enough, there was Kennedy, looking real down and discouraged, and he asked me what I thought. I said I thought he had a helluva good chance but he better start scrambling. He just looked at me unbelievingly and said how could I say he had any kind of chance at all when he had no organization, no obvious support except from New England, and all the big states like New York and Pennsylvania had their own candidates. I told him he better stop talking statistics and get on a horse and ride because he had a lot of support he didn't know anything about, 'especially from the South,' I emphasized. His whole face lit up after that and he asked me to help him and I told him why I couldn't, and then off he went, but he now had a lot of fresh hope in his face."

Political bandwagons don't simply start rolling. Somewhere, somehow, somebody has to give the first push.

"When I got to Jack's hotel room," said Jack's brother-in-law Robert Sargent Shriver, a tall handsome man who headed Chicago's School Board, Joseph Kennedy's huge Merchandise Mart, and later organized the Peace Corps, "there was Jack and Bobby and Eunice and Jean and Pat and Teddy and it looked like a family conference up at the Cape instead of a political meeting, except there were Ted Sorensen and Bailey and a few others. There was Bobby with a yellow pad in his hand, writing down the states and the delegates and Jack would say, 'I think I can get four or five of those delegates,' and Bailey would say, 'I can bring in that state,' or something like that. It was all pretty amateurish.

"And then somebody rushed in to say that Georgia had an early caucus and came out for Kennedy. We all knew how anti-Catholic they were in Georgia, and Jack said, just like that, 'Gee, if Georgia went for me, then I may really have a chance. O.K. then, I'm a candidate.' And that's when he really decided, just like that, at that moment."

The rooms filled up fast, and soon the suite was all confusion, people sitting on beds, chairs, tables, sprawled on the floor, men and women of every level in politics, all of them political salesmen for Jack Kennedy. Out of the disorder, somebody would say he knew somebody who knew somebody else on this or that delegation, and somebody else would say, "Fine, then you take care of him."

"And, finally, John Bailey jumped up," said young Representative Ed Boland of Massachusetts, "and Bailey said, 'This isn't the way to do this thing.' And then Bailey started to assign state delegations to specific people for them to contact before the balloting started the next day. I got Ohio, Michigan, Florida, and Indiana."

"I know I didn't change clothes all night," said John Bailey. "I don't suppose many of the others did."

"It's true we didn't sleep that night," said Sorensen, "but frankly we didn't accomplish very much. It was hectic, not very well organized, too many people packed into my bedroom who were just like me—green, completely green. I couldn't have been greener. I didn't talk to many people because I didn't know too many people. What I did do was to arrange for the nominating and seconding speeches and things like that. But otherwise we really didn't accomplish very much that night."

Earlier, Jack Kennedy and a friend walked out of an elevator into the jam of press and politicians, when Kennedy suddenly spotted Carmine DeSapio, boss of the New York State delegation of ninety-eight votes. "Think I ought to talk to him?" Jack asked his friend.

"Sure, why not, what have you got to lose?"

So Jack raced back to catch up with DeSapio, then said loudly, "Mr. DeSapio, I'm Jack Kennedy. Can I speak to you for a minute?"

The reporters all roared.

Now in the confusion of the suite, somebody realized that Carmine DeSapio was patiently waiting in one of the bedrooms for somebody to talk to him.

"He had been sitting around waiting for a half hour," said Jack Kennedy, "and nobody even knew who he was."

"We didn't talk long," said DeSapio, a tall heavy-set man whose tinted glasses are almost a trademark. "It was the first time we really talked together in that convention, and it was the last time. Maybe the whole thing took ten minutes, no more. He knew what my situation was. Mayor Wagner was our favorite son and we would ride with him on the first ballot. Then if he wasn't going anyplace, we'd have to make a decision. I made no promises and he didn't ask for any. But he knew I wanted a Catholic on the ticket because it would help us in New York. I would say we had a pleasant meeting."

Then Kennedy made some more calls. At 2:30 A.M. he asked his good friend Senator George Smathers to rush right over, but Smathers persuaded him to postpone their meeting until breakfast.

There were also transatlantic phone calls—Jack's father, the former Ambassador to Great Britain, Joseph Kennedy, was on the Riviera and wanted to know, "How's my boy doing?" He not only spoke to his family but to the officials of his Merchandise Mart, telling them to help in any way they could, and he also spoke to his former political cronies of the Roosevelt Administration then at the convention. One of them passed on the word that the elder Kennedy was not terribly pleased about his son's efforts for the Vice-Presidency at this time.

"That was the only advice I ever gave him," said the elder Kennedy afterward, "not to run for the Vice-Presidency in 1956. But he didn't take that advice. I told him it was a terrible mistake and then I went over to Europe and I stayed there, so there was no question of any interference. I knew Stevenson didn't have a chance. I felt that if Jack ran with him, it would be a terrible mistake, because it was hopeless."

"Before the convention opened, I was in charge of receptions for delegates' wives," said Eunice Shriver, who looks and acts like an exact female counterpart of her brother Jack Kennedy, "but this speechmaking to delegates was a lot different than talking to the women, because these delegates didn't seem to care as much. But I also went to the Alabama, Arkansas, and Mississippi delegations and told them how intelligent Jack was and things like that, and they did listen, and thank me, and some of them did switch to Jack because we did very well in those states."

Even though every supporter was assigned somebody, it wasn't that simple.

"The worst thing about a convention is the lack of communication," said Connecticut's boss John Bailey. "It's so hard to get ahold of somebody when you want to talk to him."

But the Kennedy clan made an impressively good-looking team working together as tightly as they did. At their Hilton suite that night there seemed to be a Kennedy at everybody's elbow, the three lovely daughters—Pat, Jean, and Eunice—and two of the husbands, Sargent Shriver and Hollywood star Peter Lawford, and then Jack's two younger brothers, Bobby and Ted.

"I took Jack's sister Eunice with me," said Representative Frank E. Smith of Mississippi. "I remember she told the South Carolina delegation how many college degrees Jack had and how many books he had written and how much he traveled all his life, and so I suggested that next time she leave all that out, and so then she talked about her family traditions and how they had been lucky in material things and how they had been dedicated to public service and she made a nice little speech along that line. No issues. It made a nice little impression."

"I'm secretary of the Alpha Phi Delta fraternity," said Joe De-Guglielmo, another Massachusetts Kennedy campaign worker, specializing in the foreign-language press in 1952, "and I had quite a few friends around the country who were delegates at that convention, so I started looking them up. All Jack told me was, 'Joe, you just talk to the people you know.' "

"Jack did ask me to do one special thing for him," said De-Guglielmo. "There were lots of messages that Senator Albert Gore of Tennessee was hunting for Jack and I was told to find Gore, and I did. I remember that he and Jack went into the same room alone together and they talked quite a long time, but I don't know what they were talking about. After I found him, I went to bed."

One key South Dakota delegate complained that Kennedy people called him repeatedly, waking him up at 4 A.M., 5 A.M., and 6 A.M.

It really started early Friday morning, the convention's last day, and its most unforgettable.

It was a morning of caucuses.

The Oxford English Dictionary defines a caucus as "a meeting of wire-pullers." And some say caucus is a corruption of the word "calkers"—men who drove oakum and rope into ships' seams to make them watertight.

But there's nothing watertight about a caucus once the wire-pullers are through.

One observer likened a caucus meeting to the squabbling of kids at a little boy's club meeting, everybody talking at once, parliamentary procedures enforced with difficulties, often only the chairman knowing which delegate has been recognized by the chair, a vocal minority remaining loud to the end. They met everywhere, from ballrooms to bedrooms, and kept quiet only to listen to the celebrity candidates.

These were the men and women from every level of American life, selected as delegates by state primary or state convention, a few by state committee (Alabama, Arizona, Arkansas, Connecticut, Georgia, Louisiana, Washington, Wyoming). Some have a full vote but most of them have only a half-vote each. A state was awarded two votes for each senator and representative in Congress, four bonus votes for any state that went Democratic in the 1948 presidential election, two votes for each congressional district lost by a state as a result of the reapportionment following the 1950 census, and four additional bonus votes for any state that either went Democratic in the 1952 presidential election or elected a Democratic governor on or after November, 1952.

The marvel of it is that this group of people, from everywhere and every background, in an almost haphazard, casual way, are the instruments that pick the candidate for the most important job in the world.

Here's how haphazard it is: Governor Orval Faubus of Arkansas held his caucus which picked Humphrey, then, at convention time, got up and announced all their votes for Kennedy instead of Humphrey.

"Everybody was running around," said Kennedy. "My sister Eunice worked on Delaware. I had breakfast with some of the California delegation. I went to a lot of caucuses. I got nothing from Ohio, of course, but I did talk to them. We got Virginia because Governor Battle's son was in the Navy with me. And we got Louisiana because their delegation sat right next to ours and they had a lot of bright young fellows with whom we got real friendly.

"I talked to Lyndon, too," Kennedy continued, "but he gave me a kind of noncommittal answer. Maybe Hubert thought Lyndon was for him and maybe Symington thought the same thing and maybe Gore thought that, too, and maybe Lyndon wanted them all to think just that. We never knew how that one would turn out."

Florida's Senator Smathers also talked to Lyndon Johnson about Kennedy that morning, "but he never let on what he was going to do." Smathers also talked to personal friends among the Ohio and California delegates, but got nowhere.

"I couldn't help him much in Florida, even though it was my home state," said Smathers, "because Kefauver had picked up most of the delegates, but I did get him some. And I helped him in North Carolina by talking to Governor Luther Hodges—I was born in North Carolina."

Smathers reasoned that southern support for Kennedy was mostly anti-Kefauver rather than pro-Kennedy. "But, then, the South is always more apt to go for a northerner who doesn't know any better than for a southerner who should know better, but doesn't."

"I can't be sure that we went to the Arkansas caucus," said Massachusetts Congressman Torbert Macdonald, Jack Kennedy's Harvard roommate, "but Oren Harris was helping me in that delegation, and Harris worked on Governor Faubus and introduced Jack to Faubus and that helped win over Arkansas."

"Here's the kind of thing you run into when you talk to delegates," said Representative Ed Boland. "I went to see Senator McNamara of Michigan and he said he was against Jack because Jack voted for the Taft-Hartley law. Well, I checked with Jack right away and he said McNamara was all wrong, so I went back to McNamara, but he said he was against Jack anyway right now. So then I talked to Walter Reuther. Reuther said he liked Jack, thought he was a bright young man, but for the future, not for now. Well, that was it with Michigan, what else could you do?"

"Bobby Kennedy was supposed to be floor manager for Jack at the convention, but that's a lot of crap," said one supporter. "There was no floor manager, there was just nobody in control. Everybody was out on his own, talking to anybody and everybody he could, and there was a helluva lot of overlapping."

But amateurish as it was in many ways, the Kennedy campaign for the Vice-Presidency seemed highly professional in the preliminaries: Ted Sorensen's trip to see Sharon and Finnegan, Governor Ribicoff's national publicity when he endorsed Kennedy early at the Governors' Conference, the organization of a New England bloc of votes, the highly effective Bailey Report, the deploying of Kennedy friends in Chicago a week before the open convention announcement. (There was even a special group of young volunteers, organized by Judge Bill Toohey's son, who did all kinds of things, from running messages to reprinting and circulating a *Chicago Sun-Times* editorial plugging for a Stevenson-Kennedy ticket.) Compare this with the fact that Hubert Humphrey, an openly announced candidate for the Vice-Presidency months before, admittedly didn't even know the names or faces of most of his Minnesota delegation, mostly Kefauver people who had not been active in party politics before.

However, here and now, on the convention floor, Kennedy organization was minimal.

One favorite target was Governor Robert Meyner of New Jersey, with thirty-six votes.

"I went with a guy to see Meyner," said Ken O'Donnell, "and

this guy had gone to school with Meyner, and so his pitch was also personal. Meyner listened to him, then said he'd like to do it, but the farmers in his state were against Jack on the farm issue, and my friend said, 'Bull, there aren't twenty farmers in your state and you know it.' Meyner just shrugged his shoulders and finally said, 'Well, you know, he'd have to go along with New York.' So then we went to see Jim Farley and Farley said no. And my friend said to Farley, 'When you were going down the drain as a presidential candidate in the 1944 convention, the one man who stayed with you until the finish was Jack's brother Joe Kennedy, and this is the way you repay him. . . .'

"So Farley sent us to see DeSapio."

Carmine DeSapio was another target with ninety-eight votes, but this was his first national convention and not too many people knew him. Kennedy already had seen and settled with DeSapio, but he also decided on a visit with New York City's Mayor Robert Wagner who listened politely to Kennedy's strong selling speech on himself, then said, without smiling, "You know, of course, I'm a candidate myself."

Said Rhode Island's former governor Dennis Roberts, "During the Convention, a member of the South Carolina delegation came up to see me and asked, 'Will this fellow campaign in South Carolina?' And I said, 'Do you want him?' He said he did and I asked, 'What about his religion?' And the South Carolina delegate said, 'It won't make any difference. The thing is, he'll bring young people back into the party.' "

But if the Catholic issue didn't hurt him in South Carolina, it threatened to elsewhere.

"When we met with Sam Rayburn," said Roberts, "and asked him to support Kennedy, Rayburn's answer was, 'Nothing doin' . . . you fellows are too young to remember the Al Smith thing . . . I've been through it.' " And Roberts then made a throw-away gesture to indicate the phrase, Never Again.

If the Catholic issue had weight, it was mostly silent weight. Kefauver floor worker, Bill Haddad, who was everywhere at once, admitted that never once in all that day did he run into an out-spoken anti-Catholic remark against Kennedy.

Kennedy people ran into it when they probed for it.

"I got it mostly from liberal individuals," said Representative Frank Smith. "One man from Wisconsin said Kennedy would lose everything in the state outside of Milwaukee because he was a Catholic. And the only other man who brought it up in any way was Governor Clement to the Tennessee delegation; he said he was not a candidate and he said religion was not an issue . . . pretending to be broad-minded but planting the idea just the same.

"There was some feeling and talk in the Texas delegation about it, but it was a question of Kennedy and Kefauver, and they sure didn't want Kefauver."

Kennedy came from Massachusetts, but not all Massachusetts delegates were for him, just as not all Tennessee delegates were for Kefauver, just as not all Minnesota delegates were for Humphrey.

Making his fight talk to the Massachusetts delegation, Johnny Powers, an old-time politician, didn't blarney about Kennedy's qualifications but said simply that if Kennedy were part of the national ticket, the Democrats would sweep every Massachusetts House and Senate seat and make the Republican party extinct in that state.

The nomination speech is another piece of political strategy. It's not like getting a best man for a wedding; it's part of a convention showcase to show the widespread strength of your support.

"Jack didn't even know who was going to make his nominating speech," said Senator Smathers, "and he asked me if I would do it and I told him I didn't think I was the one because I didn't think he should have somebody from the South because it might hurt him—but I told him I'd be glad to make a seconding speech. So then he asked me, 'How about Abe?' [Governor Abraham Ribicoff of Connecticut], and I said sure, then they tried to find him and couldn't so it looked like I might have to make that nominating speech after all." But they did find him.

"Here were we, about to go to the convention," said Ribicoff, "an hour before it was all to begin, and nobody had been selected to make the nominating speech. Somebody finally said, 'Who's going to make the nominating speech?' and Jack said, 'If anybody deserves to make the nominating speech, Abe does.' Nothing had been written or anything and there was less than an hour to prepare some remarks and get out to the convention hall."

Back at the hall, Fishbait Miller, of Pascagoula, Mississippi, a sergeant-at-arms of the House and a parliamentary fixture at all Democratic conventions for the past thirty years, had the job of keeping water glasses full, escorting speakers to the platform, handing them their speeches, and telling freshman candidates what to do when.

"I do remember Senator Kennedy's brother Robert coming to see me," said Fishbait, "just after the senator was nominated, and asking me, 'What do we do now?'

"I told him very politely to get the hell back to his seat and a whole bunch of police and detectives would be coming right there to escort them to a room at the Stock Yard Inn.

"That's the proper procedure, and that I know."

One of those back rooms was a meeting at the Blackstone Hotel that Jack Kennedy never forgot. It was a room filled with Roosevelts: Mrs. Franklin D. Roosevelt, two of her sons, James and Elliott, and Elliott's wife. They were all in the bedroom and the phones never stopped ringing.

(The meeting had been first discussed at a lunch in Washington at which James Landis, lawyer for Kennedy, Sr., discussed ways and means with his firm members of Landis, Cohen, Rubin and Schwartz on how to attract convention liberals to Kennedy. Abba Schwartz, long-time friend of Mrs. Roosevelt, set up this meeting with Kennedy.)

"When Jack and I arrived," said Abba Schwartz, Washington lawyer, friend of both the Roosevelts and the Kennedys, "there was also a young lady typing in the corner. Mrs. Roosevelt was rushed. She hadn't planned to be very active at this convention, but she was. This was eleven-thirty in the morning and she had to go on television at twelve. Quite a few grandchildren came in, and she told them, 'Just sit on the beds—I'm busy.' They had come for their convention tickets."

"It was a lawyer for Kennedy's father—I forget his name [James Landis]," said Mrs. Franklin D. Roosevelt, "who asked me if I would see Senator Kennedy, and I said I would, so he came up to my room. I admit there was a lot of confusion—as he says there was—but all I did was to ask him one question—why he hadn't taken a stand on McCarthyism. And the answer he gave me just wasn't enough of an answer for me, that's all."

"I told her, 'That was so long ago,'" said Jack Kennedy, "but she must have misunderstood me because what I meant was that the bill of particulars against McCarthy was long before the censure movement. My position was that we couldn't indict a man for what happened before he was seated. If he was guilty of those things, the time to stop him was before he was seated.

"Besides, the room was so noisy and it was such a short interview, and it was hardly a place or a basis for judgment."

"No, the room wasn't too noisy," said Representative James Roosevelt, later a strong supporter of Kennedy for President. "There were a few other people, but it wasn't really noisy, no. I introduced Jack to my mother and then I went over and sat on the bed and I wasn't really listening. But it was a very short interview.

"After it was over, mother told us what she had said. She asked Jack if he didn't now feel that he should have taken a stronger position against McCarthyism and would he do so now. Something like that. And she just wasn't satisfied with what he said, that's all."

It was the kind of meeting that can kill a whole future.

Elsewhere the campaign had never stopped.

"I had no particular argument for Kennedy when I talked to people about him," said one of his campaign workers. "I simply said it was either him or Kefauver because Gore didn't have a chance. . . ."

It seemed so strange. Here was a senator from Tennessee who stirred up none of the hate against himself that the South saved for Kefauver; here was a conscientious liberal with a record of Senate crusade that matched Hubert Humphrey; here was a man of broad knowledge and Senate achievement that far surpassed Kennedy. He was also young, good-looking, popular, aggressive, and yet it became a curious convention question: what happened to Al Gore?

What happened was this:

Kefauver was running, Clement was considering, and you just can't have three candidates for Vice-President from a single state. Plus that, politics had its own elaborate etiquette of priorities.

Clement, as governor, commanded first support from his delegation as their nominee. Earlier, like others, he had politely ruled himself out of the running, but now, like others, he was "humble and grateful."

After a long talk with Stevenson, he was much more humble and much less grateful.

"I took Al before the Oklahoma delegation," said Gore's strongest supporter, Oklahoma's Senator Mike Monroney, "and Al made a fine statement and they chose to give him their support. We talked to a few other people but there wasn't much time. And the other candidates had been working all night on delegations. But how could we? We didn't even know whether he was a candidate."

Critical help at critical moments came from all kinds of Kefauver people, including the man who long before had persuaded a worker in the printing company that made the convention floor tickets to run off a few extras, including the cards to get on the convention floor; another, who searched Kennedy staff wastebaskets for revealing memos; a certain unofficial delegate from a certain midwestern state who pocketed all telegrams in favor of other candidates and circulated to the delegation only those telegrams favoring Kefauver. Convention consciences are the easiest to wrestle.

418

"I remember, though, that the Kennedy people were so professional and so beautifully organized compared to us," said Kefauver worker Esther Coopersmith, who had also been a Wisconsin convention delegate in 1952. "Their placards were all printed and everything. Ours were hand-lettered and we stapled them onto poles. But we had the kind of support you couldn't buy. We had supporters so rabid they wouldn't wear Stevenson-Kefauver tags—they kept on wearing KEFAUVER FOR PRESIDENT buttons to the very end."

The convention floor was a reporter's dream. He would see several big shots in heavy conference, stick his head into the group to listen until somebody would see him suddenly, and say, "What the hell are you doing here?"

"I remember walking by the New York delegation and seeing Lehman, Farley, and Prendergast having a huddle, so I joined in," said N.B.C. reporter Herb Kaplow. "They were discussing whether to support Kennedy or Kefauver. Then Prendergast began to poll the delegation, calling each name. When it was Lehman's turn, Lehman looked at a delegate named Lester Martin and said, 'I don't know . . . I'll listen to what Lester says. What do you say, Lester?' And Lester said, 'I'm sticking to Kefauver. He's been all right to me.'"

"Politics is a cold, tough, practical business," said Hubert Humphrey, "and I never had a better demonstration of it than when two of my closest New York political supporters and friends —men who would have preferred me on the ticket and on whom I counted for support—looked me straight in the eye and told me they couldn't help me because they were committed to support Estes Kefauver. Mrs. Humphrey felt upset about it and thought that was terrible and I pointed out to her that this is a hardheaded business and personal feeling sometimes can't enter into decisions.

"I know that these friends felt that in order to elect Adlai, they had to heal the breach with the Kefauver people," added Humphrey. "Those primaries had been mean, tough, rough and tumble fights and the damage had to be repaired. The experienced politician doesn't take these things personally. After a fight, there's another job to be done. But the people for Kefauver were avid and livid. They were fighters; they'd scratch and bite. If he was through, they were through. They had to be placated. I can understand that. But it's strange, isn't it? I hadn't been fighting *against* Adlai in the primaries—I'd been fighting *for* him. But the man they wanted, the man they needed was the one who had been fighting *against* him."

"Ours was a Kefauver delegation," said Representative Quentin Burdick of North Dakota. "We had babes, zealots, people like that, people who had never been to a convention before. We had eight votes, sixteen half votes, and I think four of them with two votes were for Humphrey—so all of it went to Kefauver under the unit rule. They all liked Humphrey and maybe they would have preferred him, but they didn't think he had a chance against Kennedy."

As Senator Monroney observed, "They can say that you are a liar, a cheat, a crackpot, and a licentious old man, and most politicians don't care. But if they say you can't win, you're through."

Former Democratic vice-presidential candidate John Sparkman of Alabama met his would-be successor, Hubert Humphrey, in a hotel lobby accidentally and Sparkman had some advice: Humphrey should visit a lot of southern delegations, let them have one look at him, and he'd be surprised to find a lot of friends there, particularly among Senators who had worked with him.

"Sparkman also said frankly that it wasn't going to be easy to sell me to some members of southern delegations," said Humphrey, "and I said to him, 'Johnny, don't give me that stuff . . . do you think YOU were easy to sell in the North last time?' When he was the nominee, I had to give the Minnesota delegation a real going over and I told them, 'Listen, Stevenson wants him and I'm for him and you're going to go out there and vote for him.'"

The question now was: how much did Stevenson want Humphrey?

"The question on Adlai's mind was this," said Humphrey. "Can the South stomach Humphrey? Not whether I would be their choice, but whether they could stomach me. And I proved that they could. Lyndon Johnson was one who said that they could and I had a LONG talk with Lyndon and he promised to help me all he could and I believe that he did although some people are now trying to convince me that he didn't."

Once Stevenson made it, Lyndon Johnson did busy himself more among his delegation, talking up Humphrey for Vice-President. "He came to some of us," said Representative James Wright, Jr., of Fort Worth, Texas, "and asked whether we thought the delegation would accept Hubert Humphrey and we told him we didn't think that was the mood of the delegation, that they didn't know Hubert, and that they didn't want to take him. Too many Texans could only think of Hubert as the one who caused all that civil rights commotion with his loyalty oath at the 1948 convention, so he got nowhere."

Lyndon had made his pitch, made no move. Texas held its first caucus for Vice-President at its hotel, plunked for Clement, later learned he wasn't a candidate, and switched to Gore.

Meeting privately with leaders, Humphrey found that nearly all of them supported him and almost every one of them would have accepted him, but very few of them could or would get into an open fight to sell him. Not so in Missouri.

"I was talking to Hubert," said Symington, "and I said, 'Did you hear about the Missouri delegation? We've just voted to support you.'"

"Yes, but that's not enough," replied Humphrey. "I want you to nominate me."

Symington said he wanted to think about it a minute, put down the phone, and walked into the next room to talk it over with his closest adviser, Stan Fike. Symington and Humphrey had served together on several Senate committees, and Humphrey had helped Symington, had participated in some hearings on Missouri farm problems.

"Stan, do you know any reason why I shouldn't do it?"

"You're for him," said Stan, "so why not?"

"So I went back in," said Symington, "and Hubert was holding the phone and I said I would do it and then I asked him what about a nominating speech and when would it all happen? And he said, don't worry about that, we'll have a speech all ready for you when you come over. Nominations started at noon, he said. It was then eleven thirty-five."

Some of the most worrisome words in politics: "Don't worry about that. . . ."

Humphrey's request to Symington wasn't as impulsive as all that. His first choice was Pat Brown of California. But Brown developed voice trouble at the last minute and begged off. It's remotely conceivable, according to some critics, that Brown's voice trouble coincided with Humphrey's dipping chances and Brown's own growing preference for Kennedy.

From the Sherman Hotel to the Hilton in noonday Chicago traffic means a fifteen-minute ride, and by the time Symington and Fike barged into Suite 906, the speech was ready.

Symington read it quickly.

"This isn't me," he said. "Using it would be like using someone else's toothbrush. Give me three girls and I'll go to work."

He started dictating to one secretary. As soon as she finished a page, she went out to type it while another secretary took over. And then another secretary. One copy immediately went to the TelePromTer people. Fike was also on the phone, arranging for a police escort.

Humphrey had gone to the Amphitheater and now called from his room behind the platform, "Get Stuart out here, Stanley, it's time for him to go on."

Fike and Symington then rushed downstairs. Their chauffeur was waiting, but no car. The cops wouldn't let him drive it up and he had parked it three blocks away. And the police escort hadn't yet arrived.

But there was a nearby police car and Fike rushed over.

"Look, this is Senator Symington and he has to get out to the

BALLOTS & BANDWAGONS

convention hall to nominate Senator Humphrey for Vice-President, and we're late. . . ."

"Hop in."

Events were already under way at the Amphitheater.

Convention tradition stands strict: candidates will keep out of the convention hall during the balloting. Teetotaler Gore watched it on TV at a bar across the street. Humphrey planted himself in Speaker Rayburn's room behind the platform, and Kefauver and Kennedy stayed in small rooms at the Stock Yard Inn, about 500 feet from the Amphitheater.

Staying with Kennedy in Room 104 were Tom Winship, a *Boston Globe* newspaperman, and Ted Sorensen.

"Everything was all taken care of that we could think of," said Sorensen, "so we took off our shoes, stretched out on the beds, turned on the television, and there it was, the culmination of everything."

And it was all so fairyland unreal. Kennedy, lying on his bed in undershorts, had a pillow supporting his shoulders, his left hand behind his head, and he lay there watching, his bare toes twitching, his face serious. The tub was running.

"What had been merely interesting to me," he said, "now became important."

As always, the convention day started with a prayer:

"Let us pray, Almighty and Most Merciful Father, through the long hours of committee, caucus and convention, we pray for continued guidance and strength. . . .

"Make us understand that we cannot solve all the problems now but that we can keep the road open for new insights, new leaders. . . ."

Then "The Star-Spangled Banner," and then the hard business.

"May I have your attention, and this is very important," said Permanent Chairman Sam Rayburn. "Those who expect to be placed in nomination for the Vice-Presidency will send to the platform the name of the man who is to make a nominating speech, and those who are to make the seconding speeches.

"The Chair now wants to make a unanimous consent. There are going to be several gentlemen placed in nomination for the Vice-Presidency. If the time for the nominating speeches and the seconding speeches are long, we will be here all afternoon and into the night before we ever get to a vote. And we have three very important speakers coming on the platform this evening. Having that in mind, I ask unanimous consent that nominating speeches be limited to five minutes and that there be

(APPLAUSE)

—and that there be two seconding speeches limited to two minutes. Is there any objection?

(CHORUS OF NOES)

"The Chair hears none."

Rayburn also put a ban on demonstrations and, after some speakers proposed resolutions on various subjects, interrupted to complain that the vice-presidential nominators were slow in coming up to the platform, "Up to this time, the Chair has only one. . . ."

But soon he was ready. "The clerk will call the roll of the states for nomination for the office of Vice-President."

Tennessee's Lieutenant Governor Jared Maddux nominated Gore ". . . who uncovered the Dixon-Yates contract, co-author of the Federal Highway Bill, author of Atomic Power Bill, Reciprocal Trade program fight . . . and would be acceptable to every section of the country. . . ." Toledo's former Mayor Mike DiSalle nominated Kefauver, and DiSalle opened with the story of the man who had two sons; one who went to sea and the other who became Vice-President—and neither was ever heard of again. But then DiSalle quickly added that times had changed, that the Vice-President was now a co-partner with the President, and that Kefauver was ". . . not only a great legislator but a great human being. . . ."

Then came Kennedy's: "The Chair is pleased to recognize a former colleague of the House of Representatives and a great governor of the state of Connecticut, Abraham Ribicoff."

Ribicoff kept his speech punching:

"John Kennedy of Massachusetts is a great Democrat. John Kennedy of Massachusetts is a successful campaigner and a successful candidate every time he has run for public office. John Kennedy is something new. John Kennedy brings the vigor and youth and fresh breeze that blows through this great nation of ours. John Kennedy has a voice and personality that appeal to independent voters. John Kennedy has a personality that will appeal to the many Democrats and his record shows that he is unusually successful in making converts in the Republican ranks, too."

For a seconding speech, Rayburn introduced "an outstanding young man who has great promise in my opinion in the politics of the United States, Senator George Smathers of Florida."

Smathers started, thinking that his was the only seconding speech and he could therefore use the full five minutes.

"But when I was halfway through," said Smathers, "Rayburn started poking me in the back with the point of his gavel. I had the clock right in front of me so I knew I had plenty of time, but he kept poking and poking, and that thing can get pretty uncomfortable; so I finally turned around and told Rayburn I still had two minutes left, and he whispered loudly, 'McCormack.' I found out later that Ted Sorensen had been working on McCormack, who had been a little bit reluctant, but I guess he finally decided he better not be left out. So I finished up fast and McCormack came on."

One observer claimed that McCormack practically had to be pushed toward the platform.

Rayburn's introduction was most flowing: "Next, I present for a seconding speech, a great leader, one of the greatest leaders that I have ever known in the House of Representatives, my beloved friend, my co-worker, that great Democrat and patriot, John W. McCormack. . . ."

If Governor Ribicoff's nominating speech had the name "John Kennedy" in every sentence, McCormack's seconding speech never even mentioned his candidate's name until the very last sentence, and one of his strongest statements was: "It is time to go East for a vice-presidential candidate."

Meanwhile, Symington and Fike had raced in a "commandeered" police car, sirens screaming, to the Stockyards with the speech placing Humphrey's name in nomination. The forty-minute ride took only eleven minutes. While they speeded, Symington sat crowded in the corner of the car, working on the speech, making changes and corrections.

At the Amphitheater, Humphrey quickly glanced over the speech, changed one paragraph, and then off Symington went to be made up for TV.

"And I took his only copy of the speech," said Fike, "and dashed madly back downstairs through the orchestra pit and to the TelePrompTer people to get the corrections made." There he discovered that the original speech hadn't even been typed up yet on the TelePrompTer roll . . . an inexperienced technician had been assigned to do it.

"And so there I was," said Stan. "The speech wouldn't be on TelePrompTer, and the senator didn't know it. And I had the only corrected copy."

He ran to the second floor to check timing when he heard the convention clerk call for Minnesota, heard Minnesota yield to Missouri, and then Speaker Sam Rayburn introduce "the junior senator from Missouri."

It was an introduction with real warmth. "Members of the convention, I am going now to present one of the most attractive men in public life, a great businessman, a great officer of the federal government, a great senator from the state of Missouri, my friend, the people's friend, Stuart Symington. . . ."

This was Symington's first appearance before the convention and the ovation was loud and long. During the applause, Stan dashed back to the TelePrompTer setup in the orchestra pit, shuffled the unnumbered pages of the speech into what he hoped was the correct order, then headed for the platform.

But he didn't have a platform pass. Four big policemen blocked his way. They had heard every excuse and they weren't listening to his. But then a friend spotted him, identified him, and Fike raced over to Fishbait Miller, handing him the speech for Symington.

"Luckily the ovation was tremendous and the Senator was taking bows for three or four minutes, or I would never have gotten it to him in time," said Fike. "And luckily he had his reading glasses, or he wouldn't have been able to read it."

Symington said that he had known Humphrey for many years, had the honor of serving with him on three committees, including the Senate special subcommittee on disarmament, in which "our objective is peace, peace with honor and justice and freedom. To obtain that objective we must be dedicated in our belief and practice of democracy. We must build a shield of strength for our defense against the able and aggressive force of communism. The only war we seek is a war against inequality and disease and poverty and fear . . . these are the breeding grounds of world strife and communism. They represent the world-wide challenge."

And then he again promoted Humphrey as the champion of the rights of labor and the rights of small business ". . . a man of tireless energy . . . and high character. . . ."

There were also a scattering of favorite sons: Wagner of New York, Hodges of North Carolina, Collins of Florida.

Symington himself kept out of the vice-presidential nominations. A national magazine wrote that Stevenson had vetoed Symington as a running mate in a secret meeting. Symington promptly got a note from Stevenson:

". . . I am distressed by this report. . . . Actually, as I think you know, I have had not only the warmest personal regard for you for many years, but also the utmost admiration for your record in the many capacities in which you have served our country."

"I am sure you have put no credence in this absurd story," Stevenson wrote Symington and added a P.S.:

"Perhaps I am also a little indignant because to say such a thing in a large meeting (I think there were twelve or more present) hardly credits me with normal intelligence."

Rayburn surrendered his gavel to McCormack, and the drama began at 2:32 P.M. on Friday afternoon, August 17.

"The convention will be in order. The clerk will call the roll of the states in connection with the vote for the nomination of Vice-President. Call the roll."

Then the reading clerk called: "Alabama, twenty-six votes . . ."

"Mr. Chairman, Alabama passes temporarily."

And so it began.

Alaska, six votes for Kefauver ("As Alaska goes, so goes the nation"); "Arizona, voting under the unit rule, casts her sixteen votes for Estes Kefauver"; Arkansas, twenty-six for Gore; California, thirty-three for Kefauver, ten and a half for Kennedy, twenty-three and a half for Humphrey, one vote for Brown (laughter and applause).

Humphrey supporters screamed when Governor Faubus gave twenty-six votes for Gore—because Arkansas had caucused and voted for Humphrey, and because of that vote, Arkansas Senator Fulbright had made a seconding speech for Humphrey.

"Canal Zone casts its three votes for Kennedy. . . ."

Watching it on TV in his room at the Stock Yard Inn, Kennedy turned to plainclothesman, big Ed Agnew, assigned to him during the convention, and confided, "I never went there."

And so it went quickly, most states splitting their votes, a few voting intact under the unit rule, some still inserting other candidates.

When Illinois announced strongly for Kennedy, giving Kefauver only twelve and a half of their sixty-four votes, Kefauver turned to one of his supporters in his room at the Inn and asked, "What do you make of that?"

And his friend answered with the classic political phrase, "Don't worry about that. . . ."

(Later, somebody wanted to know how Illinois boss Jack Arvey had voted in caucus. "Me?" said Arvey. "We had two meetings and I voted for Wagner both times. I kept remembering what I had said to Estes and I didn't want anybody pointing a finger at me saying I had made a deal. This way I was in the clear. Besides, I liked Wagner. But I would have loved to have voted for Kennedy. Why? Well, we had a big lesson to learn from 1952—we just didn't get the big-city Catholic vote, and we needed it, and Kennedy could have gotten it for us.")

Pennsylvania gave Kefauver fifty-four of its seventy-four first-ballot votes, New York stayed with favorite-son Wagner, Texas went for Gore, and Humphrey backers screamed again when Minnesota passed.

That alphabetical first ballot went quickly, all less than an hour. Somebody had taken down the tote board (which electrically kept instant score during the presidential balloting), and delegates were keeping score on backs of envelopes, stray paper, anything they could find—and everybody's score seemed to be different.

There was nothing deliberate about taking down that scoreboard. Nobody had planned it (after all, nobody expected a contest for second place), but the psychological cost to Kennedy was crucial. But scoreboard or no scoreboard, at the end of that first ballot the 5,000 onlookers and the more than 4,000 delegates and alternates inside the largest roofed convention hall in the world felt the first unexpected shock waves of a dramatic fight. Discounting the usual sprinkling of favorite sons, the sudden support of the South for Kennedy made him the surprise challenger.

This was the convention buzz while the organist played "Linger Awhile" and officials retired to double-check that first-ballot count. It added up to 483½ for Kefauver, 304 for Kennedy, 178 for Gore, and 134½ for Humphrey.

Gore and Humphrey both pinned faraway hopes on another second-ballot deadlock and then wholesale switching to them on the third ballot. Kefauver knew his whole future hinged on that second ballot.

"I marked out two red lines under the box stands nearest our delegation," said Kefauver's floor worker, a young man of hyperthyroid energy, Bill Haddad. "That was our headquarters, and I had two phones set in right there. Tennessee was in the center of the front row, with Missouri on our left and Minnesota on our right, and these phones were right next to Minnesota. And guess who was sitting in the boxes right over our phones: the Kennedy family. I knew the Kennedy sisters and we had been pretty friendly but things got a little strained toward the end. Bobby Kennedy used to come around every once in a while and yell over our heads to the sisters, 'Things are going just great.'"

"To tell the truth," added Haddad, "when we first came to that convention hall, we didn't have the slightest idea that our chief opponent would be Kennedy. I don't think anybody did."

What made the sweating Kefauver hall workers particularly bitter was to hear one of their own leaders, Howard McGrath, standing in their red-lined area right under the Kennedy box, saying, "We're beat." After he left, somebody said weakly, "He's just kidding."

It takes time to sell the switchers and everybody hopes for a long recess after the first ballot. But Permanent Chairman Rayburn started the second roll-call ballot at 3:27 P.M.

The convention chairman's power is a thing of enormity. However, to the TV audience, seventy-four-year-old Sam Rayburn, pounding his gavel for convention attention, was a small bald man who always looked as if he had just swallowed something sour.

But at the House of Representatives where he was respectfully known as "Mr. Sam" or "The Speaker," Rayburn demanded a sense of decorum and dignity, and got it without raising his voice. His was such a sense of tradition that he openly disapproved of any congressman who wore odd coat and trousers on the House floor.

But a national political convention has little decorum, less dignity. For some convention delegates this is a one-time fling of fun and duty without a sense of continuity. They feel minimal responsibility to each other, much less to the chairman. To them he is a faraway man with a gavel. To him they are an undisciplined mass. Rayburn tried to act as if the huge Amphitheater was a congressional chamber, and it wouldn't always work:

". . . those who desire to walk or talk will cease walking and talking or else retire from the chamber. . . .

". . . the man who did that will be removed from the chamber. No banner not justified will be allowed in the hall while I am chairman. . . .

". . . unless better order is restored in the chamber, not many of you will know what's going on. . . ."

Not many of them knew the mystery of McCormack of Massachusetts. The mystery was: "WHO DID JOHN McCORMACK REALLY *REALLY* WANT FOR VICE-PRESIDENT?" And the mystery subtitle was, "AND THE SAME GOES FOR SAM RAYBURN."

There was no question that McCormack, at different times, had done important service for the Kennedy cause in his Senate race.

There was no question that McCormack had helped Jack Kennedy, mostly on the behest of Jack's father, an old friend of McCormack's.

Then what was the truth of the rumor that McCormack had the shiv out, ready to slip it into Jack's back at some quiet, critical moment?

"I was with John McCormack myself after that first ballot, and I saw him swing into action," said Representative Ed Boland. "I was with him when he went to the New York delegation and talked to Farley and some of the others, and to the Pennsylvania delegation—of course there was no chance there. And then we went to Michigan, Ohio, Florida, up and down the aisle, and he really talked.

"And I went up to the chairman's platform with him. I didn't have a badge but he pulled me right through the cops with him and I heard McCormack with my own ears ask Rayburn to recognize South Carolina, and Rayburn did, and of course South Carolina was for Kennedy."

Political cynics twist the story another way:

Maybe McCormack did work for Jack on that second ballot, but he didn't do anything until *after* the first ballot, until it looked like Jack might make it anyway and he didn't want to be left on an empty road. And look at the states he talked to—mostly all the hopeless ones that any practical politician *knew* would never go for Kennedy. And everybody knew how reluctant he was to make a seconding speech for Jack, how they almost had to push him up there. As for telling Rayburn to recognize South Carolina, maybe he did. But what if you were John McCormack, and just supposing you didn't want Kennedy, wouldn't it make sense to establish this with Rayburn so that when you later told him to recognize another state, at a more critical time, he might still feel that was also a Kennedy state—when it wouldn't be? Isn't this all just remotely possible?

"Well, then came the second roll call," said Ted Sorensen, "and the manager of the Stock Yard Inn gave us a bigger room, and everything started to look different and get really exciting. But Jack was still pretty calm about it."

But Gore wasn't and Kefauver wasn't and Humphrey wasn't.

If somebody ever tells you that politics is a cold-cut business— laugh. Maybe it cuts cold, but the blood runs warm.

Hubert Humphrey sat in Rayburn's small room in back of the platform with a group of close friends, and one of them remembered:

"Kennedy was pushing ahead and Soapy [Governor G. Mennen Williams of Michigan] and Neil Stabler [State Chairman] both rushed in and started pleading with Hubert, almost on bended knees, just begging him to throw his support to Kefauver. They both pointed to Freeman [Governor Orville Freeman of Minnesota] standing nearby and argued that Freeman couldn't win his race for re-election and Soapy couldn't win his race for re-election if Kennedy was on the national ticket . . . that they'd lose their vital votes among farmers and labor. . . .

"Even while they talked, Kennedy kept gaining all the time and Soapy and Neil were just begging Hubert and somebody else was saying, 'Stick it out, Hubert . . . we can make it on the third ballot, stick it out, we can get Texas and Rhode Island. . . .' and

Eugenie Anderson was there, shouting at all of them, 'Leave Hubert alone . . . he's got to make his own decision, so leave him alone. . . .' And everyone was crying. Eugenie was crying and I was crying and the tears were just pouring out of Stabler. . . ."

Humphrey's only hope was a deadlock that would push things into a third ballot. But almost everything was against that hope, including history—only three Democratic vice-presidential nominees since the Civil War had to go through more than one ballot to gain nomination.

The first big break for Kennedy on the second ballot came when Arkansas switched twenty-six votes from Gore to Kennedy. Just before that, Kennedy said, "Estes is going to win." Now he leaned back on his bed, obviously surprised. "I'll be!" he said, and nervously slapped his leg. Then he turned to Sorensen, "Ted, I wish we had a comparison of this roll call with the last." Ted smiled. "We do."

Delaware switched its ten votes to Kennedy. "I spoke to their caucus this morning," Kennedy said. "I think I got those then."

Ted suggested that maybe he better go down to the hall and find out "what the procedure is in case anything happens." Kennedy agreed, "I think maybe you better."

Kennedy gained another of Florida's twenty-eight "sun-shine votes" but Idaho, "putting all its potatoes in one basket," stayed intact for Kefauver. The "Prairie State of Illinois" added three and a half more for Kennedy, and Iowa "and its tall corn" countered with three more for Kefauver.

Maine added one and a half more for Kennedy, and Minnesota, "the land of a thousand lakes," came back with thirteen and a half more for Kefauver. The obvious southern build-up for Kennedy became clearer when Mississippi turned its twenty-two votes from Gore to Kennedy. Kefauver gained two in Missouri and five and a half in the "Treasure State of Montana."

Somebody gave a thin cheer in Kefauver's room because the Montana vote was the first Kennedy slip in any delegation—a single vote.

Kennedy then picked up two and a half votes in Nevada, and Kefauver came back with two and a half in the "Granite State of New Hampshire." Then came the important tip-off from New Jersey, "the Garden State," which gave Kennedy a twenty-nine and a half gain. New Mexico then added nine and a half for Kefauver.

But the Kefauver room was soon all gloom as the TV camera picked out Harriman and Farley huddling together just before New York switched ninety-six and a half votes from Wagner to Kennedy. Some of the gallery started chanting, "We want Kennedy . . . we want Kennedy. . . ." and Kennedy's brother Bobby passed in front of the chairman's platform, making the smiling sign of V for Victory.

Kennedy lay stretched out on his bed. "I'm bushed," he said. "Two hours' sleep in the last two nights." Ted announced that his wife, Jacqueline, was on the phone, and Jack went into another room to take the call. He was still in his shorts when some TV men arrived, and he said. "Please, no, don't take any pictures." Then he turned up the TV louder and made a few comments, "If we don't make it after this one, it'll be a close one, I think. . . . Figure Humphrey will go to Kefauver before too long." Then he climbed into a tub.

"That guy was cool," said Shriver. "He has this wonderful quality of self-containment. I was on the convention floor and I got the word from DeSapio that New York would switch ninety of its ninety-eight votes to him on the second ballot and that Texas was also going to switch to him and I didn't need much arithmetic to add up the fact that this would put Jack over 600 on the second ballot and that no candidate had ever lost before with 600 votes so I ran up to Jack's room and there he was stretched out on the bed, wiggling his toes, watching TV, and I told him about the expected switching of New York and Texas and 600 votes and nobody had ever lost before with that many votes and he better get dressed and think of something to say."

Kennedy looked at Shriver and Sorensen and said, "Not yet."

"We were watching the TV," said Sorensen, "and somebody came running in to say that Kefauver was out looking for Humphrey, and so Jack suggested that I better hunt for Humphrey, too, and suggest that he and Kennedy get together. Well, I went to several places and I couldn't find him, and finally I got into an elevator and there was Gene McCarthy [then Congressman, now Senator Eugene McCarthy of Minnesota] and I told him what Kennedy had said. All he answered was that we should forget it because they only had Protestants and farmers in his state. Later McCarthy told people that Kennedy had sent a boy to see him."

"Now suppose you were Hubert Humphrey, running hard for Vice-President of the United States," said Gene McCarthy, "and you had this little room in back of the stands, watching the balloting on TV, watching the chances go down the drain and feeling real lousy about it, and in comes this young man with the announcement that Senator Kennedy would like Senator Humphrey to come across to the Stock Yard Inn to see him, almost as though you were being offered an audience with Kennedy. And suppose, minutes later, Estes Kefauver himself comes running up those two flights of stairs and says, 'Hubert, can you help me?' Now suppose you were Hubert Humphrey, which one would you help?"

Such is the intertwined way of politics that Representative Torbet Macdonald thought this: "I thought Minnesota would switch to us. Gene McCarthy was a good friend of mine in the House, and he said he'd do all he could. He was confident Minnesota would give us a lot of votes after Humphrey withdrew. You can ask him. He was working on it for us."

If he was once, he wasn't any more.

"I've just about forgotten everything about that convention except one incident which I'll never forget," said A.B.C. commentator Martin Agronsky.

"Kennedy started running ahead of Kefauver, way ahead, and I saw Governor Orville Freeman making a dash for the back. I didn't know where he was going but I tagged right behind him. He went right into Mr. Sam's little room and went right up to Humphrey and said, 'It's all over.' And Hubert was crying, really sobbing, and so were some of his friends. I knew Minnesota would switch now and I saw Kefauver coming and so I ran as fast as I could back into the convention hall, waved my handkerchief to signal our control booth, and they flashed a light twice which meant I was on the air and I reported that Minnesota was about to switch from Humphrey to Kefauver and this meant that the tide had been stemmed and Kefauver would now undoubtedly take the lead and hold it. The tote board was down so I didn't known how close Kennedy was from getting it and I remember the director said to me on the intercom, 'Do you realize how far your neck is out?' And I told him, 'I never made a bum report for you yet, did I?' I just didn't know how lucky I was. . . ."

Meanwhile, Estes Kefauver was in that back room, pleading for himself.

"Hubert, you've just got to help me . . . you've GOT to help me. . . ."

"Everyone was crying," said one witness, "grown men all crying. Jiggs Donohue was sobbing uncontrollably. The way Hubert answered all this was to tell Symington and Fulbright, 'I'm for Kefauver.' I don't know when Symington got the word, but you know what happened when Missouri announced for Kefauver, they really turned the tide. Looking back at it, I think Hubert really made his move primarily because of Williams. . . . But I'll never forget the water gushing in that room. . . ."

When Hubert Humphrey finally decided to switch to Kefauver, he raced out into the hall but couldn't get through the mob to the Minnesota people. He entered the convention hall from under the platform, and when he couldn't get to his delegation, he stood on a chair and signaled to them. He finally made contact.

If you want to stay in politics, you have to be very careful about the rules.

If a state has a favorite son and the delegates want that favorite son, the chairman had better announce for that favorite son.

Chairman Robert Short of Minnesota passed on the first ballot.

On the second ballot he announced something about Estes Kefauver, Minnesota's choice, releasing his delegation to support its favorite son, Hubert Humphrey.

The language wasn't very proper.

In Minnesota now, Robert Short is on the outside looking in.

That's the way the game is played.

On the convention floor the game of politics reached a tension peak. "New Mexico, the land of enchantment," had just voted.

"New York, ninety-eight votes."

DeSapio was at the microphone, "Mr. Chairman, New York gives one and a half votes for Kefauver, ninety-six and a half votes for the next Vice-President of the United States, John Kennedy."

"That's got it," said Shriver, in Kennedy's room.

"Unbelievable," said Sorenson.

Up in Kefauver's room somebody said, "That wraps it up. . . ."

But in the next vote, Ohio gave fifty-one and a half votes for Kefauver, five and a half for Kennedy, and Senator Jack took off his coat and lay down again.

North Carolina passed to resurvey the scene. Ohio added one more vote for Kefauver, Pennsylvania a gain of ten. Pennsylvania had started to crack down on the dissidents. South Carolina came in to Kennedy with ten and a half and South Dakota put in one more for Kefauver.

Governor Clement got the first "boos" of the day when he announced that the Tennessee "Volunteers" would stay with Gore.

Before the convention, Gore spoke at Lincoln Park, just outside Fall River, Massachusetts. He said then that Kennedy belonged on the national ticket and that he would support him. That morning a Kennedy friend reminded Jack of this, but Jack shook his head and said no, Tennessee would stick with a favorite son.

The heavy, almost critical, psychological blow came from Texas. "I was in amongst the Texas delegation," said Representative Hale Boggs. "They'd originally been for Clement and he didn't run, so they went for Gore and they saw that Gore couldn't make it. So I was the one who got them to switch to Kennedy."

"I remember when we left the convention floor to caucus," said Representative Frank Ikard, "we had to walk behind the platform, and one of the delegates told me that in no circumstances whatsoever would he vote for Kennedy. He was dead set against it. Some of us were working for Kennedy and we wouldn't have been doing it if the Speaker wasn't for him. We were working for him without any great success and then Johnson spoke for him and the Speaker came in and said a few words to the point." (A reporter quoted Rayburn as saying, "I don't know about the rest of you but Sam Rayburn is voting for Kennedy.") "Finally they called a vote and they said, all in favor of Kennedy raise their hands, and this man who told me he would never vote for Kennedy was THE first to get his hand up."

It was a dramatic announcement, and Lyndon Johnson milked it: "Texas proudly casts its fifty-six votes for the fighting sailor who wears the scars of battle. . . ."

In the Kefauver camp somebody commented weakly to the press, "Texas is an awful big state, isn't it?"

In the Kennedy camp, Senator Jack heard the Texas news and let loose a big grin.

"Oh, there's Jean on TV," he said. His sister and his wife and more of the Kennedy clan were sitting in a box directly behind Nancy Kefauver.

"Luckily I had arranged for a couple cops to stand in front of Jack's hotel room," said Shriver, "because the press had figured out what I had figured out and what everybody else had figured out and they had started rushing over. Jack's room had a back porch running to Charlie Potter's suite down the hall. He runs the Inn. Anyway, I ran down and barged in on him and told him about the reporters and asked him if we could move into his suite. So he and his friends moved downstairs. I went back and told Jack, and he raced down that porch in his underwear and somebody else brought his clothes."

Ed Agnew, the plainclothesman, handed Kennedy a shirt and a necktie and commented, "Looks pretty good."

438

BALLOTS & BANDWAGONS

But Kennedy's only comment at that time was, "Too early, don't you think?"

On the floor, brother Bobby raced up and down the aisles, thanking everyone for his help in the victory. At Kennedy's suite the reporters really started piling outside in the hall, noisier and noisier now, and Senator Jack finally said, "Well, maybe now we better think about what we're going to say."

"Ted and I had been putting some words down on paper," said Shriver, "and we showed them to him and he looked at it and said, 'Yeah, that sounds all right, but what do I say if I lose?' Hell, New York and Texas had switched to him, nobody in that room thought he could possibly lose—it just never entered our heads. And there he was saying a thing like that."

Utah came in with two more for Kefauver, the Virgin Islands posted one more for Kennedy, and then Kefauver got one more from Washington, two more from West Virginia, and two and a half more from Wyoming.

Kefauver floor workers were using the whole Kansas delegation as runners racing to all the delegations, asking them to please squeeze a few more votes for Kefauver. The sweat was on. This was crack-down time for the political bosses.

Alabama had passed, now gave a gain of eleven votes for Kennedy, putting Kennedy well ahead. California, which also had passed, added fourteen and a half more votes for Kennedy. Governor Soapy Williams of Michigan had left Humphrey's room and pushed over to the California delegation, now telling Paul Ziffren and James Roosevelt about the Humphrey switch to Kefauver, and Ziffren and Roosevelt were both yelling at Chairman Pat Brown.

Kennedy now added a vote from Indiana and seventeen and a half from North Carolina. Then Kentucky demanded recognition, shouting that it had consistently voted with the minority throughout the convention and now wanted to join the majority, switching thirty votes from Gore to Kennedy.

Gore was at the saloon across the street, still a teetotaler, but now obviously a ripe candidate for a stiff one. When Committeewoman Martha Ragland found him there, Gore looked a little glassy-eyed, still dreaming of a deadlock. Ragland already had asked Clement to release Tennessee delegates to Kefauver, but Clement said it was Gore's decision. So here in this noisy saloon she asked Gore to release the delegates, and he said quickly and flatly, nothing doing, he was in this to the finish.

"I called them both the night before and told them to get up here quick, we need you badly," said Dixon Donnelly, a long-time Kefauver supporter who stayed behind at the Hilton Hotel to feed optimistic Kefauver reports from various delegations to the TV, radio, and newspaper people. Dixon never got to the convention floor, but his wife was there working the phone near the podium, relaying messages everywhere.

"Our good friend Bullard flew in," said Dixon, "and got to the convention hall in a helicopter, bribed his way onto the floor, had a handful of ten-dollar bills, and handed one to everyone who got in his way. Evans was there, too." Both were key Tennessee political powers.

Those who claim to have overheard the conversation, which was not conducted in a conversational tone, say that Bullard threatened to pour a million dollars into the 1958 campaign to unseat Gore, and Evans took Gore by the lapels and worked him over with rough language, saying, in effect: we helped make you and we'll help break you if you don't release the delegation to Kefauver.

Gore still hoped that neither Kennedy nor Kefauver would make it on that ballot or the next, and by then the tide would turn to him. But even as he spoke, Kennedy's lead became much more considerable and Ragland warned him that Kennedy might win in a matter of minutes, and then Gore would face the charges in his 1958 re-election fight that he had helped defeat a favorite son.

Gore said nothing, but reluctantly agreed to return to the Amphitheater.

"Tennessee couldn't switch to Kennedy—no matter what happened—as long as I was in the race," said Kefauver. "The State Democratic Convention had decided that it had to stick to a favorite son. Clement had had his chance, and then Gore, and if Gore withdrew, it would have to be me. But what Gore could do, and what we were worried about was that he might hold out until the bitter end. We didn't know how long he would hold out. That was the important pressure point."

Even Senator Mike Monroney of Oklahoma, Gore's strongest backer, had given up. "I knew Gore wasn't going to pick up any more strength," he said. "I got that from the newsmen and they gave it to me straight. You know I used to be a newspaperman myself."

Standing next to Gore at the delegation, the listener had good ears and the words he heard were loud and clear. Gore had just told Clement that it now had to be Estes Kefauver, and Clement moaned, "Oh, no, not Estes. . . ."

But in back of Clement's loud regret was the quiet knowledge that it could be worse; that if Kefauver did get the nomination, and win, there would be a United States Senate seat vacant in Tennessee and Governor Clement could quickly become Senator Clement by resigning and getting himself appointed. The importance of this for Clement was that there was no other political place for him to go—Tennessee governors cannot succeed themselves. The best view was elsewhere.

Sit in Room 264 of the Amphitheater and see what a TV director sees—three television sets, monitoring the N.B.C. cameras focused in all directions on three different parts of the convention floor, a view usually restricted to TV network control rooms. Only this wasn't a TV director, this was Colonel William Roberts working for Estes Kefauver. Besides the TV sets, he had plug-in phone connections to every part of the floor, loose-leaf folders detailing the who, why, and wherefore of every delegation on that floor.

"I knew Gore was certain to switch to Estes," said Roberts, who is a prominent Washington lawyer, "and I could see the Tennessee delegation was one big madhouse. And I could see, at that same moment, on another TV set, Mrs. Maybelle Kennedy of Pawhuska, Oklahoma, working on Senator Bob Kerr and Governor Ray Gary of the Oklahoma delegation. Maybelle was co-chairman of the Kefauver-for-President Committee and I knew Kerr liked Estes, always did, but the delegation had gone for Gore on the first ballot. I could catch Maybelle's excitement and I could see her succeeding, and finally I could see that she had convinced them and she was heading for the Tennessee delegation to tell them the news, to tip them over fast.

"The moment was crucial. If Rayburn would recognize Tennessee, then Oklahoma, the tide would turn. I called the floor, told them to get runners down to Rayburn's platform, and yell, 'Tennessee is going for Kennedy . . . Tennessee is going for Kennedy. . . .' because I knew Rayburn never like Kefauver. It worked. Clarence Cannon on the platform heard the runners and told Rayburn, 'Tennessee, Tennessee. . . .' And Rayburn recognized Tennessee, and there it was, that was the beginning. That's politics."

Tennessee millionaire Bullard had a similar diagnosis, a similar remedy—with a willing wallet of ten-dollar bills. He gently placed a ten-dollar bill onto the palm of an anxious woman, convincing her that she should rush down to the platform, yelling at Rayburn, "Tennessee is switching to Kennedy . . . Tennessee is switching to Kennedy. . . ."

If the shortest distance between two political points was not a straight line for Bullard and Roberts, it zigzagged a little bit for Bill Haddad, too.

"When I saw Tennessee waving for recognition, I didn't know what they were going to do," said Haddad, "but I ran up and down the aisles, yelling to all the delegations, 'Better jump on the bandwagon . . . Tennessee is going to switch to Kefauver. . . . You can be the one to help Kefauver win. . . . Do it now. . . . Switch now. . . .'

"Mayor Daley of Chicago—he was for Kennedy—grabbed me and physically held me for a while, but I broke loose and kept running and yelling. My two brothers, Fred and Sid, were also running and yelling, and a Humphrey man told me later that he was running right behind me, yelling, 'It's not true . . . It's not true,' but then he said, 'Every time I turned around, I bumped into another Haddad.' "

The Haddads had been sprinting, conferring, informing, transmitting, yelling with the whole Kefauver crowd in one long, sustained now-or-never effort. Suddenly, there was nothing more they could do. It was over. Either they had made it or they hadn't. If there was a split second of silence in this spree of frenzy, nobody heard it. Rayburn was about to recognize Tennessee, but who could be sure it would be Tennessee, for that split second who could be sure of anything? Bill Haddad went up front, right under the rostrum, and stopped behind a friend, Charlie Bartlett of the *Chattanooga Times*. Charlie said, "Well, it's all over." And Bill said, not sure, not knowing, not truly believing, "No, it isn't. Wait and see . . . Tennessee is going to switch to Estes. . . ."

Until that dramatic moment, from the beginning of the second roll call of the states, Speaker Rayburn had surrendered the Chair to his friend, Senator Warren Magnuson of Washington. Magnuson had recognized Kentucky, "which has consistently been with the minority all through this convention, enthusiastically joins the majority and changes its vote to John Kennedy. . . ."

And just then, at that peak of tension, Rayburn stepped in again, grabbed the gavel, rapped it, boomed out: "Does the state of Tennessee desire recognition?"

"Mr. Chairman," said the Tennessee spokesman, "Tennessee requests the opportunity for candidate Albert Gore to make a brief announcement."

Now there were some tangible seconds of silence.

"The Chair recognizes the senator from Tennessee by unanimous consent only." Then Gore, at the microphone, jammed, pushed, sweating. "Mr. Chairman, with thanks to this great, free Democratic convention, I request that my name be withdrawn in favor of my colleague, Senator Estes Kefauver. . . ."

"I'll never forget that look on Rayburn's face as long as I live," said Haddad. "He was so shocked, he really lost his composure for a moment."

If Sam Rayburn was shocked, why?

Who was he for, anyway?

Everybody knew how he hated Kefauver, how hard he had fought against him in the 1952 convention.

Everybody also knew of his serious concern about having a Catholic on the ticket. "This is no time to tinker with that," he had said.

The political translation of the tinkering remark was that Rayburn felt Democrats had enough worries about Eisenhower, that a Catholic on the ticket would only complicate the campaign.

Then what's the explanation for one newsman's report that Rayburn went to his Texas delegation and said, "I don't care what the rest of you do, but I'm voting for Kennedy"? Who *did* talk to Rayburn during that whole second roll call when he was away from the Chair? His southern friends who wanted to stop Kefauver at all costs, or the pols which felt Kefauver alone could best help the ticket?

Did Rayburn recognize Tennessee because people below him were yelling that Tennessee was switching to Kennedy, or simply because Tennessee was smack in front of him, in the front center of the hall, impossible to ignore?

Rayburn never said, but two good friends of his have conflicting ideas:

"Mr. Sam is a party man, first, last, and always," said newsman Frank McNaughton. "And when he's up there, he doesn't do things accidentally. He knows exactly what he's doing. When he recognized Tennessee, he must have known what Tennessee would do from one of his floor workers."

"Anybody who knows the Speaker," said Senator Mike Monroney, with indignation, "knows that he would not be capable of such corruption."

What was it? Politics or imagination?

Whatever it was, it was pivotal. It broke the back of a bandwagon, created a new one.

Here were two Rayburn views by Kennedy supporters:

"Let's remember one thing: we had North Carolina and some other states ready to switch to Kennedy, and who does Rayburn recognize one, two, three, but Tennessee, Oklahoma, and Missouri, all of them switching to Kefauver. That's what killed us."

And the other Kennedy view:

"Rayburn? Rayburn wasn't for either one. We were just all played out of votes and I just couldn't think where we could get any more. My evaluation is that there just weren't but two or three scattered votes here and there in the whole hall we could get. At that point I don't think there were any switches for Kennedy that Rayburn could recognize. It was all finished. We were played out of votes."

But nobody is ever played out of votes when a bandwagon rolls.

The bandwagon is a fever that takes statistics out of the definition of politics. It's a thing of chemistry that boils blood, jumps feet, waves hands, shouts voices, bangs fists, and heightens hangovers. It parts from reason in the same way that love does or hate does. It is a mass orgy of feeling that sweeps with the fervor of a religious revival. It is the Fourth of July on Christmas morning.

In the Indiana delegation, all was frenzy.

If, if, if, if, if.

If Indiana had been recognized and allowed to switch when it requested recognition. . . .

Indiana already had voted on the second ballot: Twenty for Kefauver, three and a half for Kennedy. But, suddenly, came the shocker—New York switching ninety-six and a half votes to Kennedy.

Indiana delegates mobbed their chairman, Charles Skillen:

"Let's get on the bandwagon. . . . Let's get on the bandwagon. . . ."

Kennedy's vote kept jumping: 550, 574, 599½, 612, 648, only forty more votes and Kennedy was in, and Indiana could give him more than half of those votes.

"Let's get on the bandwagon. . . ."

This is panic pressure and even a high-strength metal mind can resist only so long, and Skillen finally yielded, grabbed the microphone, and yelled, "Mr. Chairman, Mr. Chairman, Indiana wants to change its vote to Senator Kennedy. . . ."

There was no immediate answer from Mr. Chairman.

Former Congressman Andrew Jacobs of Indianapolis, a strong Kefauver man, pulled Skillen's arm and said, "You're not switching my vote to Kennedy."

Skillen hesitated, then said he'd poll the delegates.

The drawn-out poll cooled the panic, and most of the delegates decided to stick with Kefauver.

A moment later, Chairman Rayburn was saying, "Does the state of Tennessee wish to be recognized?" And the trend turned.

If Indiana had been recognized instead of Tennessee, then only one more state could have put over Kennedy.

That one state could have been California. Chairman Pat Brown had caught the bandwagon fever, started swinging his California standard for recognition, and Jimmy Roosevelt pulled Brown's jacket and asked him what he was doing. The man who would be governor in 1958 then said to the man who had tried to be governor that he knew the delegation was now unanimous for Kennedy and he was switching it. Somebody nearby then overheard Roosevelt say loudly that he was for Kefauver and that Brown had better poll the delegation, "or I'll break your leg." Brown polled, and a sizeable number of votes still stayed with Kefauver.

The new chant from the jammed gallery was: "We want Estes. . . . We want Estes. . . ."

Cool and composed again, Chairman Rayburn boomed out, "Does Oklahoma desire recognition?"

Why Oklahoma? Because he saw them next? Or because he thought that Oklahoma might follow Texas and switch to Kennedy?

"Mr. Chairman, Oklahoma desires to change its vote from Senator Gore, since he has released us, to Senator Estes Kefauver."

The roar from the gallery, the buzz of the bandwagon. The chant, picking up, beat like a drum. "We want Estes. . . ."

Oklahoma meant twenty-eight more votes.

"Does Minnesota desire recognition?"

Surely Rayburn knew what Humphrey was going to do. Or did he?

"Mr. Chairman, the great junior senator of Minnesota, asks that Minnesota cast its entire thirty votes for the next Vice-President of the United States, his good friend Senator Estes Kefauver."

Almost an hysteria now. The state banners waving madly. Everybody wanting to be recognized. So much noise that almost nobody could be heard. And one of the banners waving most furiously was Tennessee. What did Tennessee want now? Was it going to switch again?

"Just a moment now," said Chairman Rayburn, banging his gavel. "Does Tennessee desire recognition again?"

For a moment, confusion. What was going on? Tennessee again? The whole emotion of the floor seemed strangled for a second.

"Mr. Chairman, Senator Gore made his announcement, but we want the opportunity to officially request permission to change Tennessee's thirty-two votes from our distinguished junior senator to our distinguished senior senator, Estes Kefauver."

A parliamentary technicality. The convention normalized again to its original hysteria.

"Does the state of Missouri desire recognition?"

Again the question, why Missouri? The Missouri delegation sat right next to Massachusetts on the convention floor and it was true that some of the Missouri delegates had told some of the Connecticut delegates, who were hot for Kennedy, "Don't worry, if we switch from Humphrey, we'll switch to Kennedy." Did Rayburn's floor workers give him this information?

The Missouri delegation probably would have switched to Kennedy because their feeling was so strongly anti-Kefauver. But what did happen inside that Missouri delegation?

"Well, Rayburn might well have thought that we would switch to Kennedy," said Missouri delegate Jim Meredith, "because there was a lot of miscellaneous information floating around that we would. I couldn't help in tracing it or even explaining it except to say that some of it was natural . . . there were some Catholics on the delegation, Kennedy did have friends there, and he did get some votes in our caucus. But that wouldn't account for that miscellaneous information that was getting around and I'm damned if I know who was promoting it."

Another Missouri delegate, a top state official, gave another twist to the tangent:

"Kennedy had a lot of support in the Missouri delegation and he lost it not because of the Protestants but because of the Catholics. There were, I believe, eleven Catholics on the delegation and I believe that, to a man, they were not only against a Catholic getting the nomination, but violently against it. I have never seen such determined opposition in my life."

Nobody knows how much of this "miscellaneous information" reached Rayburn. One newsman insisted (and McCormack denied) that Missouri's Senator Hennings told McCormack that Missouri was switching to Kefauver and that McCormack ran to the platform, yelling at his long-time associate speaker Rayburn, "Sam! Sam! Missouri!"—and Rayburn recognized Missouri.

Another observer, Representative Hale Boggs of Louisiana, said, "Not fifteen minutes before it was all over, I went up to the platform and spoke to the Speaker, and he looked over the whole hall and told me, 'Far as I'm concerned, it's fielder's choice.' Meaning? Meaning comme ci comme ça, six of one half, a dozen of the other, take your pick."

The ones who favor the McCormack theory point out that there was still a fresh, lingering bitterness because Kennedy had openly fought and badly beaten McCormack for control of the state delegation.

Whatever the reason, there was Missouri, which had given Kefauver only one vote on the first ballot, three on the second ballot, now yelling into the microphone, "Mr. Chairman, the state of Missouri desires at this time to change its vote to thirty-seven votes for Estes Kefauver. . . ."

The time was 4:14 P.M.

The floor became a bandwagon mass of shouting men and women, waving banners, stamping feet, with Rayburn banging his gavel and protesting: "The reading clerk cannot understand what the delegates are saying. It seems that you all could be quiet for a few moments."

It didn't take much longer than that.

"I'll never forget Bobby Kennedy during the balloting," said North Dakota's Quentin Burdick, "standing in front of our delegation with tears in his eyes, pleading for our support. It didn't do any good. Jack had voted for sliding-scale supports and they don't like sliding-scale supports in our country. He stood there trying to explain his brother's voting position but we said we were sorry and the delegation wouldn't listen to him. . . ."

Michigan added four more. Florida squeezed out another half vote for him. Illinois came back with five more for Kennedy, but Pennsylvania countered with ten more for Kefauver, giving him all of its seventy-four votes.

The strength of a political boss is the strength of his crackdown. Pennsylvania's boss, Dave Lawrence, declared the bulk of his state voted for Kefauver on previous ballots, but a number of scattered votes still courted Kennedy. Then came the crackdown, which went something like this: all right, boys, we've let you have your fun, but now you must vote with the rest of us, or else.

"Or else" are two of the strongest words in the political language.

Finnegan felt what Lawrence felt.

"I was in Stevenson's Skyway Suite with Finnegan, watching the balloting on TV," said John Sharon. "Since the last time I had made my pitch to him about the open convention, we had never again discussed the subject. He knew what I had done and I thought I knew what he had done. But I never asked for the updated story and he had never volunteered it. I still don't know the whole story of how it finally happened. But when the balloting got very close and Kennedy pulled ahead, Jim showed his deep

feeling about it. 'This is a bunch of goddam nonsense,' he said."
"I think you're wrong, Jim," said Sharon.

What upset Finnegan was his feeling that this was hurting the party. This was his great sensitivity because his devotion to the Democratic party was obvious and great. "But Jim wasn't the kind of guy who said something was wrong and then, after the decision was made, would try to talk Stevenson out of it. He wasn't that kind of a guy at all," said his lovely, brainy, blonde assistant Jean Gildea. Once a decision was made, he backed it. But deep down he couldn't help feeling what he did.

But as the southern states started switching to Kennedy, Finnegan relaxed a little as he thought of something. "How do you like that," he said, "the Ku Klux Klan voting for Kennedy." Then he thought of something else which caused another smile, "Well, at least the Catholics can never claim that we used Jack as bait for their vote because the delegates are picking him themselves."

When New York switched to Kennedy, Finnegan said, "Kennedy has it," and he walked out of the room. Soon afterward a cheer went up as Tennessee switched to Kefauver and the trend changed. Finnegan poked his head in again asking what happened, and somebody told him Kefauver was out front again. Finnegan came back, sat down, still shaking his head, and watched the rest of it, upset about the possible intraparty bitterness being generated.

The final clinchers were small Kefauver gains in Iowa, Montana, and the District of Columbia. After taking its new poll, California announced a new line-up that subtracted seven from Kennedy and added twelve and a half for Kefauver. The body blows came from Delaware switching ten votes to Kefauver, West Virginia giving him fifteen more, and New England's Maine turning all its nine votes from Kennedy to Kefauver. (Governor Muskie had left the convention a day earlier.)

Soaping himself in the bathtub, Jack Kennedy kept busy thinking up words to accept the vice-presidential nomination. But as he put on his medium-blue suit and a soft-collared white shirt with a red-dotted light gray tie, his brother-in-law Sarge Shriver rushed in with the bad news, putting a comforting arm around his shoulder, telling him that the trend had turned against him.

TV soon confirmed the fact.

"When Kefauver got it," said Sorensen, "the Senator looked at me and said, 'Let's go.'"

"We all raced down the back stairs," said Sarge Shriver, who was also there, "and we got into the Amphitheater through a back door, without any cops. In fact, the cops stopped us at the platform, and somebody recognized us and told the cops to let us through. While we were running, Jack and I talked over what he should say. We got up there on the platform, sat down, and somebody told Rayburn we were there and then he recognized Jack and introduced him."

Out of the packed place came a roar as Kennedy stood there, picking at some invisible dust on his boyish, handsome face, drywashing his hands, waving to yelling friends nearby, his smile tentative but warmly appealing, his eyes slightly wet and glistening.

He spoke without notes, and his words were short, gallant, touching.

"Ladies and gentlemen of this convention, I want to take this opportunity first to express my appreciation to Democrats from all parts of the country, north and south, east and west, who have been so generous and kind to me this afternoon. I think it proves, as nothing else can prove, how strong and united the Democratic party is.

"Secondly what has happened today bears out the good judgment of our Governor Stevenson in deciding that this issue should be taken to the floor of the convention. Because I believe that the Democratic party will go from this convention far stronger for what we have done here today. And therefore, ladies and gentlemen, recognizing that this convention has selected a man who has campaigned in all parts of the country, who has worked untiringly for the party, who will serve as an admirable running mate to Governor Stevenson, I hope that this convention will make Estes Kefauver's nomination unanimous. Thank you."

"Mr. Chairman, I move that we suspend the rule and make the nomination of Estes Kefauver by acclamation."

And so it was done.

"Those in favor of the motion," said Rayburn, "will vote aye."

(CHORUS OF AYES)

Chairman Rayburn: "No Noes."

(LAUGHTER AND APPLAUSE)

"The ayes have it."

For the TV millions, those moments were magic, the kind of magic that gets remembered a generation later as a sticking fact of history, the kind of magic that gave the first full rub of presidential promise to John Fitzgerald Kennedy.

The photographers had had it hard and hectic. They flocked first with Kefauver because he had the odds. They switched fast to Kennedy when he started racing in on the home stretch. Then they double-tracked in a hurry back to Kefauver when he put on the final burst of speed for the tape.

The Kennedy suite that had been massed with photographers and well-wishers was now empty, and brother-in-law Sarge Shriver said out loud, "Talk about fleeting fame. . . ."

"Something I'll never forget," said Mrs. Dixon Donnelly, a dedicated Kefauver worker, "was Nancy Kefauver and the beautiful Jackie Kennedy in their boxes during the voting. There was no one around Nancy, and Jackie was surrounded by people. Then Estes won and suddenly there was no one with Jackie. She was left by herself at the end. She was pregnant and she just stood there and she was a very sad and forlorn figure."

"After it was all over," said one of Kennedy's friends, "some of us went back to Jack's room and there he was, sitting on the bed, not saying a word. He's like all the Kennedys—once they're in something, they don't like to lose."

To his close friends, Kennedy said, "I feel like the Indian who had a lot of arrows stuck in him and, when he was asked how he felt, said, 'It only hurts when I laugh.'"

Congressman Ben Smith was crying.

"I ran into Smathers and I chewed him out for a couple moments," said Representative Torbet Macdonald, "and then I was sorry I did. He was supposed to be one of our strongest supporters, but he didn't break his back."

"After Jack lost," said Senator Smathers, "I went back with him and Jackie to their hotel room. I've never been to an Irish wake before, but I guess maybe this was it. The three of us just sat around the room, all of us glum, none of us saying very much. We were there about an hour and a half and all Jack could think of were all the different things he might have done that might have made the difference. He was hurt, deeply hurt. The thing is, he came so close. . . ."

"If I had been there," said Jack Kennedy's father, the former Ambassador, "I would have won that nomination for Jack. How? I would have had a recess after the first ballot, and that would have given us enough time to organize and win."

Jack's brother Bobby similarly pinned it on procedures. "There are all sorts of things that can be done if you know how to use them. For example, if we had known parliamentary procedures, we could have stopped things after Tennessee switched. It's always possible to have the floor and interrupt things long enough to stop a trend and add things up. With that tote board down, nobody knew exactly how close we were. If they knew, the momentum would have carried us over. We could have interrupted things long enough to get around to the delegates and show them that Kennedy was within thirty-eight votes of a majority. You have to know parliamentary procedures. You have to know the rules cold."

Back at the Stevenson suite in the Blackstone, somebody standing close to Stevenson watched him carefully as the TV scoreboard announced Kefauver the winner.

Stevenson's remark, clearly audible, was printable—but a phrase not generally regarded as an expression of high joy.

The next morning, Hubert Humphrey's phone rang. It was Adlai Stevenson. "Hubert, maybe I'd better be reading the Scriptures this morning."

Hubert was politely cold. But the next day Hubert Humphrey bounced in on his staff and said, "Now what can we do to help get Stevenson elected?"

A professional politician takes a licking, fixes up his wound, wipes a tear from his eye, chokes back a sob, and then gets on with his business of politics.

"I went out there as a delegate," said Dave Talbot, who had helped organize Franco-American groups in Massachusetts for Kennedy. "Well, it was a different trip out than it was back. On the way out we had a plane with New England delegates, and Governor Muskie got on and took off his coat and said, God, what a dead bunch, let's have some songs and he started singing and we all joined in. But coming back, nobody was singing. I sat right next to Bobby Kennedy and he was bitter. He said they should have won and somebody had pulled something fishy and he wanted to know who did it."

Political post-mortems come quickly.

The convention floor was still unswept when one delegation chairman started getting his report ready about some of his delegates:

". . . ran out on us, deserves no consideration, tried to climb back on after Harriman had lost. . . . She is however still important in the state and we shall have to be somewhat kind. . . ."

". . . very friendly to us. . . ."

". . . unfriendly to us but co-operated because of our support for Stevenson. . . ."

". . . young and inexperienced, lost his temper and went home when he saw Harriman would lose. Thinks I am sort of gangster. . . ."

". . . very poor loser, still mad, was rooting for Kennedy. . . ."

". . . a fine gentleman who was sincerely for Harriman, but wanted Estes for veep. . . ."

". . . a real phony, played all sides of all issues. Was finally bludgeoned into supporting Stevenson after riding with the Harriman people all week. . . ."

". . . the only other delegate besides myself truly with any loyalty for the senator. However he was for Harriman and quite bitter when Estes withdrew in favor of Stevenson. . . ."

"The basis we worked on was that we would not poll the delegation or even ask for opinions, just cast the vote for Estes and God help the one that raised his voice. . . ."

The second-ballot tally before the acclamation was 751½ for Kefauver, 582 for Kennedy, 17½ for Gore, and 8½ for Humphrey.

After it was all over, one of the Stevenson secretaries decided that the time had come for a party for the low-level volunteers. These are the special people of the world who are tied together by the tightest thing there is—a dedication so deep that they deprive themselves of family, friends, love, sleep, time, memory. Their whole world has suddenly fit into a hard, short frame where nobody else can enter unless their blood is true and their eyes are wide and their heart is full. In this frame there is more heart than head, more hope than knowledge, more fervor, more faith, more love than anybody deserves.

They scheduled the party in Finnegan's secret two-room suite, two floors above the Skyway, and one of the girls opened a drawer searching for a bottle opener when she found the tickets.

Convention tickets were so scarce that even Hubert Humphrey's wife couldn't get one and President Truman himself was rationed. They were so scarce that most of these faithful low-level volunteers who gave all their days and all their nights to their dedication never even got to see the living convention.

And yet here they were, dozens and dozens of them, for every night in the week, forgotten lost tickets once worth their weight in political passes.

Their screeches were half moans and then out came the tickets thrown into a pile in the center of the room with everybody staring at them in strange fascination. Then one of the girls started to dance around this pile of tickets and the girls all joined in. Their dance was macabre, almost primitive, and the laughter had a choking quality about it.

A collector of complaints mentioned two items:

A delegate named Sam Coward who ran a drugstore in Tennessee had complained because he hadn't brought more of the store's stock with him—particularly the hangover pills.

And a woman who sold hot dogs at the convention:

"Every time I opened the bun side and the frank side, I got a shot of steam," she said. "That's two burns for every hot dog. And do you know how many hot dogs I made? Eight thousand. That's 16,000 burns."

If the delegates felt understanding about the hangover pills, and if they sympathized with anybody else who got burned, they also knew that in 1960 it would all begin again—huge hopes and expensive promises, a roomful of candidates crying real tears, hoopla mixed with weariness, desperate power plays and unanswered question marks—the high fever and high jinks inside this political pressure cooker called the national convention—the movement of it, the fun of it, the love of it.

And yet underneath all this façade of circus drama, giving it blood and bone, is the strong full purpose of the dedicated, those men and women—of both political parties—who think more of America than of themselves, those people who ultimately are the ones who make democracy work.

REPUBLICAN NATIONAL CONVENTION OF 1900

PAGES 17–20 The relationship of President McKinley and Mark Hanna with Theodore Roosevelt has been dealt with briefly, but not adequately, in many places. Of the two main biographies of Hanna, *Marcus A. Hanna* by Herbert Croly (Macmillan, 1912) and *Hanna* by Thomas Beer (Knopf, 1929), Croly seems to have supplied the better detail. Another biography, *Mark Hanna* by Solon Lauer (Cleveland, 1901) is a slim book of small consequence. An article in *Harper's Weekly* (February 27, 1904) sheds little fresh light and John T. Flynn adds a little more in *Scribner's Magazine* (August, 1933) but not so much in this area. More informative was Henry L. Stoddard's two books, *As I Knew Them* (Harper & Row, 1927) and *It Costs To Be President* (Harper & Row, 1938). The first book is the more basic.

From the McKinley view, Margaret Leech's *In the Days of McKinley* (Harper & Row, 1939), an otherwise excellent biography, devotes only short space to this, however well documented, and even shorter space to the convention itself. H. H. Kohlsaat's *From McKinley to Harding* (Scribner's, 1923), while writing from a more intimate view, is good. Most disappointing of all, in this area, especially in view of his relationship to Mark Hanna, was James Ford Rhodes' otherwise fine history, *The McKinley and Roosevelt Administrations* (Macmillan, 1922).

PAGES 21–24 Platt's story here comes partly from *The Autobiography of Thomas Collier Platt* (Dodge, 1910) which sharply differs from Theodore Roosevelt's own *Theodore Roosevelt: An Autobiography* (Scribner's, 1926). Henry F. Pringle in *Theodore Roosevelt* (Harcourt, Brace & World, 1931) offers his view on this compactly, and very well. *A Short History of New York State*, by David Ellis, James Frost, Harold Syrett, and Harry Carman (Cornell, 1957) offers added light on this.

BALLOTS & BANDWAGONS

PAGES 25–28 The Penrose material mostly comes from *Power and Glory: Life of Boise Penrose* by Walter Davenport (© 1931 by Putnam's & Coward-McCann), and Davenport really has caught the language and flavor of the man. *The Letters of Theodore Roosevelt* edited by Elting Morison (Harvard, 1954) are absolutely invaluable here, as they are throughout the rest of this chapter. The two volumes of *Selections from the Correspondence of Theodore Roosevelt and Henry Cabot Lodge, 1884–1918* (Scribner's, 1925) pinpoint this focus even more sharply.

PAGES 29–32 An excellent descriptive source of material is Mark Sullivan's *Our Times: The Twenties*, Vol. 1. (Scribner's, 1926). *The Republican Roosevelt*, by John Blum (Harvard, 1954), *The Short History of New York State* and *Theodore Roosevelt* by William Roscoe Thayer (Houghton Mifflin, 1919), are also of some use.

PAGES 33–34 Much of this material is from newspapers and periodicals of that time. The best is from the *New York Times* beginning with June 16, 1900 and continuing throughout the convention. Without question, these reports, interviews, caucus details—which have not been reported before in any book that I know—constitute the most valuable source material I found about this convention.

PAGES 35–39 Nicholas Murray Butler's *Across The Busy Years* (Scribner's, 1935) supplies an excellent account of what happened here. L. White Busbey, in *Uncle Joe Cannon*, (Henry Holt, 1927) provides a footnote, but, much more valuable are the *Papers of J. D. Long*, edited by Gardner, Weld and Allen (Massachusetts Historical Society Collection, 1939). Again, the reports from the *New York Times* of these dates, form the heart of this material.

PAGES 40–45 References here are from the autobiographies of both Platt and Roosevelt.

PAGES 46–52 The description of the convention itself is from the *New York Times*, and the "Official Proceedings of the Republican Convention of 1900" (Library of Congress).

PAGES 53–57 William Allen White's *Masks In A Pageant*, (Macmillan, 1928) has excellent material on McKinley and Hanna, as does Matthew Josephson in *The President-Makers* (Harcourt, Brace, 1940) and *The Politicos* (Harcourt, Brace, 1938), particularly on Hanna. In addition to the *New York Times*, reports there come from the *New York Journal*, the *New York Tribune, Harper's Weekly* of June 30, 1900, and *The Nation* of June 28, 1900.

REPUBLICAN NATIONAL CONVENTION OF 1912

PAGES 60–64 Pringle's *Roosevelt* is useful here, but the dramatic material comes from Kohlsaat, Stoddard's *As I Knew Them*, and his *Presidential Sweepstakes* (Putnam, 1948). Also highly important are Pringle's two volumes of *The Life and Times of William Howard Taft* (Holt, Rinehart and Winston, 1939). The Lodge letters come from his *Selected Letters* and from *The Letters of Theodore Roosevelt*.

PAGES 65–68 Herbert S. Dufy's *William Howard Taft* (New York, 1930) is useful here. Much more so is Mark Sullivan's *Our Times* Volumes III and IV (Scribner's). William Allen White's *Autobiography* (Macmillan, 1946) and the *Selected Letters of William Allen White* edited by Walter Johnson (Henry Holt, 1947) are also very good. The two volumes of *Taft and Roosevelt: The Intimate Letters of Archie Butt* (Doubleday, 1930) are absolutely vital here. Also of high importance is Victor Rosewater's *Backstage in 1912,* (Dorrance, 1932). Pringle's *Taft* has use throughout.

PAGES 69–72 References here are to Butt, White, Pringle, Stoddard and Rosewater. Two other books of considerable importance here are George Mowry's *Theodore Roosevelt and the Progressive Movement,* (Madison, 1946) and *Released for Publication,* by O. K. Davis (Houghton Mifflin, 1932).

PAGES 73–77 *The Growth of the American Republic,* by Samuel Eliot Morison and Henry Steele Commager (Oxford, 1950) offers a good account of this period. Roosevelt's *Letters* here are very revealing. The La Follette material comes partly from Mowry, but mostly from his *Autobiography* (Madison, 1911), his *A Personal Narrative of Political Experience* (Madison, 1913) and the two volume biography, *Robert M. La Follette* by Belle and Fola La Follette (Macmillan, 1953).

PAGES 78–83 Butt and Kohlsaat are liberally referred to here. Also useful is *Recollections of Full Years* by Helen H. Taft (Dodd, Mead, 1914) which supplies the intimacy of shared conversations. Mowry, Pringle, and particularly Davis provide excellent research for this part. Henry Adams also provides some references from his letters, *The Selected Letters of Henry Adams,* edited by Newton Arvin (Farrar, Straus and Young, 1951), as do Archie Butt's letters.

PAGES 84–88 Owen Wister's, *Roosevelt, The Story of a Friendship,* (Macmillan, 1930) has only slight value here. Lyman Abbott's *Reminiscences,* (Houghton Mifflin, 1915) has somewhat more value. More important are the Roosevelt letters, and his articles in *The Outlook* magazine. Reports in the *New York Times* become increasingly important at this time, as do the La Follette biographies again. Reference is also made to Thayer.

PAGES 89–93 Much of the material here comes from periodicals, such as *Harper's Weekly, Colliers,* and newspapers such as the *New York Times,* the *New York Tribune,* the *Philadelphia Evening Telegraph,* the *Louisville Courier-Journal* and the *New York Sun.* I also have included a reference from *The American Political Tradition* (Vintage, 1958) by Richard Hofstadter and further referrals to Sullivan, Josephson and Mowry.

PAGES 94–97 Pringle's *Taft,* Stoddard, Mowry and Rosewater all supply background for this section. So does William Allen White, the *New York Sun,* and Thayer.

PAGES 98–106 The heaviest part of this material comes from newspaper clippings, again mostly from the *New York Times.* Davis deals with the primaries of this convention in the greatest detail. Both Mowry and Pringle's *Taft* are also worth reading.

PAGES 107–111 The Penrose quote comes from Davenport and the Bryan report is spelled out in a valuable book, *Tale of Two Conventions* (Funk and Wagnalls, 1912). Victor Rosewater now begins to become a major reference.

PAGES 112–118 For the whole story of the fight in the Credentials Committee, Rosewater is a primary source of reference. Coupled with this in importance is the "Official Proceedings of the Republican National Convention of 1912" (Library of Congress) and the daily reports in the *New*

BALLOTS & BANDWAGONS

York Times and the *Chicago Tribune.* In this particular instance, the *Chicago Tribune* reports are more detailed.

PAGES 119–132 The best reports of this preliminary time in Chicago, just before the convention opening comes from the several books of William Allen White, Davis, some of the Roosevelt letters, and the *Chicago Tribune.*

PAGES 133–144 No other source is comparable to the Official Proceedings on the actual details of the convention itself. But this is excellently supplemented by the *New York Times,* the *Chicago Tribune,* and best of all, the account by Richard Harding Davis in *Scribner's Magazine* of September, 1912.

PAGES 145–149 Beveridge and the Progressive Era by Claude G. Bowers (Houghton Mifflin, 1932) offers a vital view of this time. *Third Parties in American Politics,* by Howard P. Nash, Jr., (Public Affairs Press, 1959) outlines the area well but without adding fresh facts. Bryan has more weight, as do William Allen White's books. And the *Chicago Tribune.*

PAGES 150–156 Rosewater, Richard Harding Davis, the "Official Proceedings," Bryan, and Nicholas Murray Butler supply the main research here.

PAGES 157–159 Most of the material here is based on reports from the *Chicago Tribune* and the *New York Times.* Also, references are made to White's autobiography, to Rosewater, and to *The Presidency,* by Stefan Lorant (Macmillan, 1951). The Taft anecdote comes from *Jumbos and Jackasses,* by Edwin Palmer Hoyt, Jr. (Doubleday, 1960). Although necessarily brief, Hoyt's descriptions are both interesting and colorful.

PAGES 160–164 W. O. Hart's *Progressive Convention of 1912,* a slim pamphlet packed with interesting observations, has specific value. Pringle's *Taft* and Bryan add material here but the most fascinating report in these pages is the one from Davis. Lawrence Abbott in his *Impressions of Theodore Roosevelt* (Garden City, 1915) supplies a shorter, but equally interesting, companion anecdote for the Davis story.

PAGES 165–172 The "Official Proceedings," the *Chicago Tribune,* the *New York Times,* Davis, the White books, Mowry, Pringle, and Stoddard, are all necessary here.

PAGES 173–174 Bower's biography of Beveridge is most revealing about the birth of the Progressive party. Hofstadter also has pertinent comment. And White's *Autobiography* is excellent on this. The final quote comes from Helen H. Taft.

REPUBLICAN NATIONAL CONVENTION OF 1920

PAGES 176–179 The opening Harding quote comes from an interview in the *New York Herald* of October 31, 1920, and I don't believe it's appeared anywhere else before. Penrose on Roosevelt comes from a small, but excellent pamphlet, *Warren G. Harding, An Account of His Nomination for the Presidency by the Republican Convention of 1920,* by Ray Baker Harris, 1957. The second Penrose quote is in *Rise of American Civilization,* by Charles and Mary Beard (Macmillan, 1937), and the Roosevelt quote is from Pringle. Most of the Lowden material is best found in *Lowden of Illinois: The Life of Frank O. Lowden,* by William Thomas Hutchinson (University of Chicago Press, 1957); *The Unchosen,* by Charles Judah and

Winston Smith (Coward-McCann, 1962), which does a fine job of pulling much information together; Kohlsaat's book; and Volume Six of Mark Sullivan's *Our Times*. Walter Lippmann's comment on Lowden was in the *New Republic Magazine*, April 14, 1920.

PAGES 180–182 Background on the other candidates can best be found in Sullivan, Judah and Smith, and Samuel Hopkins Adams', *The Incredible Era* (Houghton Mifflin, 1939). The Adams book is basic for this whole period, because few books deal as completely with it. H. L. Mencken's *On Politics*, (Johns-Hopkins, 1956) is also sharp on all candidates. The Hoover material comes from his *Memoirs, 1920–1933, The Cabinet and The Presidency*, Vol. 1, (Macmillan, 1932).

PAGES 183–184 *Teapot Dome* by M. R. Werner and John Starr (The Viking Press, 1959) is good on the Daugherty background and so is Adams.

PAGES 185–189 Freshest source on the early Harding is a long, intimate interview found in the *New York Times*, June 27, 1920. Adams and Werner and Starr are also informative here. Another interesting source is *The Mirrors of Washington*, by Anonymous, (©1921 by Putnam's & Coward-McCann). A more excellent work is Karl Schriftgiesser's *This Was Normalcy* (Little Brown, 1948). Harding's Senate record is also treated in detail by Schriftgiesser, Adams, and Sullivan. The quote by Harding's Senate secretary can be found in *The Aspirin Age*, by Isabel Leighton (Simon & Schuster, 1949). The *New York World* of August 1, 1920, also has fine comment on this time.

PAGES 190–193 Sullivan outlines the 1916 Republican convention, and Adams has the story on Penrose and Harding. The memorable discussion of Daugherty and Harding comes from *The Inside Story of the Harding Tragedy*, by Harry M. Daugherty and Thomas Dixon (The Churchill Company, 1932). The quote on Harding's political philosophy was in *The Independent* magazine, November 13, 1920.

PAGES 194–198 Daugherty, Schriftgiesser, and Adams are all good on the primaries, but the best material comes from the *New York Times*. The Mencken observation is from *On Politics*. The Harding quote on policy is in *The Mirrors of Washington*. Mrs. Harding's soothsayer story is from *Liberty Magazine*, April 9, 1938, and also reported in Adams.

PAGES 199–204 The Harris pamphlet is best on the campaign expenditures exposé. Daugherty is good, but partisan. Malcom Moos in *The Republicans* (Random, 1956) gives a more objective picture of this. Werner and Starr are also helpful and Schriftgiesser, again, is excellent. The Daugherty prophecies are in *Our Times*, and originally printed in the *New York Times* of June 13, 1920 and later in the *Washington Post* of February 27, 1921. Hoover's position here is well described in *American Political Tradition* by Richard Hofstadter, as well as in Hoover's *Memoirs*. The Penrose quote is in Stoddard's *It Costs to be President*. Harding's reluctance for the Presidency is described in *Our Times*.

PAGES 205–210 Political processes of alliance are explained in *The Politics of National Party Conventions*, by Paul T. David, Ralph M. Goldman, Richard C. Bain (Brookings Institute, 1960). Jake Hamon is well discussed in Sullivan, Werner and Starr, and Daugherty. Excellent material of the breakdown of delegates can be found in Harris, background color in *Masks In A Pageant*, and other material in Sullivan, Daugherty, Stoddard, and Leighton. Best of the color again comes from the newspapers, particularly the *New York Times*, the *New York World*, and the *Chicago Tribune*. This also applies to the start of the convention itself. The "Official Proceedings" are, of course, basic.

PAGES 211–214 Mencken's quote is from *On Politics*. The Credentials contests are well described by Adams and Harris. William Allen White vividly described the action in the Resolutions Committee in his *Autobiography*, and Judah and Smith and Adams furnish a few more specifics. Frelinghuysen's incident with Wood was told by Stoddard in *It Costs to be President*. The Penrose anecdote was in Werner and Starr.

PAGES 215–222 The "Official Proceedings" plus accounts in the *New York Times* and the *Chicago Tribune* furnish much of the material in this section. The reference to Polsby and Wildavsky more specifically refers to *Decision Making at the National Convention*, by Nathan Polsby in the *Western Political Quarterly*, September, 1960 and Dr. Aaron Wildavsky's article in "Vital Issues of June 1960." Sullivan and Butler deal with the Harding-Wood mood and William Allen White describes the process of the Allen nominating speech for Wood.

PAGE 223 White's description of Harding is in *Masks In A Pageant*. The Penrose stories are from Davenport and Werner and Starr. The Beveridge note was in Bowers.

PAGES 224–230 Harris provides one of the best sources on the smoke-filled room. Werner & Starr, and Adams and Sullivan all are also good, and Wesley Dabby's "The Smoke Filled Room and the Nomination of Warren G. Harding" in the *Mississippi Valley Historical Review*, March, 1955, is especially interesting and informative. *Mirrors of Washington*, supplies a short pithy biography of George Harvey, Herbert Agar in *The People's Choice*, (Houghton Mifflin, 1933) also has pertinent comment on a Harvey judgment of Harding, and *The President Makers* offers further background on him. The story of Harding's mistress is discussed in Leighton and Adams and there is also a book by Nan Britton herself, *The President's Daughter*, (Gould, 1927). Discussion of the charge that Harding had Negro blood is also discussed in Leighton and in Moos. The anecdote on Harding and Johnson was mentioned in Werner and Starr.

PAGES 231–232 White in his *Autobiography*, tells of the Kansas caucus, Daugherty and Adams tell of the Penrose illness, and Harris discusses the Harding family breakfast.

PAGES 233–238 The most detailed analysis of the convention balloting comes from Harris. The Lowden-Wood taxi ride is well-detailed in Judah and Smith and *It Costs To Be President*. Adams also has information to add. Nan Britton describes her emotions in her own book and Daugherty tells the Mrs. Harding story.

PAGES 239–241 Harris provides the breakdown on the votes of the key Senators. The Harding interview appeared in the *New York Herald* of October 31, 1920.

PAGES 242–245 The best report of the vice-presidential nomination comes from Sullivan and White's *Autobiography*. The *New York Times* and the *Chicago Tribune* are similarly fine.

PAGES 246–248 Stoddard, *The Outlook* magazine, Mencken, *The Nation*, the *New York Times*, *The Independent* (of July 3) all provide needed comment here. The letter to the editor of the *New York Sun* was on July 2, 1920. *The Nation* reference was June 26, 1920, and the *New York Times*, a day later. The *New York Sunday Times Magazine* also had a highly interesting sum-up of Harding on July 18, 1920. And the *Literary Digest* summed up the other press comment in its issue of June 26. That odd prediction of Harding's death is in *Fighting Years,* by Oscar Oswald Garrison Villard (Harcourt, Brace, 1939).

DEMOCRATIC NATIONAL CONVENTION OF 1932

PAGES 250–254 The Roosevelt Papers and the Louis Howe Papers at the Franklin D. Roosevelt Library in Hyde Park, N.Y., furnish the great part of material in this section. Two of the presidential prophecies appear in John Gunther's, *Roosevelt in Retrospect,* (Harper, 1950) and the other one, told to the *New York Times,* comes from, *The Human Side of F.D.R.,* by Richard Harrity and Ralph G. Martin (Duell, Sloan & Pearce, 1960). Aside from the Louis Howe Papers, Lela Stiles' biography, *The Man Behind Roosevelt* (World, 1954) and *Roosevelt and Howe,* by Alfred B. Rollins (Knopf, 1962) furnish important facts. So do the private papers of Louis Howe's daughter, Mrs. Mary Baker. So do Edward G. Flynn in *You're the Boss* (The Viking Press, 1947) and Raymond Moley in *After Seven Years,* (Harper, 1939). Mrs. Eleanor Roosevelt provides other material on Howe, and also on the Smith phone call to Roosevelt. Some of this is in *Eleanor Roosevelt,* by Richard Harrity and Ralph G. Martin, (Duell, Sloan & Pearce, 1958). His election as Governor is well covered by James A. Farley in *Behind the Ballots,* (Harcourt Brace, 1938).

PAGES 255–257 Henry Morgenthau tells his part of the story in *The Morgenthau Diaries, Years of Crisis, 1928 to 1938,* Vol. 1 by John Morton Blum (Houghton Mifflin, 1959). Samuel I. Rosenman's *Working With Roosevelt,* (Harper & Row, 1952) is an excellent source on this early period. Farley and Flynn are similarly important.

PAGES 258–260 The analysis of the other presidential candidates is largely based on an article in the *New York Times* of July 5, 1931. A more detailed description of Ritchie and Murray are in Arthur M. Schlesinger's massive research job, *Crisis of the Old Order,* (Houghton Mifflin, 1957). Equally important here and elsewhere are Roosevelt's personal letters, *F.D.R. His Personal Letters, 1928–1945* edited by Elliott Roosevelt and Joseph P. Lash, (Duell, Sloan and Pearce, 1950).

PAGES 261–263 Roosevelt's feud with Smith is ably dealt with by Farley as well as by Rollins and Flynn. For a different view, strictly partisan, one must read, *The Happy Warrior,* by Emily Smith Warner, with Hawthorne Daniel, (Doubleday, 1956). The poem from the Program of the Albany Legislative Correspondents Dinner is in Rollins. Extremely important, much more so later, is Arthur Mullen's *Western Democrat,* (Wilfred Funk, Inc., 1940).

PAGES 264–269 The Tammany investigation is considered in detail in Frank Freidel's, *Franklin D. Roosevelt, The Triumph* (Little Brown, 1956) part of an impressively researched multivolume biography. A greater specific focus on the subject comes from Herbert Mitgang in his excellent biography of Judge Samuel Seabury, *The Man Who Rode the Tiger,* (Lippincott, 1963). The Baruch anecdotes come from Schlesinger. There's an interesting article on Louis Howe in the *New York Sunday Times Magazine* of November 27, 1932. Another, on November 9, in the *New York Times* is a good roundup of this Tammany period. Farley and Friedel both background the field workers very well. Friedel is also good on the Howe-House relationship. The Roosevelt vote polls are completely detailed in the *New York Times* of March 30, and in Friedel. Byrd's letter about Shouse, March 21, 1932, is from the Roosevelt Library in Hyde Park. Other Shouse material comes from *Selections of Nominees for the Presidency*, by Charles E. Noyes, an Editorial Research Report dated June 19, 1939. Roosevelt's comments on his proposed field workers are in his personal letters.

PAGES 270–273 The Farley Elks tour is best described in *Behind the Ballots* and also in *Jim Farley's Story* (Whittlesey, 1948). He has supplemented this material in a lengthy interview. The Kiplinger Letter, dated July 10, 1931 is at the Roosevelt Library.

PAGES 274–275 The House-Howe letters, from the Louis Howe Papers at the Roosevelt Library, must be read for any further digging into this, also, Roosevelt's personal letters. The Mullen material comes from *Western Democrat*, which has other facts I have found nowhere else. The full story of that Roosevelt health report will be found in the Roosevelt papers at the Roosevelt Library.

PAGES 276–284 More on the Smith story is, again, found in the Roosevelt papers, and this applies to the full text on the Howell letter. That letter was dated Dec. 2, 1931 and can also be found in Roosevelt's personal letters. Warner, Flynn and Farley also must be read for more on this. Mitgang offers the best documentation on Seabury. The full Roper correspondence is at the Roosevelt Library. Farley is best on the nomination announcement in *Behind the Ballots*. Roosevelt's letter to Shouse, in full, is in his personal letters, and so is his letter to Byrd. Farley is also best on the National Committee meeting.

PAGES 285–290 The Garner-Hearst story is well treated in *Garner of Texas*, by Bascom N. Timmons (Harper & Row, 1948), *Citizen Hearst*, by W. A. Swanberg (Scribner, 1961), and *Mr. Sam*, by C. Dwight Dorough (Random, 1962), which offers a more specialized point of view. Of the three, the Timmons book is best. But the *New York Times* is also especially good on its reporting of this. An article in the *New York Times* of July 3, 1932, and an interview by Anne O'Hare McCormick in the September 11, 1932 issue are worth reading in full. For the Seabury details, again see Mitgang, and Rollins. The Farley memos are detailed in the Farley papers at the Roosevelt Library. T. M. Storke amplifies the McAdoo story in *I Write for Freedom* (McNally & Loften, 1963).

PAGES 291–292 Rosenman and Moley present the Brains Trust story fully in their books. Rexford Tugwell in his *The Democratic Roosevelt* (Doubleday, 1957) is more sprawling with his material, but still worth reading. On the Jefferson Day Rally in Minnesota, the best account I found was in the *New York Herald Tribune*, April 20, 1932.

PAGES 293–304 Without question, the most detailed sources on the primaries are the Roosevelt papers in the Roosevelt Library, which deal definitively with each one. The best sum-up of this material is Friedel, while Farley, Schlesinger, Mullen, and Timmons all have details to add. But the best supplement is the reporting in the *New York Times*.

PAGES 305–307 Farley must be read on this preconvention period, with Tugwell on the critical side, and Warner on the Smith delegates. Claude G. Bowers has an interesting story to tell on the nominating speech in, *My Life, the Memoirs of Claude Bowers*, (© 1962 by Simon and Schuster). Also see the Louis Howe Papers, Roosevelt's personal letters, and Flynn. On the Smith-Roosevelt rift, Mark Sullivan had an excellent analysis in the *New York Herald Tribune* of January 17, 1932.

PAGES 308–313 The Roosevelt Library, Farley, Flynn, Warner, Mullen, Rollin, Stiles, Schlesinger, Friedel, all should be consulted. Add to this an interesting article by George Creel in the *Woman's Home Companion* of August, 1932 and Walter Lippmann's *Interpretations* (Macmillan, 1932).

PAGES 314–319 Both Farley books should be read here. They overlap, but they do add extra facts. This is particularly true of the story of the two-thirds rule. Flynn gives another balance to the picture. And Mullen adds still another. Lippmann and Schlesinger have further pertinent comment.

PAGES 320–325 The "Official Proceedings of the Democratic National Convention of 1932," (Library of Congress) furnishes the basic detail of the convention itself. *The New York Times* reports are necessary and supplemental. Lippmann offers fine comment and reporting here and so do Bowers, Farley, and Mullen.

PAGES 326–331 In addition to the "Official Proceedings" of June 30, 1932, the *New York Herald Tribune* has a detailed, informative story on the repeal plan. Farley and Schlesinger both treat this issue colorfully and well; Bowers and Storke have descriptions worth reading.

PAGES 332–337 Bowers is worth reading on all the candidates. A fuller story on the "Happy Days" song can be found in Rollins, Flynn and Farley —most of them disagreeing with each other. Dorough and Timmons must be read for more of the Garner story. Stiles is wonderfully intimate on the Howe story and Rosenman presents the complete story of the convention from the Roosevelt view, including the Huey Long phone call.

PAGES 338–347 James A. Farley, in a lengthy interview, has amplified much of this material, some of which has been in his books. See Roosevelt's personal letters for this period. There's also some first-class reportage by Thomas L. Stokes, in *Chip Off My Shoulder* (Princeton, 1940), and there's a story by Arthur Krock in the *New York Times* of July 2, 1932 that's worth reading for both its analysis and description. Friedel, Schlesinger and particularly Mullen should also be read. Timmons has the best account of Mayor Walker's vote.

PAGES 348–349 Marion Dickerman, a long-time friend of the Roosevelts, as well as a delegate to the 1932 Democratic convention, pulled anecdotes out of her memory, and the Roosevelt Library would do well to visit Miss Dickerman with a tape recorder, because hers is a special kind of history. The other material can be amplified from Stokes, Farley, the Louis Howe Papers and Stiles.

PAGES 350–357 The California story is the critical one of the convention, and Storke fills in many of the missing links. Farley, Swanberg, Timmons, Warner and Dorough, also have necessary facts to add.

PAGES 358–364 A great part of this section is from Storke, the "Official Proceedings," the Roosevelt Papers at the Roosevelt Library, the *New York Times* (with some excellent reporting by Arthur Krock), Bowers, Farley, Mullen, and Friedel.

PAGES 365–366 Timmons has the best report on the Garner vice-presidential nomination. The *New York Herald Tribune* of July 3, 1932 has a fine article on convention color and Farley's books are still necessary for further information.

466

BALLOTS & BANDWAGONS

PAGES 367–371 Most complete reporting of the Roosevelt flight to the convention can be found in the *New York Times* of July 3, 1932. There's an excellent account of Smith's departure in the same issue. The Bowers comment on Smith's exit is in *My Life*. James Roosevelt and Sidney Shallet's book, *Affectionately F.D.R.* (Harcourt, Brace & World, 1959) has several anecdotes of interest for this period, but not too many. Farley is again necessary here, and Lippmann has comment worth reading, and Stokes is very good on all this. See the Louis Howe Papers for further material, including the Moley letter of November 12, 1932. *The Human Side of F.D.R.*, (Duell, Sloan and Pearce) by Richard Harrity and Ralph G. Martin, has additional fresh anecdotes of this time.

THE DEMOCRATIC NATIONAL CONVENTION OF 1956

PAGES 373–455 This entire chapter has been researched completely from interviews with participants on all levels. Their names are noted in the acknowledgments. There is a reservoir of rich research material in the files of James Finnegan, campaign manager for Adlai Stevenson, and I am deeply grateful to Jean Gildea for making them available to me.

Index